Penguin Handbo
Jewish Cookery

Florence Greenberg was born in London in
1882 and was educated at day school in England,
followed by boarding school in Germany.
She gained her cookery experience when she left
school and helped her sister do most of the
cooking for a household of twelve.

In 1911 Florence Greenberg decided to fulfil
her one ambition and become a trained hospital
nurse. Her training was only just completed
when the First World War broke out and
she joined the Army Nursing Service and was
sent out East. She received a Mention in
Dispatches for her work at Gallipoli.

Back in England, she met her late husband,
who was Editor of the *Jewish Chronicle*. They
married in 1920. From then until 1962 Mrs
Greenberg wrote cookery articles every week for
his paper. She also gave talks on the B.B.C.
from 1941 to 1946 on various household and
culinary topics and contributed a section
on Jewish cookery to *Newnes' Home Management*
and to the last edition of Mrs Beeton's *Cookery
and Home Management*.

Florence Greenberg

Jewish Cookery

Penguin Books

Penguin Books Ltd, Harmondsworth,
Middlesex, England
Penguin Books Inc., 7110 Ambassador Road, Maryland 21207,
Baltimore, U.S.A.
Penguin Books Australia Ltd, Ringwood,
Victoria, Australia

First published by Jewish Chronicle Publications, 1947
Revised 1949, 1951, 1953, 1955, 1963
Published in Penguin Books 1967
Reprinted 1968, 1791, 1974
Copyright © Florence Greenberg, 1963

Made and printed in Great Britain by
C. Nicholls & Company Ltd
Set in Monotype Walbaum

Contents

Recipes

Publisher's Note

This is the seventh edition of *Florence Greenberg's Jewish Cookery Book*. Once again the author has made extensive revisions and, while retaining many of the old favourites, has added a number of new recipes, all of which, as is her practice, she has carefully tried and tested. In order to make room for the additions and yet not to impair the handiness of the volume some recipes which can readily be found in general cookery books have been omitted.

All recipes are in accordance with Jewish dietary laws. Instructions for koshering meat and poultry as well as useful cookery hints for both novice and expert are again included.

The Kitchen

The kitchen is the workroom of the household, and upon its efficiency, comfort, and accessibility depends the success of the cooking that is done there. While the inclusion in your kitchen of every labour-saving device may not make a good cook of you, and while it may be quite possible for you to prepare both nourishing and appetizing meals without any of the newest culinary advantages, there is little doubt that modern inventions have enabled cookery to make considerable advances in the past few years.

The separation of the Jewish kitchen into respective departments for meat and milk must govern its actual planning and arrangement. And while subsequent developments of these plans must follow the lines indicated by the distinction between foods, this in itself can be made an admirable basis upon which real efficiency and order can be established.

The concentration of articles likely to be required simultaneously or in sequence must be the first aim in planning the kitchen. The best results can be achieved with a minimum of both effort and time, if care and forethought are employed to arrange things in the smallest possible space, without either overcrowding or neglecting to allow for a good clear working space at the principal table. Order and visibility in storing all goods are important factors in saving time and maintaining working space.

Lighting plays a vital part in every efficient kitchen, as it does in any other workroom. The most up-to-date method of indirect but very powerful lighting, arranged so that it is available precisely where work has to be done, is now a feature of the well-arranged kitchen. The maximum use should be made of daylight, and both sink and work-table so situated as to necessitate artificial lighting only after nightfall.

If possible, choose a table with an enamelled iron top; failing this, cover it with Formica, American cloth, or a light linoleum. A closed-in dresser is essential if plates and dishes are to be kept free of dust. If the regulation kitchen cabinet is not used, then all groceries, etc., must be kept in clearly marked containers.

A very useful item of kitchen equipment is a step-stool. It can be used for sitting on when preparing vegetables, picking fruit, etc., or for steps when required, and takes up very little room when not in use.

A cupboard for brooms, brushes, and dustpans is often built into a kitchen, but where this is lacking, a special revolving cupboard can be bought for this purpose. One section, reaching to the top of the cupboard, is used for the long-handled brooms, and the other sections are fitted with shelves which can be used for boot and stove brushes, cleaning materials, etc.

There are also on the market several inexpensive fitments suitable for hanging up the brooms and brushes.

The Sink. The sink must be kept spotlessly clean and where the surround is not tiled, it should be well painted, so that splashes can be easily washed off. It is important to use washable paint.

Where two sinks are not available for the washing-up of meat and milk dishes, separate bowls must be kept for this purpose and the dish cloths and tea towels employed should have borders of distinctive colourings.

The Kitchen Cooker. Whether the stove used is a gas or electric cooker, a modern coal range, or an oil stove, the manufacturer's instructions are issued with it, and these should be carefully studied and carried out if the best results are to be obtained. When the cooker is installed, see that it is raised sufficiently from the floor, so that there is no necessity to stoop when working at it. To give good service it is absolutely essential that the stove should be kept scrupulously clean inside and out.

The Larder. An ideal larder is made with tiled walls and fitted with slate or marble shelves. Failing this, the walls should be painted. If only wooden shelves are available, cover them with Formica or linoleum and put a slate or marble on one of them to hold milk and dairy produce. The window should be fitted with wire gauze. A rack should be used for storing vegetables and wire or muslin dish covers for covering the food.

The larder must be swept and the shelves washed daily. Bread pan, vegetable rack, meat hooks, and covers must all be thoroughly washed and scalded at least once a week.

No food should ever be put away on the dish on which it was served.

Inspect the larder daily and see that it is in good order; examine its contents and plan menus so as to include all left-overs.

Storage of Food
PERISHABLE FOODS

Where a refrigerator is available the problem of preserving perishable foods is automatically solved, but where this facility does not exist, they must be stored in the coolest part of the larder.

Meat. Cover with a wire gauze frame; see that the frame fits the dish tightly, so that flies are unable to enter. Covers must be kept scrupulously clean.

Milk. In hot weather place bottles of milk in a basin of cold water. Cover bottles with muslin, the ends of which should rest in the water. Stand in a draught.

Cheese. Wrap in greaseproof paper, then in damp muslin and hang in a cool airy place. Or simply wrap the cheese in muslin wrung out in vinegar. For cooking, leave ends of cheese till really dry, then grate them, place in a screw-topped jar, and keep in refrigerator or cool larder.

Vegetables. Keep vegetables in a vegetable rack. Wrap green vegetables in newspaper and put lettuces in a saucepan or bowl, cover, and stand in a cool place or store in plastic bags. Remove the tops of carrots, turnips, parsnips, and radishes before placing in the vegetable rack. Put onions and shallots in a string bag and hang them where the air can get at them.

DRY STORES

Glass jars with screw-top lids are best for dry stores. It is easy to see what is in them and whether the food is keeping well. Never put new supplies on top of old ones. Wash and dry containers thoroughly before refilling. Either have the shelves of the store cupboard painted or cover them with Formica or linoleum; it will then be an easy matter to keep them free of dirt and dust. Turn out the store cupboard every week.

CANNED FOODS

There is a good variety of excellent canned foods available and it is advisable to keep a stock of these in the store cupboard. They will help to vary the daily menu and are an excellent stand-by for emergency meals. The food is ready to serve cold or only needs heating.

There are many varieties of fish, meats, soups, vegetables, cereals, and fruit from which to choose, in addition to evaporated milk and cream.

Store the tins in a cool dry place, mark them with the date on which they were bought, and use them in the order in which they were purchased.

Never use the contents of a tin that is bulging, as this indicates fermentation. If on opening the contents are discoloured or give off a bad odour, the tin should be discarded.

Length of Time for Keeping Canned Foods

Milk	1 year
Fruit	1 year
Vegetables	2 years
Honey and Jam	2 years
Meat	5 years
Fish in oil	5 years
Fish in Tomato Sauce	1 year

Herbs and Spices

Spices, dried herbs, mustard, pepper, etc., should always be kept in airtight containers, otherwise the flavours will deteriorate.

Parsley, chives, mint, etc., can be grown at home, even if there is no garden, for they do quite well in window-boxes or pots.

Small quantities of the following should find a place in the store cupboard:

Bay leaves	Cinnamon	Mace	Pepper and
Capers	Cloves	Mustard	peppercorns
Cayenne pepper	Curry powder	Nutmeg	Sage
Celery salt	Ginger	Paprika	Mixed spice

In addition to ordinary malt vinegar, keep small bottles of tarragon, chilli, and garlic vinegar, a little of which often improves the flavour of savoury dishes. Also include a bottle each of Worcester sauce, Yorkshire relish, tomato ketchup, and liquid vegetable extract.

Quantities to Allow in Catering

PROVISIONS FOR TWO PEOPLE

When cooking for two people, buying in small quantities is not always advisable, especially as regards meat.

If a refrigerator or very cool larder is available, plan ahead and buy and cook for several meals. A chicken or joint can be served hot for one meal, cold the next, and many recipes will be found in the meat section for utilizing left-overs. Stews, hot-pots, and pot-roasts, are all excellent for using small quantities of fresh meat.

In the following list the approximate quantities required per meal are given. It is not possible to give exact amounts, because individual appetites and tastes vary. Also there may be times when certain foods are in short supply, but it will be some guide for the inexperienced housewife.

Fish

Whole fish 1–1½ lb.   Cutlets ¾–1 lb.   Fillets 8–12 oz.

Meat

Breast and neck of lamb or mutton 1 lb.	Steak 10–12 oz. Liver 6–8 oz. Mince ½ lb.	Sliced cooked meats 6–8 oz.

Vegetables

Artichokes, Jerusalem, ¾–1 lb.	Cabbage 1 lb.	Parsnips ¾ lb.
Broad beans 1–1½ lb.	Carrots ½ lb.	Peas 1½ lb.
French and runner beans ½–¾ lb.	Cauliflower, a small one	Potatoes 1 lb.
Brussels sprouts ¾ lb.	Celery 1 head	Spinach 1–1½ lb.
	Greens 1 lb.	Swede 1 lb.
		Turnips 1 lb.

Soup, ½–¾ *pint.*   *Sauces and gravies,* ¼ *pint.*
Milk puddings, blancmange, fruit salad, ½ *pint.*

Weights and Measures

It is most important to weigh or measure all ingredients accurately. Weighing is more accurate than measuring provided really good scales are used. Should these not be available, then use a standard cup measure.

Throughout this book when a 'spoonful' is mentioned in a recipe, it is taken to mean a rounded spoonful, that is, with as much above the rim of the spoon as below.

LIQUID MEASURE

60 drops	= 1 teaspoonful	4 gills	= 1 pint
2 teaspoonfuls	= 1 dessertspoonful	2 pints	= 1 quart
2 dessertspoonfuls	= 1 tablespoonful	4 quarts	= 1 gallon
10 tablespoonfuls	= 1 gill		

SOLID MEASURE

	oz.		oz.
2 level tablespoonfuls flour =	1	1 level tablespoonful sugar =	1
2 level tablespoonfuls coffee =	1	1 level tablespoonful syrup =	2
2 level tablespoonfuls breadcrumbs =	½ oz.		

CUP MEASURES
(*British and American*)

The British Standards Institution has designed a measuring cup, the capacity of which is ½ pint. The American cup measure is smaller than ours: whereas the British pint is 20 fluid ounces, the American is 16.

Here are the respective weights of various ingredients when lightly spooned into the cup and not shaken down. Breadcrumbs and cheese will vary slightly, being lighter when stale and dry.

Ingredient	*British*	*American*
Breadcrumbs	2½ oz.	2 oz.
Bread (soaked and squeezed)	7 oz.	6 oz.
Butter and shortening	8 oz.	7 oz.
Candied peel, chopped	6 oz.	5 oz.
Cheese, grated	3½ oz.	3–4 oz.
Coconut, desiccated	4 oz.	3 oz.
Currants and sultanas	6 oz.	5 oz.

Flour	5 oz.	4 oz.
Margarine and cooking fat	8 oz.	7 oz.
Oatmeal	8 oz.	7 oz.
Rice	9 oz.	8 oz.
Rolled oats	4 oz.	3 oz.
Suet, chopped	5 oz.	4 oz.
Sugar, brown	7 oz.	6 oz.
Sugar, granulated	10 oz.	8 oz.
Sugar, icing	5 oz.	4 oz.
Syrup and treacle	16 oz.	12 oz.

Kitchen Utensils

Always choose utensils of good quality; it is false economy to buy inferior articles which soon wear out.

The following list will act as a guide when equipping a new kitchen; these are not all essential, and the choice of articles bought will be limited by one's means, kitchen space available, and size of the family. Many things will have to be duplicated for meat or milk cooking.

Set of saucepans with lids
Milk saucepan
Steamer
Two frying-pans, small and large
Omelette pan
Small and large kettle
Cooking plates
Set of cake tins and patty tins
Sandwich tins
Baking trays
Roasting pan
Colander
Grater
Funnel
Flour dredger
Set of skewers
Mincing machine
Tin opener
Apple corer
Corkscrew
Strainers, round and conical
Sink basket
Measuring jug
2 or 3 jugs (various sizes)

Mixing bowls
Bowls for washing up
Two pie dishes
Fireproof glass dishes
Casseroles with lids (various sizes)
Egg whisk
Pastry board (not essential if enamel top table in use)
Rolling pin
Chopping board
Bread board
Bread tin or crock
Potato peeler
Two sharp knives
Vegetable knife
Chef's knife
Palette knife
2 forks
2 teaspoons
2 tablespoons
2 dessertspoons
Ladle
Fish slice
Long-handled fork

Stainless if possible

Long-handled basting spoon
3 wooden spoons
Pair of scissors
Sieve
Pastry brush
Standard cup measure
Containers for dry stores
Scales
Lemon squeezer
Salt and pepper containers
Set of pudding basins (various sizes)

Knife sharpener
Set of biscuit cutters
Pie funnel
Potato masher
Cake tray (wire)
Vegetable rack
Clock
Refuse bin
Pressure cooker
Deep fat pan with frying basket

Food Values and Menu Building

It is undoubtedly true that our health depends very largely on our diet.

Just as an engine requires fuel to enable it to work properly, so the body needs certain food elements to keep it in proper working order, and it demands that these food elements should be supplied in certain proportions. If any one of these foods is absent or given in wrong proportion, ill health will be the result. Therefore, in order to be able to plan correctly balanced meals, it is essential to have some knowledge of the classification of different foods and their comparative food values.

Foods do three main things:

(1) Build up tissue and repair it.
(2) Provide heat and energy.
(3) Supply substances called vitamins, which help to give fitness, vitality, and resistance to disease.

PROTEINS

The following are the principal foods containing sufficient protein to be of value in the diet:

Meat (including liver and kidney)
Poultry
Fish and fish roe
Eggs
Cheese

Pulse foods (dried peas, beans, and lentils)
Nuts (especially peanuts and almonds)

Milk
Wheat flour
Barley meal
Soya flour
Bread
Green peas

CARBOHYDRATES

Sugar	Oatmeal	Soya flour
Syrup	Bread	Rice
Honey	Potatoes and root	Haricot beans
Jam	vegetables	Butter beans
		Dried peas

FATS

Butter	Olive oil	Cream
Margarine	Oily fish (herrings,	Meat fat and bone
Cooking fat	salmon, mackerel,	marrow
Suet	sprats, and	Egg yolk
Dripping	sardines)	Cheese
Cod liver oil	Nuts	

CALCIUM

Milk	Black treacle	All green vegetables
Cheese	Sprats	Sardines
Eggs		

IRON

Lentils	Turnip-top greens	Wholemeal bread
Liver	Scotch kale	Pulse foods
Oatmeal	Meat	Black treacle
Spinach	Dried fruits	Almonds

VITAMINS

There are four vitamins especially that must be included regularly in the diet for health. These are vitamins A, B, C, D.

Vitamin A. Found in butter, cream, cod liver and halibut liver oil, some margarine, egg yolks, milk, whole wheatmeal, oily fish, such as herrings, salmon, and pilchards, green vegetables, carrots and liver.

Vitamin B. Found in yeast and yeast extracts, oatmeal, wholemeal bread, dried peas, beans, lentils, nuts, kidney and liver, eggs, milk, cheese, and a small quantity in vegetables.

Vitamin C. Chiefly from citrus fruits, tomatoes, green vegetables, watercress, parsley, swedes, potatoes, lettuce. Orange juice concentrate, blackcurrant and rose-hip syrup are all very rich in vitamin C.

Vitamin D. Found in cod liver and halibut liver oil, butter, vitaminized margarine, fat fish, such as pilchards, herrings, salmon, etc., eggs, and milk.

To keep an individual in good health an ordinary diet should contain about 4 oz. protein, 2 or 3 oz. fat, 14 to 16 oz. carbohydrates, and 1 oz. mineral salts daily; but these quantities will vary according to age and occupation, and are also influenced by climate and seasons of the year. Those engaged in heavy manual labour and adolescents require more food units than those engaged in sedentary occupations. Elderly people require less food, as their powers of assimilation and physical activities are less. In hot weather a smaller quantity of the heat-providing foods is required. Fats and proteins can be reduced and a corresponding increase in fruit, vegetables, and salads should be taken instead.

In planning the daily menu see that something from each of the foregoing groups (protein, carbohydrates, fats, foods that give calcium and iron, and those containing vitamins A, B, C, and D) is included.

Fruit, salads, and vegetables should be eaten every day. When fruit is in short supply, make up with extra salads and green vegetables.

The cheaper cuts of meat and the cheaper kinds of cheese give as much food value as the more expensive.

Herrings and mackerel have a higher food value than white fish.

Meals should look good, as well as taste good. Simple garnishes take very little extra time. A little finely chopped parsley or watercress sprinkled over a colourless dish makes all the difference. Sliced tomatoes and grated raw carrot are also excellent when a touch of colour is required.

Cookery Methods

To Bake Blind. To bake a pastry case before adding the filling. (See Fruit Flans, page 258.)

To Baste. To spoon fat (or other liquid) over food during baking to keep it moist.

To Blanch. There are two methods of blanching:
(1) Dip the food for a minute in boiling water, then plunge into cold water. This makes it easy to remove the skins of tomatoes, peaches, almonds, etc.
(2) Put the food into cold water and bring to the boil. Then remove the food, put immediately into cold water, and cool quickly. Sweetbreads, calf's head, etc., are always blanched like this before cooking. (See section on meat.)

To Braise. A combination of roasting and stewing. (See page 141.)

To Clarify Dripping (or other fat). Melt the fat and strain into a large bowl. Then pour over double the quantity of boiling water. Stir well and leave till cold and set. Remove the cake of fat from the top of the water, scrape off any sediment from the bottom of the cake, then melt the fat and pour into a clean basin.

To Cream. To beat fat with a wooden spoon till light and fluffy.

To Dredge. To coat lightly with flour or sugar.

To Egg and Crumb. To dip food in beaten egg, then coat with fine breadcrumbs – fresh or dried. Used for coating fish, cutlets, rissoles, croquettes, etc., before frying. Use fresh breadcrumbs for raw food, and browned crumbs (raspings) for food that is already cooked and only needs heating through, such as rissoles or fish cakes.
Note. When eggs are in short supply, use an eggless coating batter (see page 427) in place of beaten egg.

To Fold In. A process of combining beaten mixtures with other ingredients so that they retain their lightness. (See page 337.)

To Fry. (See page 142.)

To Grill or Broil. (See page 143.)

To Marinate. To stand meat or fish in a mixture of vinegar, oil, herbs, and spices for a short time before cooking to improve the flavour.

To Poach. To cook just below boiling point in hot liquid in an open pan.

To Prove. To leave yeast dough in a warm place to rise after it has been shaped into a loaf, rolls, etc.

To Purée. To rub cooked fruit or vegetables through a sieve to remove skins, pips, etc.

To Render Fat. Use any trimmings of raw or cooked fat. Either cut into very small pieces or put through the mincer. Then put into a baking tin and bake in a slow oven until all the fat is extracted and only crisp, brown pieces remain.

Or place in a saucepan, add a spoonful or two of water, and place over a very gentle heat till the fat is extracted; then strain.

To Roast. (See page 140.)

To Rub In. A method of mixing flour and fat used in cakes and pastry. (See page 337.)

To Sauté. To brown lightly in shallow fat.

To Sieve. When rubbing through a sieve, always place the sieve with the shallow side uppermost. Use a wooden spoon to rub through, and hold it firmly with the first two fingers on the edge of the bowl of the spoon. This will enable you to use a firm pressure downwards and at the same time towards you. In this way the mixture will be quickly rubbed through.

To Simmer. To cook at a temperature below boiling point. Used for soups, stews, and sauces. Bring to the boil, then adjust heat so that the liquid is kept just moving.

To Steam. To cook over boiling water.

To Stew. To cook slowly in a small quantity of liquid. (See page 144.)

Cookery Terms

Au Gratin. Any dish covered with a sauce and topped with breadcrumbs or cheese and afterwards browned under the grill or in the upper part of a hot oven. A shallow dish should be used and the food served in the dish in which it is cooked.

Bouquet Garni. A bunch of herbs used for flavouring stocks, soups, and stews. It consists of 2 sprigs of parsley, a small bay leaf, and a sprig of thyme, tied together with thread. Sometimes a small strip of lemon peel is also added. Remove as soon as the dish is sufficiently flavoured.

Canapés. Small pieces of toast, fried bread, or pastry, on which little savouries are served.

Consistency. The thickness or texture of a mixture, such as a cake or pudding.

Croquettes. Savoury mixtures of meat, fish, eggs, or vegetables, rolled into cork shapes. These are coated with egg and breadcrumbs and fried a golden brown.

Croûtons. Bread cut into dice and fried. Used as a garnish for soup. (See page 47.)

Dough. A mixture of various ingredients, flour, liquid, etc., kneaded together.

Panada. A thick paste used for binding mixtures such as croquettes and quenelles (see Binding Sauce, page 204), and the basis of hot soufflés and choux pastry.

Quenelles. Portions of savoury mixture bound with a panada, shaped with a spoon, and poached in boiling water or stock.

Raspings. Fine browned breadcrumbs, used for coating rissoles, fish cakes, etc. (See page 427.)

Rissoles. Savoury mixture of meat, fish, etc., enclosed in pastry and fried.

Stock. Liquid made from meat, vegetables, fish, or poultry and used as a foundation for soups, sauces, and stews.

Useful Hints and General Information

To Make Breadcrumbs. (1) Grate stale bread on a fine grater.

(2) Remove crusts from stale bread, then with the palm of the hand rub through a sieve or colander. For raspings, see page 427.

To Stone Raisins. Put the raisins in a basin and cover with boiling water; leave for 2 or 3 minutes, then the stones can be pinched out.

To Weigh Golden Syrup. Dredge the scale thickly with flour, then pour in the syrup, which will slip off the scale without sticking.

If measuring a spoonful, dip the spoon in boiling water first.

To Make Onion Juice. Cut a slice off the root end of an onion, then either grate it or squeeze on a lemon squeezer specially kept for this purpose.

To Dissolve Gelatine. Moisten gelatine with *cold* water and stand the container in a saucepan of water. Heat gently, stirring occasionally till gelatine has dissolved.

To Chop Suet. Sprinkle the suet liberally with flour whilst chopping – it will then not stick to the chopping knife.

Suet may be melted and strained into clean jars. Leave in a cool part of the larder or the refrigerator, and when required for use, grate it, and use in place of fresh suet.

To Prevent a Disagreeable Odour from Green Vegetables while Cooking. Put a crust of bread in the water, or add a teaspoonful of vinegar.

White Vegetables. When cooking white vegetables, such as cauliflower, artichokes, and sea-kale, put two lumps of sugar in the water. This will keep them a good colour.

Oranges. When peeling for fruit salad, etc., put in a bowl, cover with boiling water and leave for 2 or 3 minutes. The oranges will then peel quite easily, and all the pith will come away with the peel.

Lemons. Heat thoroughly before squeezing, and you will get double the amount of juice.

Acid Fruits. When stewing acid fruit, such as rhubarb,

gooseberries, plums, etc., if $\frac{1}{2}$ teaspoonful of bicarbonate of soda to each lb. is added, much less sugar will be required. Bring the fruit and water to the boil, sprinkle in the bicarbonate of soda, simmer gently for a minute or two till the froth has disappeared, then sweeten to taste and continue cooking till the fruit is soft.

New Bread. Cut new bread and cakes with a knife dipped in boiling water.

Sausages. (1) Prick with a fork and roll in flour before frying. This prevents them bursting.

(2) Cover with boiling water for a couple of minutes, then drain and dry before frying.

Mustard. When mixing mustard add a few drops of olive oil.

Dry Mustard rubbed on the hands will remove any disagreeable odour. After peeling onions, wash the hands first in *cold* water. 'Oniony' knives should also be washed in cold water before washing them in hot.

Kitchen Scissors. Use these to 'top and tail' gooseberries, to trim the skin and fins from fish, and to chop parsley, etc.

To Chop Parsley. Pinch the tufts of parsley tightly between the thumb and the first two fingers of the left hand, then cut across finely with your kitchen scissors. It is much quicker than chopping on a board.

To Chop Mint. Wash and dry the mint, cut off the leaves with your scissors, then sprinkle the leaves with granulated sugar before chopping.

To Remove Saltiness from Soup or Stew. If a soup or stew is too salty, either add a teaspoonful of sugar or a little grated raw potato, and cook gently for a few minutes.

To Boil a Cracked Egg. Wrap the egg in tissue paper, and put a tablespoonful of salt in the water in which it is cooked.

To Season Saucepans. Before using new saucepans or casseroles, fill with cold water and heat till the water boils. Then remove from the heat and leave with the water in till cold.

To Clean the Frying Pan. Strain left-over fat into a jar for future use. Rub the pan with paper before washing.

To Clean an Omelette Pan. This should *not* be washed. Sprinkle with salt and rub well with paper. Then give a final rub with a coarse kitchen cloth.

To Clean Saucepans and Other Cooking Utensils. Soak all utensils as soon as you have finished with them. Those which have been used for mixing cakes, flour mixtures, milk or eggs should be soaked in *cold* water. Hot water hardens these foods and makes them difficult to remove. Anything used in the preparation or cooking of fish should be soaked in cold water to which a little vinegar has been added.

If food has stuck to a saucepan, soak it well before attempting to clean it. Use a pot scourer or saucepan brush, and avoid scratching the pan during cleaning.

For Burnt Saucepans. Put cold salt water into the pan, bring slowly to the boil, and boil for a few minutes. Repeat the process until all burnt particles of food can be easily removed. Do not use soda for burnt pans, or they will burn more easily next time they are used.

Oatmeal. Toast oatmeal in the oven or under the grill for a few minutes before using. It gives it a nutty taste.

To Turn Out Steamed Puddings. When the pudding is cooked, remove it from the saucepan but leave it for a few minutes before turning it out. This will prevent the pudding from breaking.

To Soften Butter or Margarine. If the butter is too hard for spreading, the quickest way to soften it, without oiling, is to put it on a warm plate and invert over it a cup or basin that has been rinsed with boiling water. In a very few minutes it will be just the right consistency for spreading.

To Kosher Meat and Poultry

The meat or poultry should be put into a bowl especially reserved for this purpose, entirely covered with cold water and left to soak for ½ hour. Wash every particle of blood from the meat before removing from the water. Then place it on a smooth wooden board with holes in it, and lightly sprinkle with salt. Let it drain for 1 hour, then rinse thoroughly in cold water.

Poultry must be drawn before being koshered. Liver must be cut through and washed thoroughly. Sprinkle with salt, grill for a minute or two on each side, then use in any way required.

These instructions are according to ritual requirements and should be carried out independently of and before those given for the preparation of individual meat recipes.

Oven Temperatures

	Degrees Fahrenheit	Regulo (for gas cookers)	Degrees Centigrade
Very slow	240–80	¼–½	115–35
Slow	280–320	1	135–60
Warm	320–40	3	160–70
Moderate	340–70	4	170–85
Fairly hot	370–400	5–6	185–205
Hot	400–40	7	205–25
Very hot	440–80	8–9	225–50

Recipes

Breakfast Dishes

Whether a cooked or light breakfast is being served, whenever possible include some kind of fruit or fruit juice. Fresh or dried, raw or stewed, there is a good variety from which to choose. Ring the changes, too, with different kinds of bread.

Apple Muesli

This dish, which is of Swedish origin, is an ideal first course for breakfast. Allow per person:

Rolled oats 1 level tablespoonful   *Water 3 tablespoonfuls*
Chopped nuts 2 teaspoonfuls   *Condensed milk 2 teaspoonfuls*
Lemon juice 1 teaspoonful   *An apple*

Soak the oats in the water overnight. Just before serving, mix with the sweetened condensed milk and lemon juice, grate the unpeeled apple on to it, mix thoroughly and sprinkle the nuts on top.

Top milk, sweetened, can replace the condensed milk.
Any soft fruit in season can replace the grated apple.

Any of the following dishes are suitable for breakfast, and recipes for them will be found under their respective sections:

Any Egg Dishes and Omelettes   Fish Cakes
Fried or Grilled Fish   Kedgeree
Fried Cod's Roe   Kippers and Bloaters
Any Herring Dishes   Smoked Haddock
Savoury Toasts

Hors-d'Oeuvres and Cocktail Savouries

Hors-d'oeuvres are small dainties served as the first course at lunch or dinner. They should stimulate and sharpen the appetite and must be small, daintily served, and very piquant in flavour.

These dishes, to the thoughtful cook, present one of the best opportunities of showing her skill and originality in combination and garnish; and as they can be put on the table before the guests arrive, they can add greatly to the attractive appearance of the table.

Odd scraps of meat, fish, and vegetables can all be utilized; and there are many hors-d'oeuvres that can be bought in tins or bottles ready for serving, and a stock of these can be kept in the store cupboard. Amongst the latter are the following:

Artichokes in oil	Olives
Anchovies	Cucumbers
Brislings	Gherkins
Fillets of herring	Pimentos (small red peppers)
Rollmops	Macédoine of vegetables
Sardines	Mayonnaise sauce

The most generally used vegetables are peas, potatoes, carrots, beans, cauliflower (which are usually dressed with mayonnaise sauce); celery, which should be shredded; tomatoes, cucumber, and beetroot, cut into thin slices and dressed with oil and vinegar; fresh green salads, silver onions and radishes.

Then we have smoked salmon, sliced sausages of various kinds, and salted and devilled almonds, so there is certainly a good selection from which to choose.

In place of hors-d'oeuvres, grapefruit, iced melon, or fruit cocktails may be served.

Fruit Cocktails

The success of a fruit cocktail depends on its being served icy cold and on the correct blending of the fruits. Choose a mixture of bitter and sweet fruits, keeping it rather sharp, not syrupy like fruit salad.

Grapefruit and pineapple, or grapefruit, strawberries, and peaches make a good combination.

Thoroughly chill the fruit, and arrange in fruit cocktail or melba glasses.

Garnish with a maraschino cherry, blackberry, raspberry, strawberry, or a sprig of fresh mint.

Tomato Juice Cocktail

Tomato juice ¼ pint   *Lemon juice 2 teaspoonfuls*
Worcester sauce ¼ teaspoonful   *Salt ¼ teaspoonful*
Sugar 2 teaspoonfuls

Mix all ingredients and serve ice cold in small glasses.

Grapefruit

Allow half a grapefruit for each person. Cut the fruit in halves with a stainless knife. Remove all the pips, and with a curved grapefruit knife cut all round the fruit, severing the pulp from the skin. Also cut along the skin in between the sections, then cut out the core. Sprinkle each half with a teaspoonful of sugar and, if possible, chill in the refrigerator before serving. Place a cherry in the centre of each and serve in grapefruit glasses or on a small plate.

Or the pulp and juice may be removed from the skin and put straight into the glasses.

Grilled Grapefruit

Remove pips and centre core from grapefruit halves and loosen the sections. Pour 2 teaspoonfuls of sherry over each half and sprinkle them liberally with brown sugar.

Grill under a moderate heat till hot through and lightly browned.

In place of sugar the fruit can be spread with honey, then sprinkled with cinnamon, dotted with margarine, and browned lightly under a moderate heat.

Melon

Chill thoroughly. Cut into wedges and remove the seeds. Serve on individual plates and hand separately caster sugar and ground ginger.

Mixed Hors-d'oeuvres
(*Hors-d'oeuvres Variés*)

Special divided dishes are made for serving mixed hors-d'oeuvres, but if one of these is not available, use a set of small dishes, placing them on a large dish or on a tray; or, if preferred, put the hors-d'oeuvres directly on to a large dish, separating the individual items with a garnish of small cress or watercress.

Having the various items all together simplifies serving and it makes the choice easier for the guests. It is usual to serve about six varieties and here are some suggestions:

1 Herring Salad
Egg Mayonnaise
Sliced Sausage
Radishes
Gherkins
Potato Salad

2 Pickled Herring
Russian Salad
Red Cabbage
Sweet Corn Mayonnaise
Cucumber
Mushrooms (in oil)

3 Smoked Salmon
Celery and Beetroot Salad
Olives
Liver Sausage
Stuffed Eggs
Potato Salad

4 Anchovy Eggs
Olives
Sardines
Sliced Tomatoes
Asparagus mayonnaise or
Asparagus tips (tinned) in
cucumber rings

To Serve with Cocktails

Salted almonds or other nuts; olives, plain and stuffed; radish roses; salted potato crisps; chipolata sausages, served hot or cold on cocktail sticks; small cheese biscuits or canapés with savoury topping; cheese straws; stuffed celery sticks; savoury éclairs; savoury fish balls; savoury meringues; savoury prunes.

For recipes, see this section and pages 295-9.

Canapés

Canapés can be served hot or cold.

To Serve Cold. Cut thin slices of buttered toast into fingers, triangles, or into small rounds with a biscuit cutter.

(1) Spread with bloater cream or some kind of fish paste with half a stuffed olive or rolled anchovy in the centre.

(2) Smoked salmon sprinkled with finely chopped parsley or chopped chives.

(3) Slice of hard-boiled egg, garnished with pimento or tiny piece of curled anchovy.

(4) Sardines pounded with a little vinegar, Worcester sauce, or finely chopped pickle. Garnish with sliced tomato sprinkled with finely chopped parsley or slices of stuffed olive or pickled gherkin.

(5) Thin slices of rollmop; garnish with tiny tufts of watercress.

(6) Cream cheese; add chopped capers or gherkin and garnish with a pinch of paprika *or* add finely chopped heart of celery to the cheese and garnish with celery leaves.

(7) Chopped tongue; moisten with tomato ketchup, garnish with cocktail onions.

To Serve Hot. (1) Chutney Cheese. Cut some bread into small rounds or fingers and toast on one side. Cover the other side with chutney sauce and sprinkle with grated cheese. Place for 2 or 3 minutes under the grill till the cheese is melted.

(2) **Tomato and Cheese.** Cut bread into small rounds with a biscuit cutter. Toast one side then butter the other. Cut slices of small firm tomatoes ¼ inch thick, place on the buttered side, season with salt and a speck of grated onion. Sprinkle liberally with grated cheese and place under the grill till lightly browned.

Eggs Stuffed with Olives

3 eggs	*Beetroot*
Olives (chopped) 1 tablespoonful	*Butter 1 teaspoonful*
Small cress	*Seasoning*

Boil the eggs hard, then cut them across lengthwise and remove the yolks. Put the yolks in a basin and pound them thoroughly with the teaspoonful of butter or margarine; season with salt and pepper, and add the finely minced olives. Return the mixture to the egg cases, smoothing them over with a knife dipped in water. Place a layer of small cress or lettuce (previously tossed in French dressing) at the bottom of a shallow bowl. Cut 6 slices of beetroot, trimming the edges with a fluted cutter, place them on the cress, and put half of an egg on top of each.

For **Anchovy Eggs**, proceed as in previous recipe, substituting 1 teaspoonful of anchovy essence for the olives.

For Sardine Eggs, use 3 or 4 pounded sardines and a few drops of vinegar in place of the olives.

Egg Mayonnaise

Cut sufficient hard-boiled eggs in halves or quarters, season with salt and pepper, and coat with mayonnaise sauce (see page 212). Garnish with small cress and sliced tomatoes.

Chopped Herrings

2 salt herrings	Chopped onion 1 tablespoonful
Large sour apple	Vinegar 2 tablespoonfuls
Thick slice of bread	Salad oil 2 teaspoonfuls
1 hard-boiled egg	Lettuce leaves

Soak herrings in cold water for 24 hours. Then wash thoroughly, remove bones, and chop finely. Soak the bread in the vinegar, then break up with a fork, mix with the herring, and add the finely chopped onion, apple, the salad oil, and a little pepper. Serve on lettuce leaves and sprinkle with chopped hard-boiled egg.

Herring Salad (1)

2 salt herrings	Chopped olives 1 dessertspoonful
1 hard-boiled egg	Chopped cucumber 1 dessertspoonful
1 boiled potato (medium)	Capers 1 teaspoonful
Chopped onion 1 dessert-	Pepper
spoonful	Beetroot
Mayonnaise	

Soak the fish in cold water for several hours, then remove the skin and bones and chop the fish finely. Chop up the egg and potato and mix all ingredients together. Add sufficient mayonnaise to moisten and garnish with capers and chopped beetroot.

Herring Salad (2)

4 pickled herrings with soft roes	1 small onion
2 large apples	Capers 1 tablespoonful
Chopped beetroot 2 tablespoonfuls	Vinegar ¼ pint

Soak the herrings for several hours in cold water, then remove skin and bones and chop the fish. Peel and chop apples, onion, and beetroot, and add to the herring, together with the capers. Mix thoroughly and season with salt and pepper.

Pound the soft roes of the herrings to a paste, add the vinegar and pour over the salad, mixing well.

Chopped Liver

Chicken livers 6–8 oz.	1 hard-boiled egg
Small onion	Breadcrumbs 1 tablespoonful
Chicken fat	Salt and pepper

Cook livers in chicken fat a few minutes till tender. Then, using the finest cutter of the mincing machine, mince it together with the onion and hard-boiled egg, mix with the breadcrumbs, season with salt and pepper, and add sufficient chicken fat to form a paste.

Note. Calf's liver can be used in place of chicken livers.

Smoked Salmon

If served as the only hors-d'oeuvres, the thin slices can be put on individual plates, either flat or rolled up; sprinkle very lightly with chopped parsley.

If served with mixed hors-d'oeuvre, then arrange on a small dish, the slices overlapping each other, and garnish with sprigs of parsley.

Soups
GENERAL DIRECTIONS FOR MAKING STOCK

Stock forms the basis of all soups, stews, sauces and gravies.

The chief object in making stock is to draw into the water the goodness from the materials employed in making it.

Except when a clear brown stock is required it is not necessary to use fresh meat. There will generally be sufficient trimmings of meat and bones, both cooked and uncooked, that can be used for this purpose. The water in which mutton or brisket has been boiled, the bones from a rolled rib of beef or any boned joint, poultry carcasses, etc., all make excellent soup stock.

Always use a saucepan with a tightly fitting lid and when the stock is sufficiently cooked, strain it into a bowl and leave it overnight, either in the coolest part of the larder or in the refrigerator. The following day remove the cake of fat that has formed on top, which can be clarified (see page 19) and added to your dripping.

The stock will keep for several days, but in hot weather it should be reboiled daily; in winter every second day will do.

For Bone and Meat Stocks allow 2 quarts cold water to 2 lb. bones or meat and bones. Bones should be chopped up and any meat used cut into small pieces. Put them together in a saucepan, add a little salt, bring slowly to the boil and skim off the scum as it rises. Then simmer gently for about 4 hours. Two hours before straining the stock, add flavouring vegetables washed and peeled (or scraped). The most generally used are carrots, turnips, celery, onions and leeks.

Brown stock is made from beef or beef and knuckle of veal. White stock is made from veal, poultry, calf's head and calves' feet. If a dark coloured stock is required, brown the meat and chopped bones in a little dripping before adding the water.

Vegetable Stocks also make good soups.

Note. Do not add potatoes, green vegetables, macaroni or other starchy materials to stock, unless it is to be used immediately.

Bone Stock

Beef, mutton or veal bones 2 lb.	*3 or 4 peppercorns*
Cold water 2 quarts	*2 or 3 sticks celery*
2 medium carrots	*2 medium onions*
Salt 2 teaspoonfuls	*Small turnip*

Put the washed and chopped bones in a saucepan with the cold water and salt, bring very slowly to the boil, then boil quickly for a minute till the scum has risen, then skim. Add ½ cup of cold water, bring to the boil and skim again. Cover closely and simmer gently for 3 hours. Add the peppercorns and washed, peeled and thickly sliced vegetables and continue simmering for another hour. Strain and store as directed.

General Stock

Add any available cooked bones to liquor in which mutton or beef has been boiled. Proceed as for Bone Stock, adding vegetables and seasoning in the same proportion.

Fish Stock

Put a washed cod's head, or bones, skin, and trimmings from any white fish in a saucepan (used only for fish). Add a quart of cold water and bring to the boil. Then add a small onion or leek, a slice of parsnip, and a medium-sized carrot washed, peeled, and cut in pieces, also a sprig of parsley, a stick of celery, half a bay leaf, a clove, and a few white peppercorns. Add salt to taste and simmer for 1 hour. Then strain.

Vegetable Stock

When making a vegetable stock use a mixture of several vegetables, any root vegetables available, celery, onions, leeks, a few spinach leaves, outside leaves of cabbage or lettuce, etc., herbs, and seasoning as for Bone Stock. Allow 1 quart water and 1 teaspoonful salt to every lb. vegetables, and cook gently for 1 hour or longer. This stock should be strained and used while it is fresh, especially when starchy and green vegetables are used.

Vegetable Waters. All vegetables contain valuable mineral salts, which are easily dissolved in boiling water. Therefore the water in which they are cooked should be saved and utilized for soup. This includes water from carrots, turnips, peas, beans, cauliflower, asparagus, spinach, etc., as well as that from rice, barley, macaroni, and pulse foods. These waters can be mixed with ordinary stock for making thick soup and sauces, or without meat stock for making vegetable purées and milk soups.

To Clear Soup Stock

Remove all fat from the stock and turn it into a saucepan. For every quart add the slightly beaten white of an egg and the shell broken in small pieces. Whisk over a moderate heat till boiling, boil for 2 minutes, then cover and *simmer gently for 20 minutes*. Skim, and strain through muslin.

CLASSIFICATION OF SOUPS

Soups can be divided into four classes:

(1) **Clear Soup or Consommé.** Clarified meat stock, garnished according to fancy.

(2) **Purées.** The solid material is rubbed through a sieve, reheated with the liquor, and a little flour or cornflour added.

(3) **Thickened Soups.** Made of meat, fish, or vegetable stock and thickened with some cereal, such as flour, cornflour, or arrowroot, or, in the case of fish or vegetable stock, a liaison of eggs and milk.

(4) **Broths.** These contain meat, vegetables, and cereal, but no additional thickening. They can be garnished with vegetables, rice, barley, etc.

QUANTITY OF SOUP PER HEAD

One third of a pint is the usual allowance, but if a substantial soup is to furnish the principal part of a meal, allow half a pint per head.

Consommé

Consommé or clear soup is generally clarified (see above) and then garnished according to fancy, the consommé taking its name from the garnish. The following recipe should, however, give an absolutely clear soup, if cooked sufficiently slowly.

Gravy beef 2 lb.	*1 clove*
1 carrot	*1 blade of mace*
2 sticks celery	*Salt and peppercorns*
1 onion	*Water*

Remove all fat from the meat and cut up into small pieces, put into a saucepan with 1 teaspoonful salt and sufficient water to cover completely, and bring very slowly to boiling point. As soon as it boils, skim it and add ½ cup cold water, again allow to come to the boil and add another ½ cup of water, and continue in this way until 1½ pints cold water have been added. Prepare and cut up the vegetables, add to the soup, also the seasoning, and simmer *very gently* for 2 hours, then strain through muslin. This soup can be served hot or cold.

A flavouring of sherry, 1 teaspoonful per portion, is a great improvement. Add this just before serving.

Consommé à la Julienne. Clear soup garnished with cooked carrot, turnip, onion, and celery, cut into match-like strips.

Consommé à la Jardinière. Vegetables as above, but cut into small dice, and a few cooked green peas and tiny sprigs of cauliflower added.

Consommé à l'Italienne. Clear soup garnished with cooked macaroni cut into rings, or vermicelli, spaghetti, or fancy shapes of Italian pasta.

Consommé Royale. Clear soup garnished with dice of savoury custard (see page 50).

See also Etceteras for Soups (pages 47–50).

Apple Soup

Apple purée ⅓ pint   *Cooked rice 1 teacupful*
Stock 2 pints   *Salt, pepper, ginger*

Sieve the apple purée, which should be slightly sweetened, and add it to 2 pints of well-flavoured stock. Bring to the boil, add the cooked rice, season with salt, pepper, and a pinch of ginger, and simmer for 2 minutes.

Artichoke and Potato Soup

Jerusalem artichokes 1 lb.   *Stock 3 pints*
Potatoes 1 lb.   *Flour 1 tablespoonful*
2 sticks celery   *Margarine 2 oz.*
1 onion   *Seasoning*

Prepare vegetables and cut them into slices. (Drop artichokes immediately into cold water, to which a teaspoonful of lemon juice had been added, to preserve their colour.)

Melt the margarine in a saucepan, add vegetables, and cook for a few minutes, with the lid on the saucepan and shaking the pan or stirring occasionally, so that they do not brown. Then add the stock, bring to the boil, add seasoning, and simmer till the vegetables are tender; then rub through a sieve. Return to saucepan, reboil, then add the flour mixed smoothly with a little water. Stir while it simmers for 5 minutes. Serve with croûtons.

Beetroot Soup (1)
(Borscht)

3 or 4 large beetroots	Yolks of 3 eggs
Water 1 quart	Sugar
Meat or chicken stock 1 quart	Salt
Lemon juice	

Scrub, peel, and slice beetroots, put in a saucepan with the water, cover, and simmer till tender. Then strain. Mix this liquor with the stock, and add salt, sugar, and lemon juice to taste. Beat up the eggs with a little cold stock. Boil the remainder, remove from heat, add the beaten eggs, and stir for a minute or two over a very gentle heat, but do not reboil.

Beetroot Soup (2)
(Borscht)

Use bone stock or liquor from boiled meat. For 2 quarts stock take 1 breakfastcupful each *grated* cooked beetroot, raw potato, and sour apple, and the same quantity of finely shredded white cabbage.

Put all ingredients together in a saucepan, season with salt and pepper, add 2 teaspoonfuls of sugar, and boil gently for 30 minutes. Then add lemon juice or citric acid to taste and serve very hot.

Cabbage Soup
(Sweet and Sour)

Stock 3 pints	Sieved tomatoes or tomato juice ¼ pint
Small cabbage	Sugar
1 lemon	3 apples
1 onion	Salt and pepper

Shred the cabbage finely; peel the apples and onion and grate them. Put the stock and tomato juice in a saucepan and bring to the boil; add the cabbage, apple and onion, cover and cook gently for $\frac{1}{2}$ hour. Season with salt and pepper, and before serving add the juice of the lemon and sugar to taste.

Chicken Broth

(1) Use an old boiling fowl or stewing chicken. Wash thoroughly, cut it into joints, and break up the carcass. Scald and skin feet and gizzard and wash neck. Put the chicken into a saucepan, add 4 or 5 pints cold water and a little salt, bring to the boil, and skim. Add a cut-up onion, carrot, and stick of celery, and simmer gently for 3 hours or until the chicken is tender. Then strain and when cold remove the fat. When required, reheat and add vermicelli, noodles, or rice, and cook till tender. Rice will take about 20 minutes, fine vermicelli and noodles about 10 minutes. The chicken can be used in salad or croquettes, or warmed through in thick gravy or tomato or egg and lemon sauce.

(2) Use the carcass of a cooked chicken. Break it up into small pieces, put it in a saucepan with a cut-up onion and 2 or 3 sticks of celery. Cover with water, add salt and pepper to taste, and simmer gently for 2 hours, then strain.

Giblet Soup

Two sets of giblets	*Flour 1 oz.*
1 carrot	*Dripping or chicken fat 1 oz.*
1 onion	*Seasoning*
Stock 3 pints	

Wash and clean giblets, scald and skin the feet, and put into a saucepan with the cut-up carrot and onion, pour over the stock, add salt and pepper to taste, bring to the boil, and simmer gently for 2 hours. Then strain and cut up the giblets into small pieces and put aside. Melt the fat, stir in the flour smoothly and gradually add the stock, stir till boiling, add the reserved giblets, season to taste, and simmer for 5 minutes.

Cooked rice can be added for a change, or small meat balls. (See page 49.)

Danish Giblet Soup

Make as previous recipe, but add with the chopped giblets 1 teacupful of apple purée and 8 or 10 cooked and chopped prunes and simmer for 10 minutes.

Lentil Soup

Lentils 1 pint	*Stock or salt beef liquor 2 quarts*
2 onions	*Flour 1 oz.*
2 carrots	*Chopped parsley*
A small turnip	*Salt, pepper and a bay leaf*
2 or 3 sticks celery	

Wash lentils thoroughly, prepare the vegetables, cut them up and put all ingredients except parsley together in a saucepan. Bring to the boil and simmer gently for 1½ hours. Remove bay leaf and rub the cooked vegetables through a sieve. Return to saucepan, reboil, add the flour mixed smoothly with a little cold water, stir till boiling and simmer for 5 minutes. Add a little chopped parsley before serving.

This soup is nicest made with liquor in which salt beef has been cooked, but bone or vegetable stock can be used if this is not available, in which case a small piece of worsht cooked in the soup is an improvement. Cook this about ¾ hour, then cut up in small dice and serve in the soup.

Minestrone Soup

Heart of a small cabbage	*A small onion*
Tomato pulp (fresh or tinned) ¼ pint	*2 leeks*
Olive oil 4 tablespoonfuls	*Clove of garlic*
2 sticks celery	*Rice 1 oz.*
Small turnip	*Macaroni 1¼ oz.*
Medium carrot	*Water 4 pints*
Chopped parsley	*Salt and pepper*

Prepare the vegetables, crush the garlic; dice the carrot, turnip and onion; shred leeks, celery, and cabbage. Heat the oil in a saucepan, add the carrot, turnip, onion, leek, and garlic, cover, and cook over a gentle heat 5–10 minutes without browning, keeping it well stirred. Then add the water and seasoning, and, when boiling, the remaining ingredients except the parsley. Cook gently for ¾ hour, add the chopped parsley, and serve. If too thick, add a little more water or stock.

Onion Soup

3 Spanish onions   *Stock 3 pints*
Dripping or cooking fat 2 oz.   *Seasoning*
Flour 1 tablespoonful

Peel the onions and slice them thinly. Melt the dripping in a saucepan, put in the onions, cover, and fry gently till golden brown. Keep them well stirred, so that they brown evenly and do not burn. When the onions are brown, stir in the flour smoothly, then gradually add the stock. Stir till boiling, then cook gently for 1 hour. Rub through a sieve, season to taste, and reheat.

Hungarian Onion Soup

2 Spanish onions   *Stock 3 pints*
Margarine 2 oz.   *Noodles or vermicelli*
Paprika 1 teaspoonful   *Salt and pepper*
2 tomatoes

Peel and thinly slice the onions and cook gently in the margarine (or cooking fat) until golden brown, stir in the paprika, add the cut-up tomatoes (or a little concentrated tomato purée) and pour over the stock. Bring to the boil and cook gently for ½ hour; then rub through a sieve, return to saucepan, bring to the boil and add a little vermicelli or noodles. Season and simmer for another 10–15 minutes.

Pea Soup

Make this when you have been boiling a piece of smoked beef, tongue, or worsht.

To 3 pints of liquor allow ½ lb. split peas, a carrot, turnip, and onion, and a few sticks of celery. Soak the peas overnight, then put in a saucepan with the prepared and cut-up vegetables, and cook slowly till the peas are soft – about 2 hours.

Then rub through a sieve. Return to the saucepan, and when hot add 1 tablespoonful flour mixed smoothly with a little cold water. Stir till boiling, season to taste, simmer 5 minutes, and add a little chopped or dried mint before serving.

Potato Soup (1)

Potatoes 2 lb.	*Small piece worsht or a few sausages*
3 or 4 leeks	*Flour 1 oz.*
2 or 3 sticks celery	*Chopped parsley*
Vegetable or bone stock 2 quarts	

Prepare and cut up vegetables and cook in the stock till tender; then rub through a sieve. Return to the saucepan, add the worsht cut up in small dice, and simmer for ½ hour. Then season to taste, add the flour mixed smoothly with a little cold water, stir till boiling, simmer another 10 minutes, and add chopped parsley before serving.

If sausages are being used, remove the skin and with floured hands roll into tiny balls. These will only need cooking about 10 minutes.

Potato Soup (2)

Make this when you want some soup in a hurry. Warm some well-flavoured stock and grate into it a few peeled potatoes. Stir till boiling, cook for 10 minutes, and add a little chopped parsley before serving.

Purée of Haricot Beans

Make this like the lentil soup, substituting haricot beans for lentils. But the beans must be soaked in cold water overnight, and should be cooked till soft before sieving.

Scotch Broth

Neck of mutton 1¼ lb.	*1 large carrot*
Pearl barley 2 oz.	*1 small turnip*
1 onion	*A few sticks of celery*
2 leeks	*Water 2 quarts*
Chopped parsley	*Salt and pepper*

Trim all fat from the meat, put meat in a saucepan, pour the water over, and bring slowly to the boil, skim well, and add the seasoning and washed barley. Simmer for 1 hour. Prepare the vegetables, cut into dice or chop finely, add to the soup, and continue cooking for another hour. Take out the meat, remove the bone, cut the meat into dice, return to the broth, reheat, and add a little chopped parsley.

Spring Soup

Lettuce leaves
Young carrots 4–6 oz.
A small bunch spring onions
Chicken broth or meat stock 2 pints
Salt and pepper

Scrape and dice the carrots, trim the onions and slice them thinly, and shred a few lettuce leaves finely. Bring the stock to the boil, add the vegetables, cover and simmer gently till tender – about 30 minutes. Season with salt and pepper to taste.

If available a little diced cucumber can be added to the other vegetables.

Tomato Soup

Fresh tomatoes 1 lb. or a small tin
Vegetable or any light stock 3 pints
Margarine 2 oz.
Chopped parsley 1 tablespoonful
Salt, pepper, sugar, and mace
Onions ¼ lb.
1 large carrot
Flour 1 tablespoonful
Sago 2 tablespoonfuls

Peel and slice onions, scrape and slice the carrot. Melt the margarine, put in the onion and carrot, and fry over a gentle heat for 5 or 6 minutes; then add tomatoes (cut-up, if fresh ones are used), pour on the stock, and season with salt, pepper, and a pinch of mace. Simmer gently for 1 hour, then rub through a sieve. Return to saucepan, add ½ teaspoonful sugar, and the flour mixed with a little cold water. Stir till boiling, sprinkle in the sago, and cook gently for another 15 minutes, keeping it well stirred. Add chopped parsley just before serving.

Vegetable Soup

Vegetable stock or water 4 pints   *Margarine 2 oz.*
2 or 3 sticks celery   *1 leek*
2 medium carrots   *1 small turnip*
2 or 3 sprouts   *2 onions*
(or finely shredded spinach or cabbage leaves)   *Rice 2 tablespoonfuls*
Salt, pepper, bay leaf   *Chopped parsley*

Prepare vegetables, using the green leaves of the celery and green of the leek. Cut carrots, turnip, and onion into small dice, and celery, leek, and sprouts into thin slices. Melt the margarine, add vegetables, and cook gently with the lid on the saucepan for 10 minutes. Keep well stirred and do not let them brown. Then add the stock or water, washed rice, salt and pepper to taste, and a bay leaf. Bring to the boil and simmer gently about 1½ hours. Remove bay leaf and add chopped parsley just before serving.

MILK SOUPS

Artichoke Soup

Artichokes 2 lb.   *Milk 1 pint*
2 onions   *Water 2 pints*
Margarine 1 oz.   *Seasoning*
Flour 1 oz.

Peel and cut up the artichokes and onions. Put in a saucepan with the water, adding salt to taste, and simmer till the vegetables are tender. Rub through a sieve, return to the saucepan, add the milk, and bring to the boil. Mix the flour smoothly with the melted margarine, cook a minute or two, add to the soup, stir till boiling, and simmer for 5 minutes. Serve with croûtons.

Celery Soup

A large head of celery   *1 onion*
Vegetable stock 2 pints   *Flour 1½ oz.*
Milk ¼ pint   *Margarine 1½ oz.*
Chopped parsley   *Seasoning*

Prepare and slice the celery and onion and sauté in the margarine for 5 minutes, keeping it well stirred, then add the stock, season to taste, bring to the boil and cook gently until the vegetables are quite soft – about 45 minutes. Then rub through a sieve and return to saucepan, add the flour-blended with the milk, stir till boiling, simmer for 2 or 3 minutes, and add chopped parsley before serving.

Cheese Soup

Milk 1 pint	*1 onion*
Cheese 2 oz.	*Clove of garlic (optional)*
Margarine 1 oz.	*1 egg yolk*
White vegetable stock 1 pint	*Salt, peppercorns, cayenne*
Flour 1 oz.	

Chop the onion and crush the clove of garlic, if it is being used, and cook gently in the margarine for a few minutes without browning. Add the stock and seasoning, bring to boil, simmer for 10 minutes, add the flour mixed smoothly with a little of the milk, stir till boiling, simmer for 5 minutes, then strain. Return to the saucepan, add the milk mixed with the beaten egg and the finely-grated cheese, stir over a gentle heat, and make very hot, but do *not* boil or the egg will curdle.

Chicory Soup

Chicory 1 lb.	*Margarine 2 oz.*
Potatoes 1 lb.	*Milk ½ pint*
Onions ¼ lb.	*Chopped parsley*
Water 2 pints	*Salt and pepper*
Cornflour 2 teaspoonfuls	

Prepare and cut up the vegetables. Melt the margarine in a saucepan, add the vegetables and cook over a gentle heat for a few minutes, stirring 2 or 3 times. Then add the water, season with salt and pepper, and cover and cook slowly until the vegetables are tender; then rub through a sieve, return to the saucepan, add the milk and bring it to the boil, and add the cornflour blended with cold water. Stir till boiling, simmer gently for 5 minutes, then add a little chopped parsley.

This can be served with croûtons or grated cheese.

Mushroom Soup

Mushrooms ½ lb.
A small onion
Margarine or butter 2 oz.
Flour 2 oz.
Vegetable stock 1¼ pints
Milk ½ pint
Salt and pepper

Peel and chop mushrooms and onion, put in a saucepan with the stock, cover and simmer gently for 20 minutes; then rub through a sieve. Melt the butter in a saucepan, add flour, then gradually stir in the mushroom purée and milk, stir till boiling, season, and simmer for 5 minutes.

Onion Soup

Onions 1 lb.
Margarine 2 oz.
Milk 1 pint
Flour 1 oz.
White vegetable stock 2 pints
Salt and pepper
Cheese croûtes

Peel the onions and chop finely, or put through the mincer. Melt the margarine, add the onions, and cook over a gentle heat for a few minutes without browning. Pour on the stock, season to taste, and cook gently for 30 minutes. Add the flour mixed smoothly with a little water and the milk, stir till boiling, and simmer for 5 minutes. Put a cheese croûte (page 47) in each soup cup and pour the soup over.

Or, in place of the cheese croûtes, cut some slices of bread about ⅓ inch thick, then cut into pieces about 2 inches by ½ inch. Dip these quickly in milk, sprinkle with salt, lay them on a greased tin, and bake till crisp. Place one of these sippets in each plate or cup and pour the soup over.

Potato Soup

Potatoes 1½ lb.
A few sticks of celery
Water 3 pints
Salt and pepper
3 large onions
Milk ½ pint
Flour 1 oz.
Chopped parsley

Prepare and slice the vegetables and boil them in the water till quite soft, then rub through a sieve. Put back in the saucepan, add the milk, season with salt and pepper, and reheat. Mix the flour smoothly with a little cold water, add to the soup, and stir while it simmers for 5 minutes. Add chopped parsley and serve with croûtons.

Tomato Soup

Tomatoes 1 lb. or a small tin	*1 onion*
Water 1½ pints	*1 carrot*
Milk ½ pint	*1 stick celery*
Cornflour 1 tablespoonful	*Margarine 1 oz.*
Chopped parsley or watercress	*Salt, pepper, sugar*

Slice tomatoes and other vegetables. Melt the margarine in a saucepan, add the tomatoes and vegetables and cook over a gentle heat for 2 or 3 minutes. Then add the water and season with salt and pepper. Bring to the boil and cook gently until the vegetables are soft – about 40 minutes. Then rub through a sieve, return to pan, add the cornflour blended with the milk and stir till boiling. Add ½ teaspoonful sugar and simmer for 2 or 3 minutes. Just before serving add a little chopped parsley or watercress.

Note. A little diced ridge cucumber cooked in stock or water till just tender is also very good served in this soup.

Quick Vegetable Soup

Make this when you have some left-over vegetables – potatoes, carrots, beans, artichokes, etc. Any mixture will do. Rub them through a sieve. To 1 pint vegetable purée allow ½ pint vegetable stock, ½ pint milk, 1 oz. margarine, and 1 oz. flour.

Melt the margarine, stir in the flour smoothly, then gradually add the milk, vegetable stock, and purée. Stir till boiling, season to taste, and simmer for 5 minutes. Add chopped parsley before serving.

ETCETERAS FOR SOUPS

Bread Balls

2 thick slices of stale bread
Chopped onion 1 tablespoonful
Dripping or chicken fat 1 tablespoonful
Breadcrumbs
1 egg

Chopped parsley 2 teaspoon-
    fuls
Grated lemon rind
Mixed herbs (optional)
Salt and pepper

Soak the slices of bread in cold water, then drain and squeeze
very dry and beat up with a fork. Fry the onion a golden brown
in the fat, then add to the soaked bread, together with the
chopped parsley, grated rind of half a lemon, and, if liked, a
pinch of mixed herbs. Season with salt and pepper, add the
beaten egg and sufficient breadcrumbs to absorb any moisture.
Roll into tiny balls, drop into boiling soup, and simmer 15–20
minutes.

Croûtons

Cut stale bread into dice, fry a golden brown in a little very
hot fat. Drain and serve with thick soups.

Cheese Croûtes

Cut a stale roll or the end of a French loaf into very thin
slices. Or cut thin slices from an ordinary loaf and cut into
rounds with a biscuit cutter. (The left-over pieces can be dried
for crumbs or used in puddings.)

Bake these in a slow oven till quite crisp and lightly tinted,
then cover with grated cheese and brown under the grill.
These are particularly good in onion soup.

Crisped Bread

(1) Cut stale bread wafer thin and bake till crisp and brown in
a moderate oven.

(2) Cut stale bread into slices $\frac{1}{3}$ inch thick, then into $\frac{1}{3}$-inch

sticks. Bake till crisp and brown. Or the bread can be cut into tiny dice.

Crisped bread keeps well if stored in a tin with a closely fitting lid.

Liver Balls
(*Liver Kloese*)

Calf's or chicken's liver 4 oz.	*Breadcrumbs 1 oz.*
Grated onion ¼ teaspoonful	*Stock 6 tablespoonfuls*
Salt and pepper	*Half an egg*

Mince the liver finely. Put the breadcrumbs and stock into a small saucepan and stir over a gentle heat till cooked to a paste. Mix with the liver, add the onion and beaten egg, season with salt and pepper and mix thoroughly. Roll into tiny balls and drop into boiling soup. Cover and boil for 10 minutes before serving.

Egg Balls

2 hard-boiled eggs	*Breadcrumbs 1 tablespoonful*
1 raw egg yolk	*Salt and pepper*

Rub the hard-boiled eggs through a sieve, add the raw egg yolk, breadcrumbs and seasoning. With floured hands roll into tiny balls. Drop into boiling soup, then simmer 5–10 minutes. If preferred, these can be cooked in boiling salted water, then added to soup just before serving.

Einlauf

Flour 3 tablespoonfuls	*1 egg*
Water 3 tablespoonfuls	*Pinch of salt*

Mix the flour and salt, add the beaten egg and water, and beat till smooth. Pour *very slowly* from the end of a spoon into boiling soup. Cover, and boil quickly for 3 minutes. Add a little chopped parsley to the soup.

Kreplech

Make dough as for noodles (see below), but cut it into smaller
squares – about 2 inches. Fill as for ravioli (page 121). When
quite dry, drop into boiling soup (or salted water) and cook for
15 minutes.

Filling. Mince finely any left-over cold meat and to 1 cupful add 2 teaspoonfuls each grated onion and chopped parsley.
Season with salt, pepper, and ginger, and moisten with a
spoonful or two of thick gravy.

Mandeln
(*Soup Nuts*)

Flour 6 oz.   *Cooking oil 3 dessertspoonfuls*
2 eggs   *Salt 1 level teaspoonful*

Beat eggs slightly and mix all ingredients to a soft dough.
Leave in a cold place (fridge if available) for ½ hour. Then with
floured hands form into pencil-thin rolls and cut into ½-inch
pieces. Place on well-greased baking tins and bake in a
moderate oven (375°, Regulo No. 4) till golden brown –
about 20 minutes. Shake the tins occasionally to brown
evenly. When made in advance, reheat before serving in soup.

Meat Balls

Raw beef 4 oz.   *Chopped parsley 2 teaspoonfuls*
Breadcrumbs 2 oz.   *Salt, pepper, and nutmeg*
Grated onion 1 teaspoonful   *Grated rind of a lemon*
1 egg

Mince the meat very finely, add the crumbs, onion, parsley,
and lemon rind; mix well together, bind with egg, and season
with salt, pepper, and grated nutmeg. Roll into little balls the
size of marbles, and cook in boiling soup 15–20 minutes.

Noodles

Beat up 2 eggs with a little salt, pepper, and a pinch of ground
ginger, and add enough flour to make a stiff paste. Knead
thoroughly, roll out *very thin* on a floured board, and leave for

a couple of hours to dry. Then cut into 3-inch strips, place the strips one on top of another and cut across into match-like sticks. Toss lightly with the fingers to separate them and spread out on a board to dry. If not required for immediate use, store, when thoroughly dry, in airtight jars.

Add to boiling soup and boil for 10 minutes.

Noodle Puffs. Make noodle dough as above and when moderately dry fold over in halves. With a tiny floured cutter or thimble cut into rounds, pressing well so that the edges stick together. Fry in deep fat till golden brown. Place a few in each soup cup or plate, and pour the hot soup over.

Pfarvel

Beat up an egg with a little salt and add flour until the mixture forms a stiff ball. Grate on a coarse grater and leave on a board to dry. Add to boiling soup and cook for 10 minutes.

Potato Croûtons

Peel 2 or 3 potatoes, cut into small dice, put into cold water for 15 minutes, then drain and dry in a cloth.

Melt a little fat in a frying pan and fry the potatoes over a moderate heat, shaking the pan from time to time until they are just golden brown and crisp outside. Remove from pan and sprinkle with salt before serving with thick soups.

Savoury Custard

Yolks of 2 eggs	*Salt and cayenne*
Clear stock ¼ pint	

Beat up the egg yolks, pour on the hot stock, and season with salt and pepper. Turn into a small greased basin, cover, and steam slowly till very firm – about 15 minutes. Then cut into dice and put a few in each soup cup or plate, and pour the soup over. (See Consommé Royale, page 36.)

Fish

Fish can be used with advantage to vary the daily menu, either as a separate course at a meal or as a substitute for meat. Freshness is the most important quality of the fish. In purchasing, see that the eyes are bright, the flesh firm, gills red, and fish well covered with scales. An unpleasant smell is sure indication that the fish is not fresh. The spots on plaice should be bright red and not dusky brown.

Fish can be boiled, baked, steamed, grilled, fried, stewed, or cooked *en casserole*, but whichever method is employed it must be borne in mind that fish, more than any other food, requires very careful seasoning and flavouring. The more tasteless varieties, such as haddock, whiting, cod, hake, and lemon soles, need piquant sauces to accompany them; whereas the well-flavoured fish like salmon, halibut, and trout require only simple sauces and a minimum of seasoning.

Fish must be well cleaned. See that all blood is removed from the backbone, and remove any black skin in the cavity of the fish by rubbing with salt. Wash thoroughly under running water, and dry in a clean cloth.

Fresh-water fish is the only fish that requires soaking; never leave other fish lying in water.

The fishmonger usually cleans the fish and fillets and skins it, as required, but there are occasions when this has to be done at home, in which case the following hints will be useful.

To Clean. Lay fish on paper or a board, cut off the tail and fins (this is best done with kitchen scissors), and also the head. Scrape off scales with a knife from the tail end, holding this firmly with the left hand, then cut through the skin of the abdomen and remove the entrails. Flat fish are cleaned by making a small cut on the dark side of the fish just below the gills.

To Fillet. Place the fish flat on a board with the tail towards you. Cut round the head, round the fins, and across the tail, then down the middle, cutting only as deep as the bone.

With a sharp, pointed knife remove the fillet on the *left* side of the fish, cutting in long sharp cuts and keeping the fish as flat as possible.

Now turn the fish round, so that the head is towards you, and remove the second fillet. Turn the fish over and remove the other two fillets in the same way.

To Skin. Place the fish skin side downwards on a board. Make a small slit at the tail end, between the skin and the flesh, and then holding the tip end of the skin firmly with the left hand, work the knife along to the other end of the fillet until it is entirely separated from the skin. If the fingers are dipped in salt, they are enabled to hold the skin more firmly.

To Boil. (1) This method should only be used for cooking large, whole fish or large pieces of fish, such as salmon, hake, halibut, etc. If available use a fish kettle with a strainer, otherwise tie the fish in muslin and place it on a plate at the bottom of the saucepan.

Clean and wash the fish and rub it over with lemon juice. Place in salted water or court bouillon (see page 54) – just sufficient to cover – that is not quite boiling, and add a teaspoonful of vinegar or lemon juice. Bring to the boil and simmer gently till done. Never let fish boil fast.

It is not possible to give the exact time the fish will take to cook, for a thick fish will take longer than a thin fish of the same weight. But allow 6 to 10 minutes to the pound, according to the thickness, and for a large fish 10 minutes extra.

Test by running a wooden skewer into the fish near the bone. If it parts easily from the bone, the fish is done. Dish immediately it is cooked.

(2) Small pieces of fish can be cooked in a frying pan or small saucepan. Place the fish in hot salted water, cover, and cook very gently until done. This will take about 10–15 minutes, according to the thickness of the fish. If a frying pan is being used, cover it with a large saucepan lid or an enamel plate.

To Serve. Drain thoroughly, place on a hot dish, garnish with parsley and cut lemon, and hand the sauce separately.

Any of the following sauces can be used with boiled or steamed fish: anchovy, caper, egg, fennel, lemon, mayonnaise, mustard, parsley, piccalilli, tartare, tomato.

To Steam. (1) Prepare as for boiling. Wrap in muslin and place in a steamer over a saucepan of boiling water. This will take longer to cook.

(2) Another very good method of steaming small fish or fillets, which is specially suitable for invalids and children,

is to do it between two greased plates. After preparing the fish, sprinkle with salt and lemon juice and dot with butter. Put on one plate, cover with the other, and place over a saucepan of boiling water. It will take 20–30 minutes to cook, according to its size and thickness. If preferred, omit lemon juice and pour a little milk over the fish instead.

To Bake. Fish may be baked whole or in fillets or steaks. Whole fish can be stuffed with a savoury filling. Detailed recipes are given later.

To Fry. Almost any kind of fish adapts itself to this mode of cooking. Small fish can be fried whole, the larger ones filleted or cut into steaks.

After washing in cold water, the fish must be thoroughly dried; it must then be coated with some preparation that will prevent the fat soaking in.

There are two different methods of frying fish: (1) in deep fat; (2) in shallow fat. For the first method a deep saucepan and a frying basket are required, and the saucepan should be half filled with clarified fat or oil. This is suitable for small pieces of fish, fish cakes, whitebait, etc. For shallow frying, use a frying pan and sufficient oil or fat just to cover the fish. The oil should be heated until a faint blue smoke begins to rise.

Do not let the pieces of fish touch each other, nor put in too many pieces at a time, since if the oil is cooled below a certain temperature it will soak into the fish and make it sodden.

To Fry Fish to be Served Cold. Use method (2). Use frying oil whenever possible. Should this at any time not be procurable, then vegetarian cooking fat can take its place.

On one plate put plain flour seasoned with salt; on another beat up one or more eggs, according to the quantity of fish to be fried.

Dip each piece of dried fish in the seasoned flour, then coat with egg, and when the oil is the right heat, fry each piece a golden brown, first one side then the other, turning carefully with a fish slice. Always put skin side of fillets downwards first, so as to prevent curling. When cooked, drain thoroughly on soft paper.

The oil or fat should be strained into a jar, covered, and used again.

To Fry Fish to be Served Hot. Prepare the fish as above, but after dipping in flour and coating with egg or eggless batter (see page 427), the pieces of fish should be dipped in dried breadcrumbs. Put a little mound of the crumbs on a piece of kitchen paper, dip the egged fish in these, coating it all over. Pat crumbs down with a knife, then shake fish lightly to get rid of loose crumbs.

Fish Fried in Batter. After dipping the pieces of fish in seasoned flour, coat with frying batter (see page 226, coating batter (1)). Have sufficient oil in the pan to float the fish, but do not use a frying basket, as the batter would stick to it.

To Grill. Herrings, mackerel, plaice, and sole are suitable fish to grill, also cutlets of thick fish, such as halibut, hake, salmon, and cod.

Small whole fish should be cut across in three or four places to allow the heat to penetrate, or the outside will dry before the inside is cooked.

Make the grill hot, grease the grill rack and place prepared fish on it, lower heat slightly and cook rather slowly so that the fish is cooked through without burning. Handle carefully when turning, as the flesh breaks rather easily. Insert the back of a knife next to the bone to see when the fish is cooked; it is done when the flesh leaves the bones easily.

Before serving, sprinkle with lemon juice and chopped parsley and garnish with watercress. Serve a savoury sauce separately.

Cutlets should be 1–1½ inches thick. After washing, dry thoroughly, sprinkle with salt, pepper, and lemon juice, and brush over with cooking oil or melted butter. Cook as above, turning once or twice, until the fish is done, when the flesh will be opaque and leave the bone easily.

Court Bouillon
(Stock for Boiling Fish)

Water 2 quarts	*2 bay leaves*
2 onions	*12 peppercorns*
2 carrots	*2 cloves*
Stick of celery	*Juice of a lemon or*
2 sprigs parsley	*¼ teacupful sugar*

Prepare and cut up vegetables, and simmer all ingredients gently for 1 hour. Then strain and use. If liked, a clove of garlic can be added.

SAUCES TO SERVE WITH BOILED OR BAKED FISH

Anchovy, caper, celery, cheese, curry, egg, fennel, hollandaise, horseradish, lemon, mayonnaise, mustard, mushroom, neapolitan, parsley, piccalilli, sweet and sour, tartare, tomato.

For recipes, see pages 196–205. In making the sauce, use for the liquid half fish stock and half milk.

STUFFINGS FOR BAKED FISH

Savoury Stuffing

Breadcrumbs 4 oz.
Margarine 2 oz.
1 egg
Salt and pepper

Grated onion 1 tablespoonful
Chopped parsley 1 tablespoonful
Grated rind and juice of ½
* lemon*

Melt margarine and mix all ingredients. Milk can be used in place of the egg if preferred.

Rice Stuffing

Cooked rice 1 breakfastcupful
Curry powder 1 teaspoonful
Margarine 1 oz.
2 small onions

2 tomatoes
Juice of ½ lemon
Salt and pepper

Peel and chop onions. Skin and cut up tomatoes. Melt margarine and fry onion till golden brown, stir in curry powder and tomatoes, cook for a minute or two longer; then add to rice, together with the lemon juice and seasoning.

Bloaters

Bloaters can be baked, fried, or grilled.

To Prepare. Remove heads, split down the back, and remove the bones. Wipe fish with a damp cloth.

To Bake. Put in a greased tin, put a small knob of margarine on top of each, and bake in a moderate oven about 15 minutes.

To Fry. Put very little fat into frying pan and fry over a gentle heat.

To Grill. Put on to greased grill, skin side up. Grill slowly for 5 minutes, turn over, and cook another 5 minutes.

If preferred, the bloaters can be left whole, just removing the heads. Cook by any of above methods, but for grilling score the skin across diagonally two or three times on both sides.

Bream

Fresh-water Bream. Boil. Serve with tartare or Dutch sauce.
Sea Bream. Bake, boil, fry, grill, or stew.

Bream with Egg and Lemon Sauce

Cook like halibut (see page 66).

Baked Bream

Stuff the fish with savoury stuffing (see page 55). Place on a greased baking tin, dot with margarine, cover with grease-proof paper, pour ½ cup of water into the tin, and bake in a moderate oven 40–50 minutes.

Dish on to a hot dish and serve with parsley, anchovy, or any sauce preferred. In making the sauce, use any liquor from the tin in which the fish was cooked.

Brill

Brill can be boiled, baked, or fried. See methods for cooking plaice.

Brown Stewed Fish

Salmon, carp, shad, or bream
1 onion
1 lemon
Raisins or sultanas 1 oz.
2 or 3 cloves
Flour 1½ oz.

Water ¾ pint
Vinegar ¼ pint
2 bay leaves
Gingerbread 2 oz.
Brown sugar or golden syrup 2 oz.

Stone raisins, slice lemon and onion, and put in a stewpan with the water and vinegar, cloves, and bay leaves, bring to the boil, lay in the fish, and simmer gently till cooked. Then lift the fish on to dish, add the crumbled gingerbread, sugar (or syrup), and flour, mixed smoothly with water, to the liquor in the pan, stir till boiling, simmer 10 minutes, then pour over.

Serve cold. Amount of sugar and vinegar used can be varied.

Carp

Carp are fresh-water fish and inclined to have a muddy flavour. They should be soaked for some hours in salt water and then washed very thoroughly in vinegar and water. When cooked, serve with a piquant sauce. Carp can be baked, boiled, fried, or stewed.

Soused Carp

1 medium-sized carp	*Cloves and allspice*
Vinegar ½ pint	*Salt, pepper, cayenne*
Water ½ pint	*Clove of garlic*

Wash fish in vinegar and water. Cut it up and put in a stewpan. Add 3 or 4 cloves and allspice, clove of garlic, and salt, pepper, and cayenne to taste. Pour over vinegar and water. Cover and cook very gently until the fish is done — about 20–30 minutes. Put the carp on a dish and strain the liquor over.

Cod

Cod can be boiled, steamed, fried, grilled, baked, or cooked *en casserole*. See also recipes for left-over fish (pages 78–80).

Baked Cod with Chutney Sauce

A tail of cod	*Milk ½ pint*
1 lemon	*Chutney 1 tablespoonful*
Margarine 1 oz.	*Flour 1 oz.*
Salt and pepper	

Season the fish with salt and pepper, lay in a greased fire-proofed dish, sprinkle with lemon juice and dot with the margarine. Bake in a moderate oven till cooked – about 30 minutes.

Mix flour to a smooth paste with a little cold milk. Heat remainder, pour it over and mix well. Turn into a small saucepan, stir till boiling, simmer 2 or 3 minutes, then add the liquid from the fish, the chutney, 1 tablespoonful lemon juice, and salt and pepper to taste. Pour over the fish and serve in the dish in which it was cooked.

Note. Hake and haddock can be cooked like this, and steaks or fillets used instead of a tail of fish. These take about 20 minutes to bake.

Baked Tail of Cod

Tail of cod 2 lb.
Grated cheese 2 oz.
Breadcrumbs 2 tablespoonfuls
Chopped gherkin 1 table-
spoonful
Margarine 2 oz.
Chopped parsley 1 tablespoonful
Vinegar 2 tablespoonfuls
Salt and pepper

Place the cod on a greased fireproof dish; pour over the vinegar and spread half the margarine on top. Cover with a greased paper and bake in a moderate oven for 20 minutes. Then remove the skin from the top of the fish. Season with salt and pepper, then sprinkle over the grated cheese, chopped parsley, and chopped gherkin. Cover with breadcrumbs and dot with the remaining margarine. Return to the oven for 15 minutes.

Cod Fillets with Savoury Sauce

Cod fillets 1½ lb.
Milk ½ pint
Fish stock ½ pint
6 stuffed olives
Margarine 1½ oz.
Flour 1½ oz.
Tomato purée 1 tablespoonful
Dry mustard 1 teaspoonful
½ lemon
Chopped parsley 2 teaspoonfuls
Salt and pepper

Cook the cod in salted water for 10 minutes. Then drain the cod, remove the skin, divide it into flakes and put it into a baking dish. Pour over the sauce and heat it through in a moderate oven for about 15 minutes.

For the Sauce. Melt the margarine, stir in the flour and mustard, then gradually add the milk and fish stock. Stir till boiling, add the tomato purée, grated rind and juice of the lemon, sliced olives, parsley and salt and pepper to taste. Simmer for 2 or 3 minutes.

Cod Provençal

Cod steaks or fillets 1¼ lb.	*White sauce ¼ pint*
Chopped capers 1 tablespoonful	*Lemon juice*
Chopped gherkins 1 tablespoonful	*Salt and pepper*

Season the fish with salt and pepper, sprinkle with lemon juice, place on a greased fireproof dish, cover with a greased paper, and bake in a moderate oven 20–30 minutes.

Make the white sauce (see page 196), stir in any liquor from the fish, add the chopped gherkins and capers, and pour over the fish.

Cod in Sherry Sauce

4 small cutlets of cod	*Margarine 3 oz.*
2 small onions	*Flour 1 oz.*
Mushrooms 2 oz.	*Milk ¼ pint*
Sherry 4 tablespoonfuls	*Salt, pepper, lemon juice*
Chopped parsley	

Season the fish with salt, pepper, and lemon juice.

Peel the onions and slice thinly, then fry gently in 2 oz. margarine until tender. Remove from the fat and put them in the bottom of a fireproof casserole and lay the cutlets of fish on top. Peel and slice the mushrooms and fry for 5 minutes in the margarine left from the onions, then place on top of the fish with any remaining margarine.

Melt 1 oz. margarine, stir in the flour, gradually add the sherry, then the milk, stir till boiling, add 2 teaspoonfuls of chopped parsley, and season with salt and pepper. Pour over the fish, put the lid on the casserole, and bake in a moderate oven for ½ hour.

Note. Cutlets of haddock or hake can be cooked in the same way.

Fried Cod's Roe

Wash the roe, tie it in muslin and cook in boiling salted water
for 15 minutes. Then remove the muslin and leave to get
cold. Cut into thick slices, dip in seasoned flour, coat with
beaten egg, and fry in very hot oil. Serve hot or cold.

Baked Fish with Almonds

Fillets of white fish 1½ lb.　　*Margarine 1 oz.*
Almonds 1½ oz.　　*Flour*
Cooking oil 1 tablespoonful　　*Seasoning*
Lemon juice

Season the fillets with salt, pepper, and lemon juice, and coat
lightly with flour. Place on a greased baking dish, pour over
the melted margarine, and bake in a moderate oven, 20–25
minutes.

Blanch, dry and shred the nuts finely and fry over a gentle
heat in the oil for 3 or 4 minutes until just coloured, keeping
them well stirred. Season with celery salt and pepper and
sprinkle over the fish.

Baked Fish with Cheese Crumble

4 cutlets of cod or haddock　　*Flour 4 oz.*
Margarine 2 oz.　　*Grated cheese 2 oz.*
Salt and pepper　　*Lemon juice*

Season the fish with salt, pepper and lemon juice and place it
in a single layer in a well-greased baking dish.

Rub the margarine into the flour until it looks like fine
breadcrumbs, then add the grated cheese and mix thoroughly.
Sprinkle this over the fish and bake in a moderate oven until
the fish is cooked and the top golden brown – about 30 minutes.

Note. Fillets of fish can be used in place of cutlets.

Baked Fish with Oranges

4 cutlets of cod or haddock　　*Margarine 1 oz.*
2 oranges　　*Brown crumbs*
Grated onion 1 tablespoonful　　*Salt and pepper*
Grated cheese 2 tablespoonfuls

Place the fish in a single layer in a greased fireproof dish, season it with salt and pepper and pour over the juice of the oranges; then sprinkle the cutlets with grated orange rind and grated onion, followed by the cheese and brown breadcrumbs. Dot with margarine and bake in a moderate oven for 35–40 minutes.

Fish Florentine

Small fillets of plaice, whiting, or lemon sole	*Grated cheese 2 oz.*
	White sauce ½ pint
Cooked spinach 2 lb.	*Salt and pepper*

Take 6 or 8 small fillets of fish and remove the skin. Season each fillet with salt, pepper, and a few drops of lemon juice; roll up, place on a greased baking dish, cover with a greased paper, and bake in a moderate oven for 10 minutes.

Boil and drain the spinach, and either chop finely or rub through a sieve, season, and place on a greased oven dish. Arrange the cooked fillets on top. Make ½ pint coating white sauce (see page 196), stir in the cheese, with the exception of 1 tablespoonful, and any liquor that came from the fish whilst baking. Coat the fish with the sauce, sprinkle over the remaining cheese and a few brown crumbs, and return to oven till lightly browned.

Gefillte Fish

Use bream, cod, or haddock, or a mixture; ½ lb. of carp can be included, if available.

Fish 2 lb.	*Parsley 1 tablespoonful*
2 eggs	*Ground almonds 1 tablespoonful*
2 or 3 onions	*Fresh breadcrumbs or matzo*
A large carrot	*meal to bind*
A stick of celery	

Remove skin and bones from the fish and put these in a saucepan with an onion, a piece of carrot, and the celery, pour over 1½ pints cold water, season with salt and pepper, simmer for ½ hour, then strain.

Put the fish and remaining onion through the mincing machine – or, if preferred, chop by hand. Add the parsley,

ground almonds (these are optional), and beaten eggs, season
with salt and pepper, and add sufficient fresh breadcrumbs or
matzo meal to bind. With floured hands roll into balls.

Slice the carrot thinly, add to fish stock and bring to the
boil, simmer for 10 minutes, then lay in the fish balls. Cover
the saucepan and cook very gently for 1 hour. Lift the balls out
carefully on to a serving dish and place a slice of carrot on each.
Spoon over a little of the fish stock, which should set in a jelly
when cold.

This can also be served hot with egg and lemon sauce (see
page 201).

Fish with Potato Border

Cooked white fish 1 lb.   Margarine 1 oz.
Thick white sauce ½ pint   Milk 4 tablespoonfuls
Potatoes 2 lb.   Anchovy essence
1 egg   Salt and pepper
Chopped parsley

Boil the potatoes, then mash very thoroughly with the
margarine, milk, and three quarters of the beaten egg. Season
with salt and pepper. Keep out about 3 tablespoonfuls of the
potato, and line a greased soufflé dish or deep casserole with the
remainder, making the sides about ¾ inch thick. Brush over
with beaten egg.

Flake the fish, add three quarters of the sauce, the chopped
parsley and anchovy essence, season with salt and pepper, and
turn into the centre of the dish and put remaining sauce on
top.

Roll the rest of the potato into tiny balls and put these on
top of the potato border, brush over with egg, bake in a
moderate oven till the fish is heated through and the potato
lightly browned – about ½ hour.

Paprika Fish

4 cutlets of cod or haddock   Margarine 3 oz.
Paprika 2 teaspoonfuls   Salt and pepper
Capers 2 teaspoonfuls   Lemon juice
Mushrooms 2 oz.

Wash the fish and season it with salt and pepper; then place it in a greased casserole and sprinkle it liberally with lemon juice.

Skin and chop the mushrooms. Melt the margarine in a small saucepan, add the mushrooms, cover the pan and cook gently for 5 or 6 minutes, then stir in the paprika and chopped capers and pour over the fish. Cover the casserole and bake in a moderate oven (375°, Regulo No. 4) for 30–40 minutes.

Fish Risotto

Smoked fillet 8 oz.   *Rice 4 oz.*
Grated cheese 1 oz.   *Margarine 2 oz.*
A small onion   *Paprika*

Place the fish in tepid water, bring to the boil and cook slowly till tender; then drain and flake. Cook the rice with the onion and when soft drain and remove the onion. Mix the rice and flaked fish and add the melted margarine. Turn into a greased fireproof dish, sprinkle over the grated cheese and dust with paprika. Cook on an upper shelf of a hot oven till lightly browned.

Fish Soufflé

Cooked white fish ¾ lb.   *Grated cheese 1–2 oz.*
Hot milk ¼ pint   *2 eggs*
Butter or margarine 1 oz.   *Salt and pepper*
Flour 1 oz.

Remove skin and bone from the fish and shred it very finely. Melt the butter in a saucepan, stir in the flour, and gradually add the hot milk. Stir till boiling and continue stirring while it simmers for 2 or 3 minutes. Remove from the heat, cool slightly, then add the fish, cheese, and seasoning, beat in the egg yolks one at a time and mix very thoroughly.

Whip the whites of the eggs to a stiff froth and fold them in very lightly. Turn the mixture into a greased soufflé dish and bake in a moderate oven (400°, Regulo No. 5) about 30 minutes. Serve immediately.

Smoked Haddock Soufflé. Use about ½ lb. cooked smoked haddock in place of the white fish and omit the cheese.

Gurnet

Gurnet can be cooked according to any recipe given for haddock. It is particularly good baked and stuffed.

Haddock

Haddock can be boiled, baked, fried, or cooked by any of the methods used for cod.

Stuffed Baked Haddock

The head is usually left on for baking, but many people object to its appearance, so it must be left to individual taste whether it is removed or not. Wash and dry fish and season with salt and pepper. Fill with savoury stuffing (see page 55), and, if the head has been left on, curl the fish round in a circle or in the shape of an 'S'. Place on a greased oven dish or baking tin, dredge with flour, dot with margarine, and pour ¼ pint water into the tin. Bake in a moderate oven 30–40 minutes, according to the size of the fish. Baste from time to time.

Serve on a hot dish with any fish sauce preferred, using the fish liquor made up to the required amount with milk.

Baked Haddock with Mushroom Stuffing

Fresh haddock 1½–2 lb.   *Margarine 3 oz.*
Mushrooms 3 oz.   *Lemon juice*
Breadcrumbs 3 oz.   *Top milk 2 tablespoonfuls*
Salt and pepper   *Brown crumbs*

Have the haddock filleted. Place one half in a well-greased baking dish, sprinkle with lemon juice, season with salt and pepper, and spread the stuffing over it. Place the other half on top, season, pour over the top milk, sprinkle with brown crumbs, dot with margarine, and bake in a moderate oven about 30 minutes. Serve it in the dish in which it was cooked.

For the Stuffing. Skin and chop the mushrooms and sauté in 2 oz. of margarine for 5 or 6 minutes, then add the breadcrumbs and lemon juice, salt and pepper to taste, and mix thoroughly. If at all dry, add a spoonful or two of milk.

Haddock with Cheese Stuffing

Prepare and cook fish as in the previous recipe, but add 2 oz. grated cheese and 2 teaspoonfuls of tomato ketchup to the savoury stuffing. Serve with cheese or watercress sauce.

Smoked Haddock

Smoked haddock can be boiled or baked, and any left over is very good in fish cakes and puddings (see pages 79–80), or in salad (see page 222).

To Boil. Trim off the fins and wash in warm water. Put in a frying pan or enamel baking tin, pour over sufficient warm water to cover, bring slowly to the boil and simmer gently 8–10 minutes. Lift out with a fish slice on to a hot dish and put a few small pieces of butter or margarine on top.

To Bake. Put fish in a small greased oven dish, pour over ¼ pint of warm water, cover with a greased paper and bake in a moderate oven about 20 minutes.

Smoked Haddock with Poached Eggs

Haddock about 1½ lb.   *4 poached eggs*
Margarine or butter 1 oz.   *Flour 1 oz.*
Milk and water ¾ pint   *Salt and pepper*

Cut the haddock through in halves down and across and put the four pieces in a frying pan or saucepan, pour over the warm milk and water. Cover, bring slowly to the boil and simmer gently about 10 minutes. Put on a hot dish, pour the sauce over and place a neatly poached egg on each portion.

For the Sauce. Melt margarine in a small saucepan, stir in the flour smoothly, and gradually add the liquor in which the fish was cooked. Stir till boiling and simmer 2 or 3 minutes.

Another method is to plainly boil or bake the fish, dot with butter or margarine, and place the poached eggs on top.

Hake

Cook like cod or haddock.

Halibut

Halibut can be boiled, fried, grilled, or baked. See recipes for cod or haddock.

Halibut Stewed with Egg and Lemon Sauce

Head and shoulders of halibut   *Oil 2 tablespoonfuls*
2 onions   *Chopped parsley*
Liver balls   *Salt and pepper*
Egg and lemon sauce

Cut up the fish into convenient-sized pieces for serving. Slice the onions. Put the oil in a stewpan, add the onions, and fry very gently till just coloured. Then lay in the fish, sprinkle with salt and pepper, and pour over sufficient warm water to barely cover. Put the lid on the saucepan, bring slowly to the boil, simmer gently for 10 minutes, lay in the liver balls and continue to simmer slowly for another 15–20 minutes.

Lift out the fish with a fish slice, put in the centre of a dish with the liver balls around, pour over the egg and lemon sauce, and serve cold sprinkled with finely chopped parsley.

Liver Balls. Boil ½–¾ lb. cod's liver in salted water, then strain and chop finely. Add a little chopped parsley and a beaten egg, then sufficient fresh breadcrumbs to bind. Season with salt and pepper, and with hands dipped in flour roll into small balls.

Egg and Lemon Sauce. Mix 2 teaspoonfuls cornflour or arrowroot smoothly with the strained juice of 2 lemons, add ¾ pint of the hot fish stock, and stir over a gentle heat till boiling, and simmer for 3 minutes. Remove from the heat, and when slightly cooled pour on to 2 lightly beaten eggs. Turn into a double saucepan and stir till it thickens but do *not* reboil or it will curdle.

Halibut Mayonnaise

Middle cut halibut 2 lb.   *Chopped shallot 2 teaspoonfuls*
Salad oil 4 tablespoonfuls   *Cooked peas and carrots*
Vinegar 2 teaspoonfuls   *1 breakfastcupful*
Chopped parsley 2 teaspoonfuls   *Mayonnaise sauce ¼–½ pint*
3 large tomatoes   *Lettuce and cucumber*

Put the fish on a greased fireproof dish, cover with a greased paper, and cook in a moderate oven till done – about ½ hour. When cooked, remove the skin, taking care not to break the fish. Put it on a dish and pour over the oil, vinegar, chopped parsley, and shallot, and leave till cold.

Cut the tomatoes across in halves, scoop out the centres (reserve for soup, sauce, or stews), mix the peas and carrots with a little of the mayonnaise, and heap up in the tomato cups.

Put the fish in the centre of a dish, coat with the remaining mayonnaise, put a border of shredded lettuce with the tomato cups at intervals and garnish with thinly sliced cucumber.

If preferred the fish can be boiled instead of baked, but cook it very slowly tied in muslin and dish it carefully, so that it remains whole.

Hake, cod, or salmon can also be served in this way.

Herring

The herring is the most nourishing of the cheaper varieties of fish, for it contains a large percentage of fat.

Herrings can be fried, grilled, baked, or boiled.

To Boil. Remove head and clean thoroughly. Put into salted water, to which add a spoonful or two of vinegar, and simmer gently for 5 minutes. Serve with mashed potatoes and mustard sauce.

To Fry. The herrings can be split and boned, or left whole with just the heads removed. If the latter, score the skin across diagonally 2 or 3 times on both sides. Wash and dry very thoroughly, season with salt and pepper, dip in oatmeal and fry in a small quantity of smoking hot fat, browning lightly on both sides. Serve with cut lemon or mustard sauce.

To Grill. Split and bone or leave whole, scoring across as for frying. Dry thoroughly, season, brush over with melted margarine or frying oil, and grill under a moderate heat 3 or 4 minutes on either side.

Baked Herrings

(1) Split and bone herrings, season with salt and pepper, and sprinkle with vinegar or lemon juice. Put together in pairs on a

greased tin, cover with a greased paper and bake in a moderate oven 15–20 minutes.

(2) Remove heads from herrings and score across both sides. Mix 2 teaspoonfuls mustard with 2 tablespoonfuls each vinegar and water, add 1 teaspoonful of salt and a little pepper. Place herrings in a greased oven dish, pour over the vinegar mixture, cover with greased paper and bake in a moderate oven about 20 minutes.

Baked Herrings with Apples

4 herrings	*Margarine 1 oz.*
3 or 4 potatoes	*Salt and pepper*
2 sour apples	

Split and bone the herrings and cut each into two fillets; peel the potatoes and cut them into thin slices; peel and chop the apples.

Grease a baking dish very thoroughly and arrange sliced potatoes, standing up, right round the sides. Put half the fillets in the bottom of the dish, season with salt and pepper, and sprinkle with chopped apple. Repeat the layers, cover with sliced potato, sprinkle with salt and dot with margarine.

Cover and cook in a moderate oven about 45 minutes, removing the lid for the last 15 minutes.

Baked Stuffed Herrings (1)

4 herrings	*Breadcrumbs 2 oz.*
Small onion	*Melted margarine 1 oz.*
1 egg or a little milk	*Chopped parsley 1 tablespoonful*
Salt and pepper	*Juice of $\frac{1}{4}$ lemon*

Split and bone herrings and divide each into two fillets. Grate the onion and mix with the breadcrumbs, melted margarine, parsley, and lemon juice. Season with salt and pepper and bind with a beaten egg or a little milk. Season the herring fillets with salt and pepper, spread with the stuffing, roll up tightly, securing with a thread of cotton. Put in a greased baking dish, cover with a greased paper, and bake in a moderate oven about 30 minutes.

Serve hot or cold; if hot, accompanied with potatoes baked

in their jackets. Baked tomatoes, either plain or filled with a little of the fish stuffing, go very well with this dish. So does hot beetroot (see page 85).

When eaten cold, sprinkle with chopped capers and a little vinegar or lemon juice. Serve with potato salad and any green salad available.

The herring roes can be served as a separate dish (see Savouries, page 297), but if there are any soft roes amongst the herrings, chop one finely and add it to the stuffing in place of the margarine.

Baked Stuffed Herrings (2)

Split and bone the herrings, dip in seasoned flour and place on a greased baking dish inside uppermost. Put a little stuffing down the centre of each, cover with a greased paper and bake in a moderate oven for 30 minutes.

For the Stuffing. For 4 herrings allow 4 tablespoonfuls breadcrumbs, 2 chopped gherkins, 2 tablespoonfuls chopped apple, 2 sticks chopped celery, pinch of mixed herbs, salt and pepper. Mix all ingredients and add sufficient milk to bind.

Grilled Herrings with Parsnip Fritters

The flavour of parsnips goes extremely well with herrings.

Cut a few cooked parsnips lengthwise in quarters, coat with beaten egg or eggless batter (see page 427) and dip in brown crumbs. Fry a golden brown in deep fat and serve with the grilled herrings (see page 67) and mustard sauce (see page 197).

Marinated Herrings

Take as many Dutch pickled herrings as required, remove the heads, split and bone. Lay in cold water with the soft roes overnight.

Divide the herrings into two fillets, roll up and place in a stone jar in layers with sliced onion and sliced lemon in between. Sprinkle with peppercorns and mustard seeds and add a few bay leaves. Boil together for 2 or 3 minutes sufficient vinegar and water to cover, using two thirds vinegar and one third water, and add 1 tablespoonful of sugar to each pint. Leave till cold.

Pound the soft roes to a paste, and add to the cold boiled vinegar. Pour over the herrings and cover.

Keep in a cool place. They can be used after 5 days, but will keep some time.

Soused Herrings

Split, bone, and clean as many herrings as required, sprinkle with salt and pepper and roll up, commencing at the thick end. Pack close together in a deep fireproof dish. Add a couple of bay leaves and a few peppercorns and allspice. Cut some onions into thin rings and place on top of the herrings. Pour over sufficient vinegar and water in equal quantities to just cover. Put the lid on the casserole and cook in a slow oven about 45 minutes. Serve cold with potato salad.

Rollmops

Remove the heads from the herrings, split, bone, and wash them and cover with cold brine, using 2 oz. salt to each pint of water. Let them soak for two hours, then rinse in cold water and dry them. Put a little shredded onion on each herring, season with salt and pepper, and roll up, starting at the head end. Secure with a pointed match or half a cocktail stick and put into a screw-top jar. Sprinkle a little pickling spice and sugar in between the rolls, using a level teaspoonful of each to a pound of herrings. Add a bay leaf, and pour over sufficient white vinegar to cover. Screw down and store in a cool place. They will be ready in 4 or 5 days, but will keep 4 or 5 weeks.

A glass-top preserving jar makes a very good container. If preferred, each herring can be divided into two fillets before rolling up. The herrings should not be packed too tightly in the jar.

Kippers

Kippers can be grilled, fried, steamed, or baked. Cut off the heads and wipe with a damp cloth.

To Grill. Put kippers on a hot grill, skin side uppermost, and grill for 1 minute. Turn over, put knob of margarine on each, and grill for 2 or 3 minutes.

To Fry. Put a little margarine or cooking fat into a frying pan, and when hot put in one kipper, skin side down, put a knob of margarine on it, and place another kipper skin side up on top of it. Cover with a plate, cook gently for 2 or 3 minutes, then turn the two over and continue cooking, keeping them covered, for a few minutes longer.

To Bake. Place in pairs as for frying, with a knob of margarine between, on a greased oven dish. Cover with a greased paper and bake in a moderate oven 10–15 minutes.

To Steam. Put the kippers into a jug or pie dish, pour over boiling water, cover, and let stand for 5 minutes.

Mackerel

Like herrings, mackerel are nourishing, fat fish. It is essential they should be eaten very fresh. They can be grilled, fried, or soused like herrings.

To Boil. Remove heads and fins from 3 or 4 mackerel. Peel and slice an onion and a carrot and put into a pan or fish kettle. Put in the mackerel, add salt to taste and a few peppercorns, and sufficient cold water to just cover. Bring to the boil and simmer gently till the fish is cooked – about 15–20 minutes. Lift out, place on a hot dish, garnish with watercress and cut lemon, and serve with mustard sauce (see page 197) or gooseberry sauce (see page 201).

Baked Mackerel

2 large mackerel　　　　　　　*Breadcrumbs 2 oz.*
Grated onion 1 tablespoonful　*Vinegar 1 tablespoonful*
1 egg　　　　　　　　　　　　*Chopped parsley 1 tablespoonful*
Salt and pepper　　　　　　　*Margarine 1 oz.*

Cut off the heads of the mackerel, remove the roes, and wash thoroughly. Boil roes in salted water for 5 minutes, then drain and chop. Mix with the breadcrumbs, vinegar, grated onion, and chopped parsley. Season with salt and pepper and bind with the egg. Stuff the mackerel with this forcemeat, place them on a greased oven dish, dot with margarine, cover with a greased paper, and bake in a moderate oven about 30 minutes. Serve with mustard or piccalilli sauce.

If preferred, the fish can be split and boned. Lay one mackerel skin down on a greased oven dish, spread over the stuffing and put the other fish on top, skin side up.

Mullet

Red mullet is a delicate fish and superior in flavour to grey mullet.

Cook grey mullet like haddock and serve with Dutch, caper, or tomato sauce. The liver is considered a great delicacy and should always be left in the fish.

Red mullet should be grilled or baked.

Baked Red Mullet

2 red mullets	Chopped parsley 1 tablespoonful
Juice of ½ lemon	Margarine 1 oz.
Breadcrumbs	Salt and pepper

Score both sides of the fish. Grease a fireproof dish, sprinkle over some breadcrumbs and a little chopped parsley. Season the fish with salt and pepper and lay it in the dish, pour over the lemon juice and sprinkle with breadcrumbs and parsley. Dot with margarine and bake in a moderate oven about 20 minutes. Serve in the dish in which it was cooked.

Perch

Perch is a fresh-water fish. It is rather difficult to scale, so should be left in boiling water for 2 or 3 minutes, when the scales may be scraped off.

Perch can be boiled, fried, grilled, or stewed.

Pike

Pike is a river fish. It is inclined to be dry, so should be served with a good sauce. It is better baked than boiled. Always discard the roe.

Baked Pike

A large pike   *Margarine 2 oz.*
Savoury stuffing   *Salt and pepper*
Tomato or anchovy sauce *Lemon and parsley*

Scale, skin and wash the fish, stuff it with savoury stuffing (see page 55), and curl it round with the tail in the mouth.

Season with salt and pepper and place on a greased oven dish. Dot with the margarine, and cover with a greased paper. Bake in a moderate oven ¾–1 hour, keeping it well basted. Serve with tomato or anchovy sauce.

Plaice

Plaice can be boiled, steamed, grilled, fried, or baked.

Small plaice called dabs can be cooked whole. The larger ones can be filleted or cut across. Fillets can be cooked by any of the recipes given for sole, haddock, or whiting.

Salmon

The more simply salmon is cooked the better, so that the fine flavour of the fish is not spoilt.

Boiled Salmon

Any part of the salmon can be used for boiling – middle cut, tail, or head and shoulders – or whole small fish.

Clean, scale, and wash the fish. Put it in the fish kettle with salt and a few peppercorns, and cover with boiling water. Simmer until the fish will leave the bones when tested with a fork.

The housewife must use her own judgement in the matter of the length of time required for cooking. A thick piece will sometimes take longer to cook than a whole small fish. However, the average time is 10 minutes to the pound and 10 minutes over.

If cooked before it is required, put on a hot dish and cover with a folded cloth.

Garnish with cut lemon and parsley, and serve with plain melted butter, hollandaise sauce, or parsley sauce.

Boiled potatoes, green peas, and cucumber salad are the usual accompaniments.

Grilled Salmon

For grilling, use slices 1 inch in thickness. Wash and dry and then dip in salad oil or melted butter. Make the grill thoroughly hot, place fish on greased grid, lower heat slightly, and cook the fish about 10 minutes on each side; if it gets dry brush over again with more oil or butter. Garnish with cut lemon and watercress. Serve with any fish sauce, or put a pat of parsley butter on top of each cutlet.

For the parsley butter, add half a teaspoonful of chopped parsley and lemon juice to 1 oz. of butter, mix thoroughly, and form into pats.

Salmon Mayonnaise

(See Halibut Mayonnaise, pages 66–7.)

Fried Smelts

Wash and trim as many smelts as required. Dry them and roll in seasoned flour, then brush over with beaten egg and coat with fine white breadcrumbs, pressing them on firmly. Fry in deep fat in a frying basket till golden brown.

If preferred, the smelts can be dipped in seasoned flour, and then fried in a small quantity of oil or cooking fat till crisp and lightly browned on both sides.

Sole

Soles can be boiled, steamed, fried, baked, or grilled; cooked whole or filleted.

Baked Sole

Lemon sole (or plaice)
Juice of ¼ lemon
Chopped parsley 2 teaspoonfuls

Chopped onion 1 tablespoonful
Margarine 1 oz.
Salt and pepper

Cut the fish across into convenient-sized pieces for serving. Grease a flat fireproof dish, lay in the fish in its original shape, sprinkle over the onion, parsley, and lemon juice, and season with salt and pepper. Add 2 tablespoonfuls of water and dot with margarine. Cover with a greased paper and bake in a moderate oven 20–30 minutes. Serve in the dish in which it was cooked.

Baked Fillets of Sole

Dover or lemon sole filleted
Juice of a lemon
Margarine 2 oz.
Brown crumbs
A few small mushrooms
Chopped onion 1 tablespoonful
Chopped parsley 2 teaspoonfuls
Salt and pepper

Lay the fillets on a greased shallow baking dish, season with salt and pepper, and pour over the lemon juice.

Skin and chop the mushrooms, chop onion finely. Put the margarine in a small saucepan with the mushrooms, onion, and parsley, and make quite hot. Then pour over the fish, sprinkle lightly with brown crumbs and bake in a moderate oven about 30 minutes.

Grilled Sole

The sole should be skinned and the fins cut off. Wash and dry, brush over with melted butter and season with salt and pepper. Place it on a hot greased grill and cook for 7–10 minutes, turning the fish over so that it is browned on both sides. Have the grill really hot before starting, and when putting the fish under, lower the heat slightly.

Garnish with sliced lemon and parsley or watercress.

Sole Matelote

Any flat fish can be prepared in this way, which is a favourite method in Normandy. Remove the black skin from the fish and trim off head and fins. Put in a greased baking dish, season with salt and pepper, and half cover the fish with equal quantities of cider and water. Bake in a moderate oven for 20 minutes.

Strain off the liquid. Melt 1 oz. margarine, stir in ½ oz. flour smoothly, then gradually add the liquid. Stir till boiling, simmer for 2 minutes, then pour over the fish.

Sole Meunière

4 fillets of sole
Butter 2 oz.
Flour
Lemon juice
Chopped parsley
Salt and pepper

Remove the skin from the fillets, then season with salt and pepper and coat lightly with flour.

Melt the butter in a frying pan and when really hot, lay in the fillets and reduce heat. After 1 minute turn the fish over and continue cooking until the fish is done – about 5 minutes. Place the fillets on a serving dish and sprinkle with lemon juice and chopped parsley. Add a little fresh butter to the pan and when just beginning to brown, pour over the fish.

Fillets of Sole with Pineapple

Dover or lemon sole about 2 lb.
Small tin pineapple cubes
Margarine 1 oz.
Flour 1 oz.
Fish stock
Salt and pepper

Have the fish filleted. Put the bones and fins in a saucepan, add salt and pepper to taste, cover with warm water, bring to the boil, and simmer for ½ hour, then strain.

Season the fillets with salt and pepper, lay in a casserole, cover with the pineapple cubes, pour over half the juice, cover the casserole and bake in a slow oven (350°, Regulo No. 3) 20–30 minutes. Pour off the liquid from the dish and make up to ¾ pint with fish stock. Melt the margarine, stir in flour smoothly, and gradually add the liquid. Stir till boiling, simmer for 3 minutes, then pour over the fish.

Fillets of plaice or brill can be cooked in the same way.

Sole Véronique

4 fillets of sole
White wine or cider ¼ pint
Fish stock ¼ pint
White grapes 4–6 oz.
Flour 1 oz.
Margarine 1 oz.
Salt and pepper

Skin the fillets, season with salt and pepper, and fold in three. Place in a saucepan, pour over the wine (or cider) and fish stock, cover and cook very gently until the fish is cooked – about 10 minutes.

Place the fish on a serving dish and keep hot. Melt the margarine, stir in the flour smoothly, and gradually add the liquid in which the fish was cooked, made up, if necessary, to $\frac{1}{2}$ pint. Stir till boiling, season to taste with salt and pepper, and add the grapes, skinned, stoned, and cut in halves. Simmer for 1 minute and pour over the fish.

Sprats

Dry thoroughly and coat with seasoned flour. Lay about 12 at a time in a frying basket and fry in deep fat (cooking fat or oil) 2–3 minutes. Serve with cut lemon.

Baked Sprats. Put sprats into an oven dish, add a few peppercorns and a bay leaf and a little thinly sliced onion. Cover with equal quantities of vinegar and water and bake in a slow oven about 30 minutes. Serve cold with potato salad.

Trout

Sea Trout. Treat like salmon. Small trout can be split or left whole and either grilled or fried. If left whole, score across diagonally 2 or 3 times. Medium-sized trout take 15–20 minutes to fry or grill. Serve with tartare sauce or mayonnaise.

Fresh-water Trout are best fried. Roll in fine oatmeal seasoned with salt and pepper, and fry in butter. Serve with cut lemon.

Or roll in flour and fry in butter – about 5 minutes on either side. Add lemon juice and chopped parsley to the butter in which they were fried and pour it over the fish.

Whitebait

Frying is the usual method of cooking whitebait.

Wash the fish, handling lightly. Drain in a colander, then turn on to a cloth to dry. Put some seasoned flour on another cloth or on kitchen paper, and toss the fish in this a few at a time until evenly coated and separate one from the other. Then turn them into a frying basket and shake off any loose flour. Plunge them into a saucepan of very hot fat sufficient to cover the fish, and fry 2 or 3 minutes, when they should be crisp and lightly browned. Keep shaking the basket gently to keep the fish separated. Drain on soft paper and sprinkle with salt. Proceed in this way till all the fish are fried.

Serve with thin brown bread and butter and sections of lemon.

Whiting

Whiting can be fried, steamed, or baked. For frying whole have it skinned and curled (i.e., the tail drawn through the head).

Baked Fillets of Whiting

3 whiting	*White sauce ¼ pint*
Margarine 2 oz.	*Yolk of an egg*
White wine 1 tablespoonful	*Seasoning*
Tomatoes ¼ lb.	

Fillet the fish and put the fillets in a greased fireproof dish. Sprinkle with salt and pepper, dot with margarine, and pour over the wine. Bake in a moderate oven for about 15 minutes. Cut up the tomatoes and put them in a small saucepan with 1 oz. margarine. Cover and cook gently for 10 minutes, then rub through a sieve. Add this purée to the white sauce, also the beaten yolk of an egg, and the liquor from the fish. Pour this sauce over the fish. Return to the oven for 5 minutes and serve in the dish in which it was cooked.

Any fillets of white fish can be used instead of whiting, and tinned tomato purée can be used instead of fresh tomatoes.

LEFT-OVER FISH

Fish with Cheese Sauce

Flake any left-over white fish and put in a greased fireproof dish. Cover with cheese sauce, sprinkle with grated cheese and brown crumbs, dot with margarine or butter, and bake in a quick oven till hot through and nicely browned – about 20 minutes.

Fish Cakes

Use equal quantities of cooked fish and mashed potato. If the potatoes have not been mashed with margarine, then add a little melted – about 1 oz. to $\frac{1}{2}$ lb. each of fish and potatoes. Add a little finely chopped parsley and season with salt and pepper and a little anchovy sauce. With hands lightly floured shape into small flat cakes. Brush over with beaten egg and coat with brown crumbs. Fry a golden brown on both sides.

Curried Fish

Cold cooked fish about 1 lb.   *Margarine 1$\frac{1}{4}$ oz.*
Flour 1$\frac{1}{4}$ oz.   *Curry powder 2 teaspoonfuls*
Milk and fish stock $\frac{3}{4}$ pint   *Chopped onion 1 tablespoonful*
Chutney 2 teaspoonfuls   *Cooked rice*

Remove skin and bone from the fish and either flake it or cut it up into convenient pieces for serving. Melt the margarine in a small saucepan and fry the onion a golden brown, stir in flour and curry powder smoothly, cook for a minute or two, then gradually add the liquid. (If no fish stock is available, use all milk, or milk and water, or milk and vegetable stock.) Stir till boiling, add chutney, simmer for 5 minutes, then warm the fish through in it. Pour this into the centre of a hot dish and put a border of well-cooked rice around.

The fish can be garnished with quarters or slices of hard-boiled egg.

Kedgeree

Cooked fish $\frac{1}{4}$ lb.   *2 hard-boiled eggs*
Cooked rice 4 oz.   *Chopped parsley*
Butter or margarine 2 oz.   *Salt and cayenne*

Flake the fish and mix it with the cooked rice. Melt the butter in a saucepan, add rice and fish, and stir over a gentle heat till thoroughly hot. Season with salt and cayenne and add the chopped white of egg.

Heap up on a hot dish and garnish with the sieved yolk of egg and chopped parsley.

Fish Pie

Cold cooked fish 2 breakfastcupfuls   *Margarine 2 oz.*
Mashed potato 2 breakfastcupfuls   *1 egg*
Chopped parsley 1 tablespoonful   *Cornflakes*
Small grated onion   *Salt and pepper*
½ lemon

Remove skin and bone from the fish and chop finely. Add the mashed potato, grated onion, chopped parsley, and grated rind and juice of the lemon. Melt the margarine, except ½ oz., and add this together with the beaten egg. Season with salt and pepper and mix thoroughly.

Turn into a greased fireproof dish, smooth the top with a knife, and sprinkle with slightly-crushed cornflakes. Dot with remaining margarine and bake in a moderate oven 30–40 minutes.

If preferred, brown crumbs can be used in place of the cornflakes.

Fish Pudding

Cold cooked fish 1 lb.   *Chopped parsley 1 tablespoonful*
Cooked rice 1 breakfastcupful   *½ lemon*
Anchovy essence 2 teaspoonfuls   *1 egg*
Margarine 1 oz.   *Salt and pepper*

Remove skin and bone from the fish and flake it finely. Mix it with the rice, add the anchovy essence, grated rind and juice of half a lemon, and the chopped parsley. Then stir in the melted margarine and beaten egg. Mix thoroughly and turn into a greased basin; cover with a greased paper and steam for 1 hour. Turn out on to a hot dish and serve with anchovy or caper sauce.

Pickled Salmon

Remove the bones from some left-over cold boiled salmon, pour over spiced vinegar, and leave till the following day. Garnish with sliced cucumber.

For the Spiced Vinegar. Put in a saucepan $\frac{1}{4}$ pint each of vinegar and the water in which the salmon was boiled, add a bay leaf, $\frac{1}{2}$ teaspoonful salt, and a few peppercorns and allspice. Bring to the boil, simmer gently for 10 minutes, then leave till cold. Strain and pour over the salmon.

Savoury Fish Toasts

4 rounds of buttered toast *Fish sauce 2 tablespoonfuls*
Smoked haddock 4 tablespoonfuls *2 hard-boiled eggs*

Remove all skin and bone from the fish and mince it finely. Mix with the sauce, add pepper to taste, and make very hot. Heap up on the buttered toast and garnish with the hard-boiled eggs cut into quarters.

Smoked Fish in Batter

Cooked smoked fish $\frac{1}{2}$—$\frac{3}{4}$ lb. *Flour 4 oz.*
Margarine or cooking fat 1 oz. *Milk $\frac{1}{2}$ pint*
Water 1 tablespoonful   *1 egg*

Make a smooth batter with the flour, egg, and milk, add the water, and let stand for 1 hour. Remove skin and bone from the fish and break up into flakes. Put the margarine into a baking dish and place in the oven till melted and really hot, then put in the fish and pour over the batter, and bake in a hot oven about 45 minutes.

Vegetables

It is only comparatively recently that we, as a nation, have become conscious of the very important part that vegetables play in our daily diet. They provide vitamins and mineral salts that are absolutely essential for bodily health and fitness. But in order to retain these health-giving salts and vitamins they must be prepared and cooked correctly.

Whenever it is possible to serve vegetables uncooked, this should be done; the addition of uncooked vegetables to salads makes a palatable and highly nutritive adjunct. They should be finely shredded or grated just before serving. If for any reason this is not possible, then, after preparing, put into a basin and cover with a plate, so that they are not exposed to the air. Place in a refrigerator or cool place till required. All vegetables should be used as fresh as possible. If they have lost their crispness, soak in cold water for not more than 15 to 30 minutes after washing.

They should be cooked in a covered saucepan, in a minimum of water and as quickly as possible. Do not use soda, and after straining use any left-over vegetable water in soup, gravy or sauces.

Note. If using a pressure saucepan, which is excellent for vegetables, cooking times are considerably shorter.

Details for the preparation and cooking of green and root vegetables are given in this section. For vegetable dishes suitable to serve as vegetable entrées, supper and luncheon dishes, see recipes, pages 114–31.

Globe Artichokes

Strip off the larger outside leaves, cut off the stalk and trim base neatly. With a pair of kitchen scissors snip off the end of each leaf to within a couple of inches of the base. Wash thoroughly and soak for 30 minutes in cold water to which a little vinegar has been added, then rinse in fresh water and drain. Add a teaspoonful of lemon juice to a saucepan of boiling salted water, put in the artichokes head downwards, boil rapidly for 5 minutes, then simmer gently till the bottom is quite tender, 30–40 minutes. Drain and serve hot, accompanied by hollandaise or tartare sauce.

Artichoke Bottoms

Prepare and cook as above, then remove the leaves and chokes, leaving the round, white, soft piece at the bottom. Reheat in a well-seasoned white sauce.

Artichoke bottoms can also be fried. Brush over with egg and breadcrumbs and fry in deep fat; or let them soak in a marinade of oil, lemon juice, salt, pepper, and chopped chives until required, then dip them in a light batter and fry in deep fat.

They may also be stuffed with any kind of forcemeat or a mince of any kind of poultry or meat, baked and served as a vegetable entrée; or filled with cooked green peas, creamed spinach, or asparagus points, and used as a garnish.

Jerusalem Artichokes

Artichokes can be boiled, fried, baked, mashed, curried, or made into soup. In fact they are good cooked in almost any fashion.

To Prepare. Wash thoroughly and peel thinly with a potato peeler, dropping each one as it is peeled into a bowl of cold water to which a little lemon juice or vinegar has been added, as they turn black very quickly if exposed to the air. *Or* scrub very thoroughly, cook in their skins till tender, then remove skin and finish off as desired.

To Boil. Cook in boiling salted water till tender, 20–35 minutes depending on the size, drain, and serve with white sauce.

To Purée. Cook till tender, drain and mash to a purée with a little margarine, salt and pepper.

To Sauté. Boil for 15 minutes, cut into thick slices and fry in shallow fat till golden brown.

Chips. Prepare and fry like potato chips in deep fat. Serve with grilled steak or hot fried fish.

To Roast. Boil for 10 minutes, then cook round the meat the same as roast potatoes.

Asparagus

Select freshly cut asparagus if possible, but it will keep for a day or two in a cool place if the ends of the stalks are kept in water. Wash and scrape the stalks from the green part downward. Cut to a convenient length and tie in bundles with tape, keeping the heads together. Soak in cold water for 1 hour. Have ready a saucepan half filled with boiling water and large enough to allow the asparagus to lie flat and boil gently until the green part is tender, about 20 minutes.

When cooked, drain well and dish on a folded napkin or a large slice of toast.

Serve with oil and vinegar, melted butter, mayonnaise or hollandaise sauce.

A special asparagus cooker can be bought. This is a saucepan designed so that only the stalks of the asparagus are cooked in the water, the green part being cooked by steam.

To Serve Cold. Arrange on an asparagus or entrée dish, sprinkle a few drops of tarragon vinegar over, and keep in a cool place or on ice till required. Serve with oil and vinegar or mayonnaise sauce.

Aubergine (Egg Plant)

Aubergines can be baked, boiled, or fried and, when stuffed, make a good entrée (see page 114).

Remove the stalks, put the aubergines in a pan of boiling water and boil for 20 minutes. Remove from the pan and, when cool, cut through lengthwise (if the seeds are large these should be removed). Place them on a greased fireproof dish, dot with margarine, and bake in a moderate oven till soft – 20–30 minutes. Serve with tomato sauce or grated cheese.

To Fry. Cut a large aubergine into ¼-inch slices crosswise, season with salt and pepper, and coat lightly with flour. Sauté in a little hot fat until tender and golden brown on both sides.

Broad Beans

Broad beans are very nutritious and are rich in vitamins A, B, and C. They can be served as an accompaniment to the meat course or as the main dish for a light meal, and they are equally good hot or cold in salads.

To Boil. Remove from pods and cook in boiling salted water. Cook gently till the skins begin to crack – 20–30 minutes. If the beans are old, the outer skins should be removed first. Put the beans in a bowl, cover with boiling water and leave for 5 minutes, after which the skin will rub off easily. When cooked, drain (saving the water for soup) and serve plain or with parsley sauce.

To Cook like Runner Beans. When the beans are still very young and the pods green, treat them just like scarlet runners. Trim off the ends and a thin slice from each side and cut through pod and bean into thin shreds. Cook in boiling water till tender – about 20 minutes.

French Beans

Cut off the ends of the beans and remove strings from the sides. If quite small leave them whole, otherwise break across into 2 or 3 pieces. Cook in boiling salted water till soft – about 20 minutes – then drain (reserve water for soup).

Runner Beans

Prepare and cook like French beans, but unless very small and young, slice finely.

To Salt Beans for Winter Use

Use stoneware jars, a large crock, or glass jars. Glazed earthenware is *not* suitable. The salt affects the glaze and makes the vessel porous.

The beans must be young, fresh, and quite dry. For 3 lb. beans, 1 lb. salt will be required. One of the chief causes of failure is using too little salt. String the beans and slice finely.

Put a good layer of salt in the bottom of a large jar. Put a layer of beans on the salt and fill the jar with alternate layers of salt and beans, pressing the beans down well to avoid air pockets. Finish with a *good layer* of salt, and tie down with thick paper. The beans will sink a little, so in a few days uncover and add more beans, always taking care to finish off with a thick layer of salt. Retie the cover and store in a cool place.

To Use. Rinse the beans several times in warm water. Then put into boiling water, boil for 5 minutes, then drain this water off. Put into fresh boiling water and boil till tender.

Beetroot

To Boil. Cut off leaves and stalks, leaving about 1 inch of the

latter. Handle very carefully both in washing and cooking, so
as not to break the skin. Cook in boiling water till tender –
2 hours or longer, according to size, for old beetroot, about
1 hour for young beets.

To Bake. If preferred, the beets can be baked. Wash carefully and place in a baking tin. (If the skin has been rubbed
anywhere, cover with flour and water paste.) Bake till
tender – 2 hours or longer, according to size.

Whether baked or boiled, peel them and prepare to taste:

(1) Dice or slice, season generously with salt and pepper,
add a knob of margarine and a little vinegar or lemon juice.

(2) Dice or cut into quarters and coat with parsley sauce, to
which add lemon juice or vinegar to taste.

Beetroot Salads
(See pages 214–15)

Beetroot Tops

The young leaves of beets can be cooked like spinach (see
pages 108–9).

Broccoli

This is a variety of cauliflower and is cooked in the same way.
Sprouting Broccoli is cooked like cabbage (see below).

Brussels Sprouts

Remove any outside discoloured leaves, trim neatly, and with
a sharp vegetable knife cut across the bottom, taking care
not to cut the leaves. Wash thoroughly, put into boiling salted
water and boil rapidly with the lid on the saucepan for 7 or
8 minutes, then drain through a colander, place the colander
over a saucepan of boiling water, put a lid on the colander and
steam till tender – about 15 minutes.

Sprouts in Salad

(See general directions for Salads, pages 208–10)

Sprouts in Sandwiches

(See page 327)

Cabbage

There are several varieties of cabbage: green, red and white. Greens, kale, savoys, sprouts, cauliflower, and broccoli all belong to the cabbage family. Cabbages may be eaten raw, cooked, or pickled. Cabbages are a good source of vitamin C and mineral salts, but unless properly cooked, this most precious part of the cabbage will be completely wasted.

Remove coarse outside and discoloured leaves, cut the cabbage in quarters, and cut away the hard stalk. Wash thoroughly, leave to soak in a bowl of cold water for 15 minutes, then with a sharp knife cut across into shreds.

Put 1 inch of water in a saucepan, add 1 dessertspoonful of salt and bring to the boil, put in the shredded cabbage, put the lid on the saucepan, and boil rapidly till the cabbage is tender – about 15 minutes. Stir well after it has been cooking a few minutes.

Strain through a colander, pressing out all moisture with a greens presser (or if this should not be available, use a plate).

Paprika Cabbage

Cabbage 1–1¼ lb.	*Cooking fat 2 oz.*
Paprika 2 teaspoonfuls	*Water ¼ pint*
Vinegar 2 tablespoonfuls	*Salt*
2 small onions	

Trim the cabbage and shred it finely. Peel and chop the onions, melt the fat, add the onion and fry gently till lightly browned; then stir in the paprika, add the cabbage and pour over ½ pint of boiling water, with vinegar and salt to taste. Cover and cook gently for 20 minutes.

Cabbage with Sweet and Sour Sauce

Medium-sized cabbage	*Vinegar 3 tablespoonfuls*
Dripping or margarine 1 oz.	*Cabbage water 3 tablespoonfuls*
Sugar 1 oz.	*2 cloves*

Shred cabbage and cook in a small quantity of salted water till tender. Then drain. Boil remaining ingredients together for 5 minutes. Remove cloves and pour over the cabbage.

This is particularly good with sausages.

Stewed Red Cabbage

Red cabbage about 1½ lb.	*Cooking fat 2 oz.*
2 large cooking apples	*1 large onion*
Stock or water ¾ pint	*Sugar 1 teaspoonful*
Vinegar 2 tablespoonfuls	*Cornflour 1 teaspoonful*
Dry mustard ¼ teaspoonful	*Salt*

Remove the outer leaves and thick stems from the cabbage. Shred the rest finely, wash it and cover with boiling water, leave for 5 minutes, then drain.

Peel, core and slice the apples, skin and slice the onion.

Melt the fat in a saucepan and when hot add the cabbage, stir well, sprinkle with salt, cover the saucepan and cook very gently for 10 minutes, stirring from time to time. Then pour over the boiling stock (or water) and add the prepared apples and onion, sugar and vinegar. Simmer very slowly for 50 minutes, then strain off the liquid, put this in a small saucepan and add the blended cornflour and mustard. Stir till boiling and simmer for 2 or 3 minutes. Serve the cabbage in a hot dish and pour the sauce over.

Sausages are very good with red cabbage. Lay them on top of the cabbage for the last ½ hour and serve as a border round the cabbage.

Red Cabbage and Chestnuts

A small red cabbage	*Dripping or margarine 2 oz.*
Chestnuts 1 lb.	*Flour 1 oz.*
Sultanas 2 oz.	*Salt and pepper*
Vinegar 2 tablespoonfuls	*Water ½ pint*
Sugar ¼ oz.	

Remove the outer leaves and hard stalk from the cabbage, cut in quarters, and shred finely. Put in a bowl, cover with boiling water, and leave for 5 minutes. Then drain thoroughly.

Melt the fat in a saucepan, put in the cabbage, stir till well coated with the fat, then add $\frac{1}{2}$ pint boiling water, the sugar, and vinegar, and stew till tender.

Boil chestnuts separately and when soft, shell them and add to the cooked cabbage with the sultanas. Blend the flour with a little cold water, stir it in, season with salt and pepper, and simmer for 10 minutes.

Carrots

The carrot is one of the most valuable of all root vegetables. It is a rich source of carotene, which is converted into vitamin A, and strengthens our resistance to infection. Most children like raw carrots and should be allowed to eat them freely.

Apart from special carrot dishes, they can be used in soups, stews, salads, and sandwiches, recipes for which will be found in the various sections.

If cooked conservatively they are delicious and have the added advantage of having all their nutritive value retained.

If boiled the water should be saved and used for soup or gravy.

Scrape the carrots lightly, or they may be scrubbed and boiled and the skins rubbed off in a cloth afterwards. The length of time they will take to cook depends on the age of the carrots. If sliced: young, about 20 minutes, old, about 35 minutes. Halved or quartered: 30 minutes to 1 hour.

Boiled Carrots

Wash and scrape and, unless very young and small, cut them into slices. Put into a saucepan with just sufficient boiling salted water to cover and boil till tender – 20–35 minutes – then drain, add a small knob of margarine and a little chopped parsley, and when the margarine has melted, turn into a hot vegetable dish.

Carrots en Casserole

Carrots 1 lb.   *Salt, pepper, sugar*
Margarine 2 oz.   *Chopped parsley*
Water 4 tablespoonfuls

Scrape carrots and shred on a coarse grater. Put in a casserole,
season with salt and pepper, and sprinkle over 1 teaspoonful
of sugar. Add the margarine cut up in small pieces, pour over
the water, put the lid on the casserole, and bake in a moderate
oven about ¾ hour. Sprinkle with parsley, and serve in the
dish in which they were cooked.

Carrots and Peas

Wash and scrape some young carrots and cook in boiling
salted water till tender, then drain. Mix with freshly cooked
green peas, add a small knob of margarine, and sprinkle with
chopped mint and parsley, or coat with parsley sauce (see page
197), using half milk and half vegetable water.

Carrot Tzimmas (1)

Carrots 1 lb.   *Chicken or other fat 2 tablespoonfuls*
Brown sugar 3 oz.   *Water ½ pint*

Scrape and dice the carrots and cook in the fat till lightly
browned.
Boil the sugar and water together for 5 minutes, add the
carrots and any fat that has not been absorbed, and cook
gently till the carrots are tender. Then dredge in a little flour,
add salt to taste, and cook 2 or 3 minutes longer.

Cauliflower

Cauliflower can be eaten raw or cooked in hors d'oeuvres or
salad, as an accompaniment to the meat course, or as a vegetable entrée (see page 115). Choose a cauliflower with a fine
white head and fresh green leaves.

Boiled Cauliflower

Cut the stalk off flat at the bottom, trim off any discoloured outer leaves, place the cauliflower head downwards in salted water, and leave for ½ hour. Drain and cook in boiling salted water till just tender – 20–30 minutes.

Serve plain or coated with white sauce (see page 196), or sprinkle with breadcrumbs which have been fried brown in a little butter or margarine.

If preferred, the cauliflower can be divided into flowerets before cooking, in which case it should be ready in about 15 minutes.

Celeriac

Can be boiled or stewed like celery, added to stews, or served as salad or hors d'oeuvres.

Scrub and peel; if small leave whole, otherwise cut in halves or quarters. Cook gently in salted water or vegetable stock till tender – 1–1½ hours. Mash to a purée with a little margarine, or serve coated with white sauce.

For Salad. Cut into slices and dress with French dressing.

Celery

Can be eaten raw or cooked. It can be shredded, dressed with mayonnaise, and served as an hors d'oeuvre, or served quite plain with cheese; or cut up in vegetable salads.

It can be boiled, stewed, or braised, and is excellent for flavouring soups and stews. It is a winter vegetable and is never at its best until after a touch of frost.

Use the outside sticks in soups and stews, the green tops for the same purpose or in salads. When you have more of the leaves than you want for your immediate needs, dry them in a cool oven and keep in an airtight container for flavouring when celery is not obtainable.

To Serve Raw. Remove the outer stalks, trim the root, and cut the head of celery into quarters. Use only the white heart and clean very thoroughly, using a small vegetable brush to remove all grit. With a sharp knife cut the tops in fine strips to a depth of 2 inches. Leave in icy cold water for 1 hour, when the top ends will curl up. Serve in a celery glass with a little water.

Boiled Celery

Scrub and trim one or more heads of celery and remove the strings from back of stalks. The heads can be left whole, cut into quarters, or into pieces about 2 inches long. Cook in boiling salted water or vegetable stock till tender – about 40–50 minutes. Drain, reserving the water for soup, and serve coated with thick brown gravy or white sauce.

Braised Celery

2 large heads of celery	*Stock ¾ pint*
1 large onion	*Flour 1 oz.*
2 medium-sized carrots	*Salt and pepper*
Margarine 2 oz.	

Prepare the celery and cut into 2-inch lengths. Prepare onion and carrots and chop finely. Melt margarine (or clarified dripping) in a stewpan, add carrots and onion, and fry a golden brown; then add the celery, pour over the stock and a few drops of gravy browning, season with salt and pepper, and simmer gently till the celery is tender – about ¾ hour. Strain off the gravy and put the vegetables into a hot vegetable dish. Mix the flour smoothly with a little cold stock, add to the gravy and stir till boiling. Simmer for 2 or 3 minutes and pour over the celery.

Celery in Salad

(See page 209)

Celery Sauce

(See page 199)

Celery Stuffing

(See page 193)

Chicory

Can be eaten raw in salad, or is excellent braised.

Braised Chicory

Remove any outside discoloured leaves and wash thoroughly, leaving the heads whole. Cover with boiling water, leave for 5 minutes, then drain. Lay in rows in a well-greased, shallow oven dish, season with salt, pepper, and a squeeze of lemon juice, pour over a small cup of stock, and dot with margarine. Cover with a greased paper, and cook in a moderate oven about 1 hour. After 30 minutes turn the chicory over and remove the paper to permit browning.

Chestnuts

The husks and brown skins of chestnuts may be removed in two ways:

(1) Put chestnuts in a saucepan with water to cover, bring to the boil, and boil for 15 minutes. Take a few out at a time and remove skins with a knife.

(2) Make a slit in the chestnuts and put them on a baking tin in a moderate oven for about 10 minutes. Remove skins while hot.

To Boil. Remove skins from chestnuts and boil until tender in slightly salted water – about 30 minutes. Then drain, reserving water for soup. Can be served coated with parsley sauce or thick brown gravy.

To Purée. Mash chestnuts smoothly with a little margarine. Season with salt and pepper.

Chestnuts and Brussels Sprouts

Sprouts 1 lb.	*Margarine 1 oz.*
Chestnuts ¼ lb.	*Salt and pepper*

Prepare the sprouts; skin the chestnuts and boil separately till tender. Drain and mix together, add the margarine, salt, and pepper, and make thoroughly hot.

Chestnut Stuffing
(See page 193)

Chives

Use in place of, or with, parsley in savoury stuffings, salad dressing, sandwich spreads, omelettes, etc.

Corn on the Cob

Choose the corn as fresh as possible. Remove the outer husks, open the inner husks just enough to take out the 'silk' which covers the corn, then close the inner husks again. Put the corn into a saucepan of boiling salted water, to which add ½ oz. sugar. When the water comes to the boil again, simmer gently about ½ hour, according to the size of the corn. Lift out of the water and remove husks. Serve with fresh butter.

If you grow the corn yourself and use it when *very young*, 5 minutes should be sufficient time to cook it. And do not cut it until you are ready to cook it.

Cucumbers

Cucumbers can be served either raw or cooked; uncooked as hors d'oeuvres, in salads, and for the garnishing of cold dishes. Long strips of the rind are also used in wine cups.

Cucumber Salad
(See page 217)

Ridge Cucumbers

Ridge cucumbers can be baked, fried, or stewed, and are very good served with fish or meat dishes.

To Bake. (1) Peel and slice the cucumbers. Put a layer in a greased fireproof dish, sprinkle with lemon juice and grated onion, then with breadcrumbs, dot with margarine and repeat the layers. Bake in a moderate oven about 50 minutes, keeping it covered the first ½ hour.

(2) Choose large cucumbers, peel, cut in halves, and remove the pips. Stuff with any savoury filling (see Stuffed Marrows and Stuffed Tomatoes, pages 130–31 and 128–9), place the halves together and tie securely. Put in a baking dish with a little fat, cover with a greased paper and bake in a moderately hot oven 1–1¼ hours. Serve with thick brown gravy or a savoury sauce.

To Fry. Use small cucumbers, peel them and boil in salted water for 5 minutes, then drain and dry them in a cloth. Cut them into 4 pieces lengthways, roll them in seasoned flour, and fry them in very little fat till golden brown on both sides. These can be served with a border of fried onions, or a little sliced onion could be fried with the cucumbers.

To Stew. Peel the cucumbers and boil in salted water for 5 minutes, then cut in quarters and remove the seeds. Place in a saucepan and cover with thickened gravy or white sauce flavoured with lemon juice. Simmer gently till tender – about 15 minutes.

Custard Marrows

Custard marrows should be cut when fairly small – about 1 lb. in weight. Cut across in two, and if young and tender there is no need to remove the peel. Boil in salted water till tender and serve with tomato, cheese, or plain white sauce.

Endive

The curly-leaved endive makes a decorative salad. It can also be cooked like spinach or braised.

Braised Endive

Use a shallow wide pan, as the endives should not overlap each other.

Melt 2 oz. margarine in the pan, then add the well-washed endives with only the water that is clinging to them. Season with salt and pepper, cover the pan, and cook very gently. Turn the endives, so that they get golden brown on all sides. They should take 30–40 minutes.

Garlic

Garlic belongs to the onion family. It has a strong, pungent taste, and only very little is needed for flavouring. The small divisions are called cloves.

For flavouring salads, remove skin from one clove and cut across, then rub it round the salad bowl before making the salad.

If used in a stew, remove the skin from one clove and chop finely and fry it with the onion.

Greens

(See Cabbage, page 87)

Horseradish

Serve with hot roast beef or cold meats. As a garnish for beef, wash and peel off the outer skin, then scrape the root into shavings.

Kale or Curly Greens

Wash very carefully and remove hard pieces of stalk. Cook like cabbage.

Kohlrabi

Wash, peel, and cut the kohlrabi root into thick slices, and boil till tender – about 30 minutes.

Cook the green tops separately in boiling salted water and when tender drain and chop.

Melt 1 oz. margarine, stir in 1 oz. flour smoothly, and gradually add ½ pint water in which the vegetable was cooked. Stir till boiling and season to taste. Pour this over the root and heap up in a hot dish with a border around of the green leaves.

For Salad. Steam the root till tender and when cold remove peel and cut into slices. Dress with oil and vinegar or mayonnaise.

Leeks

Leeks belong to the onion family, but are milder and more

delicate in flavour. They are excellent in soups and stews and delicious as a separate vegetable.

They need very careful washing as they are generally very gritty.

Cut off the roots and top green (but use this green in the stock pot) and remove outer skin. Cut the top down about 1 inch to facilitate removal of grit. Cook in boiling salted water (just sufficient to cover) till tender – 35–40 minutes, according to size.

Drain the leeks (be sure to save the water for soup or gravy) and dish them on to a slice of dry toast, arranging the heads all one way.

Serve with thick brown gravy or white sauce.

For Salad. When cold, dress with French dressing.

Baked Leeks

Put some small leeks into boiling salted water, boil for 5 minutes, then drain. Cut into 2-inch lengths and put in a fireproof dish, season with salt and pepper, and add just sufficient well-flavoured meat stock to cover. Bake in a moderate oven for ½ hour.

Lettuce

Lettuces, both round and long, are mostly eaten raw as salad or in sandwiches, but they can also be cooked.

Stewed Lettuce

Trim and wash lettuce, drop in boiling salted water, cook for 5 minutes, then drain, rinse in cold water, and return to saucepan, cover with well-flavoured meat stock, and simmer gently till tender – about ¾ hour.

Or cut the lettuce into quarters after boiling and rinsing in cold water, and place in a saucepan with 2 oz. butter, pepper and salt to taste, and a dust of caster sugar. Simmer till tender, then place the lettuce on a hot dish and stir into the liquor in the pan the yolks of 2 eggs, diluted with ½ teacupful of milk.

Stir till it thickens, but do not let it boil, and pour over the lettuce.

Mint

Add a sprig to green peas and new potatoes while boiling.

Use for mint sauce, for adding to wine and fruit cups, and for garnishing fruit cocktails.

Mushrooms

Mushrooms are best prepared very simply, so as to retain their own delicate flavour.

To Bake. Skin the mushrooms and trim the end of the stalks. Place in a greased fireproof dish, stalks uppermost, put a tiny knob of butter or margarine on each, dust with salt and pepper, cover the dish, and cook in a moderate oven till tender – 20–30 minutes. Serve in the dish in which they were cooked.

To Fry. Skin; remove the stalks, which should be used in soup or sauce. Fry in butter 2 or 3 minutes on each side, season with salt and pepper, and serve on rounds of toast with the butter from the pan poured over.

To Grill. Choose large mushrooms and remove the stalks, using these for soup or sauce. Brush over with cooking oil or melted butter, and grill lightly 2 or 3 minutes on each side. Dish on to rounds of toast, season with salt, pepper, and lemon juice, and garnish with watercress.

Stewed Mushrooms

Mushrooms ½ lb.	*Milk ¼ pint*
Butter 2 oz.	*Flour 2 teaspoonfuls*
Salt and pepper	*Lemon juice 1 teaspoonful*

Skin the mushrooms and remove the stalks. Melt the butter in a saucepan, put in the mushrooms, simmer very gently for 10 minutes, then add the lemon juice, salt, and pepper, and the flour mixed with the milk. Cover and simmer gently till tender – about 15 minutes.

Water may be substituted for milk and margarine for butter. Use stalks for flavouring soups and gravies.

See also Vegetable Entrées, page 119.

Onions

There are various kinds of onions. The large ones, generally called 'Spanish', have the mildest flavour. Leeks, shallots, chives, and garlic all belong to the onion family.

Onions are invaluable in cookery for flavouring, and are excellent as a separate vegetable.

Boiled Onions

Choose onions of equal size. Peel off the outer skin and trim the root. Put into a saucepan with sufficient boiling water to cover, and cook gently till tender – ¾ to 1 hour, depending on the size. Drain, reserving the water for soup, and serve with white, brown, or tomato sauce.

Baked Onions

(1) Peel 1 lb. small white onions and cook in boiling salted water for 15 minutes, then drain thoroughly. Grease a shallow, fireproof dish, put in the onions, sprinkle with demerara sugar, salt, and pepper, and dot with margarine or dripping. Pour ½ pint stock around, and bake for 1 hour in a moderate oven, keeping them well basted with the stock.

(2) Peel some large Spanish onions and boil in salted water for 20 minutes. Drain and place in a baking dish. Sprinkle with salt, pepper, and flour, and pour into the dish sufficient milk to cover the lower half of the onions. Put a pat of margarine on top of each onion, and bake in a moderate oven until the onions are tender – about 1½ hours – basting frequently.

(3) Peel and cut into ½-inch slices 4 large Spanish onions, put into a shallow baking dish, pour over 2 oz. melted fat and ¼ pint stock or water. Season with salt and pepper and bake in a moderate oven till tender – about ¾ hour – turning over when they have been cooking ½ hour.

(4) Peel some large onions and boil for 5 minutes, then drain. Put into a casserole with sufficient hot dripping to come half-way up the onions. Cover casserole and bake in a moderate oven for ½ hour, then remove lid and continue cooking till well browned and tender – another ¾–1 hour – turning the onions over once or twice.

(5) After boiling for 15 or 20 minutes, onions can be drained and roasted round the meat.

Fried Onions

Peel and slice required amount of onions. Melt a little dripping in a frying pan, and when very hot put in the onions and stir, so that all the onion gets coated with fat. Put a plate or saucepan lid on top of the frying pan, lower the heat, and fry gently 15–20 minutes, when the onions should be soft and brown. Stir once or twice, so that the onions get browned evenly. Season with salt and pepper before serving.

For Crisp Onion Rings. Slice the onions rather thickly and divide the slices into rings with the sharp point of a vegetable knife. Season some flour with salt and pepper and coat the rings of onion with this. Drop into very hot deep fat or oil and fry till brown and crisp.

Serve with grilled steak or chops.

Fried Onions with Apples

Prepare and cook as plain fried onions, using equal quantities sliced onion and apples. Before serving, sprinkle with salt, pepper, and a little sugar.

Parsnips

The parsnip is a root vegetable belonging to the carrot family and may be cooked according to any recipe for carrots.

They can be used to flavour soups and stews, and are very good plainly boiled, then mashed and served as a purée.

Parsnips are the usual accompaniment to salt fish.

To Boil. If not too large, leave the parsnips whole. Scrub thoroughly and cook in boiling salted water till tender – about

40 minutes — then rub off the skins and serve plain or with this sauce:

Melt 1 oz. margarine, stir in 1 oz. flour smoothly, then gradually add ½ pint water in which the parsnips were cooked. Stir till boiling and add vegetable extract or Worcester sauce to taste.

Or peel the parsnips with a potato peeler and cut into quarters or chunky pieces.

To Purée. Prepare and cook as above, then mash thoroughly with a little margarine and pepper and, if liked, the juice of half a lemon.

To Bake. Peel and cut into convenient-sized pieces. Boil in salted water for 5 minutes, then drain and roast round the joint — about 1 hour.

To Fry. Dip left-over boiled parsnips in seasoned flour and fry a golden brown in hot fat.

In Salad. Shred raw parsnip finely and add to mixed vegetable salad.

Or cut cooked parsnip into neat dice and coat with salad cream. Heap up in a dish with a border of watercress and shredded lettuce.

Green Peas

Shell and, if they are young, reserve the pods for soup. Put into boiling salted water, add a sprig or two of mint and a pinch of sugar. Cover the pan and when the water has boiled again, lower the heat and simmer till the peas are tender — 15–30 minutes, according to the age of the peas. Drain (reserve the water for soup), turn into a hot vegetable dish with a knob of margarine or butter.

Green Peas – French Style

2 round lettuces	Margarine 1 oz.
Shelled peas 1 pint	Flour 1 oz.
Vegetable extract	Water ¼ teacupful
Salt and pepper	A few spring onions

Wash lettuces and separate the leaves. Grease a casserole and line thickly with lettuce leaves, put the peas and onions on top, sprinkle with salt and pepper, dot with the margarine, and dredge the flour over. Mix a little vegetable extract with the water, pour this into the dish, cover with remaining lettuce leaves, put the lid on the casserole, and cook in a moderate oven about $\frac{3}{4}$ hour.

Potatoes

Potatoes are among the fuel foods, which provide the body with heat and energy. Rich in starch, they also contain minerals, are a good source of vitamins B and C, and contain a certain amount of vitamin A.

Whenever possible, potatoes should be baked, boiled, or steamed in their jackets, as much of their nourishment lies immediately underneath the skin, and, apart from this, there is much less waste when they are cooked in their skins. If peeled before cooking, the potatoes should be peeled as thinly as possible with a potato peeler.

Boiled Potatoes

Potatoes can be boiled in or out of their jackets and can be served peeled or unpeeled.

To Boil Old Potatoes. (1) **In their jackets.** Choose potatoes of uniform size and scrub them thoroughly. Put in a saucepan, cover with boiling water, add 2 teaspoonfuls salt to every quart of water, cover, and boil *gently* till tender – 20–30 minutes, according to size. Test gently with a fork, and when easily pierced drain off the water, return the saucepan to the stove, cover potatoes with a cloth, put the lid on the pan, and leave over a very low heat for a few minutes for the cloth to absorb the steam. Serve peeled or unpeeled.

(2) **Without their jackets.** Peel potatoes very thinly and drop into cold water as they are peeled, or they will become discoloured. Unless very small, cut potatoes through lengthways, either in halves or quarters, so that the pieces are of equal size. Put into boiling salted water, using just enough water to cover. Put the lid on the saucepan and boil gently till tender –

15–20 minutes, according to size. Drain, cover with a cloth, put the lid on the saucepan, and stand over a *very* low heat for 2 or 3 minutes, shaking the saucepan gently once or twice, so that the potatoes do not stick to the bottom. If no cloth is used, then raise lid slightly, so that steam can escape.

At the end of the season, to keep potatoes white when boiling, add 2 teaspoonfuls vinegar to the water for the last 10 minutes.

To Boil New Potatoes. Choose potatoes of equal size. Scrub and scrape potatoes (if very young, the skin will rub off with a coarse cloth) and drop into cold water until all are scraped. Put in a saucepan, cover with boiling water, add salt to taste and one or two sprigs of mint. Bring to the boil, and boil steadily till tender – 20–30 minutes, according to size. Drain and leave with lid partly raised for a minute or two, and when quite dry add a knob of margarine or butter, shake gently so that all potatoes get coated, turn into a hot vegetable dish, and sprinkle with chopped parsley.

To Mash. Mash boiled potatoes free of lumps with a potato masher, add a knob of dripping or margarine (and if for a milk meal, a little hot milk), and a dash of pepper, and beat with a fork till creamy.

To vary the flavour, add chopped parsley, chives, or watercress; or an onion or two thinly sliced and fried till golden brown.

Baked Potatoes

Scrub some fairly large potatoes very thoroughly, then dry them and prick with a fork. Bake in a moderately hot oven about 1 hour – if very large, they may take a little longer. Turn the potatoes once or twice while cooking.

See also Stuffed Baked Potatoes, pages 120–21.

Potato Cakes

To 1 lb. mashed potatoes add 1 tablespoonful melted margarine and a beaten egg. Season with salt and pepper, and add sufficient flour (about 2 tablespoonfuls) to form a paste. Shape into round flat cakes and dredge with flour. Fry in shallow fat till golden brown on both sides.

Any of the following can be added for a change:

(1) Grated onion and chopped parsley.

(2) Tomato ketchup, using sufficient to give a good flavour and colour.

(3) One or two chopped cooked chicken livers.

(4) If served with a milk meal, 3 oz. grated cheese.

If preferred, the paste can be rolled out on a floured board and cut with a round cutter.

To Bake. Place on a well-greased tin, brush the top with beaten egg, and bake in a hot oven about 20 minutes.

Potato Croquettes

Cooked potatoes 1 lb.	*1 egg*
Chopped parsley 1 tablespoonful	*Dried breadcrumbs*
Margarine or dripping 1 oz.	*Salt and pepper*

Mash potatoes free of lumps or rub through a sieve. Add the beaten egg yolk, melted fat, parsley, salt, and pepper, and mix thoroughly. Shape into round balls or cork-shaped croquettes, brush over with slightly-beaten white of egg, and coat with dried crumbs. Fry in deep fat till golden brown.

Mashed Potatoes with Apples

Peel, core, and cut up 1 lb. of cooking apples and stew with very little water and a small quantity of sugar till soft, then either rub through a sieve or beat to a purée with a fork. Mash 1½ lb. of freshly-boiled potatoes, season with salt and pepper, add the hot apple purée and mix thoroughly. Serve with either hot or cold meat, or with grilled or baked herrings.

Fried Potatoes

Raw potatoes should be fried in deep fat. They can be cut into various shapes, chips, strips, ribbons, or balls. For the latter, a special vegetable cutter is necessary. Be very careful when deep frying not to fill the pan too full so that the fat overflows, remembering that it will always bubble up when the cold potatoes are lowered into it.

Chips. Peel potatoes and cut across into thick slices, then into finger strips. Soak for a short time in cold water, then drain and dry thoroughly in a cloth.

Heat fat till a faint blue smoke is rising from it, place the chips in the frying basket and lower slowly into the fat. Fry till lightly browned, then lift out the basket for a minute or two, increase the heat of the fat, and return the chips for a few more minutes till crisp and brown. Drain and sprinkle with salt and pepper.

Crisps. Very easy if you have a cutter for the slicing, though hand-cut crisps are possible. Use a very sharp knife and cut as thin as possible. Place in very cold water and let stand for half an hour before frying. Drain and dry very thoroughly in a cloth. Put only a thin layer in the basket and lower slowly into fat and fry as above. Drain on absorbent paper, sprinkle with salt, and continue until all the crisps have been fried.

Ribbons. Peel potatoes, then peel round and round as if peeling an apple, so that you have long ribbon-like pieces. Then proceed as for chips.

Pommes Anna

Peel medium-sized potatoes and slice them across thinly and evenly, about the thickness of a half-crown. Soak in cold water for 10 minutes and then drain and dry thoroughly in a cloth. Put them in a well-greased casserole in layers, pouring a little melted fat over each layer and seasoning with salt and pepper until the dish is full. Then cover with greaseproof paper, put on the lid of the dish, and bake in a moderate oven about $1\frac{1}{4}$ hours, removing the lid and paper the last 20 minutes. Pour off surplus fat before serving. They can be served in the casserole or turned on to a hot dish.

Potato Latkes

Grated raw potato 1 pint	*2 eggs*
Flour 2 tablespoonfuls	*Salt and pepper*

Choose large potatoes, peel them, and soak in cold water for $\frac{1}{2}$ hour; then grate them and drain off the liquid. Add the flour and well-beaten eggs and season with salt and pepper.

Melt a little fat in a frying pan and drop in the mixture in spoonfuls. When brown on one side, turn and brown on the other.

Variations:
(1) Serve with grated cheese.
(2) Flavour with grated onion.
(3) Omit eggs and simply add sufficient flour to bind.

Lyonnaise Potatoes

Cook in the same way as sauté potatoes, but fry a little sliced onion in the dripping till golden brown before putting in the potatoes. Sprinkle with chopped parsley, salt, and pepper before serving.

For Savoury Fried Potatoes, cut potatoes into dice instead of slices, and after frying the onion golden brown, put in the potatoes and add a tablespoonful of vinegar and a pinch of mixed herbs. Fry gently till fat is absorbed, then add seasoning and parsley.

Potato Pancake

(1) **With Mashed Potatoes.** Melt a tablespoonful of dripping in a round frying pan and when smoking hot put in seasoned mashed potato – not more than an inch deep – press down evenly, and cook over a moderate heat till well browned underneath, shaking the pan so that it does not stick. Turn over on to a plate, melt a little more dripping, slip the potato back in the pan to brown the other side. This should brown in about 7 minutes on either side.

Chopped parsley, watercress, or onion can be added to the potato before frying.

(2) **With Raw Potato.** Peel 1½ lb. potatoes and grate on a *coarse* grater. Melt 2 good tablespoonfuls of dripping in a large frying pan and when a faint blue smoke rises, put in the potatoes in a *thin* layer, season with salt and pepper, and cover with a plate or saucepan lid. Cook slowly till brown and soft – about 20 minutes.

Roast Potatoes

Peel potatoes and, unless they are rather small, cut in halves or quarters. Put into cold salted water, bring to the boil. Drain and roast round the joint for about 1 hour, turning in the fat at half time, so that both sides get equally browned. If there is no room round the meat, then cook in a separate tin of hot fat.

Potato Salads

(See page 218)

Sauté Potatoes

Slice cold, cooked potatoes and fry in a small quantity of fat. When brown on one side, turn and brown on the other.

Stewed Pumpkin

Remove rind and seeds from one or two slices of pumpkin, and cut into small pieces. Put in a saucepan with very little water, cover, and simmer till tender – about ¾ hour. Then drain through a colander and mash or sieve. Return to the saucepan, season with salt and pepper, add a little margarine or butter, and reheat.

Sage

Use to flavour stuffing for duck or goose. If using fresh sage, soak for 5 minutes in boiling water and dry carefully before chopping. It can be bought dried in packets ready for use.

Salsify

Scrape and trim the salsify, dropping each root immediately into cold water to which a little vinegar has been added, to prevent it turning black. Put into boiling salted water (to which add 2 teaspoonfuls lemon juice or vinegar), and when water has reboiled, simmer till tender – about 40 minutes.

Dish into a hot vegetable dish and coat with white sauce.

Fritters. Simmer for 30 minutes, and when cold dip in flour or frying batter and fry a golden brown in hot fat.

Salad. When cold cut into dice or finger lengths and dress with French dressing.

Sauerkraut

Sauerkraut 2 pints	*2 or 3 cooking apples*
Fat 2 oz.	*1 onion*
Water ¼ pint	*1 potato*
Sugar	*Caraway seeds*

Wash the sauerkraut thoroughly. Slice the onion thinly and peel, core and cut up the apples.

Melt the fat in a saucepan, put in the sauerkraut, apples and onion, stir together, then pour over ¼ pint boiling water. Put the lid on the pan and cook steadily for 30 minutes. Then add the finely grated potato, 1 teaspoonful of sugar and a few caraway seeds. Continue cooking until the sauerkraut is tender – about another 15 minutes.

If preferred, this can be cooked in a casserole in the oven.

Savoy

Cook like cabbage, see page 87.

Sea-kale

To Boil. Trim the bottom of the stalks to a point, wash thoroughly, and soak in cold water for ½ hour. If the sea-kale is very large it can be split in halves lengthways. Tie into bundles and put into boiling salted water, to which add 2 teaspoonfuls lemon juice, and boil gently till tender – 20–25 minutes. Do not overcook, or it will become tough. Lift into a colander, remove string, and dish on a slice of toast. Serve plain or coated with white or hollandaise sauce.

To Steam. Sea-kale is particularly good steamed; this method preserves its delicate flavour. Prepare as above and steam till tender – about 50 minutes.

Spinach

Remove the stalks and any decayed portions from the spinach and wash it in several waters, until not a particle of grit remains. Lift it out of the water with the hands and put it in a saucepan with the water clinging to the leaves – no further water is required. Add salt to taste. Place over a very gentle heat until the water in the spinach itself begins to ooze out, then boil over a moderate heat till tender – about 20 minutes. Drain well through a colander, pressing out all moisture, then either turn on to a board and chop with a knife, or rub the spinach through a sieve. Return to the saucepan, adding 1 oz. of margarine or butter to every 2 lb. of spinach. Stir over a moderate heat till thoroughly hot, then turn into a hot dish and garnish with triangles of toast or croûtons.

Be sure to save the water from the spinach for soup. With a little vegetable extract added, it makes a delicious bouillon and an extremely health-giving drink.

Stewed Spinach

Prepare and cook 2 lb. spinach as above, drain, and chop coarsely.

Melt 1 oz. margarine in a saucepan, stir in 1 oz. flour smoothly, then gradually add $\frac{1}{3}$ pint spinach water. Stir till boiling, add the chopped spinach, season with salt and pepper, and simmer very gently for 5 minutes.

See also Vegetable Entrées, pages 126–7.

Swedes

Swedes can be boiled or baked and served diced, sliced, or mashed. The juice of raw swedes is rich in vitamin C.

If no horseradish is available, use raw grated swede mixed with beetroot for 'chraine'.

To Boil. Peel thickly, cut into pieces, and cook in boiling salted water till tender – about 45 minutes. Drain and serve plain or mashed with salt, pepper, and a knob of margarine.

Left-over mashed swede can be mixed with an equal quantity of mashed potato to top a shepherd's pie.

To Roast. Cut into finger lengths, boil for 5 minutes, then drain, and roast round the meat about 1 hour.

Sweet Peppers
(*Capsicums*)

Sweet peppers, both red and green, can be fried, stuffed and
baked, eaten raw in a vegetable salad, used in soup, or a little,
finely chopped, can be added to savoury dishes of macaroni or
rice.

To Serve Raw. As the flavour is rather pungent use only one
or two spoonfuls, finely chopped (after removing skin and
seeds), in a potato or mixed vegetable salad. *Or* a small
quantity can be added to cream cheese for a sandwich filling.

To Prepare the peppers for frying or baking, cut off the
stalks, cut in half (lengthways), and remove seed and stringy
membrane.

To Fry. Put the prepared peppers (cut in halves or quarters)
into a saucepan, cover with boiling salted water, and simmer
for 5 minutes. Then drain, dip in egg and breadcrumbs, and
fry in deep fat.

Stuffed Peppers
(See pages 127–8)

Tomatoes

Tomatoes are rich in health-giving vitamins and also contain all
the mineral salts the body needs. They are a particularly good
source of iron and calcium. Growing children will greatly
benefit by a liberal supply in their diet. Serve them with
brown bread and butter for breakfast and tea, and the 'tinies'
can have them sieved.

They can be eaten raw or cooked, and also make excellent
pickle, ketchup, and jam.

To Peel Tomatoes. Drop into boiling water for half a
minute, then into cold water, and the skins can be removed
quite easily.

Uncooked Tomatoes are served chiefly as hors-d'oeuvres,

salads, or sandwiches, either by themselves or mixed with other vegetables. For recipes, see under these headings.

To Grill. Choose firm tomatoes and, if they are quite small, leave them whole and brush them over with salad oil or melted margarine. If large, cut in halves, dust with salt and pepper, and put a tiny knob of margarine on each. Grill at medium heat, 10–15 minutes. Serve with chops, steaks, eggs, or fish.

Baked Tomatoes. Choose firm tomatoes, not too small, cut a thin slice off the top of each, put on a greased fireproof dish, season with salt and pepper, put a tiny knob of margarine or butter on top of each, and bake in a moderate oven about 20 minutes.

See also Vegetable Entrées, pages 128-9.

Green Tomatoes

The smallest green tomatoes can be used in pickles and chutneys. They are very good grilled or fried; they can be baked round the joint, or added to stews or braised dishes. They make an excellent sauce for fish or vegetables and can also be used in the sweet course.

To Fry. Cut the tomatoes into thick slices, dip in seasoned flour then in frying batter, and fry a golden brown on both sides.

To Purée. Thinly slice 1 lb. tomatoes and 1 onion. Melt 2 oz. margarine in a saucepan, add the tomatoes and onion, 1 teaspoonful of sugar, and 2 tablespoonfuls of water; season with salt and pepper; cover and cook *very slowly* till soft and pulpy, keeping it well stirred. Serve with fish or meat.

Sauce. Make purée as above using half quantities, then rub through a strainer and add with 2 teaspoonfuls of chopped parsley to ½ pint white sauce. Serve with boiled or baked fish.

Turnips

Turnips can be cooked alone or in soups and stews. They need to be peeled rather thickly, as they are rather woody under the skin.

Mashed Turnips

Wash and peel the turnips and cook in boiling salted water till tender. This will take 25–40 minutes, according to the age of the turnips. Drain thoroughly, then mash them with either a fork or potato masher. Return to the saucepan, add 1 oz. of margarine to every 2 lb. of turnips, and season well with salt and pepper.

Turnip Tops

Cook like boiled cabbage, page 87.

Vegetable Marrow

Marrows can be boiled, baked, fried, or stuffed. When they are very young and small they can be peeled and cooked whole. Older marrows must be peeled, cut into pieces, and the seeds removed.

To Boil. Peel and cut up the marrow and remove the seeds. Put into boiling salted water and simmer gently till tender – about 20 minutes. Drain very thoroughly and serve plain or coated with tomato or white sauce.

To Fry. Peel and seed marrow and cut into small cubes. Peel and slice thinly 1 or 2 onions. Heat a little dripping in a frying pan, and fry the marrow and onion over a gentle heat till tender and a golden brown. Sprinkle with salt and pepper before serving.

To Bake. (1) Prepare and cut up marrow and bake round the meat for about 50 minutes.

(2) Put prepared and cut-up marrow into a greased casserole, season with salt and pepper, pour over 2 or 3 tablespoonfuls melted margarine or olive oil. Cover, and bake about 50 minutes in a moderate oven. Sprinkle with parsley before serving.

Vegetable Marrow with Caper Sauce

A medium-sized marrow
Stock or milk ¼ pint
Capers 2 teaspoonfuls
Caper vinegar 1 teaspoonful
Margarine 1 oz.
Flour 1 oz.
Salt and pepper

Peel, seed and cut up the marrow. Sprinkle it with salt and leave it for an hour; then rinse with cold water, drain thoroughly and place in a casserole.

Melt the margarine, stir in the flour smoothly, and then gradually add the liquid. Stir till boiling, add the capers and caper vinegar, season with salt and pepper and pour this over the marrow. Cover the casserole and bake in a moderate oven for about 50 minutes.

Stewed Marrow (1)

A medium sized marrow　　　*Stock or water ½ pint*
2 or 3 tomatoes　　　　　　*Flour 1 oz.*
2 medium sized onions　　　*Salt 1 teaspoonful*
Margarine or other fat 1 oz.

Peel and seed the marrow and cut it into small pieces. Skin and slice tomatoes, skin and chop onions.

Melt the fat in a saucepan, put in the onions and tomatoes, cover, and cook very gently for 10 minutes, stirring once or twice; then pour over the boiling stock and add the marrow and salt. Cover, and cook gently till tender – about 20 minutes. Pour off the liquid into a small saucepan, add the flour blended with cold water, and stir till boiling. Season to taste with salt and pepper and simmer for 2 or 3 minutes. Turn the marrow into a hot dish and pour the sauce over.

Stewed Marrow (2)

A small marrow　　　　　　　*Vinegar 1 teaspoonful*
Margarine or other fat 1 oz.　*A few caraway seeds*
Flour 1 level tablespoonful　 *Salt and pepper*
Stock ½ pint

Peel and seed the marrow and cut it into small pieces. Sprinkle with salt and let it stand for half an hour. Rinse in cold water and drain.

Melt the fat in a saucepan, stir in the flour smoothly, gradually add the stock, stir till boiling, then add the vinegar and a few caraway seeds and season with salt and pepper. Put in the prepared marrow, cover, and simmer gently till tender – about 20 minutes.

Stuffed Vegetable Marrow

(See pages 130-31)

Luncheon and Supper Dishes and Vegetable Entrées

Stuffed Aubergines

Remove the stalks and parboil the aubergines in boiling salted water for 30 minutes. Then drain and leave till cold.

Cut through lengthways, remove the seeds, then scrape out the pulp and chop finely. Mix this with veal forcemeat (see page 194) or any mixture suggested for stuffed marrow (see pages 130–31). Sprinkle with breadcrumbs, dot with margarine, place on a greased oven dish and bake in a moderate oven about 30 minutes.

Blintzes

1 or 2 eggs	*Salt*
Flour 1 breakfastcupful	*Filling*
Water 1 breakfastcupful	

Make a smooth batter with the egg, flour and water, adding a good pinch of salt. Grease a heated frying pan with oil, pour in about 2 tablespoonfuls of the batter, just sufficient to make a *very thin* pancake, tipping the pan so that the batter runs level. Fry over a gentle heat on one side only until it will just hold its shape, then turn out on to a board or cloth, the cooked side uppermost, and fry the rest of the batter in the same way.

Then put a tablespoonful of the filling in the centre of each pancake and fold over into a triangle or envelope shape, pressing edges well together. Fry a golden brown on both sides.

Fillings:

(1) **Cream Cheese.** Add a little sugar and grated lemon rind to soft cream cheese, and season with salt and pepper.

(2) **Apple.** Peel and grate ½ lb. apples and mix with 1 oz. ground almonds, 1 tablespoonful caster sugar, the grated rind and juice of half a lemon, and a pinch of cinnamon. Sprinkle the finished pancakes with sugar and cinnamon.

(3) **Meat.** Mince left-over cooked meat, add a little grated onion and chopped parsley, season with salt and pepper and tomato ketchup. Mix thoroughly, and bind with a beaten egg. Serve with tomato sauce or thick gravy.

Stuffed Cabbage

Choose a moderate-sized cabbage that has not got too tight a heart. Remove outside leaves and trim stalk. Scald the cabbage for 2 or 3 minutes in boiling water, then open out the leaves without breaking them off. Make a forcemeat with sausage meat and breadcrumbs, add a little minced onion and a pinch of herbs. Put a little of this at the bottom of every leaf, return the cabbage to its original shape, tie round with tape. Put in a saucepan, add ½ pint stock, and stew gently for 1½ hours. Dish on to a hot dish, thicken the gravy and pour around.

If preferred, this can be cooked in a covered casserole in the oven, instead of on top of the stove.

Other Suggestions for Stuffing:

(1) Any left-over minced meat, mixed with half its bulk in breadcrumbs or sieved haricot beans. Season with chopped parsley, salt, pepper, and vegetable extract, or any piquant sauce, and moisten with a little thick gravy.

(2) Cooked rice, to which add 2 or 3 tablespoonfuls each grated cheese and chopped onion. Cook the cabbage in vegetable stock and serve with cheese sauce.

Cauliflower au Gratin

Cooked cauliflower   *White sauce ¾ pint*
Grated cheese 3 oz.   *Breadcrumbs*

Break up the cauliflower into flowerets and cut the stalk in pieces and put in a fireproof dish. Add the cheese to the sauce, reserving 1 tablespoonful. Pour the sauce over the cauliflower, sprinkle with breadcrumbs and grated cheese, and bake in a quick oven till hot through and well browned – 30–40 minutes.

Artichokes, Celery, Leeks and Salsify can all be served in the same way, or a mixture of vegetables, such as cauliflower, carrots, onions, peas, beans and new potatoes.

When making the white sauce (see page 196), use half milk and half vegetable water.

Cheese Soufflé

Butter 1 oz.   2 eggs and 1 extra white
Flour ¾ oz.   Grated cheese 3 oz.
Milk ¼ pint   Salt, pepper and cayenne to taste

Melt butter in saucepan, stir in the flour smoothly, stir for a minute or two over a gentle heat, then gradually add the milk. Continue stirring till the mixture is quite thick and leaves the sides of the pan clean. Remove from heat, beat in the finely grated cheese and season with salt, pepper, and cayenne. Then beat in the egg yolks one at a time.

Whisk the egg whites till *very* stiff and fold in lightly. Turn the mixture into prepared dish (see page 273), bake in a moderately hot oven (400° – Regulo No. 5) about 30 minutes. Serve at once.

If preferred, the mixture can be put in individual paper cases (as for a large soufflé, only three-parts full). These can be baked in a hotter oven, and take only about 15 minutes.

Cheese Straws

(See pages 296–7)

Cheese Toast

Rice 3 oz.   Grated cheese 4 oz.
2 large tomatoes   Seasoning
Margarine 2 oz.

Boil rice till tender, then drain. Remove skin from tomatoes, slice them, put in a saucepan with the margarine, and cook gently for 10 minutes. Then add the cheese and rice, season with salt and pepper and a teaspoonful piquant sauce or vegetable extract. Make thoroughly hot and heap up on slices of toast or fried bread.

Curry

Almost anything can be curried – meat of any kind, poultry, eggs, fish, and vegetables (cooked and uncooked).

If cooked meats are used, they are added to the curry sauce after it has been cooked and warmed through. Uncooked meats are cooked in the sauce.

Oily fish, such as mackerel and herring, and salted or smoked fish, do not curry well.

Boiled rice is always served with curry, and chutney should be handed separately.

Boiled Rice for Curry

(See page 136)

Curry Sauce

(See page 200)

Banana and Spaghetti Curry

Spaghetti 8 oz.	*Curry powder 2 teaspoonfuls*
2 or 3 bananas	*Chopped onion 1 tablespoonful*
Margarine 2 oz.	*Flour 1½ oz.*
Seedless raisins 2 oz.	*Chutney 2 teaspoonfuls*
Milk ¼ pint	*Water ¼ pint*

Cook the spaghetti in boiling salted water till tender, then drain and keep hot.

Melt the margarine and fry the onion gently for 5 minutes, then stir in flour and curry powder smoothly, and gradually add the milk and ¼ pint of water. Stir till boiling, then add the raisins and chutney, and the bananas peeled and cut into ½-inch slices. Cover and simmer gently for 10 minutes.

Place the spaghetti in a hot dish and pour the sauce over.

Curried Vegetables

Any left-over cooked vegetables, individually or mixed, can be turned into a vegetable curry. The root vegetables, carrots, turnips, swedes, artichokes, etc., are particularly suitable, and a few left-over haricot beans or cooked macaroni can be added.

Cut the vegetables into small pieces, warm through slowly in curry sauce (see page 200), simmer for 15 minutes, and dish with a border of well-cooked rice.

For a more substantial dish, serve hard-boiled eggs, cut in half lengthways, on top of the vegetables.

See also Curry Croquettes (pages 176–7), Curried Eggs (page 302), and Curried Mutton (pages 280–81).

Liver Kugel

Cooked liver ¼ lb.	*Noodles ¼ lb.*
Chicken fat 2 tablespoonfuls	*2 eggs*
Salt and pepper	*1 onion*

Cook noodles in boiling salted water till tender, then drain. Mince the liver. Chop the onion and fry a golden brown in the chicken fat. Mix all ingredients, turn into a greased oven dish and bake in a moderate oven till golden brown.

Macaroni or Spaghetti Cheese

Macaroni (or spaghetti) 6 oz.	*Grated cheese 3 oz.*
Margarine 1–2 oz.	*Salt and pepper*

Either macaroni or spaghetti can be used. Boil till tender (see page 134), drain, and return to saucepan with the margarine and cheese. Season with salt and pepper and stir over a gentle heat till the cheese is melted. Serve extra grated cheese with it.

Another Method. Put a layer of cooked macaroni in a greased fireproof dish and coat with cheese sauce (see page 196). Repeat the layers, sprinkle the top with grated cheese, then with brown crumbs, and dot with margarine. Brown under the grill or in a hot oven. If freshly cooked, it should only take about 15 minutes to reheat, but if it has been made in advance, then it will take about 40 minutes in a moderate oven.

Variations:

(1) After boiling macaroni, reheat in curry sauce (see page 200). Garnish with green peas or any cooked root vegetables neatly diced.

(2) Add 2 or 3 tablespoonfuls of tomato purée in addition to or in place of the grated cheese.

(3) Surround the macaroni cheese (first method) with baked or grilled tomatoes or fried onions.

(4) Mix macaroni with tomato sauce, to which add a tablespoonful of chopped capers or olives.

Scalloped Mushrooms

Mushrooms ¼ lb.	*White sauce ½ pint*
Margarine 2 oz.	*White breadcrumbs*
Onion juice 1 teaspoonful	*Grated cheese*
Salt and pepper	

Peel the mushrooms and slice thinly. Place in a saucepan with the margarine and onion juice, season with salt and pepper, cover and cook gently till tender – about 10–15 minutes.

Make ½ pint thick white sauce, using the liquid from the mushrooms made up to ½ pint with milk, mix with the mushrooms, turn into individual dishes, sprinkle with grated cheese mixed with breadcrumbs, dot with margarine, and brown in the upper part of a moderately hot oven.

Mushroom Vol-au-vent

White sauce ¼ pint	*Mushrooms ½ lb.*
Lemon juice 1 teaspoonful	*Butter 1 oz.*
8 or 9 vol-au-vent cases	*Salt and pepper*

Make and bake the vol-au-vent cases (see page 248). Peel the mushrooms, remove most of the stalks (use these in soup or stew) and chop mushrooms finely. Melt the butter in a saucepan, add the lemon juice and mushrooms, cover, and cook gently for 10 minutes. Then add a bare ¼ pint thick white sauce, season with salt and pepper, and simmer another 5 minutes. Put the mixture into the cases and put on the pastry lids.

If the cases have been made in advance, warm them through before filling.

Scalloped Onions

Peel some onions and boil till soft. Drain, cut into quarters and put in a fireproof dish. Cover with cheese sauce (see page 196), using half onion water and half milk. Sprinkle the top with brown crumbs and grated cheese, dot with butter or margarine, and bake in a hot oven for 20 minutes.

If this is prepared in advance and has got cold, it will take 30–40 minutes to heat through and brown.

Stuffed Baked Onions

4 large Spanish onions	*Sausage meat 6 oz.*
Yolk of an egg	*Breadcrumbs 1 tablespoonful*
Thick brown gravy ½ pint	*Salt and pepper*

Peel the onions, put into boiling salted water, boil for 20 minutes; then drain, cut a thin slice off each stem end and with a vegetable knife carefully remove the centres, leaving good hollows, but taking care to leave the root ends intact. Chop the onion removed, and mix with the sausage meat, breadcrumbs, and egg yolk. Season to taste and fill the onions with this mixture, heaping it up slightly over the top. Put into a casserole, pour the gravy over, put on the lid and bake in a moderate oven till the onions are tender – 1–1½ hours.

Veal forcemeat (see page 194) can replace the sausage meat, if preferred. Add the chopped onion to the forcemeat and proceed as above.

Stuffed Baked Potatoes

Choose large potatoes of uniform size, scrub quite clean, prick with a fork, and bake in a moderate oven till soft (about 1 hour, but varying according to size). When cooked, cut through in halves and remove the pulp carefully, keeping the skin intact. Mash this pulp free from lumps, add 1 teaspoonful of margarine for each potato, and season with salt and pepper. Add any of the following ingredients, fill cases with the mixture, smooth over with a wet knife, put a small knob of margarine on top, and return to the oven till hot through.

Suggestions for Fillings:

(1) Flavour with curry powder or mixed herbs.

(2) Grated cheese – 1 tablespoonful to each half potato – sprinkle with grated cheese before reheating.

(3) Tomato purée – sprinkle with grated cheese.

(4) Flaked smoked haddock, tinned salmon, or any fresh-cooked fish flavoured with anchovy sauce. Allow 1 tablespoonful of fish to each half potato.

(5) Minced salt or smoked beef or tongue – allow 1 tablespoonful of meat, ½ teaspoonful of chopped parsley and of margarine to each half potato.

(6) As (5), but substitute a little finely chopped and lightly fried onion for the parsley.

For a more substantial dish place a neatly poached or steamed egg on top of each half potato.

Pilaff of Chicken Livers (I)

Rice ¼ lb.	*Chicken fat 1 tablespoonful*
Stock 1¼ pints	*Olive oil 1 tablespoonful*
Tomato sauce 2 tablespoonfuls	*Chopped onion 1 tablespoonful*
Salt and pepper	*Chicken livers*

Melt the fat with the oil in a saucepan, add the chopped onion, cover, and cook gently for 5 minutes; then add the rice, stir for a minute or two over a gentle heat, then add the boiling stock, tomato sauce, and seasoning. Cover and cook gently till the rice is soft and the stock absorbed – 20–30 minutes – keeping it well stirred.

Fry livers quickly on both sides, pile up the rice in a hot dish, and make a depression on top, in which place the livers. Or, if preferred, the livers can be cut into small pieces and mixed with the rice. (See also page 189.)

Note. Calf's liver can be used in place of the chicken livers. Or cold veal can be cut into dice and mixed with the rice 10 minutes before dishing, just long enough to heat through.

Ravioli

Make noodle dough (see page 49), and roll very thinly. Then cut into 3-inch squares. Put a teaspoonful of the filling in the centre of each, fold over into triangles, pressing the edges well together. Leave on a floured board for 1 hour or longer to dry. Drop a few at a time into boiling salted water and cook steadily for 20 minutes. Drain thoroughly, put on a hot dish, and coat with thick gravy or sprinkle with grated cheese.

Fillings:

(1) Mix together 1 breakfastcupful each minced cooked meat and sausage meat, ½ cupful breadcrumbs, and 2 teaspoonfuls grated onion. Season with salt and pepper, and bind with a beaten egg or thick gravy.

(2) Soft curd cheese, seasoned with salt and pepper, and mixed with a spoonful or two of top milk.

Savoury Batter Pudding

Flour 4 oz.	*Margarine or cooking fat 2 oz.*
Onions ¼ lb.	*1 egg*
Water 1 tablespoonful	*Salt and pepper*
Milk ½ pint	

Season the flour with salt and pepper, and make a smooth batter with the egg and milk (see Pancakes, pages 272–3). Then add the water and let stand for an hour. Slice the onions, melt the fat in a frying pan, put in the onions, cover with a plate or saucepan lid, and fry gently for 15 minutes. Turn into a shallow baking dish, with any fat that has not been absorbed, and place in a *hot* oven for 5 minutes. Then pour the batter over, return to the oven, and bake about 50 minutes – hot for the first ¼ hour, then reduce or put the pudding on a lower shelf to finish cooking.

Serve with baked tomatoes, either plain (see page 111) or stuffed (see pages 128–9).

Savoury Pancakes

Make the batter and fry according to directions given on page 272.

(1) **Cheese Pancakes.** Add 2 oz. grated cheese to ½ pint of batter. When fried, roll up and sprinkle with grated cheese.

(2) **With Onion.** Add 1 finely grated onion, 1 tablespoonful chopped parsley, and a pinch of mixed herbs to the batter. Serve with thinly sliced leeks or onions fried a golden brown.

(3) **Stuffed Pancakes.** Make the pancakes with a plain

batter, and, before rolling up, put a spoonful of hot savoury mixture in the centre.

Suggestions:

(a) Flaked smoked fish, bound with white or cheese sauce.

(b) Sieved spinach.

(c) Green peas moistened with thick well-seasoned white sauce to which add a little chopped mint.

(d) Tomato purée.

Sausages

To Fry. Prick the sausages, flour them lightly, and cook in a little hot fat until evenly browned. Sausages must be cooked gently or the skins will burst. Serve on a bed of mashed potato and fried onions.

To Grill. Prick well, place under the hot grill, and cook until browned all over, turning them frequently. They will take 8–10 minutes. Serve with mashed potatoes and grilled tomatoes.

To Bake. Prick sausages, place in a baking dish with a little dripping, and cook in a moderate oven (400°, Regulo No. 5) until browned – about 20 minutes.

Sausage Croquettes (1)

Roll out some short crust and cut into rounds. Chop up some left-over sausages and moisten with a little thick gravy. Put a little of this mixture in the centre of each round, moisten the edges and fold over in halves pressing the edges well together. Brush over with egg and roll in brown crumbs. Fry a golden brown in deep fat.

Sausage Croquettes (2)

Rice 4 oz.	Breadcrumbs
Sausages ½ lb.	Salt and pepper
1 egg	Tomato sauce

Cook rice in boiling salted water till tender. Then drain in a colander (save rice water for soup), pour cold water over it,

and drain well. Season with salt and pepper and add the beaten
egg yolk. Fry sausages lightly and cut across in halves. Form
the rice into croquettes with half a sausage in each. Brush over
with slightly whipped egg white, coat with brown crumbs,
and fry a golden brown.

Serve with tomato sauce.

Sausages with Curry Sauce

Reheat left-over root vegetables in curry sauce (see page 200)
and serve with grilled sausages and fried onions.

Sausages and Savoury Noodles

Cooked noodles 1 pint	*Sausages 1 lb.*
Made mustard 1 teaspoonful	*Tomatoes 6 oz.*
Seedless jam 2 teaspoonfuls	*Paprika ¼ teaspoonful*
Vinegar 2 tablespoonfuls	*Sugar 1 teaspoonful*
Chopped onion 3 tablespoonfuls	*Salt and pepper*
Margarine 2 oz.	

Skin and slice the tomatoes. Melt the margarine (or other fat),
add the chopped onion and tomatoes, and fry till the onions
are soft and lightly browned, then add the vinegar, jam,
sugar, paprika, and mustard, stir over a gentle heat for a few
minutes, then add the noodles, and season with salt and
pepper. Grill the sausages. Turn the noodles on to a hot dish
and place the sausages around.

Sausages with Oranges

Sausages 1 lb.	*2 oranges*
2 small onions	*Margarine 2 oz.*
Stock ¼ pint	*Flour 1 tablespoonful*
Pinch of cinnamon	*Salt and pepper*

Peel the onions and chop them finely or grate them. Melt the
margarine in a small saucepan, add the onion and the grated
rind of the oranges, cover and cook gently till the onions are
tender. Then stir in the flour and a pinch of cinnamon and
gradually add the juice of 1 orange and the stock. Stir till
boiling and simmer for 2 or 3 minutes.

Meanwhile, fry or grill the sausages, place them on a hot dish, pour over the sauce and garnish with orange slices.

Sausage and Potato Rolls

6 sausages	*Flour 1 oz.*
Mashed potato 2 breakfastcupfuls	*1 egg*
Dripping or margarine 1 tablespoonful	*Seasoning*
Thick gravy	

Mash the potatoes very thoroughly, add the flour, egg yolk and melted fat, and mix together. Divide into six portions and with floured hands press out into squares.

Fry sausages lightly, place one on each square of potato, and fold over like a pastry sausage roll. Put on a greased tin, brush over with slightly whipped egg white, and bake in a moderate oven till lightly browned.

Serve thick gravy separately.

Sausage Rolls

Pour boiling water over the sausages, leave for 2 minutes, then drain and remove skins. Cut them in halves lengthways and then across.

Roll out rough puff pastry $\frac{1}{4}$ inch thick and cut into 4-inch squares. Brush one side of the pastry with cold water, place a piece of sausage on the pastry along the damp side, fold the pastry across and press the long sides firmly together, leaving the ends open. Cut across the top 2 or 3 times with the back of a knife, and brush over with beaten egg yolk. Place on a greased tin and leave for $\frac{1}{2}$ hour. Bake in a hot oven (475°, Regulo No. 8), 25–30 minutes.

Sausage and Tomato Pie

Sausages $\frac{1}{2}$ lb.	*Dripping 1 oz.*
2 onions	*Gravy*
Tomatoes $\frac{1}{2}$ lb.	*Seasoning*
Mashed potato	

Put sausages in boiling water and simmer 2 or 3 minutes. Slice onions and fry a golden brown in the dripping. Skin and slice tomatoes and put in a fireproof dish and add the fried onion;

season with salt and pepper. Cut sausages in halves, lay them
on top of the tomato and onion, and pour over 2 or 3 spoonfuls
of gravy. Cover with mashed potatoes, and bake in a moderate
oven about 45 minutes.

Sausage and Onion Pudding

Suet crust ¾ lb.	*Margarine 1 oz.*
Sausages ¾–1 lb.	*Flour 1 oz.*
A large onion	*Salt and pepper*
Stock ½ pint	

Remove skins from sausages and roll into small balls. Peel and
chop the onion. Melt the margarine in a small saucepan, add
the onion and cook over a gentle heat for a few minutes, then
stir in the flour smoothly and add the stock gradually. Stir till
boiling, simmer for 2 or 3 minutes, then cool.

Line a greased basin with suet crust (see page 250), put in
the sausage balls and pour over the onion sauce. Put suet crust
on top, cover with a greased paper and steam for 2 hours.

Spaghetti with Bolognese Sauce

Spaghetti 6 oz.	*Concentrated tomato purée*
Thick brown gravy ¼ pint	*2 tablespoonfuls*
Mushrooms 2 oz.	*Minced raw beef 2 oz.*
Cooking oil 2 tablespoonfuls	*Sugar ¼ teaspoonful*
Red or white wine 2 tablespoonfuls	*A small onion*
(optional)	*A clove of garlic*

Cook the spaghetti till tender, then drain. Chop the onion and
mushrooms, crush the garlic. Fry the onion in the oil until
lightly browned, then add the beef, mushrooms and garlic
and cook 2 or 3 minutes longer; then add the remaining
ingredients, cover and cook gently for ½ hour. Put the spaghetti
in a casserole, pour over the sauce and mix thoroughly.

Note. Sausage meat, minced tongue, salt or smoked beef
can be used in place of the raw beef.

Spinach and Eggs

Line a greased fireproof dish with a layer of well-seasoned
chopped spinach; arrange on top as many poached eggs as

required. Cover with thick white sauce, to which 2 table-spoonfuls grated cheese have been added. Sprinkle with cheese and brown under the grill or in a hot oven.

If preferred, the hot cheese sauce can be poured over the eggs and served without browning, and plain poached eggs on spinach are extremely good without the sauce.

Spinach and Rice Mould

Cooked rice 2 breakfastcupfuls   2 eggs
Cooked spinach 2 breakfastcupfuls   Seasoning

Chop the spinach very finely or rub it through a sieve, mix with the rice, season with salt and pepper, and then add the 2 lightly beaten eggs. Grease a basin well and sprinkle with brown crumbs; add the mixture and steam for 1 hour.

Serve with brown gravy or tomato sauce.

Spinach Soufflé

Sieved spinach 1 breakfastcupful   3 eggs
Milk ¼ pint   Flour 1 oz.
Butter or margarine 1 oz.   Salt, pepper and lemon juice

Melt the butter in a small saucepan, stir in the flour smoothly, then gradually add the milk. Stir till boiling and continue stirring while it simmers for 2 minutes. Then remove from the heat, add the sieved spinach, and season with salt, pepper, and lemon juice. Add the lightly beaten egg yolks, then fold in very lightly the stiffly whipped egg whites. Turn into a well-greased soufflé dish, round which a band of greased paper has been tied to come 3 inches above the top.

Bake in a moderately hot oven (400°, Regulo No. 5) till well risen and firm to the touch – about 25–30 minutes. Remove band of paper carefully and serve immediately.

Stuffed Sweet Peppers

Cut off the stalks from the peppers, cut them in half length-ways, and remove seeds and stringy membrane. Put them in a saucepan, cover with boiling, salted water, simmer for 3 or 4 minutes, then drain. When cool, stuff each half with any savoury mixture of fish, meat, rice, or vegetables. Sprinkle with brown crumbs, dot with margarine, and bake in a hot oven in a little melted fat till tender – 30–40 minutes.

Serve with any savoury sauce preferred, or thick brown gravy.

Suggested Fillings:

(1) Mixed cooked vegetables moistened with tomato, parsley, or cheese sauce.

(2) Spinach purée sprinkled with grated cheese.

(3) Minced meat or sausage meat. Add half the quantity of breadcrumbs, flavour with grated onion and chopped parsley, and moisten with thick gravy.

(4) Cooked rice moistened with tomato or curry sauce.

Stuffed Tomatoes

Stuffed with various savoury fillings, tomatoes make excellent luncheon dishes, either hot or cold. Choose large tomatoes and either cut across in halves or cut slices off the tops. Scoop out the pulp and season cups with salt and pepper. (Any pulp that is not used in the filling can be added to stews or sauces.)

Hot Stuffed Tomatoes. For six large tomatoes:

(1) Six tablespoonfuls spinach purée, 1 tablespoonful tomato pulp, salt and pepper. Fill up tomato cases, sprinkle with breadcrumbs, and bake in a moderate oven for ½ hour.

(2) Four piled tablespoonfuls breadcrumbs, a small onion, chopped, and fried till soft but not brown, 1 teaspoonful each of anchovy essence, chopped capers, and parsley, 1 oz. margarine, and sufficient tomato pulp to moisten.

(3) Any kind of finely minced meat or poultry, well flavoured, mixed with a spoonful or two of cooked rice or breadcrumbs and moistened with tomato pulp and thick gravy.

(4) Cooked rice and curry sauce, or cooked rice mixed with an equal quantity of grated cheese and a little chopped parsley. Moisten with tomato pulp.

(5) Scald a few sausages, remove skins, and mix sausage meat with an equal quantity of mashed potato and a little chopped parsley. Moisten with tomato pulp.

Cold Fillings:

(1) Cold cooked vegetables, diced, with a little grated onion and chopped capers. Dress with any kind of salad dressing.

(2) Finely minced chicken (or veal) and tongue; add a little chopped parsley. Season to taste, and moisten with mayonnaise.

(3) Flaked cooked fish with diced cucumber, a little tomato pulp, and mayonnaise.

(4) Diced celery and apple, or diced pineapple and raw carrot, moistened with salad cream or mayonnaise.

Serve the stuffed tomatoes on a nest of mustard and cress, or surrounded with shredded lettuce and tufts of watercress.

Stuffed Tomatoes on Spaghetti

4 large tomatoes	*Spaghetti 3 oz.*
Minced cold meat 4 oz.	*2 small gherkins*
Raisins 1 oz.	*Thick brown gravy*
Grated onion 1 teaspoonful	*Salt and pepper*

Boil the spaghetti till tender, then drain. Cut the tops from the tomatoes and scoop out the centres. Mix this pulp with the spaghetti, add the raisins and a little thick gravy, season with salt and pepper, and turn into a casserole.

Mix the meat, onion and chopped gherkins, and add sufficient thick gravy to moisten. Fill up the tomatoes with the mixture, and replace the tops.

Place the tomatoes on the spaghetti, cover the casserole, and bake in a moderate oven about 30 minutes.

Vegetable Flans

Line a flan ring or deep sandwich tin with short crust, shaped well into the tin. Trim and decorate the edge. Prick the pastry at the bottom and cover with a piece of greased paper. Put a few crusts or a layer of rice on the paper and bake in a quick oven about 15 minutes. Remove paper and rice and return to oven for another 5 minutes. Fill with whatever mixture is being used and serve at once.

If the pastry case is made in advance, then after filling reheat in the oven.

Fillings:

(1) **Spinach.** Three-parts fill the pastry case with well-drained chopped or sieved spinach. Cover with a layer of thick white sauce, sprinkle with grated cheese and brown crumbs, dot with margarine, and brown in a hot oven or under the grill.

Or fill case with spinach and garnish the top with sliced hard-boiled egg.

(2) **Mixed Vegetables.** Use any cooked vegetables available: peas, beans, carrots, turnips, spring onions, etc. Cut into dice where necessary and add a little chopped parsley and just sufficient white sauce to bind. A plain sauce can be used, or for something more piquant, add a few chopped capers and a little caper vinegar.

Or use a cheese sauce and finish on top as for spinach.

(3) **Cauliflower.** Break up a cooked cauliflower into flowerets and cut up the stalk, moisten with cheese sauce, and finish off as for spinach.

Stuffed Vegetable Marrow

Choose a young marrow, preferably thick rather than a long thin one. Peel it, cut through lengthways, and remove seeds. Fill each cavity with whatever stuffing is being used, put the two pieces together, and tie round with tape. Place on a greased baking tin or dish, spread liberally with dripping or margarine, and bake in a moderate oven about 1½ hours, basting from time to time.

If preferred, the marrow can be parboiled for 5 minutes before baking, in which case it will only require 1–1¼ hours for baking. If to be parboiled, after peeling cut in halves *crossways*, remove seeds with a spoon, put into boiling salted water, and cook gently for 5 minutes. Drain and cool before stuffing.

Suggested Mixtures for Stuffing:

(1) Any kind of cooked meat, about 6 oz., minced and mixed with 3 oz. breadcrumbs. Add 1 tablespoonful of finely chopped onion and parsley, and a little piquant sauce. Bind with a beaten egg or thick brown gravy.

(2) As above, but use ½ lb. sausage meat and 1 teacupful of mashed potato in place of meat and breadcrumbs.

(3) Cooked rice, mixed with 2 or 3 skinned and chopped tomatoes, chopped parsley and onion. Season with salt and pepper, and add 1–2 oz. melted margarine. For a change add a little grated cheese.

(4) Two or three large Spanish onions. Boil till almost tender, then chop coarsely. Mix with 2 breakfastcupfuls of breadcrumbs that have been soaked in hot milk, and 2 teaspoonfuls powdered sage. Season with salt and pepper and bind with a beaten egg.

(5) Brush each hollowed half with margarine and sprinkle with grated cheese. Then fill with layers of thinly sliced onion and tomatoes. Season each layer with salt and pepper, and sprinkle with chopped parsley and brown crumbs. Do *not* put the halves together. Place in an oven dish with a little margarine or cooking fat, and after baking for 50 minutes, sprinkle the top with grated cheese and brown crumbs and return to oven till the marrow is tender – about another ½ hour. Serve with cheese sauce (see page 196).

Vegetable Sausages

Rub through a sieve sufficient cooked broad beans and green peas to make ½ pint purée. Mix this with ¾ breakfastcupful breadcrumbs, and season with salt, pepper, and sage (or mint). Add a little finely chopped parsley and bind with an egg. With floured hands form into small sausages, brush with milk, and roll in dried crumbs. Fry a golden brown and serve with grilled tomatoes.

Cereals and Pulses

Barley

Pearl barley is very good in winter soups, stews, and hot-pots (see under these headings), and can also be served in place of a vegetable. It needs slow cooking for about 2½ hours. If soaked overnight, 2 hours will probably be sufficient.

To serve as a Vegetable

Barley 4 oz.   Onion 6 oz.
Dripping 1 oz.   Tinned or bottled tomatoes 1 teacupful
Water 1 quart   Salt and pepper

Soak the barley in the water overnight, turn into a saucepan, add salt to taste, and simmer gently for 2 hours, or till tender. Peel and slice the onions and fry a golden brown in the dripping. Add them to the barley, with the dripping in which they were fried, and the tomatoes, season with salt and pepper, and simmer for 15 minutes.

If fresh tomatoes are available, use ½ lb. of these skinned and sliced in place of preserved ones.

Haricot Beans

Haricot beans, butter beans, dried flageolets, and the mottled brown Trinidad beans, can all be prepared in the same way.

They contain a large proportion of protein and make excellent meatless dishes.

Cover beans with tepid water and leave to soak for 24 hours.

They can be cooked in a casserole in the oven or on top of the stove, whichever is the more convenient.

They keep well after cooking and, if a supply is kept in the larder, they only need heating up to make an excellent emergency meal.

To Cook on Top of the Stove. Put into a saucepan with the water in which they were soaked, bring slowly to the boil and simmer gently until tender – about 2 hours. Drain (save water for stock) and serve plain or with any sauce preferred. Curry (page 200), parsley (page 197), sweet and sour (pages 204–5), or tomato (page 205) are all good.

Baked Beans

Soaked haricot beans ¼ lb.   Sugar or golden syrup
Tomato sauce 2 tablespoonfuls   2 teaspoonfuls
Salt and pepper   Mustard 1 teaspoonful

Put all ingredients into a casserole with sufficient water to cover the beans. Put the lid on the casserole and bake in a moderate oven till tender, about 2 hours.

Serve on hot toast.

Lentils

There are two kinds of lentils, the red or Egyptian lentil and the green lentil. The red lentil does not require soaking like other pulse foods, as it softens much more quickly during cooking. Lentils contain a large amount of protein and so form a good substitute for meat. When used for this purpose fat should be added in some form.

Put red lentils into a basin, cover with cold water, stir well, then pour off the water. Repeat two or three times till the water is clear, then strain and remove any black pieces.

Put the lentils into a saucepan with sufficient water to come about an inch above the lentils, cover and bring slowly to the boil, keeping them well stirred, then simmer gently till the lentils are quite soft – about 1 hour.

If any water has not been absorbed, pour this off, reserving it for soup. Season lentils with salt and pepper, beat up with a fork, and use this purée as required.

When using green lentils, wash thoroughly and soak overnight in cold water. Boil as red lentils, but they will take at least 1½ hours to get soft. Add more boiling water if it evaporates whilst cooking. Green lentils can be used in the following recipe in place of red ones.

Lentil Rissoles

Margarine or dripping 1 oz.
Red lentils ¼ lb.
1 egg
Breadcrumbs

Chopped onion 1 tablespoonful
Vegetable extract or savoury sauce
Fat for frying
Cooked rice 4 oz.

Cook lentils as in the first recipe and when strained mix with the rice. Fry the onion a golden brown in the fat and mix it in together with the yolk of the egg and a little piquant sauce or vegetable extract. Season with salt and pepper, and when quite cold, with floured hands, form into rissoles or cutlets. Dredge with flour, brush over slightly beaten white of egg, and coat with dry crumbs. Fry a golden brown in deep fat.

Macaroni and Spaghetti

Macaroni and spaghetti can be used as a garnish for soup, with fish or meat dishes, as a sweet course, as a savoury dish or in salads. For recipes see chapters under those headings.

To Boil. Cook in plenty of fast-boiling salted water with the pan uncovered. The time required will vary according to the size and variety of the pasta. The quick-cooking packet macaroni generally needs only 7 minutes (follow directions on the packet). The stick or thicker varieties need 15–25 minutes, spaghetti 12–20 minutes. Unless cut macaroni is being used, break it into short lengths. When cooked, strain through a colander (reserve the water for thick soup or sauce), run cold water over it, reheat, and use as required.

Spaghetti should be boiled without breaking it; slide it gradually into the boiling salted water and proceed as for macaroni.

Dried Peas

There are two kinds of dried peas, the split and the whole peas. They need soaking for 24 hours before cooking.

They can be used as a vegetable, and they make excellent purées and soup.

Boiled Dried Green Peas

Dried green peas ¼ lb.	*1 onion*
Margarine 1 oz.	*Dried mint*
Salt, pepper, cloves	*Water*

Wash peas and soak in warm water (to which ½ teaspoonful bicarbonate of soda has been added) for 24 hours, then drain and rinse. Put them in a saucepan, cover with cold water, and bring slowly to the boil. Peel the onion and stick 2 cloves in it, add it to the peas, season with salt and pepper, cover and cook slowly till the peas are soft – 2–3 hours. Stir from time to time, and, if necessary, add more hot water. When soft, drain the peas and remove the onion. (Reserve onion and water for soup.) Add the margarine, sprinkle with chopped mint, and when the margarine has melted, dish into a hot vegetable dish.

If the peas are bought in packets, cook according to the directions given.

To Purée. After boiling rub peas through a sieve, moisten with a little of the water in which they were cooked, return to saucepan, add margarine and dried mint and reheat.

Porridge

To make with Coarse or Medium Oatmeal. Put 1 quart water in a thick saucepan and bring to the boil. Sprinkle in 5 oz. oatmeal, stirring all the time with a wooden spoon. Continue to stir until the porridge begins to thicken and is perfectly smooth and free from lumps. Add salt to taste. Cook over a very *gentle* heat until the oatmeal is quite soft − $\frac{1}{2}$–$\frac{3}{4}$ hour − stirring frequently. Add more boiling water if required during cooking. It is a matter of taste how long it should be cooked and how thick it should be when served. If more convenient the oatmeal can be soaked in the water (cold) overnight and will then require less time to cook in the morning.

If a double saucepan is available, use it. The porridge will require much less attention and stirring but will take somewhat longer to cook.

To make with Rolled Oats. Make according to directions on the packet.

Rice

There are several kinds of rice; Carolina, Patna, Rangoon, and Java. Patna rice is the best for curry. Carolina rice makes the best puddings and moulds. Rice can be presented in a large number of dishes, both sweet and savoury; in hors-d'oeuvres, soups or salads, as a vegetable by itself or as an accompaniment to meat, fish, or vegetables.

To wash rice. Put rice in a strainer, place the strainer in a bowl of cold water, and wash rice well, changing the water two or three times, then drain.

If the grains of rice are to be kept separate, as in rice to accompany curry, then it must be boiled quickly on top of the stove, but when this is not required rice can be cooked quite satisfactorily in the oven. Some kinds of rice absorb water more quickly than others, so examine the rice after it has been cooking for 15 minutes, and if necessary, add a little more boiling water.

Boiled Rice for Curry

Patna rice ¼ lb.   Boiling salted water 2 quarts

Wash the rice as above. Add 2 or 3 teaspoonfuls salt to the water and while it is boiling rapidly sprinkle the rice in slowly so as not to check the boiling. Stir with a fork. Boil rapidly until a grain feels tender if pinched between the finger and thumb – about 15–20 minutes.

Strain through a coarse sieve or colander (save the water for soup or sauce). Pour boiling water through to separate the grains. Keep hot in the oven for 5 minutes so that it gets quite dry.

To Boil Rice in the Oven

Put 4 oz. washed rice in a greased casserole, pour over 1 pint boiling water, add 1 teaspoonful of salt, put the lid on the casserole, and bake in a moderate oven (400°, Regulo No. 5) about ½ hour.

Rice and Cheese Soufflé

Cooked rice 2 breakfastcupfuls   White sauce ¾ pint
Grated cheese 1 teacupful   2 eggs
Lemon juice   Salt and pepper

Boil rice dry as for curry; make a thin white sauce, add the cheese, and stir over a gentle heat till it has melted. Then add the rice, egg yolks, and a squeeze of lemon juice, mix thoroughly, and season to taste. Whip the egg whites to a stiff froth and fold them in lightly. Three-parts fill a prepared soufflé dish with the mixture, stand in a tin with a little hot water in it, and bake in a moderately hot oven (about 425°, Regulo No. 6) for 30 minutes.

Rice Croquettes

Cooked rice 2 breakfastcupfuls   *2 eggs*
Binding sauce (page 196) ¼ pint   *Grated cheese 3 oz.*
Salt and pepper   *Fat for frying*
Brown crumbs

Make the sauce with milk or rice water. Add it to the rice, together with the egg yolks, grated cheese, and seasoning. Mix thoroughly and leave till quite cold. With floured hands form into cork-shaped croquettes or flat rissoles, dredge with flour, brush over with slightly beaten egg white, and coat with brown crumbs. Fry a golden brown in deep fat, in a frying basket if available.

Risotto

Rice 4 oz.   *Grated cheese 2–3 oz.*
Water 1½ pints   *Margarine or butter 1 oz.*
Tomato purée ¼ pint   *Salt and pepper*

Put water in a saucepan, add 2 teaspoonfuls salt, and when boiling sprinkle in the rice, cover, and boil till tender – about 20 minutes. Strain off any water that has not been absorbed (reserve for stock). Add the margarine, tomato purée, and half the cheese, season with salt and pepper, and reheat. Turn into a hot dish, sprinkle over the remaining cheese, and serve at once.

Rice and Vegetable Mould

Add 2 or 3 tablespoonfuls chopped onion and a little vegetable extract to 2 quarts water, and when boiling sprinkle in ½ lb. washed rice, add salt to taste, and boil till tender. Then drain (reserve water for sauce or soup). Add more salt if necessary and 1 tablespoonful chopped parsley.

Thickly grease a basin (or cake tin) and sprinkle with brown crumbs. Line bottom and sides with rice, fill with vegetable mixture, cover with rice, put a greased paper or enamel plate over the top, and cook in a moderate oven about ¾ hour (or, if more convenient, steam for 1 hour). Turn out on to a hot dish and serve with curry, cheese, or tomato sauce.

For the Vegetable Mixture. About 2 breakfastcupfuls of any mixture of cooked vegetables available; peas, beans, carrots, turnips, onions, etc. Make a thick sauce with 1½ oz. margarine, 1½ oz. flour, and ½ pint mixed milk and vegetable (or rice) water. Mix this with the vegetables, add a tablespoonful chopped parsley, and flavour with curry powder, grated cheese, vegetable extract, or tomato sauce.

Savoury Rice

Rice ¼ lb.   *Margarine 2 oz.*
2 small onions   *Tomatoes ¼ lb.*
Grated cheese 3 oz.   *Salt and pepper*

Cook the rice in boiling water until soft, then strain. Skin and slice the tomatoes and chop the onions. Melt the margarine in a saucepan, add the onions, and fry for a few minutes without browning. Then add the tomatoes and simmer with the lid on for 10 minutes. Remove from the fire, add the cooked rice, the grated cheese, and salt and pepper to taste. Turn into a greased fireproof dish, sprinkle with grated cheese, dot with margarine, and brown under the grill or in a hot oven.

Semolina

Can be used for puddings, savoury dishes, and in biscuits.
For recipes see chapters under these headings.

Spaghetti

(See page 134)

Spaghetti with Bolognese Sauce

(See page 126)

Meat

CUTS OF MEAT AND THEIR USES

Beef

Bola. Roast. When boned it can be sliced and grilled or fried.

Wing Rib. Roast.

Top Rib. Roast.

Back Rib. Braise.

Brisket. Slow roast, braise or boil.

Salted Brisket. Boil.

Neck
Clod
Sticking } Stews, pies, puddings, casserole dishes, soups.
Chuck
Shin

*Rump and Fillet Steak. Grill or fry.

Lamb and Mutton

Best End of Neck. Roast, slow roast or braise. When cut into cutlets fry or grill.

*Leg. Roast, slow roast or boil.

*Loin. Roast. When cut into cutlets fry or grill.

Shoulder. Roast.

Middle Neck and Scrag. Stew or braise.

Breast. Stew. If boned it can be stuffed, and boiled or roasted.

Veal

Best End of Neck. Roast, braise or pot-roast. When cut into cutlets fry or grill.

Shoulder. Roast.

Scrag. Stew.

Breast. Stew or braise. If boned, stuffed and rolled, slow roast or braise.

*Loin. Roast or cut into chops and fry or grill.

*Fillet. Roast if whole. If sliced, fry.

*These are hindquarter meats. According to the Jewish dietary laws hindquarter meat may only be eaten if correctly purged. Until recent years it was available in the British Isles and some other countries and recipes have been included in this volume for such time as it may once more become available.

METHODS OF COOKING MEAT

The chief methods of cooking meat are baking (usually called roasting), boiling, braising, frying, grilling, pot-roasting, and stewing.

Roasting or Baking

After koshering the meat it should be dried with a cloth kept especially for this purpose.

Unless a joint is the best cut and quality and at least 2½ lb. in weight, it is usually better to slow roast, pot-roast, or braise.

Season the meat with salt and pepper and place in roasting tin with a little dripping and cook by one of the following methods.

Method 1. Start cooking the meat in a very hot oven (475°, Regulo No. 8) and cook at this heat for 10 minutes; then reduce heat to 400°, Regulo No. 5 and cook according to time-table.

Method 2. Start the joint at 375°, Regulo No. 4, and cook at this temperature until the last 15 minutes, then raise to 500°, Regulo No. 9.

Method 3. Slow Roasting. The meat is cooked the whole time in a slow oven — 350°, Regulo No. 3. This is an excellent way of roasting the cheaper cuts.

Approximate Times for Roasting

Methods 1 and 2

Beef and Mutton	Thick cut 30 minutes to the pound.
	Thin cut 25 minutes to the pound.
Lamb	30 minutes to the pound.
Veal	35 minutes to the pound.

Method 3

Beef and Mutton	Thick cut 45 minutes to the pound.
	Thin cut 40 minutes to the pound.
Lamb	40 minutes to the pound.
Veal	45 minutes to the pound.

Boiling

Use a saucepan which will hold sufficient water to cover the meat.

Fresh meat should be put into boiling salted water. Bring to the boil again, and continue boiling for 5 minutes; then skim, reduce heat, and *simmer very slowly* till cooked. If allowed to continue boiling the meat will be tough. The meat must be covered the whole time, so add more boiling water if necessary.

Salt Beef or Tongue should be placed in warm water, and **Smoked Beef or Tongue** in cold water; bring to the boil, then continue as for fresh meat.

Vegetables should be added after the scum has been removed.

The liquor from boiled meats should be used for soups and sauces.

Approximate Times for Boiling

Fresh Beef. For thin cuts 15 minutes to the pound and 15 minutes over; thick cuts, 20 minutes to the pound and 20 minutes over.

Salt Beef. 25 minutes to the pound and 25 minutes over.

Mutton. 20 minutes to the pound and 20 minutes over.

Calf's Head. 3 hours.

Ox Tongue. See detailed recipes.

Braising

Braising is a suitable method for cooking small boned joints, stuffed hearts, poultry, etc. It is a combination of pot-roasting and stewing.

Dry the meat, season and dust it with flour. Melt 2 or 3 oz. dripping in a saucepan, and when hot put the meat in and brown quickly on all sides; then remove from the pan. Put into the fat a bed of prepared thickly sliced vegetables, cover tightly, and cook over a gentle heat for 10 minutes, shaking the pan frequently. Then season, add sufficient stock just to cover the vegetables, and bring to the boil. Lay the browned meat on top, cover closely and simmer gently till the meat is tender.

Allow 25 minutes to the pound and 25 minutes over.

To Braise in the Oven. Brown meat and fry vegetables as above. Place vegetables in a casserole with sufficient boiling stock just to cover, place the meat on top, cover with a greased paper, put the lid on the casserole, and cook in a slow oven — about 325°, Regulo No. 2.

For detailed recipes see later in this section.

Frying

There are two kinds of frying — shallow frying or sautéing, and deep frying.

For Shallow Frying. Melt a small quantity of fat in a frying pan, sufficient to cover the bottom to a depth of $\frac{1}{4}$ inch. Heat until a faint blue smoke rises from it, and fry the meat a golden brown, first on one side and then the other. Reduce the heat after browning.

This method is used for chops, steaks, liver, kidneys, and sausages (see also chapter on fish).

Deep Frying. This is frying in a large quantity of fat, sufficient to cover entirely what is being fried. It is used for fritters, rissoles, croquettes, and other made-up dishes. The foods to be fried are usually coated with batter, egg and breadcrumbs, or pastry.

A deep pan with frying basket can be bought for this purpose.

General Rules. The fat must be absolutely still, with a faint blue smoke just beginning to rise, before using. A thick smoke means the fat is burning.

When the fat bubbles, it does not mean that it is boiling, but that it contains moisture which must evaporate before the right degree of heat can be obtained. Put the foods to be fried into the fat immediately the right degree of heat is reached so that the hot fat immediately forms a coating.

If the fat is not hot enough, it soaks into whatever is being fried, and a greasy taste will be the result.

Reheat the fat between each batch that is being fried.

Drain on soft paper before dishing.

Strain fat each time after using and it will keep for weeks.

Grilling or Broiling

Grilling is a simple and quick method of cooking, although not the most economical, for a comparatively large amount of heat is required to cook small portions of food, such as chops, steaks, kidneys, sausages, etc., and only good quality tender meat is grilled satisfactorily.

To ensure success the gas or electric grill should be red hot before commencing cooking.

If possible, have steaks and chops cut $1–1\frac{1}{2}$ inches thick, and brush over both sides with melted fat.

Grease the grid thoroughly. Place the meat under the grill till brown, turn, and brown the other side. Never use a fork to turn the meat because if the prongs pierce the surface the juices will escape. Use two knives, keeping them quite flat for the purpose.

When brown on both sides, lower the heat a little and continue cooking, turning once or twice, until sufficiently cooked.

Times for Grilling

Steak. 12 to 15 minutes.
Chops and Cutlets. 8 to 10 minutes.
Kidneys. 6 minutes.
Sausages. 8 to 10 minutes.

Pot-Roasting

This is an excellent way of cooking a small and not very tender piece of meat on top of the stove.

Special small roasters with lids are available for this purpose, or a really thick saucepan can be used.

The secret of success is very *slow* cooking over a gentle heat. If the meat is very coarse-grained, dip it in vinegar an hour before cooking.

Melt 2 or 3 oz. of dripping in the pan and when hot, put in the joint, brown quickly all over, put the lid on, stand the pan on an asbestos mat and cook very gently till tender (about 2 hours for a boned joint weighing 2–2½ lb.), turning from time to time.

Potatoes or other root vegetables can be cooked around the meat, adding them the last hour.

Stewing

Stewing is a slow method of cooking, and is very suitable for the cheaper cuts of meat. Long gentle cooking will make tough meat tender.

A stew can be cooked on top of the stove in a saucepan with a well-fitting lid, but it is infinitely better cooked in a casserole in the oven. Whichever method is used, the stew must be kept at a gentle simmer and not allowed to boil. Boiling will make the meat tough.

A stew generally has some kinds of vegetable added, and sometimes the meat is lightly fried before stewing.

Detailed recipes will be found in this section.

Note. If using a pressure saucepan, cooking time is considerably shortened.

Beef

Boiled Beef

Brisket 4 lb.	*6 onions*
Head of celery	*2 turnips*
3 carrots	*1 parsnip*
Salt, cloves, peppercorns	*Suet dumplings*

Prepare the meat and tie it into shape with a piece of tape or string. Prepare vegetables and cut them into large pieces.

Put sufficient salted water in a saucepan to cover the meat and bring to the boil. Put in the meat, reboil for 5 minutes, skim, then reduce the heat and simmer slowly for 1 hour. Add the vegetables, 2 or 3 cloves, and a few peppercorns, continue simmering for 30 minutes, add the dumplings, and continue cooking for another ½ hour.

To Dish. Lift the meat on to a hot dish, remove tape, and place vegetables, dumplings, and a small quantity of the liquor around. Remaining liquor will make excellent soup.

Dumplings

Flour 6 oz.	*Baking powder 1 teaspoonful*
Salt	*Chopped parsley 2 teaspoonfuls*
Suet 2 oz.	*Pepper, mixed herbs*

Sieve flour, salt, and baking powder into a basin. Add the finely shredded suet, the parsley, pepper, and a pinch of mixed herbs. Add sufficient cold water to form a fairly slack dough. With floured hands roll into small balls. Roll in flour and use as directed.

For Onion Dumplings add 2 tablespoonfuls finely chopped onion before mixing with the water.

Boiled Salt Beef

Prepare and cook with vegetables and dumplings as fresh boiled beef, but put it into tepid water (instead of boiling salted water), and for a piece weighing 4 lb. allow about 2½ hours.

For Pressed Beef. Put meat into tepid water, and when boiling, add a cut-up carrot, turnip, and onion, a few peppercorns, and a bouquet garni (parsley, thyme, and bay leaf). Simmer gently till meat is tender and the bones can be easily removed.

Take the meat out of the liquor, and after removing the bones, put between 2 boards or dishes, with a heavy weight on top, and leave till cold.

Boiled Smoked Beef

Soak the meat in cold water for 3 or 4 hours. Put it in a saucepan, cover with cold water, bring slowly to the boil, and simmer slowly for an hour. Then strain the water off, return the meat to the saucepan, cover with fresh cold water, bring to the boil, and continue simmering till the meat is tender, allowing about 45 minutes to the pound.

The meat must cook very gently. If allowed to boil it will become hard.

Braised Beef

Brisket of beef 2–3 lb.	6 peppercorns, 1 bayleaf
Carrots ¼ lb.	Small head of celery
1 turnip	Onions ¼ lb.
Dripping 2 oz.	Blade of mace
Stock	Salt and pepper

Choose a thick piece of beef and, if necessary, tie it into shape. Peel and slice onions thinly, scrape and dice carrots, clean and cut up celery, peel and dice turnip.

Melt the dripping in a stew pan and quickly fry the meat till brown on all sides. Then lift it out, put in the vegetables, put the lid on the saucepan, and cook over a gentle heat for 10 minutes, shaking the pan to prevent them sticking; then pour in sufficient stock barely to cover the vegetables. Season with salt and pepper and add the mace, peppercorns, and bay leaf tied in muslin, bring to the boil, and place the meat on top. Cover the pan tightly, and let the contents simmer very gently about 2½ hours.

To serve, place the meat on a hot dish with the vegetables around. Skim the fat from the gravy and pour it over the meat.

To Cook in the Oven. Brown meat and vegetables as above. Put the vegetables in a casserole, with boiling stock just to cover, lay the meat on top, put lid on the casserole, and cook in a slow oven (325°, Regulo No. 2), about 2½ hours, turning the meat over at half time.

Beef Olives

Steak 1¼ lb.	Veal forcemeat (page 194)
Stock or water ¾ pint	Dripping or other fat 1½ oz.
Flour 1 oz.	A small onion
Salt and pepper	A small carrot

Remove fat from the meat and cut it into very thin slices about 4 inches long and 2 inches wide, then beat thoroughly with a wet rolling pin.

Spread a little forcemeat on each slice, roll up tightly, and secure with fine string. Then roll in seasoned flour.

Heat the fat in a stewpan and fry the olives until the entire surface is lightly browned; then remove from the pan, put in the sliced onion and carrot, and fry these quickly for a few minutes. Then sprinkle in the flour, and when this is brown, gradually add the stock and stir till boiling. Replace the olives, cover with greased paper, put on the lid, and simmer gently for 1½ hours. Remove strings and dish olives on to a bed of mashed potato or sieved spinach, season the gravy and strain it over.

If preferred, after browning and making the gravy, cook in a casserole in a moderate oven for 1½ hours.

To Pickle Beef or Tongue

Brisket of beef 4–6 lb.	*Brown sugar 4–6 oz.*
or a fresh tongue	*Saltpetre ¼ oz.*
Water 4 quarts	*2 or 3 bay leaves*
Rough salt 1 lb.	

Put the water, salt, sugar, saltpetre, and bay leaves in a saucepan and bring to the boil, cook gently for 10 minutes, keeping it well skimmed, then strain into a large earthenware bowl and leave till quite cold.

Dry the meat and place it in the cold pickling solution, put a heavy plate on top to keep the meat well under the liquid, cover with muslin and leave in a cool place for 10 days, turning over once or twice.

Note. Three or four cloves of garlic can be added with the meat for those who like the flavour.

To cook, see page 141.

Carrot Tzimmas (2)

Brisket of beef 2½ lb.	*Sugar 2 oz.*
Chicken or other fat 2 oz.	*Carrots 1 lb.*
Citric acid ¼ teaspoonful	*1 or 2 onions*
Potatoes 2 lb.	*Salt and pepper*

Put the meat and onions in a saucepan, cover with boiling water, season with salt and pepper, and simmer very gently for

1½ hours. Then add the carrots, cut into thick slices, and the potatoes; if these are very small leave whole, otherwise cut in halves, and continue to cook gently until the vegetables are just tender.

Place the meat and vegetables in a large casserole; make a thick sauce with the fat, flour, and 1 pint of the liquor in which the meat was cooked, add the sugar and citric acid and pour over contents of casserole. Bake uncovered on an upper shelf in a moderate oven about 30 minutes.

Note. If preferred the potatoes can be cooked as in Prune Tzimmas, page 149, and the juice of a lemon can replace the citric acid.

Cholent

This is the traditional dish served on the Sabbath in Orthodox homes when a hot meal is required. It is prepared on Friday and cooked in a cool oven until mid-day dinner the following day.

Fat brisket or short rib 2 lb.	*Dumpling*
Haricot or butter beans ¼ lb.	*Sugar 1 tablespoonful*
Potatoes (medium size) 2 lb.	*Seasoning*
A small onion	

Use a handled saucepan or large casserole with a *tightly fitting lid*. Peel the potatoes and leave them whole. Put the beans in the bottom of the pan, add the chopped onion and half the potatoes. Place the meat and dumpling in the centre and fill up with remaining potatoes. Season each layer with salt and pepper, sprinkle over the sugar, and cover with boiling water. Place greaseproof paper over the top before putting on the lid. Place in the middle of a moderately hot oven until it comes to the boil, then turn the heat down to 250°, Regulo No. ½, and leave till required the following day.

For the Dumpling. Mix together 4 oz. flour, 1 oz. finely chopped suet (or raw chicken fat), 1 tablespoonful grated onion, 2 teaspoonfuls chopped parsley, and a fairly large grated potato. Season with salt and pepper, then form into a roll.

Hungarian Goulash

Stewing beef 1¼ lb.	*A large onion*
Paprika 1 teaspoonful	*Sieved tomatoes ½ pint*
Flour 1 oz.	*Dripping 2 oz.*
Small potatoes	*Salt and pepper*

If preferred, use a mixture of beef and veal. Cut up the meat into 1-inch cubes and roll in seasoned flour. Chop the onion. Melt the dripping in a frying pan, add the meat and onion and fry a golden brown. Then put into a casserole, add the sieved tomatoes (fresh or tinned), the paprika, and sufficient water or stock to cover the meat. Season with salt and pepper, put the lid on the casserole and cook in a slow oven about 1½ hours; then add some small potatoes and continue cooking for another 40 minutes. If the potatoes are not very small, cut them in halves or quarters.

Dumplings (see page 145) can be used in place of potatoes.

Prune Tzimmas

Brisket of beef 2¼ lb.	*Sugar 2 oz.*
Potatoes 2 lb.	*1 lemon*
Prunes ¼ lb.	*Chicken or other fat 2 oz.*
1 or 2 onions	*Salt and pepper*
Flour 2 oz.	

Soak the prunes overnight. Put the meat in a saucepan, add the prunes and onions and pour over sufficient boiling water to cover. Season with salt and pepper and cook gently till the meat is tender.

Peel and thickly slice the potatoes, place in a large casserole and put meat and prunes on top.

Melt the fat, stir in the flour and gradually add 1 pint liquid in which the meat was cooked; stir till boiling, add the juice of the lemon (or ¼ teaspoonful citric acid) and sugar and simmer for 2 or 3 minutes, then pour over the meat and potatoes.

Bake on an upper shelf in a moderate oven until the potatoes are cooked and the meat browned — about 40 minutes.

Roast Beef

See general notes on roasting, page 140.

A boned rib of beef must be rolled, skewered and tied into shape.

Serve roast beef with Yorkshire pudding, grated horseradish, and roast potatoes.

Yorkshire Pudding

Flour 4 oz.	2 eggs
Water ¼ pint	Vegetable extract
Dripping 2 tablespoonfuls	Salt ¼ teaspoonful

Add a little vegetable extract to the water.

Sift the flour and salt into a bowl, make a well in the centre, break in the eggs and 2 tablespoonfuls water. With a wooden spoon stir in a little flour from the sides. Keep stirring, gradually adding more water until half has been used. Mix to a smooth batter free of lumps and beat lightly, then add remaining water and let stand for at least ½ hour.

Put the dripping in a shallow fireproof dish or baking tin and put in the oven till *smoking* hot; then pour in the batter and bake in a hot oven 30 minutes.

It can be served in the dish in which it was cooked, or cut in pieces and placed round the meat.

Note. If Yorkshire pudding is being cooked with the meat, then roast according to method 2 (page 140).

Fried Steak

Melt about 2 oz. fat in a frying pan, make smoking hot, put in the steak, brown one side, turn and brown the other, then lower the heat. Turn frequently, using a blunt knife so as not to pierce the meat. It will take 10–15 minutes to cook, depending on the thickness of the steak. Season with salt and pepper, put on a hot dish, and pour a little thickened gravy over, flavoured, if liked, with a little mushroom ketchup or Yorkshire relish.

Serve with fried onions, potato chips, grilled tomatoes, and French mustard.

Grilled Steak

(See directions for grilling, page 143.)

Marinated Steak

For each pound of steak allow 2 tablespoonfuls olive oil, 1 tablespoonful vinegar, a small sliced onion, a piece of bay leaf, and a few peppercorns. Mix together and lay the steak in the marinade for several hours, turning over occasionally. Then grill or fry in the usual way. The marinade helps to make the steak tender.

Stewed Steak

(See page 313, omitting the pickled walnuts.)

Steak Pie

Steak 1½–2 lb.	Stock or water
Flour 2 tablespoonfuls	Short or flaky pastry
A few mushrooms	Salt and pepper

Cut the meat into 1-inch cubes. Add a teaspoonful of salt and a good sprinkling of pepper to the flour and coat the meat with it. Then put it in a casserole, add a few sliced mushrooms (these are optional) and cover with well-seasoned boiling stock or water, put the lid on the casserole and cook very gently in a slow oven till tender – 2–3 hours. Then leave till cold.

Put the meat into a pie-dish sufficiently small to allow the meat to be raised in the centre and three-parts fill with the stock in which it was cooked. Cover with pastry, decorate with leaves of pastry (see page 246), brush over with beaten egg (this is optional, but it gives a gloss), and make a small hole in the centre for the steam to escape. Bake about 40 minutes. If short crust is being used start at 450° (Regulo No. 7), for flaky pastry 475° (Regulo No. 8). As soon as the pastry is set and lightly browned – about 15 minutes – reduce to moderate, 400° (Regulo No. 5).

Heat the remainder of the gravy in which the meat was first cooked and serve separately.

Steak and Kidney Pie. When available, 6–8 oz. kidney can replace the same amount of steak, and this should be cut up into small pieces and cooked in the casserole with the steak.

Steak Pudding

Stewing steak 1 lb.   *Flour 2 oz.*
Kidney or sheep's heart ¼ lb. *Suet crust ½ lb.*
Chopped onion 2 teaspoonfuls   *Salt and pepper*

Add ½ teaspoonful salt and a good sprinkling of pepper to the flour. Cut up the meat into 1-inch cubes and the kidney or heart into small pieces and roll in the seasoned flour.

Grease a 1½-pint basin. Cut off quarter of the pastry for the lid, and roll out remainder ¼ to ½ inch thick, and lift it gently into the basin. Press to fit the sides and bottom and have a little over-hanging the top. Put in the meat and chopped onion and sufficient water to come half way up the meat. Roll out remaining pastry to fit the top of the basin. Damp the edges of the pastry, put on the lid and press edges together. Cover with a greased paper and pudding cloth and steam about 3½ hours. Serve in the basin in which it was cooked, with a folded napkin pinned round it.

Serve a small jug of boiling stock separately to add to the pudding on opening it.

Scotch Hot-pot

Stewing steak 1 lb.   *Sausages ¼ lb.*
Potatoes 2 lb.   *A large cooking apple*
3 or 4 onions   *Flour 1 oz.*
Tomatoes ¼ lb.   *Chopped parsley*
Stock or water   *Salt and pepper*

Remove skin from the sausages, add a little chopped parsley, and with floured hands roll into tiny balls.

Cut the steak into cubes. Season the flour highly with salt and pepper, and coat the meat and sausage balls with it. Slice the potatoes, onion, apple, and tomatoes (when fresh ones are not available, use tinned or bottled ones).

Put a layer of sliced potatoes in the bottom of the casserole, then one of meat and sausage balls, cover with onion, apple, and tomato, season with salt and pepper, and repeat the layers. Pour over sufficient seasoned stock or water to come three-quarters up the dish, cover with thickly sliced potatoes, dot with dripping, cover, and cook in a slow oven 2½–3 hours, removing the lid the last ½ hour.

Haricot Stew

Shin of beef or stewing steak 1 lb.　　*Haricot beans 6 oz.*
2 leeks　　　　　　　　　　　　　*Carrots ¼ lb.*
Dripping 2 oz.　　　　　　　　　*Flour 1½ oz.*
Stock 1½ pints　　　　　　　　　*Salt, pepper, vinegar*

Soak the haricots in water overnight. Cut meat into small pieces, put in a dish with 2 tablespoonfuls of vinegar, and let it soak for 15 minutes, turning it occasionally.

Prepare and slice carrot and leeks. Melt the dripping, fry the vegetables golden brown, then lift them out. Stir in flour, brown this, then gradually add the stock (or water), and stir till boiling.

Put the meat, haricots, and browned vegetables in a casserole, season to taste, pour over the thickened gravy, cover, and cook in a slow oven 2½–3 hours.

Italian Stew

Stewing beef 1 lb.　　　　*Water or stock 1½ pints*
Rice 1 teacupful　　　　　*Seasoning*
2 large onions　　　　　　*Dripping 2 oz.*
Tomatoes ¼ lb.

Slice and fry the onions in the dripping till golden brown, then add the meat cut into small pieces, and fry till lightly browned; pour over the water or stock, bring to the boil, and simmer gently for 2 hours. Add the rice and skinned and sliced tomatoes the last 30 minutes.

Stewed Ox-tail

1 ox-tail　　　　　　　　　*Stock or water*
Dripping 2 oz.　　　　　　*Lemon juice 1 tablespoonful*
Flour 2 oz.　　　　　　　　*Mace, bay leaf, cloves*
2 small onions　　　　　　*Salt and pepper*
Diced carrot and turnip

Cut the tail into joints and divide the thick part in half.

Melt the dripping in a stewpan, dry the pieces of tail, and fry them a good brown. Then take them out of the stewpan, put in the sliced onion, and when golden brown stir in the flour.

When this has browned also, add about 2 pints stock or water, and stir till boiling; then add 2 cloves, a blade of mace, salt and pepper, and the pieces of tail. Simmer gently till tender — about 3½ hours.

Arrange the pieces of tail on a hot dish, add the lemon juice to the gravy, and strain it over.

Garnish with groups of diced carrot and turnip cooked separately and triangles of fried bread.

One or two tablespoonfuls sherry can replace the lemon juice.

Boiled Ox-tongue

A smoked tongue, if very hard, should be soaked in cold water overnight; otherwise 3 or 4 hours will be sufficient.

A salted tongue fresh from the pickle need only be soaked for an hour.

Put a smoked tongue into cold water, a salted one in tepid water, and a fresh tongue in boiling salted water. The saucepan should be sufficiently large for the tongue to be completely covered with water. Add a few peppercorns, a couple of bay leaves, and cloves. Bring *slowly* to the boil and simmer very gently till tender — about 3 hours for a large salt one and about 4 hours for a large smoked one. Test with a fork at the root end. If it goes in easily it is sufficiently cooked.

Remove the skin and trim the root. If the tongue is to be served cold, skin it and fasten down to a board by sticking a fork through the root and another through the tip to straighten. When cold trim some of the fat from the root, brush over with glaze, and fasten a paper frill round the root.

To Press. After skinning the tongue while still hot, trim the root, removing any small bones and superfluous fat. Roll the tongue round and press it into a round tin (a 2 lb. cake tin will do) previously rinsed out in cold water. Press the tongue well into this, place a board or plate on it with a weight on top, and leave till cold.

To Pickle Tongue

(See page 147)

Boiled Tongue with Sweet and Sour Sauce

Cook a fresh tongue till tender, then remove skin and cut it
into slices. Return to the saucepan, pour the sauce over, and
simmer for 10 minutes.

For the Sauce

1 small onion	Chicken or other fat 1¼ oz.
Flour 1 oz.	Vinegar 2 tablespoonfuls
Stock ¾ pint	Golden syrup 1 tablespoonful
Raisins 1 oz.	Ground cinnamon ¼ teaspoonful

Chop the onion finely and fry gently in the fat till golden
brown, then stir in the flour smoothly, and when this is
brown also, gradually add ¾ pint liquor in which the tongue was
cooked. Stir till boiling, add the syrup, stoned raisins (or
sultanas), cinnamon, and lemon cut into thin slices. Simmer
for 10 minutes, then use as directed.

Note. The amount of syrup and vinegar used can be varied
to suit individual taste, and sugar can replace the syrup.

Sea Pie

Stewing beef 1 lb.	Flour, salt, pepper
Mixed vegetables 1 lb.	Stock or water
Suet crust 6 oz.	

Cut the meat into small pieces and roll in seasoned flour.
Prepare the vegetables – carrots, turnips, celery, onions,
swedes, etc. (whatever is available) – and cut these also into
small pieces.

Put meat and vegetables in alternate layers in a saucepan,
season well with salt, pepper, and, if desired, grated nutmeg,
and pour over sufficient stock or water to cover. Bring slowly
to the boil and simmer gently for 1¼ hours.

Roll out the suet pastry into a round a little smaller than the
saucepan and lay gently on top of the stew. Put on the lid and
continue to simmer for another ¾ hour.

To Dish. Lift off the crust and cut into 6 or 8 pieces. Put the
meat and vegetables on to a hot dish and place the crust on top.

Note. A little liver mixed with the beef is very good; and
neck of mutton can also be served in this way.

Sausages
(See pages 123–6)

DISHES WITH MINCED BEEF

Stuffed Cabbage Leaves (1)
(*Holishkes*)

Cabbage leaves	Brown sugar 1 oz.
Cooked rice 1 teacupful	Tomato purée ¼ pint
Raw minced beef 1 lb.	Water ¼ pint
Grated onion 1 tablespoonful	Sultanas 2 oz.
Lemon juice	Salt and pepper

Use a white cabbage, remove 12 of the largest leaves, place in a bowl, cover with boiling water, leave for 2 or 3 minutes, then drain, dry with a cloth, and cut away the tough stem end.

Mix the meat and rice, add the grated onion and a spoonful of tomato purée, and season with salt and pepper. Put a portion in the centre of each cabbage leaf, fold over the sides, roll up like a parcel and fasten with thread.

Line a large saucepan with a few more scalded leaves and place the rolls close together on top, pour over the tomato purée and water, add sugar, sultanas, and juice of a lemon, and cook over a very gentle heat 2–2½ hours. If the liquid boils away, add a little more water.

Stuffed Cabbage Leaves (2)
(*Holishkes*)

Cabbage leaves	Brown sugar 1 oz.
Rice (raw) ¼ lb.	Juice of a lemon
Raw minced beef ¾ lb.	Stock
Grated onion 1 tablespoonful	Salt and pepper
Tomato purée 2 tablespoonfuls	

Scald and trim 12 cabbage leaves as in previous recipe.

Wash the rice, mix it with the meat and add the grated onion, 1 tablespoonful tomato purée, a squeeze of lemon juice, salt, and pepper. Put a spoonful on each leaf, fold over sides, and roll up like a parcel. Then pack them closely in a large casserole, just cover with well-seasoned boiling stock, to which add remaining tomato purée, the sugar, and lemon juice. Put the lid on the casserole, and cook in a very slow oven (300–325°, Regulo No. 1–2) about 3 hours.

Meat Ball

Minced raw beef 1 lb.	*Small grated onion*
Stale bread	*Parsley 2 teaspoonfuls*
A large egg	*Salt, pepper, mace, ginger*

Soak 2 thick slices stale bread till soft, then squeeze *very* dry and beat up with a fork till free of lumps. Then mix with the meat and add the grated onion and chopped parsley. Season with salt, pepper, a pinch of mace and ginger, and bind with the egg. Mix thoroughly and roll into a ball, flatten slightly, and dredge well with seasoned flour.

Melt a little dripping in a baking tin and when quite hot put in the meat carefully. Spoon a little of the dripping over the top and bake in a moderately hot oven about 1¼ hours, turning over at half time.

Start baking at about 450° (Regulo No. 7), and after 15 minutes reduce heat to 400° (No. 5).

Serve with thick brown gravy.

Note. If preferred, use 3 oz. breadcrumbs in place of soaked bread.

Hamburg Steaks

Minced beef (raw) 1 lb.	*1 egg*
Grated onion 2 teaspoonfuls	*Breadcrumbs 2 oz.*
Flour	*Salt and pepper*

Mix meat, breadcrumbs, and grated onion, season with salt and pepper, add the beaten egg, and mix thoroughly. Form into round flat cakes about 1 inch thick, and dip lightly in flour.

Fry in shallow fat, browning quickly on both sides, then reduce the heat and cook gently for 5 minutes on each side.

Meat Cakes en Casserole with Savoury Balls

Minced beef 1 lb.	*Fresh breadcrumbs 2 oz.*
2 or 3 onions	*2 or 3 sticks celery*
2 carrots	*1 egg*
Dripping 2 oz.	*Flour*
Stock 1 pint	*Chopped parsley*
Savoury balls	*Seasoning*

Grate one of the onions and add it to the meat together with the breadcrumbs, a tablespoonful of chopped parsley, and the beaten egg. Season with salt and pepper and mix very thoroughly. Roll into small balls, flatten, and coat with seasoned flour.

Prepare and slice remaining onions, carrot, and celery.

Make veal forcemeat (see page 194), roll into small balls, flatten, and coat with seasoned flour.

Melt the dripping in a frying pan and lightly brown the onions, meat cakes, and savoury balls. Lift them out and put the meat balls in a casserole with the prepared vegetables.

Add 1 piled tablespoonful of flour to the fat in the pan, and when brown, gradually stir in 1 pint of stock (or water, to which add 1 tablespoonful liquid vegetable extract). Stir till boiling, then pour over the contents of the casserole, cover, and cook in a slow oven about 2 hours, adding the savoury balls the last half-hour.

This is a tasty and very economical dish, and will make a generous meal for 6–8 people. Any left over will be quite good reheated in a casserole in the oven.

Meat Loaf

Minced beef 1 lb.	*Grated onion 1 tablespoonful*
Fresh breadcrumbs 2 oz.	*Chopped parsley 2 teaspoonfuls*
Gravy or stock	*1 egg*
Savoury sauce	*Salt and pepper*

Add the breadcrumbs, parsley, grated onion and beaten egg to the minced beef, flavour with tomato purée or Worcester sauce, season with salt and pepper and mix thoroughly, adding a spoonful or two of thick gravy or stock.

Turn into a greased loaf tin, press down firmly, cover with a greased paper and bake in a moderate oven about 1 hour.

Serve with thick brown gravy, to which can be added a little chopped sweet pickle.

If the Loaf is to be served cold, leave in tin or basin till quite cold before slicing.

Variations:

(1) Flavour with curry powder and serve with boiled rice and chutney.

(2) Add a little sausage meat or minced smoked beef to the mixture before cooking.

(3) For special occasions place 2 hard-boiled eggs in the centre and cover well with the meat mixture before cooking.

(4) For a steamed loaf turn into a greased basin, cover and steam for $1\frac{1}{2}$ hours.

Meat Pie

Raw minced beef 1 lb. *Medium-sized turnip*
Thin gravy ¼ pint *Potatoes 1 lb.*
A large onion *Dripping, salt, and pepper*

Parboil the potatoes and cut into rather thin slices.

Slice the onion *very thinly*. Grate the turnip, mix it with the minced beef, add the gravy, season with salt and pepper, and press into a greased oven dish. Put the thinly sliced onion on top, then cover with the potato slices. Dot with dripping, and bake in a moderate oven $1-1\frac{1}{4}$ hours.

Mince with Toast or Spaghetti

Minced beef 1 lb. *Chopped onion 1 tablespoonful*
Dripping ½ oz. *Stock or water ½ pint*
Toast or spaghetti *Breadcrumbs ¼ teacupful*

Chop the onion very finely. Melt the dripping in a strong saucepan, add the onion and meat and cook over a gentle heat for a few minutes until lightly browned, keeping it well stirred. Then pour in the stock (or water flavoured with vegetable extract) and season with salt, pepper, and a little ketchup. Stir till boiling, then cover and simmer very gently for 20 minutes. Add the breadcrumbs, which will absorb any liquid fat, and cook for a few minutes longer. Turn into a hot

dish and garnish with triangles of toast or surround with a
border of spaghetti.

Mutton and Lamb

Boiled Mutton

Shoulder, neck, stuffed and rolled breast or leg can all be boiled.

Put the joint into a saucepan with sufficient boiling water to
cover, add salt to taste, cover, and boil quickly for 5 minutes,
then simmer *very gently* until the meat is cooked, allowing 20
minutes to the pound and 20 minutes over. The last hour add
2 or 3 carrots, turnips, and onions. Use small onions and leave
them whole, cut carrots and turnips through in halves.

When cooked, place the meat on a hot dish with the vegetables around. Serve with caper sauce (page 196).

Use the water in which the meat was cooked for mutton
broth.

Breast of Lamb Cutlets

Boil one or more breasts of lamb as above until the bones will
just slip out. After removing the bones press the meat between
two plates with a weight on top. Leave till quite cold, then cut
into individual portions, dip in egg or eggless batter, and coat
with dry breadcrumbs. Fry a golden brown in deep fat.

Serve with thick gravy or tomato sauce, fried or mashed
potatoes, and pickled gherkins.

Stuffed Breast of Lamb (1)

One of the best ways to serve breast of lamb is to bone and stuff
it, and then either roast it in the oven or pot-roast or braise it
(see pages 140–44).

Remove the bones with a sharp-pointed knife, spread with
any stuffing preferred, roll up, and tie securely with tape.
Season with salt and pepper, and bake in a moderate oven
(or on top of the stove if you are braising or pot-roasting).

In the same tin, roast some onions which have been peeled,

boiled for 10 minutes and drained; bake with the meat about 1½ hours. If space allows, put the onions at one end of the tin and potatoes at the other; or roast the potatoes in a separate tin.

Suggestions for Stuffings:

(1) **Veal Stuffing** (page 194).

(2) **Potato Stuffing.** Mash 1 lb. freshly cooked potatoes thoroughly with a little dripping. Add a finely grated onion and either 1 tablespoonful chopped parsley or 3 tablespoonfuls chopped watercress. Season with salt and pepper.

(3) **Sausage Meat.** Mix ½ lb. sausage meat with 1 teacupful breadcrumbs moistened with stock. Add chopped parsley and season if necessary.

(4) **Spanish Stuffing.** Mix together 1 breakfastcupful cooked rice, a few sultanas, rind and juice of half a lemon, a grated onion, a pinch of mixed spice, salt and pepper.

Stuffed Breast of Lamb (2)

Prepare and stuff the meat as above. For 2 breasts of lamb allow 2–2½ lb. potatoes. Cut the potatoes into thick slices, and put in a greased baking tin. Sprinkle with salt, and pour 1 teacupful of water over. Lay the prepared meat on top, dot with dripping, and cover the meat with a greased paper. Bake in a moderate oven about 1½ hours, removing the paper the last ½ hour.

If preferred, the breasts of lamb can be cooked without boning and stuffing. Simply season and lay the lamb on top of the potatoes, cover with greased paper, and cook as above.

Roast Lamb and Mutton

The usual cuts for roasting are leg, shoulder, saddle, loin, and best end of neck.

Lamb and mutton should be well cooked (see page 140).

Serve redcurrant jelly or onion sauce with roast mutton, and mint sauce or mint jelly with roast lamb.

Lamb and Mutton Chops

Chops and cutlets can either be fried or grilled. Cutlets can either be fried plain or first dipped in egg and breadcrumbs.

Chops are best grilled (for grilling and frying see pages 142–3).

If you are going to cut your cutlets at home, ask the butcher to saw off the chine bone. Divide the cutlets with a very sharp knife, allowing a bone to each. Trim off the fat, leaving a narrow rim round the meat, the fat removed being rendered down for dripping (see page 19).

Dry very thoroughly before cooking. Dish round a mound of mashed potatoes.

Grilled or fried tomatoes or mushrooms, green peas, or spinach purée are all excellent with chops and cutlets.

Banana Fritters are also very good with grilled chops and steak. Bananas should be not quite ripe. Split them through, sprinkle with salt and cayenne, and coat with frying batter. Fry in hot fat until a golden brown. Sprinkle with chopped parsley and serve with tomato sauce.

Cutlets with Gherkin Sauce

4 or 5 cutlets   *Stock ¼ pint*
2 or 3 gherkins   *Chopped parsley*
1 shallot   *Vinegar 1 teaspoonful*
Salt and pepper

Trim the cutlets and fry till well browned on both sides. Then pour off the fat, add the stock, the shallot (grated) and a little finely chopped parsley; season with salt and pepper. Simmer the cutlets gently in the sauce for 5 minutes. Then put them on a hot dish, add the sliced gherkins and vinegar to the sauce and pour it over.

Stuffed Shoulder of Mutton

A small boned shoulder of mutton   *Onion sauce*
Onion 2 oz.   *Sage 1 teaspoonful*
Breadcrumbs 4 oz.   *1 egg*
Chopped apple 1 tablespoonful   *Brown gravy*
Salt and pepper

Add the finely chopped onion, powdered sage and chopped apple to the breadcrumbs, season with salt and pepper, and bind with the beaten egg. Fill the boned shoulder with this forcemeat, season with salt and pepper, and tie round. Put into a baking tin with some hot dripping, and bake in a moderate oven, allowing 20 minutes to the pound and 20 minutes over. Baste from time to time. Serve with onion sauce and brown gravy.

Stuffed Shoulder of Mutton – Braised

A small boned shoulder of mutton   *Rice ¼ lb.*
Forcemeat as in previous recipe   *Onions 1 lb.*
Dripping 3 oz.

Stuff the shoulder as in previous recipe and sew up or tie round into the shape of a large sausage.

Melt the dripping in a stewpan, put in the meat, and brown all over.

Peel the onions, cover with boiling water, and leave for 5 minutes, then drain. Place them round the meat and cook over a very gentle heat about 2 hours, turning the meat and onions after they have been cooking an hour.

Cook the rice in boiling water for 20 minutes; then strain (reserving water for soup). Put the mutton on a hot dish and keep it hot. Add drained rice to the contents of the saucepan, and let it simmer for 10 minutes, keeping it well stirred. Season with salt and pepper, and serve round the meat.

Casserole of Lamb with Apples

Middle neck 1½ lb.   *Dripping 2 oz.*
Onions ½ lb.   *Sugar*
Cooking apples ½–¾ lb.   *Salt and pepper*
Stock ½ pint

Cut up the meat, trim off superfluous fat, season with salt and pepper and place in a casserole.

Slice the onions thinly, then fry them in the dripping till lightly browned, place them on top of the meat and pour the stock over.

Peel and core the apples and cut them into thin slices, place on top of the onions and sprinkle with caster sugar. Cover the casserole and cook in a slow oven about 1½ hours.

Irish Stew

Scrag or middle neck of mutton 2 lb.
Potatoes 2 lb.
Onions 1 lb.
Pearl barley 1¼ oz.
Chopped parsley
Salt and pepper

Trim off superfluous fat and cut the meat into neat joints. Place a layer of meat in a stewpan or casserole. Sprinkle with salt, pepper, barley, and chopped parsley; then cover with a layer of sliced onions and one of thickly sliced potatoes, and season these with salt and pepper. Repeat layers, finishing with potatoes on top. Pour in sufficient water to barely cover, put on the lid and simmer very gently on top of the stove or in the oven for about 2½ hours.

Lamb Stewed with Peas and Carrots

Neck of lamb 2 lb.
Peas (shelled) 1 pint
2 or 3 onions
Stock or water 1 pint
Carrots ¼ lb.
Salt and pepper

Cut up the lamb neatly. Slice the onions and carrots.

Put a layer of onions and carrots in a casserole, then one of meat, season with salt and pepper, and repeat the layers. Pour over sufficient stock or water just to cover, put the lid on the casserole, and simmer gently in a moderate oven for 1¼ hours, then add the peas and continue cooking for ¾ hour.

If more convenient, this can be cooked in a saucepan on top of the stove, but must be simmered very gently.

The vegetables can be varied – French beans, shredded celery, tomatoes, and young diced turnips are all good.

Lamb Stewed with Rice and Sultanas

Neck of lamb 1½–2 lb.
Sultanas 3 oz.
Cinnamon ¼ teaspoonful
Stock 1¼ pints
Rice 6 oz.
Salt and pepper

Cut up the meat, trim off superfluous fat, season with salt and pepper and place in a casserole. Add the rice, sultanas and

cinnamon and pour over boiling stock. Cover and cook in a
slow oven about 1½ hours.

Lancashire Hot-pot

A real Lancashire hot-pot should cook very slowly, have very
little liquid added, and the top layer of potato should form a
brown 'crust.'

The meat can be neck of lamb or thinly sliced liver, or
sheep's heart.

Cut up the meat and trim off some of the fat.

Put layers of sliced potato, carrot, onion (or leek), and
shredded celery in a large casserole, season with salt and pepper,
add the meat and a few more vegetables, pour in sufficient
water to come a quarter of the way up the casserole, and top
with a layer of *thickly* sliced potatoes. Dot with dripping, put
the lid on the casserole, and bake in a very slow oven for 2½
hours, uncovering the casserole the last ½ hour.

Cornish Pasties

A small onion	*A large potato*
Short or flaky pastry ¾ lb.	*Chopped parsley*
Mutton ½ lb.	*Salt and pepper*

Roll out the pastry and stamp into rounds the size of a saucer. Boil
the potato for 5 minutes, then cut it and the meat into small
dice, chop the onion and parsley finely, and mix all together.

Add 2 tablespoonfuls gravy and season with salt and pepper.

Put a heap of the mixture in the centre of each round of
pastry, then wet the edges, fold over in halves, press well
together, and crimp with the fingers. Brush over with beaten
egg, cut a small hole in the centre for steam to escape. Bake in
a quick oven for 15 minutes, then reduce the heat and bake
another ½ hour.

Fried Kidneys

Wash and dry the kidneys thoroughly. Cut them through
without separating the two halves. Remove skin and core and
season with salt and pepper. Fry in a little chicken or other fat,

first on the cut side; then turn and fry on the other – about 6 minutes altogether.

Serve on rounds of fried bread with fried mushrooms or tomatoes. Or cut some potatoes roasted in their jackets in halves, place a kidney on each, and pour over a little of the fat in which they were cooked.

Tomato Brady

Best end neck of lamb 2 lb. *Onions ¾ lb.*
Tomatoes 1½ lb. *Salt and pepper*

Scald the tomatoes and remove the skins. Skin and slice the onions. Cut the lamb into chops and trim off some of the fat. Put half the tomatoes in the bottom of a saucepan or casserole, then a layer of onions; put the chops on top, then another layer of onions, and finish with tomatoes. Season each layer with salt and pepper and cover tightly. Place over a very gentle heat or in a slow oven, and simmer *very slowly* for 2½ hours. The tomatoes will give sufficient moisture without adding any stock or water.

The success of the dish depends on very gentle cooking and a tightly fitting lid, so that the steam is used to cook the meat instead of escaping.

Tinned or bottled tomatoes can be used when fresh ones are not available.

Sheep's Heart

Sheep's heart can be cooked by any of the recipes given for calf's heart (pages 170–71), but will not take quite so long to cook.

For roasting. 1–1¼ hours should be sufficient.

Sheep's Heart Pudding. Make like steak and kidney pudding (see page 152).

Sheep's Tongues and Mushrooms

4 sheep's tongues *Margarine 1 oz.*
A small onion *Flour 1 oz.*
Mushrooms 2 oz. *Stock*
Chopped parsley 1 teaspoonful *Salt and pepper*
Sherry 1 tablespoonful

Soak the tongues in salt water for 2 hours, then rinse and place in a saucepan, cover with well-seasoned stock, add the onion, cover, and cook *very gently* till tender – 2–3 hours. Then take out the tongues, remove skin, trim the roots, and cut each into 3 or 4 slices lengthwise.

Melt the margarine, stir in the flour, cook till lightly browned, then gradually add ¾ pint of the liquid in which the tongues were cooked. Stir till boiling, add the peeled and sliced mushrooms, parsley, sherry, and the slices of tongue. Simmer very gently 12–15 minutes.

Note. The tongues can be cooked the previous day if more convenient, in which case, after removing the skin, return to the liquor until required.

Veal

Veal should always be well cooked. For times for roasting see page 140.

If the meat is not stuffed, roll some veal forcemeat (see page 194) into small balls, dip in flour and cook in the tin with the meat for ½ hour.

Braised Veal

Bone a breast of veal, season with salt and pepper and lemon juice, spread with veal forcemeat, roll up, and tie securely.

Then proceed as for braised beef (see page 146), cooking very gently about 2½ hours. The vegetables can be served with the veal, *or* strain off the gravy and add a little lemon juice to it and reboil, pour a little over the meat, and serve the rest separately. Use the vegetables in soup or a made-up dish.

Braised Veal with Olives

Boneless veal 2–3 lb.   *Chicken fat or dripping 2 oz.*
A few small onions   *Tomato purée 1 tablespoonful*
Stock 1 pint   *Stoned olives*

Peel the onions and leave them whole. Melt the dripping in a stewpan, put in the meat, brown it quickly all over, remove it and put in the onions whole, and cook these also till brown.

Then add the stock and tomato purée, season, and bring to the boil. Put back the meat and simmer very gently for 2½ hours, turning the meat occasionally. A few minutes before serving add a few stoned olives.

Wiener Schnitzel

Thin slices of veal steak should be well battened, so that they are really thin. Dip in seasoned flour, then in beaten egg, and coat with fresh breadcrumbs. Fry in hot chicken or other fat till golden brown on each side.

Garnish each schnitzel with a slice of lemon, with a slice of stuffed olive in the centre.

If desired, a fried or poached egg sprinkled with chopped capers can be served on each schnitzel.

Serve schnitzel and all veal cutlets with mashed or new potatoes or potato crisps. Spinach purée, grilled tomatoes, and stewed mushrooms are also good accompaniments.

Ragoût of Veal

Neck, breast or knuckle of veal 2–2½ lb.	*Flour 1½ oz.*
1 onion, 1 carrot, ¼ turnip	*Sherry*
¼ lemon	*Salt and pepper*
Dripping 1½ oz.	*Stock or water 1½ pints*

Cut up the veal into convenient-sized pieces for serving. Melt the dripping and fry the meat till lightly browned; then remove from the fat and add the sliced onion; brown this also. Then stir in the flour, and gradually add 1½ pints stock or water, and stir till boiling, add the grated rind and juice of half a lemon, and season with salt and pepper.

Put the meat in a casserole with the diced carrot and turnip, pour the gravy over, cover, and cook in a slow oven about 2½ hours. Add 2 tablespoonfuls cooking sherry the last ½ hour.

Veal Stewed with Green Peas and Savoury Balls

Neck, breast or knuckle of veal 2–2½ lb.	*¼ lemon*
Flour 1½ oz.	*Stock*
Green peas 1 pint	*Seasoning*
Dripping 2 oz.	*Savoury balls*

Cut up the meat and make the savoury balls. Melt the dripping and fry first the meat, then the balls, till lightly browned on both sides. Remove from the pan, stir in the flour and when this is brown, gradually add 1½ pints stock or water. Stir till boiling, add the grated rind and juice of half a lemon, and season with salt and pepper.

Put the meat and gravy into a casserole, cover and cook in a slow oven for 1½ hours, add the peas and savoury balls, and continue cooking slowly for another ¾ hour.

For the Savoury Balls. Make veal forcemeat (see page 194), roll into small balls, flatten, and lightly coat with flour.

Calf's Brains

1 set of brains	2 rounds of toast
Yolk of an egg	½ lemon
Flour 1 tablespoonful	Margarine 1 oz.
Seasoning	Chopped parsley

The brains must be very fresh. Wash them in cold salted water and remove the skin; then put them in fresh cold water for 1 hour.

Put them in a saucepan with sufficient cold water to cover, add 1 teaspoonful lemon juice and a little salt, bring to the boil, and simmer very gently for 15 minutes. Then strain and keep hot.

Melt the margarine in a small saucepan, stir in the flour smoothly, then gradually add ½ pint of the liquor in which the brains were cooked. Stir till boiling and simmer for 5 minutes. Add 1 teaspoonful lemon juice, cool slightly, then pour on the beaten egg yolk, and reheat without boiling.

Place the brains on rounds of toast, pour the sauce over, and sprinkle with chopped parsley.

Fried Brains

Boil the brains as above and leave till cold. Cut into slices, coat lightly with flour, then dip in beaten egg, and coat with bread-crumbs. Fry a golden brown on both sides in a little chicken or other fat.

Serve with thickened gravy or tomato sauce. Or, if something piquant is preferred, pour off all the fat from the pan, except 2 tablespoonfuls, and to this add 1 tablespoonful tarragon vinegar, 1 teaspoonful each chopped parsley and chopped capers, and when quite hot, pour over the fried brains.

Stewed Calf's Feet

2 calf's feet   Meat balls
1 onion   Egg and lemon sauce
Seasoning

Cut up the calf's feet and place in a stew pan with sufficient water to cover, add salt and pepper and the onion cut in slices. Bring it to the boil and let it simmer gently until quite tender, about 3 hours. One hour before serving add the meat balls. To serve, heap up the calf's feet in the middle of a dish, put the meat balls around, and pour over the sauce (see page 201).

For the Meat Balls. Mix together 4 oz. of chopped veal, 2 oz. of chopped suet, 2 teaspoonfuls of chopped parsley, 4 tablespoonfuls of breadcrumbs, and the rind and juice of half a lemon. Season carefully and bind with a well-beaten egg.

Calf's Heart

The heart can be braised, baked, or stewed.

To Prepare. Wash the heart very thoroughly, remove large veins and arteries, and cut through the inside division of the heart, so as to have a good space for the stuffing. Soak in salted water for 1 hour, and then dry thoroughly.

Braised Calf's Heart

A calf's heart   Veal stuffing (page 194)
A carrot, turnip, and onion   Flour 1 oz.
2 sticks celery   Blade of mace, peppercorns, bay leaf
Stock ¾ pint

Prepare the heart as directed. Fill the cavity with veal forcemeat, and keep in place by tying a piece of greased paper over the thick end.

Melt 2 oz. dripping and quickly brown the cut-up vegetables in it. Remove vegetables to a casserole, and fry the heart sufficiently to brown the outside; then place it on the vegetables in the casserole. Stir in the flour, and when brown, add the stock. Stir till boiling and season with salt and pepper. Tie the spices in muslin, put into the casserole, pour over the gravy, cover, and cook in a slow oven till the heart is tender – 1½–2 hours. Remove spices and paper from the heart, and cut it into portions before serving.

Roasted Calf's Heart

Prepare and stuff heart as for braising. Then wrap in greased paper and put in baking tin with melted dripping. Bake in a moderate oven about 1½ hours, basting at intervals, and remove paper the last 15 minutes.

Liver

Calf's liver is the best for frying. Lamb's liver is also soft and tender, but sheep and ox liver need slower and more careful cooking and are more suitable for stews and casseroles.

To Fry. Cut liver into thin slices and dip in seasoned flour. Melt a little dripping in a frying pan, and when hot add the liver and brown on both sides, then reduce heat and fry very gently till tender. Place the liver on a hot dish, pour off all but 2 tablespoonfuls of the fat, stir in 1 tablespoonful flour, and when lightly browned add ½ pint stock, bring to the boil, season, and strain over the liver.

Serve with fried onions or mushrooms and mashed potatoes.

Stewed Liver

Liver 1 lb.	*Apples ¼ lb.*
2 or 3 onions	*Potatoes ¼ lb.*
Stock or water 1 pint	*Flour 2 oz.*
Dripping 2 oz.	*Salt and pepper*

Cut the liver into small pieces and roll in seasoned flour.

Melt the dripping in a frying pan, put in the liver and sliced onions, and fry till brown; then lift out, sprinkle in remaining flour, and when this is brown gradually add the stock (or water) and stir till boiling. Season with salt and pepper.

Peel and cut up the potatoes and apples and put in a casserole with the liver and onions, pour over the gravy, cover the casserole, and cook in a moderate oven for 1½ hours.

Stewed Calves' Tongues

2 calves' tongues	*1 onion*
Tomato purée 1 tablespoonful	*Margarine 1 oz.*
Flour 1 oz.	*Bay leaf, peppercorns, salt*

Soak the tongues in cold water for 1 hour, then put in a saucepan and cover with boiling water. Add a few peppercorns, a bay leaf, 2 teaspoonfuls salt, and a cut-up onion. Cook gently till the tongues are tender – 2–2½ hours. Then remove from the liquor and skin them.

Melt the margarine in a saucepan, stir in the flour, and gradually add ¾ pint of the liquor in which the tongues were cooked and 1 tablespoonful concentrated tomato purée, stir till boiling, season with salt and pepper, lay in the tongues and simmer for 5 minutes. Serve with mashed potato and sieved spinach.

In place of concentrated tomato purée, fresh or tinned tomatoes can be used. Sieve sufficient to make ½ pint, add ¼ pint of the liquor in which the tongues were cooked, and make the sauce with this.

If liked, a little grated horseradish can be added to the sauce.

Calves' Tongues with Mushrooms and Savoury Balls

2 or 3 calves' tongues	*Mushrooms ¼ lb.*
1 onion	*Margarine 1½ oz.*
Flour 1¼ oz.	*Savoury balls*
Sherry 1 tablespoonful	*Seasoning*

Prepare and cook the tongues, as in previous recipe, till tender. Then trim the roots, skin them, and cut into slices.

Melt the margarine, stir in the flour smoothly, and gradually add 1 pint of the strained liquor in which the tongues were cooked. Stir till boiling, add a little browning and salt and pepper, if necessary, and a tablespoonful cooking sherry, and simmer for 5 minutes.

Put the slices of tongue in a casserole, add the mushrooms, peeled and sliced, and the savoury balls. Pour over the gravy, put the lid on the casserole, and cook in a moderate oven about 40 minutes.

For the Savoury Balls. Make veal forcemeat (see page 194), roll into small balls, flatten, and dip lightly in flour. Fry a golden brown on both sides, then drain and use as directed.

SWEETBREADS

To Prepare. Wash and soak in cold water for 1 hour. Then blanch them; that is, put in a saucepan, cover with cold water, bring slowly to the boil, simmer gently for 5 minutes, then drain and put in a basin of cold water. When cold trim off fat, skin, and gristle, and continue cooking as desired.

To Fry. After blanching and trimming, put in a saucepan, cover with well-seasoned stock, and simmer for ½ hour; then press between two plates till cold. Cut in slices, dip in beaten egg, coat with breadcrumbs, and fry a golden brown on both sides.

Serve garnished with green peas or macédoine of vegetables, and accompanied by mashed potatoes and either tomato sauce or thick brown gravy.

To Fricassée. Prepare and cook as for fried sweetbreads and cut into slices. For 2 sweetbreads allow 3 or 4 mushrooms, 1 oz. margarine, 1 oz. flour, ¾ pint veal stock, 1 lemon.

Skin and chop the mushrooms, cook them gently in the margarine for 5 minutes, then stir in the flour and gradually add the stock; add the grated rind of half the lemon and 1 teaspoonful of juice, and stir till boiling. Season with salt and pepper, put in the sliced sweetbread, and simmer gently for 10 minutes. Serve garnished with sliced lemon.

Sweetbread Flan. Turn the fricassée mixture into a cooked flan case and place on an upper shelf of a moderately hot oven until lightly browned.

Sweetbread Patties

Cooked sweetbread 8 oz.
Cooked tongue 2 oz.
White sauce ¼ pint
12 small vol-au-vent cases (page 248)

Mushrooms 2 oz.
¼ lemon
Margarine 1 oz.

Make a thick white sauce (see page 196), using chicken or veal stock for the liquid.

Cut the sweetbread into small pieces and chop the tongue.

Peel the mushrooms, remove the stalks (use these in soup or stew), and cut into small pieces. Put in a saucepan with the margarine and grated rind and juice of half a lemon, cover, and cook gently for 10 minutes; then add the sauce, sweetbread and tongue, and heat through very gently.

Warm the vol-au-vent cases in the oven, fill with the mixture, and put on the pastry lids.

Left-over Meat Dishes

Cottage Pie

Cooked meat $\frac{1}{2}$ *lb.*	*Potatoes* $1\frac{1}{2}$ *lb.*
Tongue, smoked beef or	*Thickened gravy*
sausage 2–3 oz.	*Margarine or dripping 1 oz.*
Small onion	*Salt and pepper*
A few sprigs parsley	

Trim off skin and gristle from the meat (put these in the stock pot). Add any oddments of salt or smoked beef, 2 or 3 cooked sausages, a small end of worsht, or root end of a tongue. Put these and the peeled onion and a few sprigs of parsley through the mincer. Season with salt and pepper and a little vegetable extract, and add sufficient gravy to make a moist, but not runny, mixture; then turn into a greased oven dish.

Boil potatoes and mash very smoothly with the margarine or dripping, season with salt and pepper. Spread evenly over the meat, slightly roughen with a fork, sprinkle with dried crumbs, dot with margarine, and bake in a moderately hot oven till hot through and nicely browned – about 1 hour.

Variations:

(1) Add 2 or 3 skinned and chopped tomatoes to the meat mixture.

(2) Mix the mashed potato with an equal quantity of cooked and mashed swede, parsnip, or turnip.

(3) Add a *grated* onion to the potato.

(4) Add $\frac{1}{2}$ lb. cut-up onions to the potatoes and boil together till soft, then drain (reserve water for soup) and mash thoroughly with salt, pepper, and margarine. Put half the

meat mixture in the dish, then a thin layer of potato and onion purée; add remaining meat, then cover with potato and onion, and finish off and bake as above.

Croquettes or Rissoles (1)

Cooked meat ¼ lb.   *Small onion*
A few sprigs parsley   *Binding sauce ¼ pint*
Seasoning   *Salt and pepper*
Egg or eggless batter   *Breadcrumbs*

Use any left-over meat available and put through the mincer with the onion and parsley; add the binding sauce (see page 214), season with salt and pepper and a grate of nutmeg and, if liked, a teaspoonful tomato ketchup or any savoury sauce. Spread on a plate and leave till cold. Then with floured hands roll into neat cork shapes or round flat cakes, dust lightly with flour, brush over with beaten egg, or eggless batter (see page 427), and coat with dry crumbs. Fry a golden brown in deep fat.

Rissoles. Roll out some short crust thinly and cut into rounds the size of the top of a tumbler, place a little of the cold mixture on one half of each round, moisten the edges with water, fold over the other half, press edges together, brush over with beaten egg, roll in crumbs or crushed vermicelli, and fry a golden brown in deep fat.

Croquettes (2)

Mix minced meat, onion, and parsley with an equal quantity of mashed potato. Season and shape, and finish as in previous recipe.

Curry Croquettes

Cold meat ¼ lb.   *Curry powder 2 teaspoonfuls*
Flour 1 oz.   *Cooked rice 1 breakfastcupful*
Stock ¼ pint   *Lemon juice 1 teaspoonful*
Small onion   *Breadcrumbs*
Dripping 1 oz.   *Salt and pepper*
1 egg

Mince the meat finely. Chop the onion quite small and fry in the dripping till lightly browned, then stir in the flour, and when this is brown add the curry powder and the stock. Stir till boiling and continue stirring while it simmers for 2 or 3 minutes. Add this thick binding sauce to the meat and rice, also the lemon juice and beaten yolk of egg. Mix thoroughly, season with salt and pepper if necessary. Leave till cold, then shape into neat even-sized croquettes. Brush over with slightly beaten white of egg, coat with dry breadcrumbs, and fry in smoking-hot deep fat till golden brown. Serve with chutney.

Note. If a mild curry flavour is preferred, use slightly less curry powder.

Devonshire Pasty

Cooked meat 10–12 oz.
Cooked potatoes ½ lb.
A small onion
Dripping 1 oz.
Gravy
Short crust ¾ lb.
Chopped apple 1 tablespoonful
Chopped parsley 1 tablespoonful
Salt and pepper

Chop the onion and fry in the dripping till golden brown. Remove all skin and gristle from the meat and cut it and the potatoes into dice.

Mix the meat, potatoes, onion, parsley, and apple together, season with salt and pepper, and moisten with a little thickened gravy. Roll out the pastry into two large rounds and line a round pie plate with one piece, put in the meat mixture, wet the edges, and cover with remaining pastry. Trim and crimp the edges, brush over with beaten egg, make a little cut in the centre for steam to escape, and bake 30–40 minutes. Start at 450°, Regulo No. 7, then after 15 minutes reduce to 400°, No. 5.

Meat and Apple Macaroni

Cooked macaroni 2 breakfastcupfuls
Minced cooked meat 4–6 oz.
Cooking apples ¾ lb.
Thick gravy ½ pint
Margarine ¼ oz.
Salt and pepper
Sugar
Brown crumbs

Mix the meat, macaroni, and gravy, season with salt and pepper and turn into a baking dish. Peel, core, and finely chop the apples and place on top. Sprinkle with sugar, then with brown crumbs, and dot with margarine. Bake in a moderate oven about 30–40 minutes.

Note. Spaghetti can be used in place of macaroni.

Meat Kedgeree

Cooked meat 6 oz.	*Margarine 2 oz.*
A small onion	*A hard-boiled egg*
Cooked rice 4 oz.	*Salt and pepper*
Chopped parsley	

Mince the meat and chop the onion finely, melt the margarine in a saucepan, and fry the onion till soft and lightly browned. Then add the cooked rice and meat, season with salt and pepper, and stir over a gentle heat till thoroughly hot. Mix in the chopped white of egg, and heap up in a hot dish. Garnish with sieved egg yolk and chopped parsley.

Note. Half a teaspoonful of curry powder can be added to the mixture.

Meat or Poultry in Aspic

(See page 223)

Meat Pie (1)

Meat mixture as for Cottage Pie	*Mashed potatoes*
(page 174)	*Worcester sauce*
Onions ¼ lb.	*Mixed herbs (optional)*
Tomatoes ½ lb.	*Salt and pepper*
Thickening gravy ¼ pint	

Boil the onions till tender, then drain (reserve water for stock) and chop. Skin and slice tomatoes.

Moisten the meat with the gravy, add a pinch of mixed herbs, if liked, and a teaspoonful or two of Worcester sauce. Add salt and pepper to taste and turn into a greased oven dish. Put the onion on top, season with salt and pepper, then the tomatoes and season these also. Cover with a good layer of mashed potato and slightly roughen with a fork. Bake in a moderate oven about 50 minutes.

Meat Pie (2)

Use meat mixture as for Cottage Pie (see page 174), and add 1 breakfastcupful mashed potato and a beaten egg, but only add 2 or 3 spoonfuls thickened gravy. Press into a greased baking dish and bake in a moderate oven 45 minutes. Serve with gravy.

This is good cold, cut in slices and served with salad.

Meat and Apple Pie

Put a layer of thinly sliced cooked meat in a pie dish, sprinkle it with grated onion, salt and pepper and cover with stewed apple. Repeat the layers, pour over a little thick gravy and cover with short crust.

Bake in a moderately hot oven for 40 minutes. Start at 450°, Regulo No. 7 and after 15 minutes reduce to 400°, Regulo No. 5.

Meat Pudding (1)

Cooked meat ¾ lb.	Shredded suet 2 oz.
1 hard-boiled egg	A small onion
1 raw egg	Breadcrumbs 2 oz.
Parsley	Stock 6 tablespoonfuls
Seasoning	Onion sauce

Put the meat, onion, and a few sprigs of parsley through the mincer. Moisten the crumbs with the boiling stock, then mix with the meat and shredded suet. Season with salt, pepper, and a little vegetable extract, and add the beaten egg.

Grease a pudding basin and line it with the hard-boiled egg, cut in slices, turn in the mixture, press down carefully, cover with a greased paper and then a pudding cloth, and steam for 1½ hours. Serve with onion sauce (see page 197).

Meat Pudding (2)

Left-over meat 6–8 oz.	Shredded suet 3 oz.
A small onion	Salt and pepper
Flour 8 oz.	

Any kind of meat can be used. Put it through the mincer with the onion. Put the flour and suet in a basin, add the meat and onion, season well with salt and pepper, and mix to a slack dough with cold water.

Put into a greased basin, cover, and steam about 2½ hours.

Serve with tomato, celery, or onion sauce, or a well-flavoured thick brown gravy.

Meat and Rice Mould

Rice ¼ lb.
Stock ½ pint
Dripping 1½ oz.
Flour 1½ oz.

Cooked meat 10–12 oz.
Tomato ketchup 1 tablespoonful
Chopped parsley 1 tablespoonful
Salt and pepper

Cook the rice in boiling salted water or stock till tender, then drain very thoroughly.

Melt the dripping (or margarine), stir in the flour smoothly, then gradually add the stock and stir till boiling. Add the tomato ketchup, season with salt and pepper, and simmer for 2 or 3 minutes. Cut the meat into dice, add to the thick sauce, together with the parsley.

Line a greased deep oven dish, bottom and sides, with rice, pour in the meat and sauce, and cover with rice. Bake in a moderate oven till hot through – about 30 minutes.

A little fried onion can be added to the rice for a change.

Meat Roll (1)

Mince finely about ¾ lb. cooked meat, having if possible about a third of it salt or smoked beef or sausages. Add 1 teacupful mashed potato, 1 tablespoonful chopped parsley, and season with salt, pepper, and any kind of savoury sauce or vegetable extract; add a well-beaten egg and mix thoroughly. If at all dry, add a spoonful or two thickened gravy.

Form into a roll, dust with flour. Put into a baking tin with 2 or 3 oz. hot dripping, and bake in a moderate oven about 40 minutes. Put on to a hot dish and pour either tomato sauce or thick gravy around.

Meat Roll (2)

Roll out short crust thinly and spread with the meat filling as for Cottage Pie (see page 174), leaving 1 inch of the pastry free all round. Damp the edges and roll up. Brush over with beaten egg, place on a baking sheet, and bake about 40 minutes. Start at 450°, Regulo No. 7, and after it is lightly browned reduce the heat.

Mince

Underdone meat ½ lb.	*Stock or gravy ¼ pint*
Margarine ¼ oz.	*Chopped parsley*
Flour ¼ oz.	*Salt and pepper*
A small onion	*Toast*
Vegetable extract or savoury sauce	

Mince the meat. Chop the onion very finely, then fry a golden brown in the margarine (or dripping), stir in the flour and when this is brown, gradually add the stock; stir till boiling, season with salt and pepper and flavour with a teaspoonful vegetable extract or mushroom ketchup. Simmer 2 or 3 minutes, then put in the minced meat, mix thoroughly and leave the pan where the contents will keep hot *without boiling* for 10–15 minutes.

Turn into a hot dish, sprinkle with parsley and garnish with triangles of toast. This is also good with a border of macaroni or spaghetti.

Meat Toasts. The same mixture can be served on rounds of toast, and for a really substantial dish put a neatly poached egg on top of each.

Curried Mutton

Cold mutton ¾–1 lb.	*Rice*
Curry powder 1 dessertspoonful	*Dripping 1½ oz.*
An apple	*Sultanas 1 oz.*
Flour 1½ oz.	*Small onion*
Lemon juice 2 teaspoonfuls	*Stock ¾ pint*
Chutney 2 teaspoonfuls	*Seasoning*

Melt the dripping in a saucepan, add the finely chopped onion and fry a golden brown, stir in flour and curry powder, cook for 2 or 3 minutes, then gradually add the stock, stir till boiling, add the finely chopped apple, sultanas, chutney, and lemon juice, and mix together. Cut the meat into cubes, mix with the sauce, cover, then bring very slowly to the boil and simmer *very gently* for 30 minutes. Serve with chutney and boiled rice (see page 136).

Stuffed Cabbage Leaves and Apples

Cooked meat 6–8 oz.
2 tomatoes
Stock ¼ pint
Juice of ¼ lemon
Tomato purée 2 tablespoonfuls

Cabbage leaves
1 large cooking apple
1 small onion
Worcester sauce
Salt and pepper

Mince the meat, skin and chop the tomatoes, mix together, add a little Worcester sauce, and season with salt and pepper.

Pour boiling water over the cabbage leaves, let stand for 5 minutes, then drain. Put a spoonful of the meat mixture in the centre of each, and fold over into parcels. Put in a casserole with thin slices of peeled apple in between, and sprinkle with finely chopped onion. Add the lemon juice and tomato purée to the stock, bring to the boil, pour into the casserole, cover and cook in a moderate oven about 40 minutes.

Stuffed Tomatoes

6 tomatoes
Cooked meat, minced, 6 piled tablespoonfuls
Chopped parsley 1 tablespoonful
Breadcrumbs

Fried bread
Grated onion
Salt and pepper

Choose large, firm tomatoes, cut a slice off each (these can be used in soup or stew) and scoop out the centre, taking care to keep the case intact. Chop up the pulp that has been removed and add it to the minced meat, together with the chopped parsley and a teaspoonful grated onion, salt and pepper.

Fill the tomato cases with the mixture, heaping it up slightly. Sprinkle with browned crumbs, place on a greased baking dish and bake in a moderate oven 25–30 minutes. Serve each on a round of fried bread.

Veal Soufflé

Minced veal 6 oz.
Flour 1 oz.
2 eggs
Seasoning

Margarine 1 oz.
White stock ¼ pint
Chopped parsley 2 teaspoonfuls

Remove all skin and gristle from the meat and put it twice through the mincing machine.

Melt the margarine in a small saucepan, stir in the flour smoothly, then add the stock gradually and stir till boiling; simmer for 2 or 3 minutes, then remove from the heat.

Separate the yolks and whites of the eggs and beat yolks one at a time into the sauce; then add the veal and parsley, and season with salt and pepper and, if liked, a little grated lemon rind.

Whisk the egg whites till quite stiff and fold them lightly into the meat mixture. Turn into a prepared soufflé dish (see page 273) and bake in a moderately hot oven (about 400°, Regulo No. 5) for 30 minutes.

Chicken Soufflé. Make as above, using chicken instead of veal.

Poultry

TO PLUCK A BIRD

Hold the bird in the left hand, breast downwards, grasp the wing farthest away from you where it joins the body, and begin by plucking off the feathers from under the wing, after which proceed with the body, taking care not to tear the skin. Then singe it.

TO SINGE A BIRD

Hold the bird by the neck with the left hand and move a lighted paper quickly all over the bird, so as to singe off any coarse hairs. Be careful when singeing not to scorch.

TO DRAW A BIRD

Cut off the head, slip the skin back from the neck, and cut off the neck close to the body, leaving a flap of skin to fold over the back. Remove the windpipe and the crop, which is a little bag of skin lying close to the neck. Insert the first finger inside the neck and loosen all the inside, breaking the ligaments that can be felt with the finger. Turn the bird round and make a deep cut across the body, between the tail and the vent, and cut out the vent, making an opening large enough for you to insert your fingers and enable you to pull out the whole of the bird's inside in one motion. Take great care that you do not break the gall bladder.

Remove the oil bag from the back of the 'parson's nose'.

Cut open the gizzard and remove the bag of stones, and also the gall bladder from the liver.

TO TRUSS A FOWL FOR ROASTING

Cut through the skin 2 inches below the leg joint, bend the leg at the cut and crack the bone, then pull out the tendons, twisting the legs to enable them to be drawn out easily. There should be seven sinews. Care must be taken not to cut through these when cutting the skin, or they cannot be removed.

Run a trussing needle and string through the centre of the two leg joints, then turn the bird on its breast, carry the string in a slanting direction between the two centre bones of the wing and catching the underneath part of the pinion. Then draw the string over the bird through the pinion and wing at the other side, where it will meet the other end of the string. Tie ends together. Now place the bird breast downwards and, holding it in the left hand, run the needle and string through the back beside the thigh bones. Now pull the legs straight out, turn the bird on its back, and carry the string over the leg, then through the breast, over the other leg, and tie the legs together.

TO TRUSS A GOOSE OR DUCK

Geese and ducks are prepared, drawn, and trussed in the same way as fowls, except that the wings or pinions are cut off at the first joint.

The feet of a goose are nearly always removed, but those of a duck are generally left on, but should be scalded and peeled. Put a folded cloth over the breast bone and flatten it with a rolling pin.

Then proceed as for a fowl, except that the wings are not crossed over at the back, and the legs are tied down close by the side of the body.

TO PREPARE GIBLETS

Remove the oil bag from the back of the 'parson's nose' and the gall bladder from the liver, taking care not to break it; if any part of the liver looks green, cut it away. Cut off the fat and membrane from the gizzard, then cut it through and remove the inner sac. The feet and neck are included in the giblets. Scald the feet in boiling water for 10 minutes, then remove the skin. Cut the neck at the joints in two or three pieces, and wash very thoroughly. The giblets can be used for gravy or soup, or turned into a pie, or served as a stew.

TIME-TABLE FOR ROASTING POULTRY

Chicken	45–60 minutes
Chicken if very large	$1\frac{1}{4}$–$1\frac{1}{2}$ hours
Duckling	25–45 minutes
Duck	1–$1\frac{1}{2}$ hours
Goose	$1\frac{1}{2}$–2 hours
Gosling	1–$1\frac{1}{2}$ hours
Turkey (small)	2–$2\frac{1}{2}$ hours
Turkey, 10 lb. or over	3–$3\frac{1}{2}$ hours

USUAL ACCOMPANIMENTS TO SERVE WITH POULTRY

Chicken or Fowl (roast). Bread sauce and brown gravy. Garnish with watercress. Potato crisps or straws, roast or new potatoes.

Chicken or Fowl (boiled). White, or egg and lemon sauce. Smoked beef or tongue.

Roast Duck. Apple sauce, brown gravy. Orange salad, green peas.

Roast Goose. Apple or gooseberry sauce, brown gravy.

Turkey (roast). Grilled or fried sausages, cranberry sauce, and bread sauce. Thickened gravy.

Turkey (boiled). Celery sauce, boiled tongue.

Boiled Chicken (Fowl)

1 boiling fowl	*1 onion and 2 cloves*
Lemon	*A few peppercorns*
Blade of mace	*Salt*

Have the fowl trussed for boiling. Rub the breast of the bird with a cut lemon, place in a saucepan just large enough to hold it, and cover with boiling water. Add salt to taste, peppercorns and mace. Bring to the boil, boil for 5 minutes, add the onion stuck with cloves, reduce heat, and simmer very gently till the bird is tender.

Time required will depend on the weight and age of the bird. A small, young bird may take only 1½ hours, but an old boiling fowl anything up to 4 hours.

To Dish. Remove trussing skewers and string, place the bird on a hot dish, coat with parsley, celery, or egg and lemon sauce, and serve more sauce separately.

To Use Left-over Boiled Chicken

Boiled chicken is excellent eaten cold with smoked tongue, or turned into chicken mayonnaise and garnished with cooked vegetables, or peas in tomato cups.

Put the chicken back into the chicken broth until it is cold; it will then remain quite moist.

It can also be used in patties (see page 331), curried (see Curried Mutton, pages 180–81), or it can be cut into neat pieces and warmed gently through in parsley, celery, or egg and lemon sauce, and garnished with forcemeat balls (see page 195).

See also following recipes.

Chicken in Aspic

(See page 223)

Chicken Croquettes

Cooked chicken ¼ lb.	*Chicken fat 1 oz.*
Chicken broth ¼ pint	*Flour 1 oz.*
Lemon juice 1 teaspoonful	*1 egg*
Salt and pepper	*Breadcrumbs*

Mince the chicken finely. Melt the fat in a small saucepan, stir in the flour smoothly, then gradually add the chicken broth and stir over a gentle heat till quite thick. Remove from heat, add the minced chicken, lemon juice, and yolk of the egg, season with salt and pepper, and mix thoroughly. Spread on a dish and leave till cold. Then, with lightly floured hands, form into cork-shaped croquettes, brush over with beaten white of egg, and coat with fine white breadcrumbs. Fry in a frying basket in deep hot fat till a golden brown. Serve with mashed potatoes and green peas.

Chicken Fricassée

Cooked chicken ¼ lb.	*Mushrooms 2 oz.*
Chicken broth ¼ pint	*Margarine 1 oz.*
Smoked tongue 2 oz.	*Flour 1 oz.*
Lemon juice 1 tablespoonful	*Chopped parsley*
Toast for garnish	*Salt and pepper*

Cut the chicken and tongue into small dice. Skin and chop mushrooms and sauté in the margarine for 5 minutes, then stir in the flour and gradually add the broth. Stir till boiling, then add the lemon juice, chicken, tongue and a little chopped parsley. Season with salt and pepper and simmer very gently for 10 minutes. Turn into a hot dish and garnish with triangles of thin toast.

Chicken Risotto

Remains of cold chicken	*Rice 6 oz.*
Chicken broth 1½ pints	*Tomato purée ¼ pint*
Chicken fat 2 oz.	*1 onion*
A few mushrooms	*Salt, pepper, mace*

Remove the bones from the chicken and cut it into dice.

Peel and slice onion and mushrooms, and fry in the hot fat for 5 minutes. Pour over the chicken broth, bring to the boil, season with salt, pepper, and a pinch of mace, and add the washed rice.

Cover the saucepan and cook gently until the rice is tender and the stock absorbed – about ½ hour. Do not stir the rice while cooking, shake the saucepan occasionally and fork it gently once or twice. Add the heated tomato purée and the chicken, and stir for a few minutes till the chicken is hot through.

Fried Chicken

Choose a small, young bird and cut into convenient pieces for serving. Dip in seasoned flour. Heat some dripping in a frying pan, brown the joints quickly all over, then lower the heat, cover the pan with a plate or saucepan lid, and cook gently till tender, turning at intervals. It should take about 20 minutes to cook.

Chicken Maryland

Cut a young chicken into joints, dip in seasoned flour, brush over with beaten egg, and coat with breadcrumbs. Place in a well-greased baking tin, and bake for 5 minutes in a hot oven, then baste with melted chicken fat, and return to oven. Baste frequently till the bird has been cooking ½ hour. Reduce heat after it has been cooking for 15 minutes.

Chicken Pie

Cut a chicken into convenient-sized pieces for serving, put into a saucepan, cover with boiling water, season with salt and pepper, and simmer gently till tender, adding a cut-up carrot and onion and 2 or 3 sticks of celery after it has been cooking for 15 minutes.

When tender remove the bones from the joints and place the chicken in a large pie-dish.

Melt 2 oz. chicken fat, add 2 oz. sliced mushrooms, and sauté for 5 minutes, then stir in 2 oz. flour, and gradually add 1 pint chicken stock. Stir till boiling, season with salt and pepper, and pour over the chicken. Leave till quite cold, then cover with pastry and bake as for steak pie, page 151.

Roast Chicken

Clean and season chicken. If to be stuffed, fill the crop end with veal stuffing (see page 194); if two kinds are to be used, put sausage meat in the crop end and fill the body with veal stuffing. Put into a baking tin containing hot fat, cover the breast with greased paper, and bake in a moderately hot oven about 1 hour, basting once or twice and removing the paper the last 15 minutes.

Remove skewers, put the chicken on a hot dish, and garnish with watercress.

Serve with bread sauce and thickened gravy.

Bake first 15 minutes at 450°, Regulo No. 7, then reduce the heat.

To Roast an Old Bird

A fowl that is no longer young should eat as tender as chicken if cooked in the following manner.

Wrap the cleaned and trussed bird in greaseproof paper, put into boiling, salted water, and simmer very slowly for $1\frac{1}{2}$ hours, or a little longer for a large bird. Leave till cold, then stuff with veal stuffing.

Melt some dripping in the meat tin, and when the fat is really hot put in the bird. If available, cover the breast with a slice or two fat smoked beef, and roast the bird slowly for $1\frac{1}{2}$ hours, keeping it well basted. If smoked beef has been used, remove it the last 15 minutes.

Fowl in Rice Border

This is a suitable way to serve an old bird.

Prepare the fowl and put it into boiling stock or salted water. (Liquor from boiled salt beef or tongue is very good to use for this.) Add an onion and a bouquet garni, and simmer very gently till tender – $2\frac{1}{2}$–$3\frac{1}{2}$ hours, according to the age of the bird.

When the bird is nearly tender, take 1 pint of liquid from the saucepan, bring it to the boil, and sprinkle in $\frac{1}{2}$ lb. rice. Simmer gently for $\frac{1}{2}$ hour, adding more liquid as the rice swells. Put the rice into a greased ring mould and leave in a warm place for 10 minutes.

Carve the chicken, turn the rice out on to a hot dish, put the chicken in the centre, and coat with egg and lemon or tomato sauce.

Chicken en Casserole
(See pages 311–12)

Pilaff of Chicken Livers (2)

Chicken livers ¼ lb.	*Cooked rice ¼ lb.*
Mushrooms 2 oz.	*Chicken fat 2 oz.*
Small onion	*Tomato sauce*
Green peas 1 cupful	*Salt and pepper*
Tomato purée 2 tablespoonfuls	

Prepare the mushrooms and livers, cut them into small pieces, chop onion finely.

Melt the fat in a small saucepan, put in the mushrooms, liver, and onion, cover the pan, and cook over a gentle heat for 15 minutes. Then add the contents of the saucepan to the rice, together with the cooked green peas and the tomato purée. (If more convenient, in place of tomato purée add 2 skinned and sliced tomatoes and 2 tablespoonfuls stock.) Mix thoroughly, turn into a greased basin, cover with a greased paper, and steam for 45 minutes. (See also page 121).

Stuffed Necks
(Gefillte Helzel)

Remove the skin from the neck of the chicken (or goose). Tie up one end, fill with the stuffing, and sew up the other end securely. Put in a small baking dish with a sliced onion and a little water, and bake in a moderate oven till crisp and brown — ¾ to 1 hour, basting occasionally.

Or it can be cooked in the tin with the chicken.

For the Stuffing:

(1) Use veal forcemeat (see page 194), adding the finely chopped heart and liver of the bird.

(2) Chop finely a little of the raw fat from the chicken (or goose). To each tablespoonful of fat add 3 tablespoonfuls flour and 1 teaspoonful finely grated onion. Season with salt and pepper, and mix thoroughly.

Giblet Pie

1 set turkey or 2 sets chicken giblets	Flaky pastry
	Stock
Steak ¾ lb.	Flour
1 onion	Seasoning

Prepare the giblets (see page 184) and wash thoroughly. Cut up the steak into small pieces. Sprinkle the giblets and steak with well-seasoned flour and put into a casserole with the finely chopped onion. Cover with stock or water, adding more salt and pepper if necessary. Put the lid on the casserole and cook in a slow oven till tender – 2–3 hours.

Put the steak and giblets into a pie dish with a little of the gravy and leave till cold. There should be enough to fill the dish. Roll out pastry and cover the pie (see page 251). Decorate with leaves of pastry, brush over with beaten egg. Make a little hole each end for steam to escape and bake as for steak pie, page 151.

Roast Duck

Have the duck trussed for roasting and fill the body with sage and onion stuffing (see page 194). Ducks are never stuffed at the crop end like chicken and turkey.

Season with salt and pepper, put in a baking tin, cover the breast with greaseproof paper, and pour over ½ pint melted dripping. Bake in a hot oven 450° (Regulo No. 7) for the first 15 minutes; then finish in a cooler oven. It will take 1–1½ hours, according to size. Remove paper 10 minutes before the bird is done.

Serve with apple sauce, green peas, and thickened gravy.

Ducklings will take only ¾–1 hour to cook.

Apples stuffed with Sage and Onions can be served in place of apple sauce. Choose even-sized cooking apples, not too large. Peel and core them, leaving the fruit whole, and remove sufficient pulp from the centre to form a good-sized cavity. Fill up with sage and onion stuffing (see page 194), place on a baking dish, and bake till the apples are just tender, but not broken – about 45 minutes.

Casserole of Duck
(See page 312)

Roast Goose

Prepare and stuff with sage and onions like roast duck.

Season with salt and pepper. Put the pieces of fat from the inside of the bird over the breast, then cover with greaseproof paper.

Put in the baking tin, pour over ½ pint hot dripping. Cook in a hot oven for the first 15 minutes, then lower the heat and cook till done, basting from time to time. A 10-lb. bird will take about 2 hours. Uncover the breast the last 15 minutes.

Dish on to a hot dish and serve with apple sauce and thickened gravy to which a few drops of lemon juice have been added.

Apple Rings. The bird can be garnished with apple rings, which can be served in place of or in addition to the apple sauce. For these choose good-sized cooking apples, peel, core, and slice them thickly. Using some of the fat from the goose, fry them on both sides till lightly browned.

Savoury Goose Pie

Put a layer of sliced cold goose in a pie dish, spread with apple sauce and add another layer of goose, then cover with cold goose stuffing. Season with salt and pepper and pour over 3 or 4 tablespoonfuls of red wine or thick gravy, cover this with flaky pastry and then brush over with beaten egg.

Bake until the pastry is cooked – about 30 minutes. Start in a hot oven 475° (Regulo No. 8) and when lightly browned reduce to moderate.

Boiled Turkey

This is quite a good way to cook a small bird.

Stuff with sausage meat and rub over with lemon juice.

Put into a saucepan of boiling salted water, add some cut-up vegetables – 2 carrots, a turnip, 2 onions, and a few sticks of celery – then cook slowly till the bird is tender. A 10-lb. bird takes about 2½ hours.

Serve masked with celery, egg, or parsley sauce and garnish with sausage balls. Hand more sauce separately. A boiled tongue is the usual accompaniment.

Roast Turkey

Prepare and dress like a chicken. Both breast and body can be stuffed – sausage meat one end and chestnut or veal stuffing the other (see pages 193–4).

Fill the crop end with sausage meat (about 1½ lb. for a 12-lb. bird), draw the flap over and secure firmly. Fill the body with the other stuffing and brush the bird all over with melted fat. Then either wrap the bird in two layers of greaseproof paper or in one layer of aluminium foil and place on a rack in a roasting tin.

Start cooking at 450°, Regulo No. 7, and after 10 minutes reduce to 375°, Regulo No. 4. Allow 15 minutes per lb. for a bird under 12 lb. and 12 minutes per lb. for a bird over 12 lb.

About ½ hour before the cooking time is complete, open the wrapping, so that the skin becomes brown and crisp.

If the bird is too large for the roasting tin, after wrapping it can be cooked directly on the grid shelf. Place the bird on its side with the greatest length crossways on the shelf. The bird must not overhang the shelf at the back of the oven. Half-way through the cooking turn the bird over on the other side.

Serve with bread sauce, brown gravy and cranberry sauce.

To Use Left-over Turkey

Use for any of the dishes suggested for cooked chicken. The carcass broken up will make excellent soup – see section on Soup Stock.

Savoury Stuffings for Meat and Poultry

Apple Stuffing

Sour cooking apples 1½ lb. *Margarine 1 oz.*
Rice 4 oz. *Yolk of an egg*
Sugar 1 oz. *Seasoning*

Peel, core, and slice apples and put them in a stewpan with the margarine and just sufficient water to prevent them burning, and stew till soft. Boil the rice till tender, then drain. Mix all ingredients and season with salt and pepper.

Use for roast goose.

Celery Stuffing

Breadcrumbs 6 oz. *1 egg*
¼ lemon *Shredded suet 2 oz.*
Chopped celery *Chopped parsley 2 teaspoonfuls*
*   1 breakfastcupful* *Grated onion 2 teaspoonfuls*
Salt and pepper

Cook celery till tender, then chop finely. Mix all ingredients, using a little celery water to moisten, and the grated rind as well as the juice of the lemon.

Use for boiled turkey.

Chestnut Stuffing

Chestnuts 1 lb. *Margarine 2 oz.*
Sausage meat ½ lb. *Breadcrumbs 3 oz.*
Stock *Salt and pepper*

After removing shells and inner skins (see page 93), put the chestnuts in a saucepan with sufficient stock to cover and boil till quite soft. Drain and rub through a sieve; add the melted margarine, breadcrumbs and sausage meat, season with salt and pepper and mix thoroughly.

Use for roast turkey.

Note. The sausage meat can be omitted and an egg added to bind the mixture.

Mushroom Forcemeat

Mushrooms 4 oz.	*1 egg*
Breadcrumbs 4 oz.	*Chicken fat or margarine 2 oz.*
Grated lemon rind ½ teaspoonful	*Chopped parsley 1 teaspoonful*
Salt and cayenne	

Wash, peel, and chop the mushrooms. Melt the chicken fat or margarine in a small saucepan, add the mushrooms. Cover and cook gently for 10 minutes. Then add to remaining ingredients and mix thoroughly.

Use for stuffing boiled or roast chicken or turkey.

Sage and Onion Stuffing

Onions 1 lb.	*Breadcrumbs 4 oz.*
10 sage leaves	*Salt and pepper*

Choose large onions, peel them, cut into quarters, and boil till just tender; then strain and chop finely.

While the onions are cooking remove stalks from sage leaves, pour boiling water over the leaves, let them stand for 5 minutes, then dry and chop finely.

If dried sage leaves are used, crush finely and use 1–1½ teaspoonfuls.

Mix all ingredients, season with salt and pepper.

Use for stuffing geese and ducks. If for stuffing a goose, a small portion of the liver, simmered for a few minutes and then finely minced, can be added.

Veal Forcemeat

Fresh breadcrumbs 4 oz.	*½ lemon*
Chopped parsley 2 teaspoonfuls	*Shredded suet 2 oz.*
Grated onion 2 teaspoonfuls	*1 egg*
Salt and pepper	

Mix all ingredients together, using the grated rind and juice of the lemon. If the mixture is at all dry add a little water, or use two eggs instead of one.

Forcemeat Balls

Make a mixture as for veal forcemeat, and with floured hands roll into small balls. Leave round or flatten slightly. Roll in flour and fry a golden brown on both sides.

Use in stews, casseroles, etc. (see recipes in these sections), or as a garnish around veal or chicken.

Sauces

No matter how good a dish may be, unless the sauce or gravy is well made the course will be spoilt. Therefore, every good cook must consider this branch of cookery as one of the most important. A good sauce will turn even the most homely fare into something really appetizing. When a sauce is required for coating, it must be thick enough to adhere to the back of a spoon; if required for pouring round a dish, it should be thin enough to flow without being lumpy.

Hot sauces must be served really hot, and cold sauces very cold.

If the sauce needs to be kept hot some time before using, place the saucepan in which it was made in another containing boiling water, and stand over a very gentle heat.

Always use a *wooden* spoon and a really thick saucepan. If the sauce is not perfectly smooth, put it through a strainer.

Sauces must be slowly and thoroughly cooked, and should simmer for 3 or 4 minutes after they have reached boiling point.

Thickening for Sauces

The basis of most sauces is butter (chicken fat, or margarine) and flour cooked together, which makes a thickening. It is important that these should be cooked for a minute or two, before adding the liquid. The pan should be removed from the heat before the liquid is added.

The liquid can be milk, milk and water, or the stock of fish, meat, or vegetables.

Sauces can also be thickened with arrowroot, cornflour, potato flour, or rice flour mixed smoothly with a little cold liquid. It is then added to the boiling liquid and simmered gently 5–10 minutes.

Or the sauce can be thickened with egg yolks. Never *boil* the sauce after adding egg yolks, or it will curdle. See detailed recipes in this section.

For a **Coating Sauce** allow 1 oz. fat and 1 oz. flour to ½ pint liquid.

For a **Pouring Sauce** to be poured round the food to be served, allow 1 oz. fat and 1 oz. flour to ¾–1 pint liquid.

For a **Thick Binding Sauce**, used when making rissoles, egg cutlets, etc., allow 1 oz. fat and 1 oz. flour to ¼ pint liquid.

SAVOURY SAUCES

White Foundation Sauce (1)

Butter (or chicken fat or margarine) 1 oz.	*White pepper*
Flour 1 oz.	*Salt*
Milk or white stock ¼ pint	*Lemon juice*

Melt the fat in a small thick saucepan. Add the flour and mix well together. Cook over a very gentle heat for a minute or two without browning. Remove the pan from the fire, pour in the liquid gradually, then stir over a gentle heat till it boils; add salt and pepper to taste, and simmer for 5 minutes. Add a squeeze of lemon juice when the sauce is off the fire. By adding distinctive flavourings to the above foundation sauce, many different sauces can be made.

For a meat meal, chicken fat or margarine and white stock will be used, instead of butter and milk.

Anchovy Sauce. Use half fish stock and half milk in making the sauce, and add 2 teaspoonfuls of anchovy essence.

Caper Sauce. Use fish stock or meat liquor, and add 1 tablespoonful chopped capers and 2 tablespoonfuls vinegar.

Cheese Sauce. Add 2 tablespoonfuls of grated cheese and a little made mustard.

Egg Sauce. Add 1 or 2 finely-chopped hard-boiled eggs to ½ pint sauce.

Fennel Sauce. Boil some fennel till tender, add 1 tablespoonful finely chopped to ½ pint sauce. Serve with mackerel.

Mustard Sauce. Add 2 teaspoonfuls dry mustard to the flour before blending with the fat, and before serving stir in 1 tablespoonful vinegar.

Onion Sauce. Cook two large Spanish onions till soft, then chop finely. Use ¼ pint of the onion water with ¼ pint of stock or milk to make the sauce, and add the chopped onion.

Parsley Sauce. Add 1 tablespoonful finely chopped parsley.

Piccalilli Sauce. Add 1 tablespoonful finely chopped piccalilli to ½ pint sauce. Serve with herrings, mackerel, or white fish.

Watercress Sauce. Add 2 tablespoonfuls chopped watercress to ½ pint sauce and use for coating vegetables or fish.

White Foundation Sauce (2)

Using ingredients as in recipe (1) above, mix the flour to a smooth paste with some of the liquid, heat the remainder with the butter or margarine, and stir on to the flour mixture. Return to the pan and stir till boiling, then simmer very gently for 4 or 5 minutes.

It is better to make the sauce by this method if using a smaller proportion of fat, and when it is necessary to economize with fat it can be made without adding any at all.

If using cornflour or arrowroot instead of ordinary flour, 1–2 teaspoonfuls, according to the thickness required, will be sufficient.

Gravy

After removing the joint from the roasting tin, pour off the fat, leaving just 1 tablespoonful and the meat essence from the joint. Add to this 1 dessertspoonful of flour and stir over a gentle heat till brown, then gradually add ½ pint stock or water (with a little vegetable extract added), stir till boiling and simmer for 3 minutes. If necessary, add a few drops of gravy browning, and strain into the gravy boat.

If a thin gravy is preferred, pour off all the fat and add

stock or water to essence in the tin, and finish off as above.

When gravy is required for grilled meat, etc., make like Quickly-made Brown Sauce (see page 199).

Seasoning for Gravies

For made-up dishes, gravies should be more highly seasoned, and for this purpose a small quantity of any of the following can be added: tomato, walnut, or mushroom ketchup, Yorkshire relish, vegetable extract, onion juice, garlic, celery salt.

Apple Sauce

Cooking apples 1 lb.   *Water ¼ teacup*
Margarine ½ oz.   *Sugar 1½ oz.*

Peel, core, and slice the apples and cook them with the sugar and water till tender. The amount of water and sugar required will vary according to the kind of apples used, but the sauce should be a little tart.

When tender, mash the apples to a pulp (or rub through a sieve) and add the margarine. Serve with duck or goose.

Bread Sauce

Chicken or mutton broth ½ pint   *1 onion*
Breadcrumbs 2 oz.   *2 cloves*
Salt, cayenne, mace   *Margarine 1 oz.*

Peel the onion and stick the cloves into it, put it in a saucepan with the broth, bring slowly to the boil, cover, and stand over a very gentle heat, till the broth is well flavoured; then remove the onion, add the breadcrumbs, season with salt, cayenne, and a pinch of mace, cook very gently till the breadcrumbs swell – about 15 minutes – stir in the margarine, and turn into a hot tureen.

Note. This sauce thickens with standing. If it becomes too thick, add a little more broth.

Brown Sauce

Brown stock ¾ pint	*2 sticks of celery*
A small onion	*A small carrot*
Margarine or dripping 1 oz.	*Sprig of parsley*
Flour 1 oz.	*Half a bay leaf*
A blade of mace	*Salt*
A few peppercorns	

Melt the fat, add the sliced onion, and fry a golden brown; then stir in flour smoothly and when this is brown also, remove from the heat and add the stock gradually. Return to the fire and stir till boiling; then add the cut-up vegetables, herbs, and seasoning. Cover and simmer gently about ¾ hour, then strain and reheat before serving.

For a Quickly-made Simple Brown Sauce. Melt 1 oz. fat and stir in 1 oz. flour, and cook over a gentle heat till brown. Then gradually add ½ pint stock and stir till boiling, season, and simmer for 5 minutes before serving. For a piquant flavour add a little mushroom ketchup, Worcester or tomato sauce.

Celery Sauce (1)

Outside sticks of 2 heads of celery	*Margarine 1 oz.*
1 small onion	*Flour 1 oz.*
Chicken broth or any kind of white stock ¾ pint	

Prepare celery and onion, cut into small pieces, and cook in the stock till tender – 30–40 minutes; then rub through a sieve. Melt the margarine, stir in the flour smoothly, cook for a minute or two, then gradually add the celery purée. Stir till boiling, season to taste, and simmer for 5 minutes.

Serve with boiled chicken or mutton.

Celery Sauce (2)

Make ½ pint white foundation sauce, and when boiling, add 1 teacupful *finely shredded* heart of celery and 1 tablespoonful of the green leaves finely chopped. Stir whilst simmering for 2 or 3 minutes and serve with boiled or baked fish. The crisp raw celery makes a change served in this way.

Chestnut Sauce

2 dozen chestnuts *Sherry 2 tablespoonfuls*
Brown gravy ¼ pint

Boil the chestnuts till soft, then remove the skins and rub through a sieve. Add them to the gravy and reheat. Remove from the stove, stir in the sherry. Serve with roast turkey.

Cranberry Sauce

Cranberries 1 lb. *Brown sugar 3 oz.*
Water ¼ pint

Pick and wash the fruit, put in a saucepan, bruise well with the back of a wooden spoon, add the water, and stew till soft. Rub through a sieve, add the sugar, and reheat.

Curry Sauce

Curry powder 2–3 teaspoonfuls *A small apple*
Lemon juice 1 teaspoonful *A small onion*
Flour 3 teaspoonfuls *Margarine 1 oz.*
Chutney 1 teaspoonful *Stock ¼ pint*
Salt

Chop apple and onion finely and fry in the margarine (or dripping) till lightly browned; then stir in the flour and curry powder and cook a minute or two longer. Then gradually add the stock and stir till boiling, add the chutney, lemon juice, and salt to taste, cover, and simmer gently for 20 minutes.

Dutch Sauce (1)
(Hollandaise)

Butter or margarine 1 oz. *Flour ¼ oz.*
Lemon juice 1 tablespoonful *2 egg yolks*
Fish or vegetable stock ¼ pint *Salt and pepper*

Melt half the butter in a small saucepan, stir in the flour smoothly, cook for a minute or two, then add the stock, stir till boiling and simmer for 2 or 3 minutes. Remove from the heat and cool. Beat up the egg yolks with 1 tablespoonful cold water and beat into the sauce. Put into a double saucepan and stir over a gentle heat till it thickens. It must not boil or it will curdle. Add the lemon juice and the remaining butter bit by bit, and put through a fine strainer.

Dutch Sauce (2)
(Hollandaise)

Yolk of 2 eggs	*Butter 2 oz.*
Lemon juice 1 tablespoonful	*Salt, pepper*

Put the egg yolks in a *double* saucepan, add the butter bit by bit, and whisk over a gentle heat till it thickens. Then season with salt and pepper, add the lemon juice and strain.

Egg and Lemon Sauce
(For Boiled Chicken)

Rind and juice of 2 lemons	*Chicken broth $\frac{3}{4}$ pint*
Cornflour 1 dessertspoonful	*Yolks of 2 eggs*
Salt and pepper	

Grate the rind of the lemons, add it to the chicken broth and bring to the boil. Mix the cornflour smoothly with the lemon juice, add to the hot broth and stir till boiling; then simmer for 5 minutes. Remove from the heat and cool. Then pour on to the beaten egg yolks, turn into a double saucepan and stir till it thickens, but do not reboil. Season with salt and pepper.

Gooseberry Sauce

Green gooseberries $\frac{1}{2}$ lb.	*Water $\frac{1}{4}$ pint*
Margarine 1 oz.	*Sugar 1 oz.*

Stew gooseberries in the water till soft, then rub through a sieve. Return to the saucepan, add sugar and margarine and reheat.

Serve with boiled mackerel or roast mutton, goose, or duck.

Glaze

Take 2 pints of bone stock and boil gently till reduced to $\frac{1}{4}$ pint, keeping it well skimmed; as it becomes reduced, transfer to a small saucepan, add a few drops of browning and when cold and on the point of setting, use as required. Wipe over the tongue or joint with a cloth wrung out in hot water, and apply the glaze with a pastry brush.

Horseradish Sauce – Cold

(1) Scrub and scrape the horseradish, then grate finely. Add sufficient white vinegar to cover and caster sugar to taste.

(2) Mix horseradish with an equal quantity grated sour cooking apple, before adding sugar and vinegar.

(3) Add 2 or 3 teaspoonfuls grated horseradish to $\frac{1}{4}$ pint mayonnaise sauce.

Serve any of these with tongue or with meat or vegetable salads.

A Good Substitute for Horseradish Sauce. Grate finely some raw swede, and to 1 breakfastcupful add 2 teaspoonfuls made mustard and sufficient vinegar to moisten.

Horseradish Sauce – Hot

White sauce (page 196)
  or brown sauce (page 199) $\frac{1}{4}$ pint
Grated horseradish 1 tablespoonful

Sugar 1 teaspoonful
Vinegar 1 teaspoonful

Add the sugar to the sauce and bring to the boil, mix the horseradish with the vinegar, and add to the sauce.

Mayonnaise Sauce

(See pages 212–13)

Mint Sauce

Chopped mint 3 tablespoonfuls
Granulated sugar 1 tablespoonful

Vinegar $\frac{1}{4}$ pint
Water 2 tablespoonfuls

Pick the leaves from the stalks, wash and dry thoroughly. Put on to a chopping board, sprinkle over the sugar and chop very finely. It is very much easier to chop the leaves if the sugar is sprinkled over them.

Put into a small basin, pour over 2 tablespoonfuls boiling water, and leave till cold; then add the vinegar.

Honey Mint Sauce. Mix together 1 tablespoonful each honey and chopped mint and 4 tablespoonfuls hot vinegar. It is best if left to stand till the following day.

Bottled Mint Sauce

(See page 403-4)

Mushroom Sauce

Fish stock or water ¾ pint	*Flour 1 oz.*
Margarine 1 oz.	*Mushrooms 4 oz.*
Mushroom ketchup 1 tablespoonful	*Salt and cayenne*

Prepare the mushrooms and chop finely. Melt the margarine in a small saucepan, add the flour, and cook over a gentle heat till lightly browned; then stir in gradually the stock or water; stir till boiling, add the chopped mushrooms and ketchup, cover and cook gently for 15 minutes. Add salt and cayenne to taste.

Serve with fish.

Orange Sauce

Brown sauce (page 199) ½ pint	*Redcurrant jelly 1 teaspoonful*
Lemon juice 1 teaspoonful	*1 orange*

Peel the orange very thinly, removing all pith from the peel, and cut it into fine shreds. Put these in a small saucepan, cover with water, and simmer gently for 5 minutes; then drain. Add them to the brown sauce, together with the juice of the orange, the redcurrant jelly, and lemon juice. Season with salt and pepper, and stir till boiling.

Serve with roast duck.

Paprika Sauce

Paprika pepper 2 teaspoonfuls	*Margarine 1½ oz.*
Chopped onion 2 oz.	*Flour 1 oz.*
Vinegar 1 tablespoonful	*Salt*
Stock ½ pint	

Melt the margarine, add the chopped onion, and cook gently till tender and lightly browned. Then stir in the flour and paprika smoothly, cook for a minute or two, gradually add the stock, vinegar, and salt to taste, and simmer for 5 minutes.

Serve with meat, fish, or sausages.

Piquant Sauce

Brown sauce ¼ pint   *Vinegar 2 tablespoonfuls*
Capers 2 teaspoonfuls   *Chopped parsley 1 teaspoonful*
1 shallot   *Salt and pepper*
1 gherkin

Chop the shallot very finely, put in a small saucepan with the vinegar, cover, and cook very gently for 10 minutes. Add the brown sauce, stir till boiling, then add the chopped capers, gherkin, and parsley, and season with salt and pepper.

Binding Sauce for Rissoles

Dripping or margarine 1 oz.   *Flour 1 oz.*
Meat or vegetable stock ¼ pint   *Salt and pepper*

Melt the fat in a small saucepan, stir in flour smoothly, and cook for 2 or 3 minutes. Then gradually add the stock, stir till boiling, season, and continue stirring while it simmers for 2 or 3 minutes, when it should leave the sides of the saucepan quite clean.

This is called a **Panada** and is used for binding rissoles, egg cutlets, etc.

Sweet and Sour Sauce

Stock or vegetable water ¼ pint   *Margarine 1 oz.*
Sugar or golden syrup 1 tablespoonful   *Flour 1 oz.*
Vinegar 2 tablespoonfuls   *Salt and pepper*

Melt the margarine, stir in the flour, and cook over a gentle heat till brown; then gradually add the stock and vinegar and stir till boiling. Add sugar or syrup to taste, season, and simmer for 5 minutes.

Serve with root vegetables, fish, or boiled brisket.

For **Sweet and Sour Onion Sauce**. Chop 4 oz. onions finely and fry slowly in the margarine till brown, then stir in the flour and finish as above.

Hot Tartare Sauce

Make ½ pint white sauce, using half milk and half fish stock for the liquid, then add 1 tablespoonful bottled mayonnaise, ½ teaspoonful vinegar, 1 small teaspoonful very finely chopped onion, and 1 teaspoonful each chopped capers, parsley, and olives, and reheat without boiling.

Serve with boiled, baked, or hot fried fish.

Tomato Sauce

Margarine 2 oz.
Tomatoes ½ lb.
Stock ½ pint
Chopped onion 1 tablespoonful

Flour 1 oz.
Sugar ¼ teaspoonful
Salt and pepper

Melt half the margarine in a saucepan, add the chopped onion and cook over a gentle heat for 5 minutes, then add the sliced tomatoes and stock and cover and cook slowly for 20 minutes, then rub through a sieve.

Melt remaining margarine, stir in the flour and gradually add the tomato purée. Stir till boiling, add the sugar and salt and pepper to taste, and simmer for 5 minutes.

Concentrated tomato purée or canned tomatoes can replace the fresh tomatoes.

Wine Sauce (1)

Thickened gravy ½ pint
Red wine 2 tablespoonfuls
Redcurrant jelly 2 teaspoonfuls

Juice of ½ lemon
Salt and pepper

Bring gravy to the boil and stir in remaining ingredients.

Serve with cutlets or roast mutton.

Wine Sauce (2)

Add 2 or 3 tablespoonfuls of cooking sherry or white wine to ½ pint slightly thickened gravy.

SWEET SAUCES

Chocolate Sauce (1)

Grated chocolate 2 oz.   *Water ¼ pint*
Cornflour 1 dessertspoonful   *Sugar 1 oz.*
Vanilla essence

Put the sugar, chocolate, and water in a saucepan and stir till boiling; add the cornflour mixed smoothly with cold water, and stir till it reboils, simmer for 5 minutes; then add a few drops essence of vanilla.

Note. Ground rice or arrowroot can be used in place of cornflour.

Chocolate Sauce (2)

Milk or water ¼ pint   *Chocolate powder 1 table-*
Cornflour or arrowroot   *spoonful*
  1 dessertspoonful   *Vanilla and sugar*

Mix the cornflour and chocolate powder quite smoothly with a little of the milk (or water). Boil the remainder and pour it over. Return to the saucepan, stir till boiling, simmer for 5 minutes, and add sugar and vanilla to taste.

Custard Sauce

Milk ¼ pint   *Sugar 1 dessertspoonful*
2 egg yolks   *Vanilla sauce*

Make the milk hot (not boiling). Beat up the egg yolks with the sugar, pour the hot milk over, strain into a saucepan, and stir over a very gentle heat till it thickens (but do not let it boil, or it will curdle). Remove from the heat and add the vanilla.

For Custard Sauce made with Custard Powder. Blend 1 dessertspoonful custard powder and the same quantity of sugar with just sufficient cold milk to form a thick paste. Heat the remainder of ½ pint, and when quite boiling, pour over the blended powder, stirring whilst doing so. It should thicken sufficiently without any further cooking.

For Coffee Custard Sauce. Add 1 tablespoonful coffee

extract to the milk. If it is a sweetened extract, halve the quantity of sugar.

Hard Sauce
(For Plum Pudding)

Margarine 2 oz.
Caster sugar 2 oz.
Brandy or rum ¼ wineglass

Beat the margarine and sugar together till creamy, then beat in the brandy or rum very gradually. Pile up in a small glass dish and chill before serving.

Jam Sauce

Water ¼ pint
Apricot jam 3 tablespoonfuls
Juice of half a lemon
Sherry 1 tablespoonful (optional)
Cornflour 1 teaspoonful

Put the jam, water, and lemon juice in a saucepan and bring to the boil. Add the cornflour mixed smoothly with a little cold water, and simmer for 5 minutes. Rub through a strainer, reheat, add the sherry, and serve in a sauce-boat or poured around the pudding.

Lemon Sauce

1 lemon
Water ¼ pint
Arrowroot or cornflour 1 teaspoonful
Sugar 1–2 oz.

Mix the arrowroot smoothly with a little cold water, boil the remainder, and pour it over. Add the grated rind and juice of the lemon and the sugar, and stir over a gentle heat till boiling, then simmer for 2 or 3 minutes.

Orange Sauce. Use the grated rind and juice of a large orange and a teaspoonful of lemon juice.

Note. When fresh fruit is not available, diluted lemon or orange squash can be used. Pour it on to the creamed arrowroot, and boil as above.

Marmalade Sauce

Orange marmalade 2 tablespoonfuls   *Sugar 1 oz.*
Cornflour or arrowroot 1 teaspoonful   *Juice of ½ a lemon*
Water ¼ pint

Mix the cornflour smoothly with a little of the water. Heat remaining ingredients in a small saucepan, and when hot, add the cornflour and stir till boiling. Simmer for 5 minutes.

Serve with steamed sponge puddings.

Syrup Sauce

Golden syrup 2 tablespoonfuls   *Cornflour 1 teaspoonful*
Juice of ½ lemon   *Ginger ¼ teaspoonful*
Water ¼ pint

Put syrup, lemon juice, and water in a saucepan and bring to the boil. Mix cornflour and ginger smoothly with a little cold water; add to the syrup, etc., and stir till boiling. Simmer gently for 5 minutes.

Serve with ginger puddings.

Wine Sauce

Margarine 1 oz.   *Sugar 1 oz.*
Flour ½ oz.   *Sherry ¼ teacupful*
Water ¼ pint

Melt the margarine in a saucepan, stir in the flour smoothly, then add the water gradually and stir till boiling. Simmer for 2 or 3 minutes, and just before serving add the sugar and sherry.

Sauces for Ice Cream

(See pages 293–5)

Salads and Salad Dressings

During the last few years most housewives have learned to appreciate the health value of fresh salads, and at the same time have discovered how much a well-balanced salad meal is appreciated by everybody. The foodstuffs from which salads can be made are almost unlimited. They include cooked and uncooked vegetables and fruit; dried vegetables, such as haricot beans and peas; nuts, cheese, fish, meat, rice, macaroni and eggs. A salad may be made from one foodstuff only or from a combination of them. The French, who are noted for their salads, do not mix ingredients nearly as much as we do, and a real French salad usually consists of one vegetable mixed with a few herbs and plainly dressed with oil and vinegar.

Salads can be served as an adjunct to another dish, when they should be quite simple, with a French dressing, or they can form the main course at a meal.

These substantial salads are generally dressed with mayonnaise or a creamy dressing, and contain some form of protein in addition to the vegetables. Detailed recipes are given later.

Do not mix a green salad until just before it is needed, or it will go limp. This does not apply to *cooked* root vegetables, which are generally mixed with mayonnaise or salad cream, and are improved by standing for a while.

Serve salads in glass or china bowls or on individual plates. Tomatoes, small round beetroots, and apples can be hollowed out to form attractive cups to hold various salads.

PREPARING SALAD VEGETABLES

It is important to have all salad vegetables fresh and crisp. If not wanted for immediate use, wrap in a damp cloth or plastic bag, and keep in a cool place if a refrigerator is not available.

Lettuces also keep very well in a covered saucepan or basin, if in a cool place.

Wash all fresh vegetables, such as cabbage, celery, chicory, endive, lettuce, sorrel, spinach, and watercress, very thoroughly. Separate leaves from the roots and wash in several waters – as cold as possible – until free of all grit. If at all limp, leave for a short time in cold water.

Shred cabbage heart (after removing the hard stalk) and spinach leaves with a sharp knife. Lettuce and endive should not be cut with a knife. If the leaves are not to be left whole, tear lightly apart with the fingers. Drain very thoroughly in a sieve or colander, then in a cloth. If a salad basket is available, use this instead. Shake well, then hang up in a cool, airy place till ready to dress and serve.

The dressing will never mix properly with the salad if the leaves are wet.

Raw Root Vegetables. Carrots, turnips, beetroot, swedes, parsnips, etc., all of which are excellent in salads, should be scrubbed, peeled, and then grated. Do not grate them until ready to mix the salad. Should this be unavoidable, put in a *covered* container and leave in a very cold place.

Decorate a mayonnaise with chopped capers, sliced gherkins, olives, the sieved yolk or chopped white of hard-boiled eggs, or mustard and cress.

Garnish green salads with sliced tomato, beetroot (cut into dice or fancy shapes with a cutter), slices of hard-boiled egg, radish roses, sliced pimentoes or cucumber.

Cucumber for garnishing. Do not remove the peel, but score downwards deeply all round with a fork, then cut into thin slices.

Radish Roses. Wash radishes and trim off the roots and all but about 1 inch of the stalk. Take a sharp pointed knife, and starting at the root end, peel the red skin down in about 5 sections, to look like petals, stopping just before the stalk. Leave in cold water for $\frac{1}{2}$ hour, when the petals will open out.

Alternatively, simply cut the radish across 3 or 4 times (according to size) starting at the root end, about three-quarters of the way down the radish.

In either case, the radish rose will open out and make a most attractive garnish for salads and cold service dishes.

For flavouring use any of the following: finely chopped chives, tarragon, spring onion, mint, thyme, rosemary, parsley.

SALAD DRESSINGS

Boiled Dressing (1)

Salad oil 2 tablespoonfuls   *Dry mustard 1 teaspoonful*
Vinegar to taste   *1 egg*
Flour 1 teaspoonful   *Water $\frac{1}{4}$ pint*
Salt, pepper, cayenne, sugar

Put the flour, sugar, and seasonings into a small basin and mix with the beaten egg; stir in the oil. Gradually add $\frac{1}{4}$ pint of boiling water, stirring all the time; then add vinegar to taste. Stand the basin in a saucepan of boiling water and stir over a moderate heat till it thickens.

Boiled Dressing (2)
(*Without Oil*)

Custard powder (standard flavour) 1 oz.	*Milk ¼ pint*
Sugar, salt and dry mustard	*Margarine ½ oz.*
¼ teaspoonful of each	*Vinegar 2 tablespoonfuls*

Blend dry ingredients with a little milk, boil remainder and pour it on. Return to saucepan and stir till boiling. Remove from heat, add vinegar and margarine, and whisk thoroughly. If too thick when cold, add a little more vinegar or boiling water.

Continental Dressing

This dressing is very good served with vegetable hors d'oeuvres and fish salads. To ½ pint French dressing add a small onion and a hard-boiled egg finely chopped and 1 teaspoonful chopped parsley.

Creamy Salad Dressing

Cold white sauce ¼ pint	*Chopped parsley 2 teaspoonfuls*
Lemon juice 1 tablespoonful	*Grated horseradish 2 teaspoonfuls*
Salad oil 1 tablespoonful	*Salt, pepper and sugar to taste*
Onion juice 1 teaspoonful	

Put the white sauce in a basin and add the other ingredients. Mix thoroughly. This sauce is excellent with mixed vegetable salads.

Egg Dressing

Yolks of 2 hard-boiled eggs	*Tarragon vinegar 1 teaspoonful*
Salad oil 3 tablespoonfuls	*Salt, pepper, cayenne, sugar*
Vinegar 1 tablespoonful	*Made mustard ¼ teaspoonful*

Sieve the egg yolks and put them in a basin with the salt, pepper, cayenne, mustard and a pinch of sugar. Mix thoroughly, gradually stir in the oil and lastly the vinegar.

Note. Chop the egg whites and use in the salad.

French Dressing

Salad oil 3 tablespoonfuls   *Vinegar 1 tablespoonful*
Salt and pepper

Season oil with salt and pepper, then mix in the vinegar. Sometimes a little tarragon vinegar is added and some people like a little mustard also.

For Vinaigrette Dressing, add a little chopped parsley, chives and capers (or gherkins). This is good with vegetable and fish salads.

Mayonnaise Sauce

Yolks of 2 eggs   *White vinegar 1 tablespoonful*
Salad oil ¼ pint   *Tarragon vinegar 2 teaspoonfuls*
Made mustard ¼ teaspoonful   *Salt, pepper and cayenne*
Sugar ¼ teaspoonful

Put the yolks of eggs into a basin with the mustard, sugar, salt and cayenne. Add the oil drop by drop, stirring all the time with a wooden spoon. When the mixture becomes really thick, add a few drops of vinegar, and then continue with oil and vinegar alternately, until the ingredients are used up. Once the sauce thickens the oil may be added more quickly, but the stirring must continue all the time.

Lemon juice can take the place of vinegar, and the amount of this or vinegar used can be varied according to taste.

Quickly-made Mayonnaise

2 egg yolks   *Sugar 1 teaspoonful*
Salad oil 1 breakfastcupful   *Salt 1 teaspoonful*
Lemon juice 1 tablespoonful   *Dry mustard ¼ teaspoonful*
Vinegar 1 dessertspoonful   *Pinch of cayenne*
Tarragon vinegar 1 dessertspoonful

Put salt, sugar, mustard and pepper into a bowl and mix smoothly with the lemon juice and vinegars. Add the egg yolks and one-third of the oil. Beat with a rotary beater till the mixture begins to thicken (about 1 minute); add half the remaining oil and beat another minute; and then the rest of the oil and beat 1 minute longer.

This makes an excellent thick mayonnaise in a minimum of time.

Salad Cream for Store

Vinegar ¼ pint
Flour 2 level tablespoonfuls
Caster sugar 1 tablespoonful
Mustard 1 tablespoonful
Salt 2 teaspoonfuls

Water ¼ pint
3 eggs
Cayenne
Margarine 1 oz.

Sieve flour, mustard, sugar and salt into a basin, add a good pinch of cayenne, and mix smoothly with a little of the water; then add the lightly beaten eggs and when well mixed stir in remaining water and vinegar. Strain into a double saucepan, add the margarine cut up in small pieces, and stir till it thickens. Turn into wide-necked jars and cork or screw down when quite cold.

This salad cream will be quite thick. When using thin down with salad oil and lemon juice or vinegar.

Additions to Salad Cream

Any of the following can be added to home-made or bottled salad dressing, and are especially good on vegetable, fish, or rice salad: chopped chives or spring onions; tiny dice of well drained, peeled, raw cucumber; French mustard; chopped capers or chopped sweet pickle; Worcester sauce; paprika; curry powder.

Tartare Sauce

To ½ pint mayonnaise add 2 teaspoonfuls each of finely chopped olives, capers and gherkins, 1 teaspoonful of chopped parsley, and 2 finely sliced spring onions.

SALADS

Apple Cup Salad

Choose red apples of equal size, polish well, and cut a slice off
the stem end. Hollow out the centres to form cups and moisten
the insides with oil and vinegar.

Dice the pulp and mix with cooked green peas. Moisten with
salad dressing and fill up the apple cups. Sprinkle over chopped
nuts and serve on lettuce leaves.

Or substitute shredded celery for the green peas.

Bean Salads

(1) Mix together 2 breakfastcupfuls sliced cooked French or
runner beans, 1 teacupful finely shredded cabbage heart, and a
small peeled and sliced apple, add salt to taste, moisten with
salad dressing and garnish with tomato.

(2) Mix beans with sliced banana, moisten with salad dressing, and garnish with tomato.

(3) Mix beans with peas and sprigs of cauliflower, dress with
French dressing, and garnish with sliced black olives and
radishes.

Beetroot Salads

Beetroots can be used in salads either cooked or raw. If the
latter, after peeling, shred on a fine grater, moisten with
vinegar, and use as a garnish for green salad. When cooked,
cut into slices, dice or any fancy shape preferred. Use as a
garnish or mixed with other vegetables, or simply dressed with
French dressing.

Beetroot and Apple. Dice and mix together a large cooked
beetroot, 2 cooked potatoes, and 2 large apples. Add 2 teaspoonfuls capers, season with salt and pepper, and dress with French
or Continental dressing.

Beetroot and Celery. Mix together equal quantities diced
beetroot and celery cut into rings. Season with salt and pepper
and dress with oil and vinegar.

Beetroot and Cauliflower. Mix diced beetroot with sprigs of cooked cauliflower. Heap up in a bowl with a border of finely shredded raw cabbage and dress with salad cream.

Cabbage Salads

Cabbages are far richer in vitamin C than lettuces and should be served frequently in salad dishes.

Choose a firm cabbage, not too large. Remove outside leaves and very hard stalk, then cut into quarters. Wash carefully and unless taken straight from the garden, crisp in very cold water for ¼ hour. Then drain and dry in a cloth. Put on a board and with a very sharp knife cut across into fine shreds.

(1) Serve plain with French dressing or any thick dressing preferred.

(2) Mix equal quantities shredded red and white cabbage, sprinkle with chopped mint, and dress with oil and lemon juice (or vinegar). Heap up in a bowl and surround with diced beetroot.

(3) Mix with an equal quantity grated raw carrot, thinly sliced celery, young spinach leaves finely shredded and cooked beetroot cut into match-like strips. Sprinkle with chopped onion, season with salt and pepper, and moisten with French dressing. Serve with a border of chopped celery leaves or tufts of watercress.

(4) Mix with grated apple and shredded celery and dress with oil and vinegar.

(5) After dressing sprinkle cabbage with caraway seeds.

Carrot Salads

Raw grated carrot can be used in any mixed green salad. If cooked, it should be diced or sliced and used in any mixed vegetable salad.

(1) Mix equal quantities of diced cooked carrots and green peas, moisten with salad dressing and sprinkle with chopped parsley or mint.

(2) Mix together 1 cup of grated raw carrot and ½ cup of sultanas, moisten with salad dressing, and serve surrounded with shredded lettuce or heart of cabbage and garnished with tufts of watercress.

(3) Slice cooked carrots, sprinkle with chopped capers,

parsley, and spring onion. Dress with French dressing. Serve on a bed of shredded lettuce and garnish with sliced hard-boiled egg.

Cole Slaw

This is an American salad and is made by adding *hot* boiled dressing to the shredded cabbage. Pour the hot dressing over the cabbage and leave till quite cold before serving.

Either of the boiled dressings, pages 210–11, can be used, or the following:

Vinegar 4 tablespoonfuls	*1 egg*
Water 4 tablespoonfuls	*Flour 1 teaspoonful*
Chicken fat or margarine 1 oz.	*Mustard ¼ teaspoonful*
Salt ¼ teaspoonful	*Sugar 2 teaspoonfuls*

Mix the mustard, sugar and salt with the vinegar and water. Melt fat in a small saucepan, stir in flour smoothly, then gradually add the vinegar mixture, stir till boiling, simmer for 5 minutes, cool slightly, then pour over the lightly beaten egg.

Chicory Salad

Remove any discoloured leaves and wash in cold water. Cut the heads through lengthways, then cut across into small pieces.

(1) Mix the chicory with peeled and diced eating apples, moisten with salad cream and garnish with sliced tomatoes.

(2) Mix the chicory with an equal quantity of diced beetroot and dress with French dressing; place in a serving dish, surround with potato salad and sprinkle over the sieved yolk and chopped white of a hard-boiled egg.

Corn Salad

Corn salad or lambs' lettuce makes an excellent salad by itself or it can be mixed with thin strips of beetroot and celery. Dress with French dressing.

Creole Salad

Arrange on lettuce leaves slices of skinned tomatoes, alternating with sliced banana. Sprinkle with chopped spring onion and dress with salad cream.

Cucumber Salad

There is no need to peel the cucumbers. Either score downwards deeply with a sharp pronged fork (a fish fork is good for this) or just cut off the peel in thin strips, leaving a small piece of green alternating with white.

Slice the cucumber very thinly, sprinkle liberally with salt, and let stand for 1 hour. Then drain thoroughly, dress with oil and vinegar, and sprinkle with chopped parsley.

Orange Salad
(*To serve with Roast Duck*)

Remove peel and all the pith from some oranges. (This is very easily done if, before peeling, the oranges are allowed to stand in boiling water for 2 or 3 minutes.) Cut into very thin slices, remove pips, and put into a glass bowl. Sprinkle with a very small quantity of caster sugar and dress with oil and lemon juice seasoned with salt and pepper.

Pineapple Salad (1)

Line a salad bowl with lettuce or endive, then arrange in the centre some half-slices of pineapple and dress with French dressing.

Serve with roast poultry. If preferred serve the pineapple on one or two lettuce leaves on individual plates.

Pineapple Salad (2)

Mix together 1 breakfastcupful of diced cooked potatoes, 3 table-spoonfuls each of small pineapple cubes and diced cucumber and 1 tablespoonful of chopped nuts; season with salt and pepper and moisten with mayonnaise. Place in the centre of a bowl, sprinkle with chopped parsley and surround with shredded lettuce and tufts of watercress.

Potato Salads

Use waxy potatoes in preference to floury ones, and of even size. When new potatoes are not available, choose the smallest of the old ones.

Scrub thoroughly and boil in their jackets slowly till soft, taking care not to overcook them. As soon as cool enough to handle, remove the skins and cut into dice or slices. Add a little finely chopped onion and parsley, season with salt and pepper, and moisten with oil and vinegar in equal parts. Leave till quite cold, then heap up in a salad bowl and top with mayonnaise.

Chopped chives or gherkins can be added if liked.

Chopped raw celery, using as much potato as celery, is also very good. Put a border around of chopped green celery leaves and garnish with diced beetroot.

A potato salad is definitely better if dressed whilst the potatoes are hot, but cold left-over ones can be used, provided they are firm.

Russian Salad

Cooked green peas ¼ pint
Diced carrot, turnip and French beans
3 or 4 new potatoes
A few anchovies

Small cauliflower
2 gherkins
Stuffed olives
Mayonnaise

Divide cauliflower into flowerets and cook all vegetables separately.

Dice the carrot, turnip, beans and potatoes, and shred the gherkins finely. Mix these together with the peas, season with salt and pepper and add sufficient mayonnaise to form a creamy mixture. Turn into a dish and garnish with sliced stuffed olives and anchovy fillets.

Spinach Salad

Young spinach leaves make a good salad either by themselves or in combination with other raw vegetables. Remove stalks and wash free of grit. Put a few leaves one on top of another and shred finely.

Dress with French dressing and sprinkle with finely chopped onion.

Spinach is particularly good with shredded cabbage. Use the spinach as a border and heap up the cabbage in the centre. The two shades of green are very attractive. Garnish with radish roses.

Tomato Salad

Blanch and skin tomatoes (see page 19) and cut into thin slices. Season with salt and pepper and dress with oil and vinegar. Sprinkle with chopped parsley and, if available, a little chopped spring onion.

Tomato Cup Salad

Cut a slice from the top of some tomatoes and scoop out the hard centre and pips (these may be used in soup or sauce), and replace with whatever filling is being used. Sprinkle with chopped parsley and serve on individual plates surrounded with mustard and cress or watercress.

Suggested Fillings:

(1) Diced canned pineapple, to which add a few chopped nuts. Moisten with mayonnaise.

(2) Diced cooked new potatoes, mixed with green peas and a little shredded spring onion. Moisten with mayonnaise.

See also Cold Stuffed Tomatoes, page 129.

Tomato Flowerets

Choose very small tomatoes of equal size. Cut across 3 or 4 times not quite to the base, then the tomato should open out like a water-lily. Put a tiny blob of mayonnaise in the centre with a pinch of chopped parsley on top. Use to garnish a mixed green salad, allowing one tomato per head.

A Winter Salad

Celery 1 head	*A small shallot*
A small beetroot	*Mayonnaise sauce or salad dressing*
2 large apples	

Cut celery into rings and beetroot and apples into dice. Chop shallot very finely. Mix together and dress with any dressing preferred.

MAIN DISH SALADS

Cheese and Fruit Salads

Fruit combines well with cheese and mixed green salad.

Tinned pineapple and stewed or raw cherries are both particularly good.

Cut the cheese into dice, use any green salad preferred, garnish with the fruit, and serve salad dressing and potato salad separately.

Cheese and Tomato Salad

Cut some tomatoes into flowerets like water lilies (see page 219), put a cheese ball in the centre of each, and place on individual plates on a bed of lettuce. Surround with potato salad, then a border of grated raw carrot with more cheese balls at intervals. Garnish with tufts of watercress and sliced radishes. Hand mayonnaise and more grated cheese separately.

For the Cheese Balls, for 4 people. Moisten 1 teacupful grated cheese with 2 or 3 teaspoonfuls milk or salad cream and mix to a paste. The amount of milk will depend on the dryness of the cheese. Add slowly, as the mixture should not be wet. With wet hands roll into tiny balls and sprinkle lightly with chopped parsley.

Soft Cream Cheese simply rolled into tiny balls can be used instead.

Cheese and Vegetable Salad

Serve this on individual (fish size) plates. Line the plate with lettuce leaves and heap up some finely-shredded spinach in the centre. Surround with little heaps of diced cooked beetroot, chopped celery, and shredded carrot; sprinkle with French dressing and heap up some small dice of cheese on top of the spinach. Sprinkle with chopped parsley and serve potato salad separately.

Chicken Salad

(1) Remove skin and bone from some cooked chicken and cut into neat pieces. Put a layer of green peas in a salad dish, cover with sliced tomato, and lay the chicken on top. Coat with mayonnaise. Surround with lettuce leaves, garnish with sliced cucumber, hard-boiled egg, and radish roses.

(2) Cut chicken into dice, add a few chopped capers and moisten with mayonnaise; heap up in the centre of a dish, surround with lettuce and garnish as above.

Any of the following can be added to the diced chicken before mixing with mayonnaise: diced tongue, diced pineapple or skinned grapes, or a few green peas.

Danish Salad

Cooked macaroni 4 oz.	*Salad dressing*
Chopped capers 2 teaspoonfuls	*1 apple*
3 hard-boiled eggs	*Small beetroot*
Chopped parsley	*2 tomatoes*

Cut up the macaroni, peel and dice the apple and beetroot, skin and slice the tomatoes.

Mix together the macaroni, apple, beetroot, and chopped capers and moisten with salad cream. Divide into six portions on individual plates, place half a hard-boiled egg on top, coat with salad cream, surround with shredded lettuce, sprinkle with chopped parsley, and garnish with the sliced tomatoes.

Egg and Cheese Salad

Boil as many eggs as required for 10 minutes. Put in cold water for a few minutes, then shell and cut in halves. Put each half on slices of cheese, arrange on a bed of lettuce and garnish with tomatoes. Dress with mayonnaise and sprinkle with parsley.

Egg Mayonnaise

(See page 31)

Stuffed Eggs

(See pages 30, 305–6)

Fish Salads

Any kind of left-over fish, fresh, smoked, or tinned, makes excellent salad. Combine with potato or rice (see Rice Salads, pages 223–4).

(1) Remove skin and bone and flake the fish, mix with diced potato, add a little finely chopped onion and capers, season with salt and pepper, and moisten with salad dressing or mayonnaise sauce. Heap up on lettuce or other green salad, sprinkle with chopped parsley, and surround with sliced tomato and cucumber.

(2) Cooked parsnips go particularly well with fish. Cut them into finger length about 3 inches long, roll each piece in finely chopped onion or shallot, and marinate in oil and vinegar for 1 hour.

Put a bed of watercress in a shallow dish. Heap up in the centre some tinned salmon or other flaked fish moistened with mayonnaise and surround with the prepared parsnips. Sprinkle with chopped parsley and garnish with diced cooked beetroot.

(3) Cook some macaroni or spaghetti till tender, then cut into short lengths and mix with an equal quantity flaked cooked fish, smoked or fresh. Sprinkle over a little tarragon vinegar, add a little finely chopped onion or chives, and moisten with mayonnaise sauce.

Heap up on a bed of green salad, surround with sliced tomatoes and cucumber, sprinkle with chopped parsley, and garnish with quarters of hard-boiled egg.

(4) Remove skin and bone from 2 cooked fresh herrings and flake finely, then mix with 2 tablespoonfuls grated raw apple, 1 breakfastcupful diced cooked potato, and 1 teacupful each of diced cooked carrot and beetroot. Moisten with salad dressing and garnish with watercress.

Cold Meat Salads

Any kind of cooked cold meat can be used – fresh, salt, or smoked.

(1) Remove any skin and gristle from the meat, cut it into dice, and marinate in a little French dressing for 1 hour. Mix with an equal quantity of potato salad, add a little grated horseradish and finely chopped onion. Line a salad bowl with lettuce leaves, add some sliced tomatoes and cucumber, and heap up the mixture in the centre. Coat this with mayonnaise and sprinkle with chopped parsley.

(2) Spread a little mustard over thin slices of tongue or salt or smoked beef, roll up into cornet shapes and place a slice of chicory or a small gherkin in the end of each. Heap up some mixed vegetable salad in the centre of a dish, surround with lettuce and place the rolled meat at equal intervals around. Garnish with sliced tomato and hard-boiled eggs.

Meat or Poultry in Aspic

Diced meat or chicken and tongue or sausages can be used.

Arrange slices of hard-boiled egg and tomato in the bottom of a basin with a few green peas, then add the diced chicken and tongue (or meat or sausages) and pour over the aspic jelly, which should be cool but still fluid. Leave in a cold place till set, then turn out on to serving dish and garnish with watercress and tomatoes.

For the Aspic Jelly. Make with agar (see Agar Jellies, page 278). For the liquid use clear stock or water, either of which should be well flavoured with liquid vegetable extract. Add a little lemon juice or vinegar if necessary.

Note. These can be made in small individual moulds.

Rice Salads

Rice is excellent in substantial salad dishes.

Cook as for curry (see page 136), then add a little finely chopped onion and parsley. Moisten with salad dressing.

Rice and Sardine Salad

After moistening the rice with salad cream, add a few capers or a little finely chopped pickle, press into a basin and leave till cold. Then turn out on to a shallow dish and put the sardines around standing against the rice. Surround with lettuce leaves or endive, with little heaps of green peas moistened with salad cream alternating with sliced tomatoes.

Pilchards can be used in place of sardines.

Smoked Fish also makes a good salad. When cooked, flake the fish and mix with the rice and arrange salad as above.

Rice and Sausage Salad

Prepare rice as above and when cold mix in lightly some sliced cooked sausages.

Heap up in a bowl, surround with shredded lettuce and little heaps of green peas or beans and diced carrot moistened with mayonnaise. Garnish with tomato and tufts of watercress.

Or surround rice and sausage with tomato cups filled with carrot and peas (see Halibut Mayonnaise, pages 66–7) on a bed of shredded lettuce.

Rice and Cheese Salad

To 2 breakfastcupfuls cooked rice add 1 teacupful grated cheese, a little grated onion, and 1 tablespoonful chopped parsley. Moisten with salad cream. Heap up on a bed of any kind of green salad, surround with grated raw carrot, and garnish with tomato or beetroot and tufts of watercress. Serve extra grated cheese and salad cream separately.

Salad in Slices

In the centre of a large flat dish put a small heap of shredded lettuce sprinkled with grated cheese. Hard boil as many eggs as required, cut through lengthways, and place each on a thin round of cheese, cut side down. Place in a circle round the lettuce.

Slice thinly some radishes, cucumber, beetroot and tomato and put a circle of each round the eggs in the order mentioned, separating the beetroot and tomato with a little mustard and cress.

Finish with an outer circle of tufts of watercress. Serve salad cream or mayonnaise separately.

Ingredients can be varied to suit individual taste. Sliced carrot and shredded heart of cabbage can be substituted for some of the other vegetables, but always work in circles and let something green alternate with a colour.

Scandinavian Salad

Mix together equal quantities of sliced cooked sausages, diced apple and cooked potato. Add a little chopped pickled cucumber and moisten with salad dressing. Heap up in the centre of a dish, surround with shredded lettuce, and garnish with tomato.

Puddings and Sweets

Included under this heading are steamed, sponge and suet puddings, milk puddings, hot soufflés, fritters, pancakes, fruit dishes and baked puddings.

Before starting to mix the pudding, have all the ingredients in readiness measured or weighed. Have the basin or dish ready greased; the water ready boiling in the saucepan, if for a steamed pudding; or the oven at the right heat if for a baked one.

For a steamed pudding fill the basin only two-thirds full, to allow the pudding to rise. Cover with a piece of greased paper and then a cloth on top.

Plan meals so that you use your stove economically. If a joint is being cooked in the oven, have a baked pudding which can be cooked the same time as the meat; if only the top of the stove is being used, have a steamed pudding. A steamed pudding is always improved by serving a sauce with it.

If a steamer is not available, place the pudding in a saucepan with sufficient boiling water to reach only halfway up the basin. As the water boils away refill with *boiling* water.

Simple Steamed Fruit Puddings

Make suet crust according to recipe on page 250. Take two thirds of the pastry and, on a lightly floured board, roll it out about $\frac{1}{3}$ inch thick. Grease a pudding basin and line it smoothly with this pastry, pressing it into the sides and bottom with 1 inch all round overhanging the top, half fill with prepared fruit, add 1 or 2 tablespoonfuls of sugar, according to the tartness of the fruit; then add the remainder of the fruit and more sugar, and pour over ¾ teacupful of water. Then roll out the remaining pastry to the size of the top of the basin, moisten the edges of the pastry in the basin with water and fit the piece on top. Press the edges together. Cover with a greased paper, then with a pudding cloth, and steam for 2½–3 hours.

FRUIT FRITTERS

Coating Batter (1)

Flour 4 oz.   *Cooking oil 1 tablespoonful*
Pinch of salt   *White of an egg*
Tepid water ¼ pint

Sieve flour and salt into a basin and make a well in the centre. Gradually add the oil and water, and beat till smooth and free from lumps. Leave the batter to stand for at least 1 hour.

Just before using, stir in the stiffly whipped white of an egg.

Coating Batter (2)

Make like Pancake Batter (see page 272), but use only ¼ pint of milk instead of ½ pint.

Eggless Batter

(See page 427)

To Cook Fritters

Use clarified dripping, cooking fat, or oil for frying. It should be about 3 inches in depth.

The fat should be heated until it has a faint blue smoke rising from it.

To test the heat, drop in half a teaspoonful of batter. If the fat is sufficiently hot the batter will rise to the surface immediately and begin to brown.

Do not put too many fritters in at once, as they would cool the fat down too much. The fritters also need room to swell.

Brown one side, then turn over and brown the other.

Drain well, dust with sugar, arrange on a hot dish, and serve as soon as possible.

To coat the fruit drop it into the batter, leave for a minute or two, then lift out with a skewer. Do not coat the fruit until ready to fry.

Apple Fritters. Peel and core the apples and cut into slices about ⅜ inch thick. Dust with sugar and grated lemon rind before coating. When cooked, sprinkle with sugar and cinnamon.

Banana Fritters. Peel, cut in halves and split each piece through lengthways. Sprinkle with lemon juice before coating.

Fig Fritters. Stew figs slowly without sugar in just sufficient water to cover. Do not cook them very soft. Drain very thoroughly and dust with flour before coating.

Orange Fritters. Divide into sections and remove pips.

Tinned Fruits. Pineapple, pears, peaches, and apricots can all be used, but must be very well drained before coating with batter.

Baked Apples

Choose good cooking apples of uniform size. Wipe them, remove the cores, but do not peel. With a sharp knife cut just through the skin all round the centre of each apple.

Put them in a fireproof dish, fill the centres with brown sugar and a little grated lemon rind. Cover the bottom of the dish with water and a teaspoonful of sugar for each apple. Bake in a hot oven 35–45 minutes (according to the size of the apples), basting with the syrup once or twice.

For a change, fill with raisins, walnuts or crystallized ginger chopped small, or substitute cinnamon for the lemon rind.

The apples can be sweetened with golden syrup in place of sugar.

Apple Charlotte (1)

Cooking apples 1¼ lb. *Breadcrumbs 4 oz.*
Brown sugar *Margarine 1 oz.*
1 lemon

Peel, core and slice the apples, add very little water and sugar to taste, and stew till soft; then add the grated rind and juice of the lemon.

Grease a fireproof dish and put in a thick layer of breadcrumbs, then half the apple; repeat the layers, making a top layer of breadcrumbs, sprinkle with brown sugar, dot with margarine, and bake in a moderately hot oven till hot through and the top is well browned – about 30 minutes.

Or, instead of using breadcrumbs, take some thin slices of stale bread and cut sufficient small triangles to line the sides of the dish. Dip these in melted margarine and place round the sides of the dish, the points coming just above the top. Fill up with stewed apple (not very much juice), and cover neatly with bread dipped in melted margarine. Sprinkle liberally with brown sugar, dot with margarine and bake as above.

Gooseberries or Rhubarb can replace the apples.

Apple Charlotte (2)

Cooking apples 1¼ lb. *Breadcrumbs 4 oz.*
Golden syrup 2 tablespoonfuls *Water 1 tablespoonful*
1 lemon *Brown sugar 1½ oz.*
Ground ginger ¼ teaspoonful *Margarine 1 oz.*

Grease an oven dish, put in a layer of breadcrumbs, then one of thinly sliced apples; repeat the layers till the dish is full.

Put the syrup, water, grated rind and juice of the lemon and the sugar in a small saucepan, and stir over a gentle heat till the sugar is dissolved. Pour this over the contents of the dish, dot with margarine and bake in a moderate oven (375°, Regulo No. 4), 1–1¼ hours.

For Rhubarb Charlotte. Make as above, using cut-up rhubarb in place of apples.

Apple Crunch

Apples 1¼ lb.
Sugar
Cornflakes 2 breakfastcupfuls

Margarine 2 oz.
Golden syrup 1 rounded tablespoonful

Peel, core and slice the apples. Put them in a saucepan with 3 or 4 tablespoonfuls of water and sugar to taste and cook over a gentle heat till just soft, then turn into a baking dish.

Crush the cornflakes slightly. Melt margarine, syrup and 1 oz. of sugar, then pour over the cornflakes. Place on top of the stewed apple and bake in a moderate oven about 15 minutes.

Note. If the sugar-coated breakfast flakes are used, then omit syrup and sugar and simply mix them with the melted margarine.

Gooseberries or Rhubarb can replace the apples.

Apple Custard

Stewed apple 1 pint
1 lemon or orange
2 eggs

Cinnamon
Sugar

Sieve the apple, add the grated rind and juice of an orange or lemon, a pinch of cinnamon and sugar to taste. Stir in the lightly beaten eggs and bake for ½ hour in a moderate oven (375°, Regulo No. 4). After it has been cooking for 15 minutes, sprinkle the top with sugar.

Boiled Apple Dumplings

6 apples
Flour 8 oz.
Suet 3–4 oz.

Salt
Brown sugar 2 oz.
6 cloves

Chop the suet finely, add it to the flour with ½ saltspoonful of salt, and mix it with cold water to a stiff paste. Put on a large pan of water to boil. Peel and core the apples. Roll out the pastry and stamp it into rounds large enough to cover the apples. Lay each apple on a round of pastry, fill up the centres with brown sugar and put a clove in each. Mould the paste over the apples and, having wetted the edges of the rounds, secure them firmly together.

Tie each in a scalded, floured cloth and boil steadily for $1-1\frac{1}{4}$ hours. Remove the cloths, place on a hot dish and sprinkle with sugar.

Apple Ginger

Cooking apples $1\frac{1}{2}$ *lb.*	*Sugar*
Water $\frac{1}{4}$ *pint*	*Lemon juice*
Ground ginger $\frac{1}{2}$ *level teaspoonful*	*Angelica*
Preserved ginger 2 oz.	

Peel, core, and cut up the apples, put in a saucepan with the water, sugar to taste, a squeeze of lemon juice, and the ground ginger mixed with a spoonful of water, cover, and cook till tender. Add the chopped preserved ginger and leave till cold. Turn into a glass bowl or individual dishes and garnish with angelica.

Apple Meringue

Cooking apples $1\frac{1}{2}-2$ *lb.*	*Sugar*
Whites of 2 eggs	*Flavouring*

Peel, core and cut up the apples and stew with *very little* water and sugar to taste, flavouring with ground cinnamon or lemon rind. When soft turn into a fireproof dish and leave till cold.

Whisk the egg whites till stiff, fold in 2 oz. caster sugar and heap up over the apple. Sprinkle with sugar and bake in a moderate oven (375°, Regulo No. 4) till the meringue is set and lightly browned — about 20 minutes.

Apple Pudding

(See Steamed Fruit Puddings, pages 225–6)

Apple Steffon

Short or suet crust $\frac{1}{2}$ *lb.*	*Cinnamon*
Apples $1\frac{1}{2}$ *lb.*	*Brown sugar*
Currants 2 oz.	*Candied peel 1 oz.*
$\frac{1}{2}$ *lemon*	*Margarine 1 oz.*

Spread the margarine thickly over the bottom and sides of a

pudding basin, then sprinkle liberally with brown sugar and line with pastry.

Peel, core and cut up apples into small pieces and put half in the basin; then sprinkle over the chopped candied peel, currants, grated rind and juice of half a lemon, a dust of cinnamon and sugar to taste; add the rest of the apples and a little more sugar. Pour over ½ teacupful of water, cover with crust, twist a greased paper over the top, and bake in a moderate oven (400°, Regulo No. 5), about 1¼ hours. Turn out on to a hot dish and serve at once.

Rhubarb, Gooseberries or Plums can be used instead of the apples, but omit peel, currants and cinnamon.

Apricot Meringue

Dried apricots ¼ lb.   *Icing sugar 3 tablespoonfuls*
Caster sugar 4 oz.   *2 eggs*

Wash the apricots and soak them overnight. Turn them into a saucepan with the water, which should be just sufficient to cover, and simmer gently till soft. Rub through a coarse sieve. Add the caster sugar and the well-beaten egg yolks, and beat up lightly. Turn into a fireproof dish and bake in a moderate oven for 20 minutes. Whip up the egg whites to a stiff froth; fold in the sieved icing sugar. Heap up over the pudding, dredge with caster sugar, and return to a moderate oven till the meringue is set and lightly browned – about 20 minutes.

Baked Puddings

The following is an excellent foundation mixture for baked puddings, and there are many ways in which it can be used to produce varied dishes.

Take 2 eggs, 3 oz. margarine, 3 oz. sugar, and 5 oz. self-raising flour (or plain flour sieved with ½ teaspoonful baking powder).

Beat margarine and sugar till soft and creamy, add lightly beaten eggs one at a time, then stir in sieved flour, and use in one of the following ways:

Fig, Date or Raisin Pudding. Add 3 or 4 oz. chopped figs,

stoned dates or raisins to the mixture, turn into a greased
fireproof dish and bake in a moderate oven (400°, Regulo No. 5)
about 50 minutes.

Eve's Pudding. Put a layer of peeled, cored and finely
chopped cooking apples in a greased baking dish, sprinkle with
sugar and the grated rind and juice of half a lemon. Spread
the mixture over the top and bake as above.

Eggless Baked Puddings

Flour 5 oz.	*Custard powder 1 dessertspoonful*
Margarine 2 oz.	*Baking powder 2 teaspoonfuls*
Sugar 2 oz.	*Milk ¼ pint*

Sieve flour, custard powder and baking powder. Cream
margarine and sugar and add dry ingredients alternately with
the milk.

Finish as suggested in previous recipe.

Baked Bananas

The bananas should be firm and just ripe. Remove skin and cut
them in halves lengthways. Place in a greased baking dish,
brush over with melted butter or margarine and sprinkle with
lemon juice. Bake in a moderate oven about 20 minutes.

Variations:

(1) Pour a little sherry or rum over the bananas.

(2) Boil a few seedless raisins in water for a few minutes,
strain and mix with the bananas.

(3) Sprinkle honey over the bananas with the lemon juice.

(4) Sprinkle bananas with white or brown sugar 10 minutes
before removing from the oven.

Baked Grapefruit

2 grapefruit	*Cinnamon 1 teaspoonful*
Margarine 2 oz.	*Crushed cornflakes 1 breakfastcupful*
Brown sugar 3 oz.	

Cut grapefruit across in halves, remove pips and core and
loosen the sections.

Melt the margarine and mix it with the crushed cornflakes, sugar and cinnamon; then heap up the mixture over the fruit. Bake 15–20 minutes in a moderate oven (400°, Regulo No. 5). Serve hot.

Blackberry Apples

4 large cooking apples *Golden syrup 2 tablespoonfuls*
Blackberries 4 oz. *Sugar*

Remove the cores from the apples, being careful not to cut through the bottom. Mash the blackberries with some sugar and fill the hollows with them. Put the stuffed apples in a baking dish, pour round the golden syrup mixed with an equal quantity of water, and bake in a moderately hot oven (425°, Regulo No. 6), till soft, basting once or twice with the syrup. The time will vary according to the size of the apples — average about 45 minutes.

Baked Bread Pudding

Stale bread 12–14 oz. *Golden syrup 2 tablespoonfuls*
Shredded suet 2 oz. *Mixed spice ¼ teaspoonful*
Candied peel 1 oz. *Brown sugar*
Dried fruit 4 oz.

Crusts of bread can be used quite well. Soak them in water till soft, then press *very dry* through a colander and beat up with a fork till free of lumps. Wash the dried fruit, stone raisins and cut up dates if being used. Shred suet finely. Mix all ingredients thoroughly. Turn into a greased pie dish, sprinkle with brown sugar, and bake in a moderate oven about 1¼ hours.

Melted margarine can be used in place of the suet, if preferred.

Steamed Bread Pudding

Stale bread 1 lb. *1 egg*
Candied peel 1 oz. *Dried fruit 6 oz.*
Golden syrup or brown sugar *Shredded suet 3 oz.*
* 3 oz.* *Mixed spice ¼ teaspoonful*

Prepare bread, fruit and suet as in previous recipe. Mix all ingredients thoroughly, turn into a greased basin, cover with a greased paper and steam 2½–3 hours.

Turn out on to a hot dish and serve plain or with marmalade sauce (see page 208).

Bread and Jam Fritters

Spread some slices of bread with margarine, then with jam. Sandwich together and cut into fingers or any shape preferred. Coat with frying batter (see page 226) and fry a golden brown on both sides.

Castle Puddings

Weight of 2 eggs in margarine,
sugar and flour
Baking powder ¼ teaspoonful

Apricot jam
Essence of lemon
Desiccated coconut

Beat margarine and sugar to a cream, add the lightly beaten eggs and a few drops lemon essence. Sieve the flour and baking powder and mix in lightly.

Half fill greased individual dariole moulds with the mixture and bake in a moderately hot oven (425°, Regulo No. 6) 15–20 minutes.

Turn on to a hot dish, pour over hot sieved apricot jam, sprinkle with desiccated coconut and put a glacé cherry on top of each.

Or the puddings can be left plain and jam sauce poured round the dish or served separately.

This quantity should make ten puddings.

Chocolate Pudding

Flour 5 oz.
Sugar 3 oz.
Margarine 3 oz.
Vanilla essence

Baking powder 1 teaspoonful
Cocoa 2 tablespoonfuls
2 eggs
Water ¼ teacupful

Beat margarine and sugar to a cream, then add the lightly beaten eggs and a few drops essence of vanilla. Mix the cocoa with ½ teacup of water and add it to the mixture; sieve flour and baking powder, stir them in lightly and mix thoroughly. Turn into a well-greased basin, cover with greased paper and steam 1¼–1½ hours.

Economical Chocolate Pudding

Make mixture as for steamed chocolate cake (see page 340). Turn into a greased basin, cover with a greased paper, and steam 1–1¼ hours. Serve with chocolate or custard sauce.

Crispy Plum Pie

Cut the plums in half and remove the stones. Put them in a pie dish with a very little water and sugar to taste. Cook in a moderate oven for 10 minutes, then completely cover the plums with thin slices of bread that have been spread with margarine, followed by golden syrup. Return to a moderate oven until the bread is crisp and lightly browned – 20–30 minutes.

Note. If preferred sprinkle the bread liberally with demerara sugar instead of spreading with golden syrup.

Date Pudding

Flour 3 oz.
Breadcrumbs 3 oz.
Stoned dates 4–6 oz.
Mixed spice ¼ teaspoonful
1 egg

Sugar 2 oz.
Golden syrup 2 oz.
Chopped suet 3 oz.
Baking powder ¼ teaspoonful

Chop the stoned dates, beat up the egg and mix all ingredients, adding sufficient water to make a soft, dropping consistency. Turn into a greased basin, cover with a greased paper and steam for 2½ hours. Turn out on to a hot dish and serve with orange or lemon sauce (see page 207).

For Fig Pudding. In place of dates use finely chopped figs, which should be soaked in cold water overnight.

Eggless Date Pudding

Self-raising flour 6 oz.   Dates 4 oz.
Sugar 2 oz.   Margarine 1–2 oz.
Bicarbonate of soda 1 level   Water ¼ pint
  teaspoonful   Mixed spice ½ teaspoonful

Cut up the dates, put them in a small saucepan with the sugar, water and margarine. Bring slowly to the boil, simmer for 3 minutes, then cool. Sieve the flour, spice and bicarbonate of soda into a basin, pour on contents of saucepan and mix thoroughly. Turn into a greased basin, cover with a greased paper and pudding cloth and steam for 1½ hours.

Or turn into a greased dish and bake in a moderate oven about ¾ hour.

Fruit Meringue

Soft fruit 1 lb.   4 sponge cakes
Water ¼ teacupful   Whites of 2 eggs
Caster sugar

Use any soft fruit available – raspberries, currants, loganberries or blackberries.

Cook the fruit with the water till soft, then rub through a sieve and sweeten to taste.

Cut up the sponge cakes, put in the bottom of a baking dish, pour over the fruit purée, and leave till cold.

Whisk the egg whites to a stiff froth, fold in 2 tablespoonfuls caster sugar and heap up roughly over the contents of dish. Sprinkle with caster sugar and cook in a moderate oven until the meringue is set and lightly browned – about 20 minutes.

Ginger Pudding

Flour 8 oz.   Shredded suet 3–4 oz.
Golden syrup 3 tablespoonfuls   Tepid water
Bicarbonate of soda 1 teaspoonful Ground ginger 1 teaspoonful

Mix the flour, ginger and shredded suet. Add the syrup and bicarbonate of soda mixed with ½ teacupful tepid water. Mix thoroughly and three-parts fill a greased basin with the mixture. Cover with a greased paper and steam 2½–3 hours. Serve with syrup sauce.

Golden Apple Pudding

Self-raising flour 4 oz.　*Apples ¾ lb.*
Breadcrumbs 4 oz.　*Shredded suet 4 oz.*
Ground cinnamon ½ tea-　*Orange or lemon rind*
spoonful　*Golden syrup 2 tablespoonfuls*

Peel and grate the apples. Mix the flour, cinnamon, suet and breadcrumbs together. Add a little orange or lemon peel, the grated apple and golden syrup. Mix thoroughly, pour in a greased basin, cover with a greased paper, and steam for 2½–3 hours.

Gooseberry Pudding

Gooseberries ½ lb.　*Breadcrumbs 1 oz.*
Self-raising flour 4 oz.　*1 egg*
Shredded suet 2 oz.　*Cold water*
Sugar 3 oz.

Top and tail the gooseberries and, if large, cut them across.

Mix all ingredients together, adding a very little cold water if the mixture seems very stiff.

Turn into a greased basin, cover with a greased paper, and steam for 2½ hours. Serve with brown sugar.

See also pages 225–6.

Gooseberry Upside-down Pudding

Gooseberries ¾ lb.　*Margarine 6 oz.*
Soft brown sugar 3 oz.　*Self-raising flour 5 oz.*
Caster sugar 3 oz.　*2 eggs*

Top and tail gooseberries and if large cut in half.

Melt 3 oz. margarine in a greased baking dish, then stir in the soft brown sugar and place the gooseberries on top. Cream the remaining margarine with the caster sugar, add the lightly beaten eggs one at a time, and fold in the flour; then cover the gooseberries with the mixture and bake it in a moderate oven (400°, Regulo No. 5) about 45 minutes.

Turn out on to a hot dish with the gooseberries on top.

Queen of Gooseberry Pudding

Gooseberries 1 lb.　　*Breadcrumbs 3 oz.*
Margarine 1 oz.　　*Granulated sugar 3 oz.*
2 eggs　　　　　*Caster sugar 2 oz.*

Stew the gooseberries with the granulated sugar and a little water till soft, then rub through a sieve. There should be about 1 pint of purée, so if necessary add a little water.

Mix the purée with the breadcrumbs, egg yolks, and melted margarine. Turn into a greased oven dish and bake in a moderate oven (375°, Regulo No. 4) for $\frac{1}{2}$ hour. Then whisk the egg whites till quite stiff, fold in the caster sugar, heap up over the pudding and return to the oven till the meringue is set and lightly browned – about 20 minutes. Serve hot.

Jam Batter Pudding

Flour 5 oz.　　*Milk $\frac{1}{2}$ pint*
2 eggs　　　　*Sugar 1 oz.*
Pinch of salt　　*Jam*

Grease a basin and cover the bottom with red stoneless jam. Make a batter with remaining ingredients and pour over the jam. Cover with a greased paper and steam for $1\frac{1}{2}$ hours. The basin should not be more than two-thirds full, to allow for rising.

Jam Layer Pudding

Self-raising flour 10 oz.　　*Shredded suet 4 oz.*
Cold water　　　　　　*Jam*

Add a pinch of salt to the flour, then the finely shredded suet and mix to a firm paste with cold water. Roll out about $\frac{1}{3}$ inch thick and cut into rounds the size of the basin. Grease the basin and put a little jam in the bottom, cover with a round of pastry, then continue with layers of jam and pastry until the basin is full. Have pastry for the top layer. Cover with a greased paper and steam for 3 hours.

Marmalade or golden syrup can replace the jam, but if the syrup is used, add to it a few fresh breadcrumbs and a pinch of ginger.

Lockshen Pudding

Cooked noodles or spaghetti
  1 pint
Sultanas 4 oz.
Candied peel 1 oz.

Cinnamon ¼ teaspoonful
Sugar 2 oz.
Margarine 2 oz.
2 eggs

Melt margarine, cut up peel, beat eggs lightly. Mix all ingredients thoroughly. Turn into a greased pie dish and bake in a moderate oven about 40 minutes, or turn into a greased basin, cover and steam 1¼–1½ hours.

Marmalade Pudding

Breadcrumbs 3 oz.
Demerara sugar 3 oz.
1 egg
Tepid water

Marmalade 3 oz.
Flour 3 oz.
Shredded suet 3 oz.
Bicarbonate of soda ½ teaspoonful

Grease a basin and sprinkle with a little of the sugar.

Mix the bicarbonate of soda with 1 tablespoonful of tepid water. Put all ingredients together in a bowl and mix very thoroughly, adding a little more water to make mixture a dropping consistency. Turn into the prepared basin, cover with greased paper, and steam for 2½–3 hours.

Mixed Fruit Pudding

Flour 4 oz.
Breadcrumbs 3 oz.
Dried fruit 8 oz.
Baking powder 1 teaspoonful
Shredded suet 3–4 oz.
Candied peel 1 oz.

2 eggs
Brown sugar 2 oz.
Mixed spice ¼ teaspoonful
Cinnamon ¼ teaspoonful
Golden syrup 1 tablespoonful

Use any mixture of fruit, dates, raisins, currants and sultanas. Wash thoroughly, remove stones and cut up dates. Cut up the peel and chop suet finely. Mix all dry ingredients, then stir in the syrup and well-beaten eggs. Mix thoroughly, turn into a greased basin, cover with a greased paper, and steam for 2½–3 hours.

Baked Orange Pudding

Self-raising flour 6 oz.　*2 eggs*
Margarine 2 oz.　*1 orange*
Sugar 3 oz.

Beat the margarine and sugar to a cream, add the lightly beaten eggs, then stir in the flour, beat lightly, and add the grated rind and strained juice of the orange.

Turn into a greased fireproof dish and bake in a moderate oven (400°, Regulo No. 5) about 50 minutes.

Steamed Orange Pudding

Self-raising flour 6 oz.　*Margarine 3 oz.*
Sugar 3 oz.　*Marmalade 2 tablespoonfuls*
2 eggs　*Orange flavouring*

Beat the margarine, sugar and marmalade till soft and creamy, then add the beaten eggs and a few drops of orange flavouring. Mix thoroughly, then add the flour. Add a spoonful or two of warm milk or water to make the mixture a soft dropping consistency. Turn into a greased basin, cover and steam for 1½ hours. Serve with marmalade or custard sauce.

Pineapple Pudding

Small tin pineapple slices　*Flour 4 oz.*
Soft brown sugar 2 oz.　*Margarine 3 oz.*
Caster sugar 2 oz.　*2 eggs*
Baking powder ¼ teaspoonful　*Arrowroot 1 teaspoonful*

Beat up 1 oz. margarine with the soft brown sugar, and spread over the bottom of a greased fireproof dish.

Drain off the syrup from the pineapple and arrange a layer of fruit on the bottom and sides of the dish.

Beat remaining margarine and caster sugar to a cream, add the lightly beaten egg yolks, then the sieved flour and baking powder.

Beat up the egg whites to a stiff froth, fold them into the mixture lightly, pour on to the pineapple in the baking dish and bake in a moderate oven (400°, Regulo No. 5) about 45 minutes. Turn out on to a hot dish and serve with pineapple sauce.

For the Sauce. Boil ½ pint of syrup from the pineapple, mix 1 teaspoonful of arrowroot with a little cold water, add to boiling syrup and simmer for 5 minutes.

Plum Pudding

Raisins 1 lb.	*Sweet almonds 2 oz.*
Sultanas 1 lb.	*Candied peel ¼ lb.*
Currants 1 lb.	*Flour ½ lb.*
Shredded suet 1 lb.	*Breadcrumbs ½ lb.*
Demerara sugar 1 lb.	*Cooking apples ½ lb.*
Salt 1 teaspoonful	*1 lemon*
Mixed spice 2 teaspoonfuls	*1 orange*
Cinnamon 1 teaspoonful	*4 eggs*
Sherry, brandy or rum 1 wineglassful	*½ nutmeg*

Use stale bread and grate it finely. Stone the raisins, wash and dry currants and sultanas. Blanch the almonds and cut them into strips. Slice the peel; chop suet finely; peel, core and grate the apples; grate the nutmeg.

Sieve the flour, salt and spices into a bowl, add all dry ingredients and the grated rind and juice of the orange and lemon, then the well-beaten eggs, and the brandy (sherry or rum) and mix very thoroughly.

Fill well-greased basin with the mixture; cover first with greased paper, then with a pudding cloth, and steam for 6 or 7 hours.

This quantity will make two large family-sized puddings or three smaller ones.

After boiling lift out on to a dish and leave till cold. Then remove pudding cloth and tie on a fresh one. If stored in a cool dry place they will keep for months. When required, steam or boil for at least 2 hours. Uncover and leave for 2 or 3 minutes for the steam to escape. Turn out on to a hot dish, sprinkle the top with sugar and serve with wine or hard sauce (pages 207–8).

Purim Fritters

Stale bread   2 egg yolks
Water ¼ teacupful   Sugar and cinnamon

Use either a stale French loaf or slices of stale bread cut into
rounds with a biscuit cutter. Cut the bread into slices about ½
inch thick. Beat the egg yolks lightly, add the water and
sweeten to taste. Dip the bread in this, drain well and fry a
golden brown on both sides in shallow fat. Drain and sprinkle
with caster sugar and powdered cinnamon before serving.

If preferred, the slices of bread can be coated with breadcrumbs after dipping in the egg, and can be served with a
spoonful of warm jam on each, instead of the sugar and
cinnamon.

Rice with Apples and Sultanas

Water 2 pints   Margarine 1 oz.
Rice 6 oz.   Apples 1 lb.
Sultanas 2 oz.   Sugar 2 oz.
Ground cinnamon ¼ teaspoonful

Bring the water to the boil, sprinkle in the well-washed rice,
cover and cook steadily for 10 minutes. Then add the apples,
peeled, cored and thinly sliced, and the remaining ingredients.
Cover and cook slowly till the rice is tender and the water
absorbed – 20–30 minutes.

Variations:
   (1) Omit the apples and serve with chocolate sauce.
   (2) Top each portion with a teaspoonful of golden syrup.

Rice and Orange Pudding

Rice 6 oz.   Margarine 2 oz.
Sugar 2 oz.   Golden syrup 1 tablespoonful
2 oranges

Boil the rice till just tender, then drain.

Melt the margarine, sugar and syrup, add the grated rind
of the oranges, pour over the rice and mix lightly.

Remove all the pith from the oranges, cut them into thin slices and remove pips.

Put a layer of rice in a greased baking dish, cover with half the orange slices and repeat the layers, having rice on top.

Bake in a moderate oven 20–25 minutes.

Roly-poly Pudding

Self-raising flour 8 oz.   *Cold water about ¼ pint*
Salt ¼ teaspoonful   *Jam or other filling*
Shredded suet 3 oz.

Sift the flour and salt into a basin, add the finely shredded suet, mix well, and add sufficient cold water to make a firm dough. Roll out into an oblong about ⅓ inch thick, and spread with jam or marmalade to within an inch of the edges; damp these with water, roll up tightly and press edges together. Wrap in well-greased greaseproof paper and then in a pudding cloth, rolling loosely to allow for swelling. Tie the ends securely. Put in a saucepan of fast boiling water and boil 1½–2 hours.

Other Fillings:

(1) **Golden Syrup.** Spread with a good layer of golden syrup, and sprinkle over 2 oz. breadcrumbs.

(2) **Apple and Dried Fruit.** Mix together a large cooking apple, finely chopped, 1 oz. chopped candied peel and 3 or 4 oz. sultanas, 1 tablespoonful of sugar and a pinch of cinnamon.

(3) **Date Spread.** Stone and cut up ½ lb. dates, put into a small saucepan with barely enough water to cover; add ½ teaspoonful ground ginger or cinnamon. Simmer gently till of jam consistency – about 10 minutes – and use when cold.

Steamed Sponge Pudding

Flour 6 oz.   *Baking powder 1 teaspoonful*
2 eggs   *Flavouring*
Margarine 3–4 oz.   *Milk or water*
Caster sugar 3 oz.

Sieve flour and baking powder. (If self-raising flour is used, omit the baking powder.)

Cream the margarine and sugar, then add the lightly

beaten eggs one at a time and a few drops of vanilla or lemon essence; next fold in the flour and if necessary add a table-spoonful or two of milk or water to give a soft dropping consistency. Turn into a greased basin, cover and steam for 1½ hours. Serve with jam or custard sauce.

Variations:

(1) Put 2 or 3 tablespoonfuls of stoneless jam or marmalade in the bottom of the greased basin, then add the pudding mixture.

(2) Add 2 oz. of halved glacé cherries to basic mixture.

(3) Add 3 oz. of sultanas and 1 oz. chopped candied peel to basic mixture. A little mixed spice can be added to the flour before sieving.

(4) **Coffee Pudding.** Add 2 oz. chopped nuts, 1 tablespoonful of liquid coffee essence and a few drops of vanilla to basic mixture.

(5) **Banana and Date Pudding.** Add 2 oz. chopped cooking dates and 2 mashed bananas to basic mixture.

(6) **Coconut.** Substitute 2 oz. desiccated coconut for 2 oz. of flour.

Eggless Steamed Sponge

Margarine 2 oz.	*Golden syrup 1 tablespoonful*
Self-raising flour 6 oz.	*Bicarbonate of soda 1 teaspoonful*
Sugar 2 oz.	*Vinegar 2 teaspoonfuls*
Milk to mix	

Rub fat into flour, add sugar and syrup, mix bicarbonate of soda with the vinegar, and add this together with sufficient milk to make a soft dropping consistency. Grease a pudding basin, put a little jam, marmalade, or dried fruit at the bottom, put the mixture on top, cover with a greased paper, and steam for 1½–2 hours.

Fatless Steamed Sponge

2 eggs	*Self-raising flour 5 oz.*
Sugar 3 oz.	*Water 2 tablespoonfuls*

Put the eggs and sugar in a basin, stand over boiling water, and beat till thick. Fold in the flour lightly and add the water. Finish off as previous recipe and steam $1\frac{1}{4}$–$1\frac{1}{2}$ hours.

Plain Suet Pudding

Self-raising flour 4 oz.
Breadcrumbs 4 oz.
Salt $\frac{1}{4}$ teaspoonful
Shredded suet 3–4 oz.
Water about $\frac{1}{4}$ pint

Mix flour, breadcrumbs, salt and shredded suet together, and add sufficient water to form a soft dough. Turn into a greased basin, cover with a greased paper, and steam $2\frac{1}{2}$–3 hours.

Turn out on to a hot dish and serve with jam, marmalade or syrup sauce – or just with plain golden syrup.

If preferred, 8 oz. self-raising flour can be used in place of breadcrumbs.

Pastry

The secret of successful pastry-making lies in observing a few simple rules.

All utensils, as well as the hands, must be cold and dry.

When rubbing in fat, use the tips of the fingers only; never handle the pastry more than is absolutely essential, and when kneading knead lightly and quickly.

Use an enamel-topped table in preference to a wooden pastry board, and roll as lightly as possible. Always roll forward and with short rapid strokes, and never roll right off the pastry.

Dust board and rolling pin with flour before rolling out the pastry, but do not sprinkle flour over the pastry.

Never stretch pastry when covering a dish, or it will shrink when baking.

Unless using a pie funnel, make an opening in the centre of pies or tarts to allow the steam to escape.

Various kinds of fats can be employed in the making of pastry: butter, clarified dripping, shredded suet, or one of the many fats which are on the market made from vegetable oils and nuts.

To Bake

Always bake pastry in a hot oven; generally speaking, the richer the pastry the hotter the oven. See detailed recipes in this section.

To Cover a Pie

(See Fruit Pies, page 251)

To Glaze

Fruit Pies and Tarts. When pastry is half cooked, brush over with beaten white of egg or cold water, and dredge with caster sugar.

Meat Pies and Patties. Brush over with beaten egg. Take care not to get any egg on the edges of the pastry, or it will not rise.

Pastry Leaves and Roses

Pastry leaves and roses are used to decorate the top of a meat pie.

Leaves. Roll out a strip of pastry about 1½ inches wide. Mark with slanting lines about 2 inches apart and cut into diamond-shaped pieces. Mark each diamond of pastry with the back of a knife to imitate the veins in a leaf and pinch the end towards the centre of the pie.

Roses. Roll out a small piece of pastry till paper thin, and cut into a square about 4 inches. Fold this into four to make a 2-inch square. Lay this over the first finger, folding all edges downwards, and cut a cross in the centre. Press the bottom edges together and open out the petals from the centre.

DIFFERENT KINDS OF PASTRY

Short Crust

Flour 8 oz.   *Fat 4–5 oz.*
Pinch of salt   *Cold water*

Sieve the flour and salt into a bowl, add the fat, cut it into the flour, then rub it in very lightly with the finger tips until the mixture resembles fine breadcrumbs. Then pour in a very little cold water, mixing with a knife, adding a little water at a time till a stiff paste is formed. Turn on to a lightly floured board, knead lightly till free of cracks, then roll out and use as required.

The fat or 'shortening' can be butter, margarine, or cooking fat, or a mixture of margarine and cooking fat.

American Baking Powder Pastry

This is a good recipe to use when fat is in very short supply, but it should be eaten hot and the same day it is made.

Flour 8 oz.	*Sugar 2 teaspoonfuls*
Pinch of salt	*Baking powder 4 level teaspoonfuls*
Cooking fat 1 oz.	

Sieve flour, baking powder, sugar, and salt. Rub in the fat and then add sufficient water to make a stiff dough. Roll out thinly, as the pastry will rise a good deal. Bake immediately in a very hot oven (475°, Regulo No. 8).

Biscuit Crust
(For Flans or Pies)

Flour 8 oz.	*Fat 4–5 oz.*
1 egg yolk	*Caster sugar 1 teaspoonful*
Lemon juice 1 teaspoonful	*Cold water*

Sieve the flour and sugar into a bowl; make like short crust, using the egg yolk mixed with the lemon juice and a spoonful or two of water for mixing.

Note. If for a savoury flan omit the sugar.

Puff Pastry

Flour 8 oz.	*Butter or other fat 8 oz.*
Pinch of salt	*Lemon juice 1 teaspoonful*
Cold water	

Sift flour and salt into a bowl, add the lemon juice and sufficient cold water – about $\frac{1}{4}$ pint – to mix to a soft dough. Knead lightly and set aside in a cold place for 10 minutes. Put the butter in the corner of a floured cloth, press out as much water as possible, and press into an oblong.

Roll out the pastry 3 times the length of the butter, and place the butter in the middle. Turn the ends of the pastry over the butter, making a fold of three. Press the edges together, half turn, press several times more with the rolling pin, then roll out to its original length. Repeat seven times in all, allowing the pastry to stand $\frac{1}{4}$ hour in a cold place after each two rollings. After the last rolling leave for a few hours in a cold place, covered with a cloth; then use as required.

Vol-au-vent

A vol-au-vent is a case of puff pastry, round or oval, which may be filled with either a savoury or a fruit filling.

To make it roll out some puff pastry $\frac{1}{2}$ inch thick and another piece $\frac{1}{4}$ inch thick.

Cut a large round or oval shape from each piece of pastry with a cutter. Then from the *thick* oval stamp out the centre, leaving an inch margin. Damp the edges of the thin oval and lay the pastry ring carefully on top. Put on to a baking sheet, brush the top ring with beaten egg, and bake in a hot oven (475°, Regulo No. 8) about $\frac{1}{2}$ hour. At the same time glaze and bake the oval that was cut out, and it can be used as a cover when the filling is a savoury one.

Use hot or cold. Even if it is to be served hot, it can be made in advance and reheated when required. Small individual cases are made in the same way, simply using a smaller cutter.

Rough Puff Pastry

Rough puff pastry is excellent for pies, patties, tarts, and tart-lets.

To $\frac{1}{2}$ lb. of flour allow 4–6 oz. of fat, 1 teaspoonful of lemon juice, and a pinch of salt. The fat can be margarine or cooking fat or a mixture of both; it must be cold and firm and the water used for mixing must also be very cold.

Sieve the flour and salt into a bowl, add the fat, cut into small pieces (about the size of a small nut) *without* rubbing it in. Add the lemon juice and enough cold water to mix to a fairly stiff dough, using a knife for the mixing. Turn out on to a floured board, press the pastry lightly together, making edges straight before rolling. Handle as little as possible and do *not* knead the pastry. Roll out into a strip about 6 or 7 inches wide, keeping edges straight and corners square. Fold in three, half turn, so that the open edge is towards you, and roll again. Repeat the folding and rolling three times more, but leave the pastry to stand in a cool place (fridge if available) for a short time after the second and fourth rollings. Then roll into shape, size and thickness required.

Flaky Pastry
(For Pies, Tarts, and Tartlets)

Flour ¾ lb. Fat 8 oz.
Pinch of salt Lemon juice 1 teaspoonful
Cold water

For the fat use butter, margarine, or cooking fat, or a mixture of any two.

Sieve the flour and salt into a bowl and rub in 2 oz. fat.

Mix to a stiff but pliable paste with cold water, to which the lemon juice has been added. Knead the paste lightly on a floured board, then roll out to a strip about 6 or 7 inches wide.

Divide remaining fat into three and spread one portion in small pieces evenly over the pastry, leaving 1 inch all round free of fat.

Then fold the paste into three like this: Place the bottom edge two-thirds up the strip and bring the top edge over, so that it lies along the folded edge. Press edges lightly together with the rolling pin to enclose cold air.

Give the paste a half turn, so as to bring the folded edge to one side. Roll out again to a long narrow strip, and repeat the process twice more. Leave in a cool place for 10 minutes, then roll out to desired size and thickness.

Choux Paste
(For Cream Buns, Éclairs, etc.)

Flour 4 oz.	*Pinch of salt*
Butter or margarine 2 oz.	*3 eggs*
Water ¼ pint	*Vanilla essence*

Use a saucepan to make the paste, one large enough to allow the eggs to be beaten in. Put in the butter, pour over the boiling water, and when the butter has melted stir in the sieved flour, mixing very thoroughly with a wooden spoon, and stir over a gentle heat until the mixture – which is called a panada – thickens and leaves the sides of the pan quite clean. Cool slightly, then beat in the eggs one at a time. Beat very well and add the vanilla essence.

Suet Crust

Shredded suet 4–6 oz.	*Salt ¼ teaspoonful*
Flour 12 oz.	*Cold water*
Baking powder 1 teaspoonful	

Remove all skin and gristle from the suet before weighing. Then chop it finely, sprinkling a little flour over it while chopping, to prevent sticking. Sieve flour, baking powder, and salt into a bowl, mix in the suet, and add enough cold water to make a soft dough. Use as required.

Fruit Pies, Flans, and Tartlets

Fruit Pies

Almost any kind of fruit may be used, or a mixture, either fresh, canned, or bottled. The soft summer fruits, currants, raspberries, and cherries, are delicious when mixed. Large fruit should be cut in pieces. Apples are improved if grated lemon rind or one or two cloves are added. Fill the pie dish with fruit and sugar in layers; the quantity of sugar will vary according to the acidity of the fruit and individual taste. Always have the top layer fruit, as sugar is apt to make the crust heavy and discolour it. Pile the fruit high in the centre and add a little water.

To Cover. Roll out some short crust about $\frac{1}{4}$ inch thick. Cut off strips 1 inch wide, wet the rim of the dish with cold water and lay the strips on, press on to the rim of the dish and join without overlapping. Brush over this strip of pastry with water, then lift the piece of pastry on the rolling pin and lay over the fruit, taking care not to stretch it. Let it lie loosely. Press the edges together and with a sharp knife carefully trim the pastry round the edge of the dish. Then ornament the edges; this can be done with an ordinary fork or teaspoon, just pressing down enough all round the rim to make an impression.

Make two small holes with a skewer to allow the steam to escape. Bake in a hot oven (450°, Regulo No. 7) for 15 minutes, then slightly lower until the fruit is cooked – about 40 minutes altogether. The time will vary according to the nature and degree of ripeness of the fruit. If soft fruit, or cooked or bottled fruit is being used, place a pie funnel or egg cup in the centre of the dish. The pie should take only 30 minutes to cook. If flaky or rough puff pastry is being used, start baking in a hotter oven (475°, Regulo No. 8) and reduce the heat after 15 minutes.

Almond Cheese Cakes

Short crust	*Margarine 2 oz.*
Raspberry jam	*1 egg and 1 extra yolk*
Ground almonds 4 oz.	*Cornflour 1 oz.*
Caster sugar 3 oz.	

Beat the egg slightly with the sugar, then add the melted margarine, the ground almonds, and cornflour, and mix thoroughly.

Line a dozen patty tins with short crust, roll out the trimmings and cut narrow strips for decoration. Put $\frac{1}{2}$ teaspoonful jam in the bottom of each pastry case, then half fill with the almond mixture. Put two narrow strips of pastry crosswise over the top. Bake in a hot oven (450°, Regulo No. 7) for 6 to 7 minutes, then reduce the heat, and continue cooking until the tartlets are a pale golden brown. Serve hot or cold.

Note. Whole almonds, blanched and finely chopped, can be used in place of ground almonds.

Apple Cake
(Apfel Kuchen)

Kuchen dough	*Margarine 2 oz.*
Cooking apples ¾–1 lb.	*Cinnamon*
Caster sugar 2 oz.	*Sultanas*

Roll out risen kuchen dough (page 378) and line a greased baking tin 8 by 10 inches. Prove for 10 minutes, then brush over with melted margarine. Peel and core the apples and cut into eighths, and place them on the dough in parallel lines. Sprinkle over the sugar, a little cinnamon, and a few sultanas, then pour over remaining melted margarine. Bake for 15 minutes in a hot oven (425°, Regulo No. 6), then reduce to 375°, Regulo No. 4 until the apples are soft and the pastry cooked – about another 15–20 minutes.

Apple Cheese Cakes

Short or rough puff pastry 6 oz.	*Apples ¾ lb.*
Margarine 2 oz.	*Sugar 2 oz.*
Yolks of 2 eggs	*¼ lemon*
Cake crumbs 1 oz.	*Water*

Peel, core and cut up the apples, put in a saucepan with the grated rind and juice of half a lemon and 4 tablespoonfuls of water, cover, and cook gently till soft, then rub through a sieve or strainer. Melt the margarine in a saucepan, add the sugar and apple purée, and stir till sugar has dissolved; remove from heat and add the beaten eggs and cake crumbs.

Roll pastry thinly, cut into rounds, and line patty tins with it, fill with apple mixture, and bake in a hot oven for 6 or 7 minutes then reduce heat and continue cooking for another 12–15 minutes.

This quantity should make 15–18 cheese cakes.

If using short crust, start cooking at 450°, Regulo No. 7; for rough puff pastry 475°, Regulo No. 8.

Continental Apple Tart

Self-raising flour 10 oz.	*Butter or margarine 5 oz.*
Caster sugar 3 oz.	*Currants 1 oz.*
Brown sugar	*Sultanas 1 oz.*
Cooking apples 1½ lb.	*Candied peel 1 oz.*
1 egg	*Pinch of cinnamon*

This tart is best made in a shallow 2-inch tart tin with hinged sides. When tart is cold, remove the pins and lift off the circular side piece. The quantities given are for a tin about 8½ inches across. Grease it well before lining with pastry.

Peel, core, and cut up the apples, and stew in *very little* water with the currants and sultanas. Cook to a pulp, then sweeten to taste with brown sugar and add the chopped peel. Leave till cold.

Rub the butter into the flour, add the sugar and egg, and knead thoroughly to a pliable dough. Leave for 20 minutes then roll out in a long strip, fold in three and roll again, and repeat once more. Line the bottom and sides of the tart tin with the paste, sprinkle with caster sugar and flour, pour in the apple, and decorate with strips of pastry. Bake in a moderate oven for 1 hour, keeping the tart covered with an enamel plate or saucepan lid for ¾ hour. Leave in tin till cold.

Crispy Apple Tart

Line a deep tart tin or round glass baking dish with thin suet crust. Cover with a thick layer of thinly sliced apples. Sprinkle with sugar and lemon juice and cover with another thin layer of pastry. Spread with golden syrup and sprinkle with brown sugar. Bake in a moderate oven about 50 minutes. The crust should be crisp and like toffee.

Crumbly Apple Pie

Apples 1 lb.	*Flour 4 oz.*
Margarine 2 oz.	*Sugar*

Peel, core, and slice the apples and put them in a pie dish with very little water and sugar to taste, then heat through in the oven. Rub margarine into the flour until it looks like fine bread-crumbs, add 2 oz. sugar and a pinch of salt, and mix thoroughly.

Sprinkle this over the hot fruit and bake in a moderate oven (400°, Regulo No. 5) until the top is golden brown and the fruit soft – about 30–40 minutes.

Rhubarb, plums, or any soft fruit can replace the apples. A small tin of pineapple pieces can be mixed with the apples.

Apple Strudel

Flour ¼ lb.	*Warm water about ¼ pint*
Pinch of salt	*1 small egg*
Olive oil 2 tablespoonfuls	*Apples 1 lb.*
Breadcrumbs 1 tablespoonful	*Currants 3 tablespoonfuls*
Brown sugar	*Lemon juice*
A few almonds	*Margarine 2 oz.*

Sieve the flour and salt into a bowl; beat up the egg, add the oil, and pour into the middle of the flour, together with a little *warm* water; do not put all the water in to start with. It depends on the size of the egg and dryness of the flour how much will be needed. Mix with a fork and then knead with the hand very thoroughly to a soft, pliable dough that does not stick to the hands or bowl. Leave on the pastry board, cover with a warm basin, and leave for ½ hour. Stretch a clean cloth over the kitchen table, sprinkle it with flour, put the pastry in the middle, roll it out into a large rectangle, and pull it with the hands until it is almost thin enough to see through.

Peel the apples, cut them into very thin slices, brown the breadcrumbs in a little margarine, mix them with the apples, cleaned currants, and chopped almonds. Sweeten with brown sugar and flavour with lemon juice. Spread over the pastry and sprinkle with a little melted margarine. Raise one side of the cloth and roll the pastry and apple like a 'roly-poly'. Form into a crescent, place on a greased baking sheet, brush over with the margarine, and bake for about 40 minutes. Start in a hot oven (450°, Regulo No. 7) and when lightly browned reduce to moderate.

For a Cheese Strudel. Mix ½ lb. any kind of curd cheese with 1 oz. melted butter and a beaten egg. Add sugar and salt to taste and use in place of the apple mixture.

Bakewell Tart

Short crust 4 oz.	*Ground almonds 2 oz.*
Margarine 2 oz.	*Caster sugar 2 oz.*
1 egg	*Almond essence*
Raspberry jam	

Beat the margarine and sugar till soft and creamy, stir in the beaten egg and a few drops almond essence, and then the ground almonds. Mix thoroughly.

Line a round shallow tin with pastry, put in a layer of jam, then spread the mixture on top. Bake in a moderate oven (400°, Regulo No. 5) until well risen and brown and the filling is set – 30–40 minutes.

Alternative Fillings:

(1) Plain cake or spongecake crumbs can be used in place of the ground almonds, in which case use about a teaspoonful of almond essence.

(2) Mix together 2 oz. each rolled oats, melted margarine, and caster sugar, flavour strongly with almond essence, and spread the mixture evenly over the jam.

Banana Puffs

Bananas	*Flaky pastry*
Apricot jam	*Lemon juice*

Split bananas through lengthways, sprinkle with lemon juice and sandwich together with apricot jam. Then cut each banana into 2 or 3 pieces.

Roll out the pastry thinly and cut into 4-inch squares. Place a piece of banana on each, moisten the edges with cold water, then fold over, pressing edges firmly together. Brush over lightly with cold water and sprinkle with caster sugar. Bake in a hot oven about 15–20 minutes.

Cheese Cake

Short or biscuit crust ½ lb.   *Filling*

Roll out the pastry and line a greased tart tin, shaping it well into the bottom and sides of the tin, and prick the bottom. Fill with the cheese mixture and bake in a hot oven (450°,

Regulo No. 7), for 10 minutes, then reduce the heat to moderate (370°, Regulo No. 4) until the pastry is lightly browned and the filling firm — about 20–30 minutes.

Filling (1)

Curd cheese 10 oz.	Lemon rind
Margarine 2 oz.	Candied peel 1 oz.
Caster sugar 1 oz.	Currants 1 oz.
1 egg	

Sieve the cheese. Cream the margarine and sugar, add the beaten egg, cheese, peel, currants, and grated lemon rind, mix thoroughly and use as directed.

If preferred, the currants and peel can be omitted.

Note. The cheese filling can be sprinkled with crushed rusk crumbs, if a brown finish is required.

Filling (2)

Curd cheese 12 oz.	Margarine 1 oz.
Flour 2 level tablespoonfuls	Sugar 3 oz.
Cream or top milk 2 table-spoonfuls	2 eggs
	Grated lemon rind

Sieve the cheese, add the flour and cream. Separate the yolks and whites of the eggs. Beat the yolks lightly with the sugar, add the melted margarine, then mix with the cheese. Flavour with grated lemon rind, then fold in the stiffly whipped egg whites.

Cheese Cakes with Kuchen Dough. If preferred, kuchen dough can be used in place of ordinary pastry (see page 378).

Grease two deep sandwich tins. Roll out the dough and line the tins with it. Leave the tins in a warm place for the dough to rise again for ½ hour. Fill with the cheese mixture and bake about ½ hour (about 425°, Regulo No. 6).

Chestnut Tartlets

Short crust	Chestnuts 6 oz.
1 egg	Caster sugar 3 oz.
Cooking sherry 1 tablespoonful	Apricot jam

Boil chestnuts till soft, then remove shells and skin and rub through a sieve. Mix with the sugar, beaten egg, and sherry.

Line patty tins with pastry, put a teaspoonful of apricot jam in each, then a tablespoonful of chestnut mixture. Bake in a quick oven (450°, Regulo No. 7) till lightly browned.

Chocolate Meringue Tart

Short crust 6 oz.	*Chocolate 3 oz.*
Cornflour 1 oz.	*Caster sugar 3 oz.*
Milk ½ pint	*2 eggs.*
Vanilla essence	

Make a flan case with short (or biscuit) pastry (see pages 246–7). Bake 'blind' and leave till cold.

Blend the cornflour with a spoonful of cold milk and boil the remainder. Melt the chocolate in a basin over hot water, then pour on the hot milk and mix with 1 oz. sugar and blended cornflour. Stir over a very gentle heat till boiling, simmer for 2 or 3 minutes, then cool slightly; then add the beaten egg yolks and return to the saucepan and stir over a very gentle heat for 2 or 3 minutes, but do not reboil. Add a few drops essence of vanilla and leave till cool, then pour into the pastry case. Whip the egg whites to a stiff froth, fold in remaining sugar (except about 1 teaspoonful), then heap up over the chocolate filling. Sprinkle with caster sugar and place in a cool oven (325°, Regulo No. 2) till the meringue is set and lightly tinted – 20–30 minutes.
Serve hot or cold.

Note. The chocolate filling can be mixed with water in place of milk.

Coconut Tart

Short crust 4 oz.	*Caster sugar 2 oz.*
A little jam	*Desiccated coconut 4 oz.*
Margarine 1 oz.	*2 eggs*

Line a deep pie plate with pastry and spread with a thin layer of jam. Melt the margarine and mix with the coconut, sugar, and lightly beaten eggs. Spread evenly over the jam, and bake

35–40 minutes, the first 15 minutes 450°, Regulo No. 7, then reduce to moderate (400°, Regulo No. 5).

Date and Apple Tart

Line a tart tin with short crust, then fill with a mixture of chopped dates and apple. Sprinkle with sugar and a little ground cinnamon. Damp the edges of the pastry and cover with a second round. Press the edges well together, trim and mark with a knife or fork. Make a hole in the centre and bake in a moderate oven (450°, Regulo No. 6) 35–40 minutes.

Rhubarb finely chopped can be used in place of the apples.

Éclairs

Make a choux paste (see page 250). Put into a forcing bag with a plain tube (about ½ inch) and force the mixture on to a greased baking tin in finger lengths, 3½–4 inches long. Cut the mixture with a knife dipped in hot water when required length is obtained. Bake in a moderately hot oven (400°, Regulo No. 5) about 35 minutes, until well risen, crisp, and of a golden brown colour.

Remove from the tin, slit down the sides with a sharp pointed knife, to allow the steam to escape, and leave on a cake tray to cool. When cold, fill with whipped sweetened cream flavoured with vanilla, or confectioners' custard (see page 270), and ice with coffee or chocolate glacé icing (see page 370).

Cream Buns. Make and bake like éclairs but put through the forcing bag in little mounds about the size of half an egg.

Fruit Flans

Use biscuit crust (see page 247) – roll out lightly and quickly ¼ inch thick.

A flan ring or deep sandwich tin can be used. If using a sandwich tin, line it with greased paper. A flan ring should be well greased and placed on a greased paper on a baking sheet.

To Bake Blind. Place the pastry inside the flan ring (or sandwich tin), press well into shape, taking care to press the pastry well down on to the tray on which it is standing. Trim off the pastry along the top edge of the tin with a sharp floured knife. Prick the bottom and place a circular piece of greased paper inside the flan, greased side against the pastry. Then put in a layer of crusts of bread or haricot beans (the beans can be used over again and should be kept specially for the purpose), in order to keep the pastry in shape while it is cooking.

Bake in a hot oven (450°, Regulo No. 7) about 15 minutes, then remove the paper and return to the oven for a few minutes to dry the bottom and finish cooking. Remove from tin, cool on a cake tray, and when cold fill as required.

Almost any kind of fruit, fresh or tinned, can be used for the filling, or a combination of fruits. After arranging the fruit neatly in the case, cover with thickened syrup or apricot glaze.

The flan can be served plain or topped with meringue or whipped cream.

To Thicken Fruit Syrup. Take $\frac{1}{4}$ pint of syrup from canned or freshly cooked fruit, add a little more sugar if necessary and bring to the boil, add 1 teaspoonful of arrowroot mixed with a little cold syrup, stir till boiling, and simmer for 5 minutes.

Apricot Glaze. Rub 2 tablespoonfuls apricot jam through a sieve, add $\frac{1}{4}$ pint of fruit juice, and bring to the boil. Blend 1 teaspoonful of arrowroot or cornflour with a little cold water, pour on the boiling syrup, return to the saucepan, stir till boiling, and simmer for 3 or 4 minutes.

Apple Flan

Fill a cooked flan case with apple purée. When stewing the apples add a few sultanas or finely chopped crystallized ginger and a pinch of cinnamon.

Or put a layer of apple purée in the case, sprinkle over a little grated orange rind and top with orange slices.

Apricot, Greengage or Plum Flan

Fruit 8–10 oz.   *Sugar 2 or 3 oz.*
Arrowroot or cornflour 1 teaspoonful   *Water $\frac{1}{4}$ pint*

Make a flan case (see above).

Cut the fruit in halves and remove the stones. Boil the sugar and water together for 5 minutes, then put in the fruit, and simmer gently till just tender, but not broken. Take out the fruit and stir in the arrowroot mixed smoothly with 1 table-spoonful of cold water, stir till boiling and simmer gently for 5 minutes. When nearly cold, fill the pastry case with the fruit and cover with the thickened syrup.

Banana Flan

Cut some bananas into slices about $\frac{1}{4}$ inch thick and arrange in circles, the pieces slightly overlapping each other, in a cooked flan case (see pages 258–9). Put a large glacé cherry in the centre and cover with apricot glaze (see page 259).

Fresh Fruit Flans

Prepare the fruit in the ordinary way; hull strawberries and raspberries and stone cherries. Put into the flan case just before serving, and spoon cold syrup glaze over.

   Syrup Glaze. Boil together 4 oz. sugar and $\frac{1}{4}$ pint water or fruit juice, flavoured with lemon juice, till thick and syrupy. Use when cold.

Grape Flan

Spread a thin layer of apricot jam in the bottom of a cooked flan case. Remove skin and pips from grapes and arrange in circles on top of the jam, then coat with apricot glaze (see page 259).

Fruit Tartlets

Make these in the same way as a fruit flan. Line patty tins with pastry and bake 'blind'. Leave till cold, then fill with fruit and glaze the tartlets as for fruit flans.

   Lemon Curd Tartlets. Fill cooked tartlet cases with lemon curd. Blanch and shred a few almonds and put in a cool oven till lightly browned, then sprinkle over the tartlets.

Pineapple Flan

Biscuit crust	*Small tin sliced pineapple*
Glacé cherries 1 oz.	*Pineapple syrup ¼ pint*
Arrowroot 1 teaspoonful	*Sugar 2 oz.*

Make the flan case (see pages 258–9) and leave till cold. Boil the
syrup, add the sugar and the arrowroot mixed smoothly with
a little cold syrup. Stir till boiling, simmer for 5 minutes, and
leave to cool.

Arrange the pineapple and cherries in the cold flan case, and
spoon the syrup over.

Spring Flan

Short crust 6 oz.	*Milk ¼ pint*
A few sticks of rhubarb	*Custard powder 1 tablespoonful*
Water ¼ pint	*Sugar*

Make and bake a flan case (see pages 258–9) and leave till cold.
Make a thick custard with the milk and custard powder, and
sweeten to taste. When cold pour into the flan case, and lay
sticks of carefully cooked rhubarb across.

To Cook the Rhubarb. Cut it into lengths the size of the
flan. Put ¼ pint of water in a saucepan, add 1 piled tablespoonful
of sugar. Boil for 2 or 3 minutes, then lay in the rhubarb and
cook *very gently* till tender, but not broken.

Crispy Gooseberry Tart

Line a deep tart or round glass baking dish with pastry; put
in a good layer of gooseberries (cut across if large), sprinkle
with sugar and cover with another thin layer of pastry. Spread
the top thinly with golden syrup and sprinkle with brown
sugar. Bake in a moderate oven about 45 minutes, the first 15
minutes 450°, Regulo No. 7, then reduce the heat till the
pastry is cooked.

Jam Tart

Line a pie plate with short crust, trim and crimp the edge,

prick the bottom, spread any kind of jam over, and cross with strips of pastry.

Bake about 20 minutes in a hot oven (450°, Regulo No. 7).

Jam Puffs

Puff or flaky pastry 8 oz.   *White of egg*
  (pages 247–8, 249)   *Caster sugar*
Jam

Roll pastry about ⅓ inch thick and cut into squares. Brush edges with water and put a teaspoonful of jam in each. Fold over to form a triangle, pressing the edges well together, so that the jam does not ooze out during the cooking. Place on a baking sheet, brush over with white of egg or cold water, and sprinkle with caster sugar. Bake in a hot oven (475°, Regulo No. 8) 15–20 minutes.

Lemon Meringue Pie

Short or biscuit crust   *Water ¼ pint*
A large lemon   *Cornflour 1 oz.*
Caster sugar 6 oz.   *Margarine 1 oz.*
Cherries and angelica   *2 large eggs*

Prepare a pastry case according to directions on pages 258–9, bake, and leave till cold.

Mix the cornflour to a thin cream with a little of the water, heat the remainder and when boiling pour on to the cornflour, add 3 oz. sugar and the grated rind and juice of the lemon. Return to saucepan, stir till boiling, and simmer for 2 or 3 minutes, then add the margarine, remove from the heat, and beat in the egg yolks one at a time, then pour into the pastry case.

Whisk the egg whites very stiffly, fold in remaining 3 oz. sugar, and heap up over the tart. Sprinkle with caster sugar and bake in a very slow oven (325°, Regulo No. 2) until the meringue is crisp and very lightly coloured.

Serve cold decorated with cherries and angelica.

Mint Pasties

Short or flaky pastry ¼ lb.	*Currants 4 oz.*
Candied peel	*Sugar 1 oz.*
Finely chopped mint 1 tablespoonful	*Margarine 1 oz.*

Melt the margarine and mix with washed currants, mint, sugar and peel.

Roll out the pastry thinly, cut into rounds and line patty tins with half the rounds. Put a little of the mixture on each, moisten the edges of the pastry with cold water and cover with another round of pastry. Brush tops lightly with cold water and sprinkle with caster sugar. Bake in a hot oven (450°, Regulo No. 7) until the pastry is cooked – about 20 minutes.

Pastry Fingers

These are quickly and easily made. Use either short or flaky pastry. Roll out quite thin and spread half with any of the following mixtures. Moisten the edges and fold the other half over. Brush the top with cold water and sprinkle with caster sugar; bake about 20 minutes. For flaky pastry 475°, Regulo No. 8; for short crust 450°, Regulo No. 7. When cooked cut into fingers and serve either hot or cold.

Fillings:

   (1) Any kind of stoneless jam, lemon curd, or mincemeat.

   (2) Sprinkle with demerara sugar and cover with currants.

   (3) Spread with honey and sprinkle with chopped nuts and dates (or figs).

   (4) **Apple Filling.** Peel and core a large cooking apple, grate it finely, add 1 oz. of stoneless raisins and the same quantity of candied peel, a pinch of mixed spice and sugar to taste.

   (5) **Apricot Filling.** Soak 4 oz. dried apricots overnight. The following day stew till tender, drain off the water, and rub through a sieve. Return the purée to the saucepan, add 2 oz. sugar, 2 teaspoonfuls of lemon juice, and stir over a very gentle heat till the sugar has dissolved. Add a few chopped blanched almonds and leave till cold.

Rhubarb Tart

Rhubarb 1 breakfastcupful	*Breadcrumbs 1 oz.*
Sultanas 2 oz.	*1 egg*
Margarine 1 oz.	*Sugar*
Half a lemon	*Short crust*

Chop the rhubarb and sultanas together, and mix them with the melted margarine, grated rind and juice of the lemon, breadcrumbs and beaten egg. Add sugar to taste.

Line a tart tin with pastry, spread over the rhubarb mixture, damp the edges and cover with another round of pastry, trim edges and press together. Make a hole in the centre for the steam to escape, and bake about 40 minutes, the first 10 minutes in a hot oven (450°, Regulo No. 7) then reduce to 375°, Regulo No. 4.

Baked Syrup Roll

Roll out short crust into an oblong strip, spread with syrup (leaving 1 inch of the pastry all round free), sprinkle liberally with breadcrumbs, damp the edges and roll up. Place on a greased baking tin and bake about 40 minutes. Start at 425°, Regulo No. 6, and, when it is lightly browned, reduce the heat.

Note. Currants or chopped sultanas can be used in place of breadcrumbs and a light sprinkling of ginger or cinnamon can also be added.

For Jam Roll. Simply spread the pastry with jam and proceed as above.

Treacle Tart

Short crust pastry 6 oz.	*Breadcrumbs 2 oz.*
Golden syrup 3 tablespoonfuls	*Lemon juice or ginger*

Slightly warm the syrup, flavour with a pinch of ginger, or a little lemon juice and grated lemon rind, then stir in the breadcrumbs.

Roll out the pastry and line a tart tin (about 9 inches in diameter) with it, trim and decorate the edge. Spread over the syrup mixture, decorate with cross strips of pastry, and bake in a moderately hot oven (425°, Regulo No. 6) about ½ hour.

Coconut Tart. Use desiccated coconut instead of bread-crumbs.

Vanilla Slices

Puff pastry ¼ lb. *Confectioners' custard ¼ pint*
Strawberry jam *White glacé icing*

Make puff or rough puff pastry (see pages 247–8), roll out ⅛ inch thick, cut into strips the length of the baking sheet and about 4½ inches wide. Bake for 15 minutes in a hot oven (500°, Regulo No. 9).

Make custard (see page 270), and leave till cold.

When the pastry is cool, spread one piece with a very thin layer of strawberry jam, then with the custard. Put another strip of pastry on top, and cover with glacé icing (see page 370). When set, with a very sharp knife cut into 2-inch lengths.

Milk Puddings, Pancakes, and Hot Soufflés

For simple milk puddings allow 1½ oz. of grain to 1 pint of milk, if to be baked; slightly more grain if to be steamed in a double boiler. Allow 1 tablespoonful of sugar or more, according to taste.

The puddings must be cooked in a very moderate heat, so that the grains become soft and swollen very gradually. For large grain this will take 2–3 hours.

Custards and milk puddings which contain eggs must never *boil*, or they will curdle.

A pudding made with 1 pint of milk is sufficient for four people.

Sago and Tapioca

Allow quantities as above. Put the washed grain with the sugar and milk in a greased baking dish. Allow to stand at least 1 hour before placing in the oven. Cook slowly 1½–2 hours, stirring from time to time.

Farina, Ground Rice, Semolina

Bring 1 pint of milk to boiling point, sprinkle in 1½ oz. grain and stir while it simmers for 5 minutes. Add the sugar, turn into a greased baking dish, and cook in a moderate oven till lightly browned – about 30 minutes.

Milk Pudding with Eggs

Cook the pudding in a double boiler till the grain is soft, then cool slightly and stir in the well-beaten eggs, allowing 1 or 2 to 1 pint of milk. Stand the dish in a baking tin with water to come 1 inch up the side of the dish, and cook in a moderate oven about 30 minutes. It must *not* boil.

Blancmange

Allow 1½ oz. cornflour and 1 oz. sugar to 1 pint milk. Mix the cornflour and sugar to a thin paste with a little cold milk; boil the remainder of the milk and stir on to the paste. Return to the saucepan and let it simmer very gently for 5 minutes.

Flavour with vanilla or other essence and turn into a wet mould till cold and set. Serve with jam, stewed fruit, or fruit syrup.

If using packet blancmange powder, follow directions given on the packet.

For Chocolate Blancmange. Add 2 oz. grated chocolate or 1 tablespoonful cocoa to the milk before boiling.

For Fruit Mould. Add 2 sliced bananas or 2 tablespoonfuls tinned pineapple, peaches, or apricots, well drained and cut into dice, after the cornflour is cooked.

Apricot Condé

Rice 2 oz.
Milk 1 pint
Arrowroot 1 teaspoonful

Sugar 2 oz.
Tinned apricots
Vanilla essence

Grease a thick saucepan with butter, put in the milk and washed rice, place over a gentle heat, and stir till boiling; cover and simmer very gently till the rice is soft and the milk absorbed – about 20 minutes. Remove from the heat, stir in the sugar and flavour with vanilla.

Rinse some small individual moulds with cold water, fill with rice and press down. Leave till cold, then turn out. Place half an apricot on each and pour cold thickened syrup around.

To Thicken the Syrup. Allow 1 teaspoonful of arrowroot to $\frac{1}{2}$ pint of the syrup. Mix the arrowroot with 1 tablespoonful cold syrup, boil remainder and pour it over. Put in a small saucepan, stir till boiling and simmer for 2 or 3 minutes.

Batter Pudding

To Steam. Make pancake batter (see page 272). Turn into a well-greased basin, cover with a greased paper and steam for 1 hour. Serve with jam or syrup sauce.

To Bake. Heat $\frac{1}{2}$ oz. butter or margarine in a shallow fireproof dish, and when smoking hot pour in the batter. Bake in a hot oven (425°, Regulo No. 6) until well risen, crisp and brown – about 40 minutes. Serve with jam, honey, or syrup.

Note. A few raisins, currants or sultanas can be added to either steamed or baked batter pudding.

Bread and Butter Pudding

2 eggs   Sugar 1 oz.
Milk 1 pint   Bread and butter (or margarine)
Dried fruit 1 oz.

Put two layers of slices of thin bread and butter in a greased baking dish and sprinkle over a few sultanas, currants or chopped dates.

Beat up the eggs, add the milk and sugar and pour into the dish. Let stand for $\frac{1}{2}$ hour for the bread to swell, then stand in a baking tin containing a little water, and cook in a slow oven till the custard is set – about 40 minutes.

Cabinet Pudding

Milk ¼ pint
Currants or sultanas 2 oz.
Thin bread and butter 4 oz.
  (or margarine)

2 eggs
Sugar 1 oz.
Flavouring

Grease a pint basin and sprinkle sultanas or currants on the
bottom. Then line with slices of bread and butter (buttered
side next to the basin). Cut up the trimmings of the bread and
butter and put in the centre of the basin with the remaining
dried fruit.

Beat up the eggs with the sugar, add the milk and a few drops
vanilla essence or a little grated lemon rind. Pour into the
basin and allow to stand for ½ hour. Cover with a greased paper
and steam gently for 1¼ hours.

Chocolate Meringue Pudding

Fresh breadcrumbs 3 oz.
Cocoa 1 dessertspoonful
Caster sugar 3 oz.

Milk ¾ pint
Margarine 1 oz.
2 eggs

Mix 1 oz. sugar with the cocoa and mix smoothly with the
milk. Turn into a saucepan and bring to the boil. Add the
margarine and then pour on to breadcrumbs. Cool slightly,
then add the beaten egg yolks. Turn into a greased baking dish
and bake in a moderate oven (375°, Regulo No. 4) until set —
about 20 minutes. Whisk the egg whites very stiffly, fold in
remaining 2 oz. sugar and heap up on top of the pudding.
Return to oven until the meringue is set and lightly browned
— about 20 minutes.

Coffee Pudding

Milk ¾ pint
4 sponge cakes
Sugar 1 tablespoonful

Coffee extract 1 tablespoonful
2 eggs
Essence of vanilla

Use stale sponge cakes and crumble them. Beat up the eggs
with the sugar, add the milk and coffee extract and a few drops
essence of vanilla, then pour over the cake crumbs. Leave to

soak for a few minutes, then mix well, turn into a greased basin, cover with a greased paper and steam for 1¼ hours.

Serve with coffee custard sauce (see pages 206–7).

Baked Custard

Milk 1 pint   *2 eggs*
Caster sugar 1 tablespoonful

Heat the milk with sugar till just tepid, then pour on to the well-beaten eggs. Strain into a greased baking dish, stand in a baking tin with water coming half-way up the dish, and bake in a slow oven till set, about 40–50 minutes. The water in the tin must not be allowed to boil, or the custard will be full of holes.

Serve hot or cold.

If a custard is to be turned out instead of served in the dish in which it was cooked, then allow 3 eggs to 1 pint milk.

For Coffee Custard. Flavour the milk with coffee essence and a few drops of vanilla.

Steamed Custard. See section on Invalid Cookery.

Caramel Custard

Caster sugar 1 oz.   *3 eggs*
Granulated sugar 2 oz.   *Milk 1 pint*
Water 5 tablespoonfuls

Put the granulated sugar and water into a small strong saucepan, heat gently till dissolved, then boil without stirring until it becomes thick and syrupy and a rich brown colour, taking care not to let it burn.

Grease a soufflé dish, pour in the caramel and turn round very quickly so as to coat the bottom and sides. Leave to cool.

Beat up the eggs and caster sugar, pour over the hot (not boiling) milk, and strain into the prepared dish. Cover with a greased paper, place in the top of a steamer and steam very gently till set – about 30–40 minutes; or cook in a slow oven standing in a tin of water.

Leave till quite cold and turn out just before serving.

Confectioners' Custard

Milk ½ pint   2 egg yolks
Sugar 1 oz.   Cornflour ½ oz.
Margarine 1 oz.   Essence of vanilla

Mix sugar and cornflour to a smooth paste with 2 tablespoon-fuls cold milk; heat remaining milk and pour it on. Return to saucepan, add the margarine, stir till boiling and simmer gently for 3 minutes. Cool slightly, add beaten egg yolks, and stir over a gentle heat till it thickens, but do *not* reboil. Flavour with essence of vanilla.

When cold use to fill éclairs or tartlets.

Eggless Fritters

Flour 4 oz.   Cooking oil 2 teaspoonfuls
Baking powder 1 teaspoonful   Milk ½ pint
Sultanas or currants 2 oz.   Fat for frying

Sieve flour and baking powder, add the oil and milk and mix to a smooth batter. Add the cleaned fruit and fry in spoonfuls in shallow fat. When brown one side, turn over and brown the other. Sprinkle with sugar and cinnamon or serve jam separately.

Nursery Pudding

Breadcrumbs 4 oz.   Milk 1 pint
1 egg   Grated rind of a lemon
Sugar 1 oz.   3 bananas

Heat the milk, pour it over the crumbs, cover and leave to cool. Then add the beaten egg, lemon rind and sugar.

Slice the bananas into a greased baking dish, pour over the bread mixture and bake in a moderate oven for ½ hour.

Queen Pudding

Milk 1 pint   Breadcrumbs 4 oz.
2 eggs   Jam
Sugar   Lemon peel

Boil the milk with some strips of lemon peel, then strain over the breadcrumbs, cover and let stand for 15 minutes. Add the beaten egg yolks and sugar to taste. Mix thoroughly, turn into a greased fireproof dish and bake in a moderate oven (375°, Regulo No. 4) till set, about 30 minutes. Then spread with stoneless jam.

Beat the egg whites to a stiff froth, fold in 2 tablespoonfuls caster sugar, heap up roughly on top of the jam, sprinkle with caster sugar and return to the bottom shelf of the oven till lightly browned – 20–30 minutes.

For Chocolate Pudding. Omit jam and lemon peel and mix 1 tablespoonful of cocoa with the hot milk.

Rice Pudding

Wash 2 oz. rice thoroughly, drain and put into a greased baking dish, sprinkle over 2 tablespoonfuls of sugar and pour on 1 pint of milk. Bake in a very slow oven for 2½–3 hours. Start at 350° Regulo No. 3, and when it has come to the boil reduce to 300°, Regulo No. 1. If something else is being cooked at the same time that requires greater heat, then put the pudding on the lowest shelf or the floor of the oven.

For Fruit Rice Pudding. Add 2 oz. sultanas or cut-up dates.

Rice and Apple Meringue

Milk 1 pint	*Rice 2½ oz.*
Sugar	*Stewed apple 1 pint*
2 eggs	*Lemon rind*

Cook the rice in the milk in a double saucepan till the rice is soft and the milk absorbed. Then remove from the heat, sweeten to taste and when cool beat in the egg yolks. Drain off any juice from the apple, and flavour with grated lemon rind. Put half in the bottom of a greased baking dish, cover with half the rice and repeat the two layers.

Whisk the egg whites to a very stiff froth, fold in 2 oz. caster sugar, and heap up roughly over the pudding. Bake on the middle shelf of a moderate oven until the meringue is set – about 20 minutes.

For Rice and Jam Meringue. Omit the apple and after

turning the rice into a baking dish, spread the top with a layer of apricot or strawberry jam before adding the meringue, and bake as above.

Serve hot or cold.

Rice and Raisin Mould

Milk 1 pint	*Sugar 1 oz.*
Rice 2½ oz.	*Ground cinnamon ¼ teaspoonful*
Raisins 2 oz.	

Wash the rice and stone the raisins. Put all ingredients into a double saucepan and cook until the rice is soft and the milk absorbed.

Turn into a wetted basin and turn out when cold.

Pancakes

Flour 4 oz.	*1 egg*
Milk ½ pint	*Pinch of salt*
Sugar	*Cooking fat*
Lemon	

Sieve flour and salt into a basin, make a well in the centre, drop in the beaten egg and add half the milk. Use a wooden spoon and work in the flour so that the batter in the centre is even and smooth all the time. When half the liquid has been worked in and all the flour is absorbed, beat well for 2 or 3 minutes to get the mixture light and airy, then stir in the remaining liquid and pour into a jug ready for frying.

To Fry. Warm a small frying pan, rub with a little salt and wipe clean with a dry cloth. This 'tempering' ensures that the pancakes will not stick – it need not be done again during the frying.

Have the cooking fat melted in a small saucepan, pour a little into the prepared frying pan and when smoking hot pour back into the saucepan. A film of fat will be left, which will be sufficient for frying the pancake.

Pour in slowly just enough batter to cover the bottom of the pan. When set and lightly browned on one side, turn or toss and cook the other. Turn out onto sugared paper, dust with caster sugar and sprinkle with lemon juice. Roll up and keep hot on a plate over a saucepan of water till all are ready.

Savoury Pancakes

(See pages 122–3)

French Pancakes

Flour 4 oz.   Caster sugar ½ oz.
Milk ½ pint   Pinch of salt
2 eggs   Grated lemon rind
Jam

Sieve the flour and salt into a basin. Separate the yolks and whites of the egg and make a light batter with the yolks and milk, as in previous recipe. Let stand at least 1 hour and just before cooking add the sugar, a little grated lemon rind and the egg whites beaten to a stiff froth.

Grease some saucers or shallow individual dishes, put a little of the batter into each, place on a baking tin and bake in a quick oven about 20 minutes.

When cooked remove from containers, put a teaspoonful of warm jam on each, fold over, and sprinkle with caster sugar.

Hot Soufflés

Before starting to mix a soufflé have everything in readiness. If it is to be steamed, have water boiling in the saucepan; if it is to be baked, have the oven at the right temperature (400°, Regulo No. 5).

Avoid opening the oven door or lifting the lid of the saucepan as much as possible. A sudden rush of cold air might cause the soufflé to fall.

To Prepare Dish. Brush thickly with butter, cooking fat, or cooking oil. Take a double band of paper long enough to fold round the dish and overlap and deep enough to come 3 or 4 inches above the rim. Brush this also with butter or oil and tie round the outside of the dish, greased side inwards. This paper is removed before serving. Only three-parts fill the dish, to allow for rising.

To Bake. Stand soufflé dish in a baking tin containing sufficient hot water to come 1 inch up the sides of the dish. Bake in a moderately hot oven (400°, Regulo No. 5), 25–30 minutes, till firm in the centre.

To Steam. Place the soufflé dish in a steamer and lay a greased paper across the paper band. Put the lid on and cook over gently boiling water, till the soufflé is set in the centre — about 40 minutes.

If a steamer is not available, place in a deep saucepan containing 2 inches boiling water, placing a large biscuit cutter under the dish to raise it slightly.

Beat egg whites immediately before folding into the mixture. They must not be allowed to stand and must be beaten really stiff.

Serve a soufflé immediately it is cooked.

Vanilla Soufflé

Butter 1 oz.	*Milk ¼ pint*
Flour 1 oz.	*3 eggs and 1 extra white*
Caster sugar 1 oz.	*Essence of vanilla ¼ teaspoonful*

Melt the butter in a saucepan, stir in the flour smoothly, stir over a gentle heat with a wooden spoon for a minute, then gradually add the milk. Continue stirring till this panada is quite thick and leaves the sides of the pan clean. Then remove from the heat and beat in sugar and vanilla.

Separate yolks and whites of the eggs and beat in the yolks one at a time. Add a pinch of salt to the whites and whisk them to a stiff dry froth; then with a metal spoon fold them very lightly into the mixture. Turn into prepared soufflé dish (about 6–7 inches across) and bake or steam. (See general directions.)

Variations:

(1) **Chocolate Soufflé.** Dissolve 2 oz. chocolate in the milk before adding to the panada.

(2) **Coffee Soufflé.** Flavour milk with coffee essence.

(3) **Fruit Soufflé.** Use a thin purée of fruit instead of milk for making the panada. Tinned peaches or apricots are some of the most suitable fruit to use.

(4) **Ginger Soufflé.** Use equal parts ginger syrup and milk for the panada and add a little finely chopped ginger to the mixture.

Cold Soufflés
(See pages 280–81)

Stewed Fruit

Fruit can be cooked in a covered casserole in the oven (see Casserole Cookery, page 309), or on top of the stove. Whichever method is used, always cook gently.

The amount of sugar and water required will vary according to the kind of fruit; allow about 3–4 oz. sugar and ¼ pint water to each pound of fruit.

Peel, core and slice or quarter apples; top and tail gooseberries; stalk cherries, plums and greengages.

To Keep Fruit Whole. Make a syrup by dissolving the required amount of sugar in the water, bring to the boil, simmer for a few minutes, then put in the prepared fruit. Cover and cook very gently till tender.

Apples cooked this way should be peeled, cored and cut into *quarters* only. Flavour with lemon juice or cloves.

To Cook Fruit to a Pulp. Prepare fruit and put in a saucepan with a little water and sufficient sugar to sweeten. Cover and cook gently till pulpy. Then either beat up with a fork or rub through a sieve.

Rhubarb will require much less sugar if a little bicarbonate of soda is added to neutralize the acid. Cut up 1 lb. rhubarb into 1-inch pieces, put in a saucepan with ¼ pint of water, and bring to the boil; add ½ level teaspoonful bicarbonate of soda, simmer gently for 5 minutes, and when it has finished frothing add sugar to taste, and continue simmering till tender.

Very acid gooseberries and plums can be cooked the same way.

Pears. Peel, cut in halves and remove the core and cook in boiling syrup till tender.

Very hard winter pears can be cooked as follows: To 1 lb.

pears allow 4 oz. sugar, $\frac{1}{2}$ pint of water, juice of half a lemon, 2 cloves and a few drops of red colouring.

Put the water, sugar, cloves and lemon juice in a saucepan, bring to the boil and simmer for 5 minutes, then add the peeled and cored pears and cook very gently till tender – at least 1$\frac{1}{2}$ hours. Add a few drops of red colouring and turn into serving dish. If preferred the pears can be cooked in a covered casserole in a slow oven, and a teaspoonful of vinegar can replace the lemon juice.

Dried Fruits. Wash thoroughly, cover with cold water, and leave to soak overnight. To $\frac{1}{2}$ lb. figs, prunes, apricots or apple rings allow 4 oz. sugar, the water in which they were soaked and flavouring. Bring to the boil and simmer very gently till soft. Add sliced lemon to prunes and apricots.

Figs can be cooked in the following manner: Wash $\frac{1}{2}$ lb. and soak overnight in sufficient water to cover. Put into a saucepan with the water in which they were soaked, the rind and juice of half a lemon, and a piece of root ginger bruised and tied in muslin. Cover and stew till tender. Then strain off the juice and measure, add half as much sugar and cook to a thick syrup. Pour over the figs and serve cold.

Cold Sweets, Jellies, and Creams

GENERAL DIRECTIONS

Creams and Mousses should be quite cold and just beginning to set before being put into the mould, otherwise the gelatine may stick to the bottom. Always rinse the mould in cold water before putting the jelly or cream into it.

Unless a refrigerator is available, make cold sweets the previous day.

Soufflés should have a band of stiff white paper tied round the outside of the dish and coming 3 inches above the top. This can easily be removed later with a knife dipped in hot water.

Gelatine should be dissolved in water, fruit juice, or syrup – not in milk, or it may curdle. Never pour boiling liquid on to gelatine. Put the gelatine in a small saucepan and pour on sufficient cold liquid to cover. Let it soak for a little while, then stand over a very gentle heat till dissolved. It should be added to the mixture when the latter is just warm and is best put through a strainer.

Note. There are different makes of gelatine and the Orthodox Jewish housewife will, of course, wish to inquire for the kosher variety. Any time that kosher gelatine is not available, vegetarian gelatine substitute should be used. See Agar Jellies, page 278.

To Decorate a Mould for Creams and Jellies

A little clear jelly will be required, and any of the following for decoration: glacé cherries, crystallized fruits, violet or rose leaves, angelica, pistachio nuts or almonds. Pistachio nuts and almonds must be scalded with boiling water and the skins removed before being chopped or cut into shreds. Angelica should be cut into thin strips, then into diamond shapes to represent leaves.

Rinse the mould out with cold water, pour in a little cold liquid jelly, and leave in a very cold place or on ice till set; then arrange the decoration on the jelly in any design preferred and spoon over, very carefully, a little more jelly, taking care not to disarrange the decoration. Then leave till set. To coat the sides of the mould, after the decoration has set, pour in a little more cold jelly and turn the mould round and round slowly, if possible on a basin of ice, till the sides are coated and the jelly set.

To Turn Out Jellies and Cold Sweets

Dip the mould in a basin of hot, but not boiling, water. Move the mould about for a second or two, then lift out. Place the serving dish on top of the mould and reverse them, holding the thumbs on mould and the fingers under the dish. Shake in a downward direction to loosen the jelly, then lift off the mould carefully. Should the jelly not leave the mould after shaking it two or three times, then dip in the water again and repeat the process.

Agar Jellies

When kosher gelatine or jellies are not available, agar can be used instead. This has great jellying powers and sets quickly.

Use the *powdered* variety, which is obtainable at many general grocers and health-food stores. Although not absolutely clear like an ordinary jelly, it is quite satisfactory both for sweet and savoury dishes.

Allow 2 *slightly* rounded teaspoonfuls of powdered agar to 1 pint of boiling liquid and ½ pint of cold water. Put the powdered agar in a basin, pour over the cold water, stir and let stand for 10 minutes, then add the boiling liquid, pour into saucepan and boil for 1 minute.

Fruit Jellies. For the pint of boiling liquid use diluted orange or lemon juice or bottled fruit squash, or left-over fruit juices sweetened to taste. When slightly cooled turn into serving dish or individual glasses. Any kind of cut-up fruit except pineapple can be added, as when making ordinary jellies.

Milk Coffee Jelly. For the liquid use strong milk coffee sweetened to taste. Garnish with chocolate granules.

Banana Snow

4 large ripe bananas　　*Caster sugar 1 tablespoonful*
Juice of a lemon　　　　*Glacé cherries*
White of 1 egg

Mash the bananas with a fork till they are pulped, then add the lemon juice and white of egg. Beat until it is like thick cream, then add the sugar and beat for another 5 minutes. Pile up in a glass dish or in individual glasses and decorate with glacé cherries.

Blackcurrant Cream

Blackcurrants 1 lb.　　*Chopped nuts*
Sugar 3 oz.　　　　　*Cream ¼ pint*
Boiled custard ½ pint　*Water ¼ pint*

Cook the currants with the sugar and water till soft, then rub through a sieve. Make a rather thick boiled custard and mix it with the currant purée. Add half the cream, whisk lightly and turn into individual glasses, decorate with the rest of the cream and sprinkle with chopped nuts.

Border Mould with Fruit

2 eggs	Flour 4 oz.
Margarine 3 oz.	Caster sugar 3 oz.
Baking powder ½ teaspoonful	Fresh or stewed fruit

Beat the margarine and sugar to a cream, add the beaten eggs, then fold in lightly the sieved flour and baking powder. Turn into a greased border mould and bake in a moderate oven for 30–40 minutes. Turn out and leave till cold. Put in a dish and fill the centre with any kind of stewed fruit or a mixture of fresh fruits. If the latter are used, then a little syrup flavoured with lemon juice or sherry should be made to soak the cake.

Charlotte Russe

Lemon jelly ½ pint	Cream or top milk ½ pint
Gelatine ¼ oz.	Caster sugar 1 oz.
Water 4 tablespoonfuls	Vanilla essence
8 to 10 sponge fingers	Cherries and angelica

Dissolve the jelly and pour a thin layer into the bottom and round the sides of a 1-pint cake tin or mould and allow to set. Decorate with cut glacé cherries and angelica, pour over a thin layer of jelly and leave till set.

Trim the sides and ends of the sponge fingers, so that they are quite straight, dip the ends in jelly and line the mould with them.

Dissolve the gelatine in warm water, strain it into the cream (or top milk), add the sugar and vanilla and whisk until thick. Pour into prepared mould and leave till set.

To unmould, dip the bottom of the mould in hot water, then turn out on to a glass dish (see page 277) and garnish with chopped jelly.

For a Chocolate Filling. Dissolve 2 or 3 oz. grated chocolate in the milk.

For a Coffee Filling. Flavour with coffee extract.

Chestnut Cream

Chestnuts 1 lb.
Plain chocolate 2 oz.
Sugar 1 oz.
Cream 2 or 3 tablespoonfuls

Milk ¼ pint
Vanilla
Chocolate granules

After removing husks and skins (see page 93) boil chestnuts till tender, then rub through a sieve. Grate the chocolate and put with the milk and sugar in a saucepan, stir over a gentle heat till the chocolate is dissolved, then bring to the boil, add the chestnut purée, flavour with vanilla and continue stirring over a gentle heat for 2 or 3 minutes. Leave till cold, stir in the cream and put it into small glasses and sprinkle with chocolate granules.

Chocolate Mousse

Block chocolate 3 oz.
3 eggs

Cream or nuts for garnishing

Cut the chocolate into small pieces and put into a basin. Put the basin over a saucepan of hot water and place over a gentle heat until the chocolate has melted, then remove from the heat and stir in the lightly beaten egg yolks. Whip the whites till quite stiff and fold them into the mixture.

Turn into individual glasses and leave till cold and set. Garnish with whipped cream or chopped nuts or desiccated coconut.

Note. This can be made with diabetic chocolate, either plain or nutty, and makes a good sweet for those on a sugarless diet.

Chocolate Soufflé

Plain chocolate 3 oz.
Milk ¼ pint
Cream ¼ pint
Caster sugar 2 oz.

3 eggs
Gelatine ¼ oz.
Water 4 tablespoonfuls
Vanilla essence

Grate the chocolate, dissolve it in the warmed milk and leave till cool.

Mix the gelatine with 4 tablespoonfuls cold water and stand in a saucepan of hot water over a gentle heat till dissolved.

Whisk the egg yolks with the sugar over a saucepan of boiling water till thick and light; remove from the heat, add the gelatine, milk and chocolate, and flavour with essence of vanilla. Whip up the cream, add it to the mixture and whisk lightly. Whip the egg whites to a stiff froth and fold them in.

Turn into a prepared soufflé dish and leave in a cold place till set. Then remove paper carefully, using a hot knife to separate the paper from the soufflé.

Decorate with whipped cream and chopped nuts.

To prepare soufflé dish, tie a band of stiff white paper round the dish to come 3 inches above the edge.

Vanilla Soufflé. Make as above, omitting the chocolate.

Coffee Soufflé. Add 1 tablespoonful coffee extract to milk in place of the chocolate.

Chocolate Soufflé (2)

Chocolate 4 oz.	Whites of 2 eggs
Milk ¼ pint	Cream ¼ pint
Water 4 tablespoonfuls	Gelatine ¼ oz.
Caster sugar 1 oz.	Chopped nuts

Grate the chocolate and put it into a small saucepan with the milk and sugar and stir over a low heat till dissolved.

Melt the gelatine in the water, then strain into the chocolate and flavour with essence of vanilla. Leave till cool. Whip the cream, add to the chocolate mixture and whisk lightly; then fold in the stiffly whipped egg whites.

Turn into prepared soufflé dish and finish off as in previous recipe.

Coffee Cream

Boiled custard 1 pint	Sugar
Coffee extract 1 tablespoonful	Vanilla
White of an egg	

Make a *thick* custard with any good custard powder, adding the coffee essence to the milk, sweeten to taste and add a few drops of vanilla.

Whip the white of egg to a very stiff froth and add to the

custard when it is nearly cold. Whisk lightly and turn into a glass dish and serve very cold.

Or omit the white of egg and, when the custard is cold, add 2 tablespoonfuls of top milk or cream and whisk very thoroughly.

Coffee Chocolate Cream

Strong coffee 1 pint	*2 eggs*
Chocolate 3 oz.	*Sugar 1 oz.*
Arrowroot or custard powder	*Vanilla*
1 tablespoonful	*Chopped nuts*

Grate the chocolate, put in a saucepan with the coffee and sugar and bring to the boil; then stir in the arrowroot (or custard powder) mixed smoothly with a little cold water, and stir while it simmers for 2 or 3 minutes. Cool, then pour on to the lightly beaten eggs, turn into a double saucepan and stir over a gentle heat till it thickens, but do not reboil. Add a few drops vanilla essence. Leave till cool, then whisk lightly, turn into individual glasses, and sprinkle with chopped nuts.

Crispy Tartlets

Cornflakes 2 oz.	*Rolled oats 2 oz.*
Margarine 3 oz.	*Sugar 2 oz.*
Golden syrup 2 teaspoonfuls	*Lemon curd or apple purée*

Crush the cornflakes and mix with the rolled oats and sugar. Melt the margarine and syrup, pour on to the dry ingredients and mix together. Put about a tablespoonful of the mixture into well-greased patty tins and press down firmly. Bake in a moderate oven (400°, Regulo No. 5) on a middle shelf about 15 minutes. Remove from the oven, leave for a minute or two to set, then remove carefully from the tins and cool on a cake tray.

Fill with apple purée or lemon curd just before serving. The apple purée can be topped with a little custard or garnished with whipped cream.

Gooseberry Fool

Green gooseberries 1 lb.   *Sugar 4 oz.*
Water ¼ pint   *Boiled custard ½ pint*

Stew the gooseberries with the sugar and water till soft, then rub through a sieve. Mix the purée with the custard, and when cold pour into custard glasses.

If preferred, in place of the custard use ¼ pint cream and 1 egg white. Whip the cream till it will hang on the whisk, then add the stiffly whisked white of an egg and add to the gooseberry purée.

For Raspberry or Strawberry Fool. Do not cook the fruit, simply rub through a sieve and mix as above.

Gooseberry Snow

Gooseberries 1 lb.   *Whites of 2 eggs*
Caster sugar   *Bicarbonate of soda*

Top and tail the gooseberries, put them into a saucepan with only sufficient water to prevent them burning and a pinch of bicarbonate of soda and stew till soft. Then rub through a sieve and add caster sugar to taste.

Whip up the egg whites very stiffly, add to the gooseberry purée and beat another 5 minutes. Heap up in a glass bowl and serve with sponge fingers.

'Haman's Ears'

2 eggs   *Caster sugar*
Oil 3 tablespoonfuls   *Oil for frying*
Flour

Beat up the eggs, stir in the oil and then mix in enough flour to make a soft dough. Knead very thoroughly, then break off small pieces and roll out on a floured board *as thin as possible*, about the size of a meat plate, and cut each piece in four. Leave for 1 hour or longer to get dry, then fry in hot oil a very light brown. Drain and sprinkle with caster sugar. Handle carefully, as they break very easily.

Jelly Trifle

6 slices Swiss roll   Cream ¼ pint
Tin of raspberries   White of an egg
Pint packet raspberry jelly Caster sugar 1 teaspoonful

Drain the raspberries from the syrup and, reserving a few for garnishing, put the remainder into a glass bowl with the Swiss roll. Add sufficient water to the raspberry syrup to make 1 pint, dissolve the jelly in this and while hot, pour over the contents of the bowl. Leave till set.

Whip the white of egg to a stiff froth and the cream till it will hang on a fork, mix the two together, add the caster sugar and a few drops of vanilla. Heap up over the trifle and garnish with raspberries.

Agar Jellies

(See page 278)

Lemon Cream

See page 422; arrowroot or cornflour can be used in place of potato flour.

Meringues

Whites of 3 eggs   Caster sugar 4 oz.
Pinch of salt   Granulated sugar 2 oz.

Line baking tins with two thicknesses of greaseproof paper and brush lightly with olive oil or melted cooking fat.

Put the egg whites in a basin with a pinch of salt; then beat with a rotary whisk until really stiff, so that they stand in peaks when the whisk is lifted out. They should also not fall out if the basin is tilted.

Add the granulated sugar and whisk again until the mixture regains its former stiffness, then with a metal spoon fold in the caster sugar lightly, agitating the mixture as little as possible.

To Shape the Mixture

(1) **With Forcing Bag and Pipe.** Fill the bag and squeeze out on to prepared tin in pyramids, round or ovals.

(2) **With Spoons.** Two dessert spoons will be needed and a knife standing in cold water.

Take a spoonful of the mixture in one of the spoons, smooth it over with the wet knife, making it egg shaped, then scoop out with the second spoon on to prepared tin. Shape the rest of mixture in the same way and dredge the meringues with a little extra caster sugar.

To Bake. Place the trays on the lower shelves of a very cool oven (230°, Regulo No. $\frac{1}{4}$) until the meringues are quite dry, firm and crisp – 2–3 hours. When done remove from the tins and cool on a cake tray. Do not leave them in a damp atmosphere.

To Fill. Whip some double cream, sweeten to taste and flavour with vanilla (or use vanilla sugar). Spread thickly on the meringues and place them together in pairs. Then put into paper cases. The unfilled ones will keep in an airtight tin and should not be filled until a short time before they are to be used. To vary the filling, flavour the cream with a little liquid coffee or add a few chopped nuts.

Orange Caramel

4 or 5 oranges	Loaf sugar 4 oz.
Caster sugar	Water $\frac{1}{4}$ pint
Sherry	Chopped almonds

Pour boiling water over the oranges, leave for a few minutes, then peel them. By scalding them all the pith should come off with the peel. Cut into slices, remove any pips, put in a glass dish and sprinkle with caster sugar and a spoonful or two of sherry.

Dip the lumps of sugar in a little of the water, put into a small strong saucepan and melt slowly over a gentle heat. Cook until dark brown, taking care not to burn it, then add remaining water and cook till thick. Pour on to a greased tin and leave to harden. Break into small pieces and sprinkle over the oranges, together with a few chopped almonds.

If preferred, instead of the caramel and chopped nuts use 2 oz. nutty hardbake. Crush this and sprinkle over the oranges.

Orange and Coconut Trifle

4 oranges   *Caster sugar*
1 tangerine   *4 sponge fingers*
Custard or cream   *Desiccated coconut*

Peel the oranges, cut into slices and remove pips. Put half in the bottom of a glass dish and sprinkle with caster sugar and desiccated coconut. Split the sponge fingers and lay them on top, then the remainder of the oranges sprinkled with sugar and coconut.

Let this stand for 2 or 3 hours, and just before serving cover with whipped cream or boiled custard flavoured with grated orange peel.

Garnish with sections of tangerine.

Pears with Chocolate Sauce

Tinned or bottled pears   *Vanilla*
Chocolate 3 oz.   *Chopped nuts*
Arrowroot 1 teaspoonful

Drain the pears and put them into a glass dish or on individual plates.

Dissolve the chocolate in ½ pint of the pear syrup, heat and when boiling add the arrowroot mixed smoothly with a little cold water. Simmer for 2 or 3 minutes, add a few drops essence of vanilla, and leave till cold. Then pour over the pears and sprinkle with chopped nuts.

For a more elaborate sauce, after removing from the heat add 2 tablespoonfuls sherry and a stiffly whipped white of egg, and whisk thoroughly.

Pineapple Cream

Boiled custard 1½ pints   *A little cream for decoration*
Small tin pineapple

Make a rather thick boiled custard with custard powder,

sweeten to taste, and leave till cold; then whisk lightly, adding a spoonful or two of top milk or cream.

Strain the pineapple and cut into small pieces. Put in a glass dish and pour over the custard.

Garnish with pineapple and whipped cream.

Rhubarb and Orange Compôte

Rhubarb 1 lb.	*Water ¼ teacupful*
2 oranges	*Sugar*

Peel the oranges, removing all the pith, cut into slices and remove the pips. Cut the rhubarb into 1 inch pieces. Put the fruit in layers in a casserole, sprinkling each layer with sugar, pour over the water, cover the casserole and bake in a slow oven until the rhubarb is tender – 20–30 minutes.

Rothe Gruetze

Raspberries and redcurrants 2 lb.	*Sugar to sweeten*
Arrowroot 2 oz.	*Water 1 pint*

Pick over and wash the fruit, and stew with the water and sugar to taste, till quite soft; then rub through a fine sieve. Mix the arrowroot smoothly with a little cold water, boil the fruit purée, stir in the arrowroot and continue stirring while it simmers for 3 minutes. Turn into a dish and leave till cold. Garnish with a few whole raspberries and serve very cold with cream or custard.

Note. 2 oz. fine sago can be used in place of the arrowroot. Cover this with cold water and let it stand for several hours. Then add it to the fruit purée, mix thoroughly and stir over a gentle heat till boiling. Simmer *very gently* till the sago is quite clear. Add more sugar if necessary and when cool turn it into a glass dish. When quite cold garnish as above.

Semolina Sponge

Red fruit juice 1 pint	*Semolina 2 oz.*
Lemon juice	*Sugar*
Jam	

Bring the fruit juice to the boil and sprinkle in the semolina, stirring all the time. Then cook over a gentle heat till the semolina is quite clear. Remove from the heat, add the juice of half a lemon and sugar to taste. Turn into a bowl and whisk until it is very frothy. Turn into individual glasses and put a little red jam in the centre of each.

Strawberry Meringue

Crush a few meringue cases and crush some strawberries, adding a few drops of lemon juice. Fill sundae glasses with alternate layers of the purée and crushed meringue, and garnish with whipped cream.

Strawberry Shortcake

For the Pastry

Flour 8 oz.   Baking powder 2 teaspoonfuls
Caster sugar 2 oz.   Butter or margarine 2 oz.
Pinch of salt   Milk about ¼ pint

For the Filling

Strawberries 1 lb.   Double cream ¼ pint

Wash the strawberries and remove their stalks; reserve a few for garnishing, slice the remainder and sprinkle them with sugar.

Grease 2 medium-sized sandwich tins. Sieve flour, baking powder and salt into a bowl, rub in the fat, add the sugar and mix to a soft dough with milk. Turn the mixture on to a board, knead lightly and divide into two. Then flatten into two rounds (a little less than ½ inch thick) to fit the tins.

Bake in a hot oven (425°, Regulo No. 6) until firm to the touch and lightly browned – about 20 minutes.

When cool put a layer of the prepared strawberries on one of the cakes and cover with the other. Place remaining strawberries on top, cover with whipped and sweetened cream and garnish with whole strawberries.

Strawberry Sponge

Strawberries 1 lb.	*A sponge ring*
Caster sugar 4 oz.	*Lemon juice 1 teaspoonful*
Pistachio nuts	*Cream ¼ pint*

Reserve a few strawberries for garnishing and crush the remainder with 3 oz. caster sugar and the lemon juice, and fill the sponge ring with this purée. Whip up the cream with the remaining sugar, and flavour with a few drops of vanilla. Heap this up over the purée, garnish with strawberries and sprinkle with finely chopped pistachio nuts.

Summer Pudding (1)

Redcurrants 1 lb.	*Sugar*
Raspberries ½ lb.	*Stale bread*

Prepare the fruit and stew till soft with ¼ pint water and sugar to taste. Cut the bread into slices about ½ inch thick, and line a basin with it. Pour in the boiling fruit and cover the top with a round of bread. Stand the basin in a cool place and put a small plate on top with a heavy weight on it, and leave till the next day.

Turn out carefully and either coat with custard or serve it separately.

Any kind of soft fruit can be used in the same way. Blackcurrants, blackberries, rhubarb are all good.

Summer Pudding (2)

Redcurrants 1 lb.	*Granulated sugar 6 oz.*
Raspberries or ripe loganberries	*Water ¼ pint*
1 lb.	*Stale bread*

Cover the bottom of a glass dish with thin slices of crustless stale bread, then put in the uncooked raspberries or ripe loganberries. Put washed currants in a saucepan with the sugar and water and boil rapidly for 20 minutes; then strain while hot over the raspberries. Serve very cold.

Trifle

4 sponge cakes	Sherry
Boiled custard 1 pint	Cream ¼ pint
Glacé cherries and almonds for decoration	Jam

Cut the sponge cakes through in halves and spread with jam.
Then arrange them in the bottom of a glass bowl, and soak
them with sherry (or fruit juice if preferred). Pour over the
custard while still hot, and leave it to get cold. Whip the cream
quite stiff with a little sugar and vanilla essence. The stiffly
beaten white of an egg may be added to the cream if desired;
it makes the cream lighter and also go further. Spread a good
layer smoothly over the trifle and with icing forcers pipe the
remainder on top. Decorate with blanched almonds cut into
strips and glacé cherries cut in quarters.

Pistachio nuts (skinned and finely chopped) or crystallized
violets can be used in place of the cherries.

Sliced Swiss roll can be used in place of the sponge cakes and
jam.

For a Fruit Trifle. Add a layer of soft fruit (tinned or fresh)
over the sponge cakes before pouring on the custard, reserving
a little for decorating the top. Tinned apricots, peaches,
raspberries and strawberries are all excellent; also sliced
bananas, but never use bananas to garnish, as they turn brown.

Vanilla Mousse

1 tin evaporated milk	Caster sugar 1 oz.
Gelatine ¼ oz.	Vanilla essence

Put the tin of milk in a saucepan of cold water, bring to the
boil and boil 3 minutes, leave in water till cold then chill
thoroughly.

Put the gelatine in a cup with sufficient cold water to cover,
stand in a saucepan of hot water over a gentle heat till dissolved.

Whisk the chilled milk with a rotary egg-whisk till very
light and frothy and doubled in bulk; then strain in the
gelatine, add the sugar and vanilla essence to taste, and whisk
another 5 minutes.

Turn into a glass dish or individual glasses and leave in a cool place till set.

For Coffee Mousse add 1 tablespoonful coffee extract when the gelatine is added.

For Chocolate Mousse. Dissolve a 2 oz. bar of plain chocolate in ½ teacupful of hot milk. When cold, add at the same time as the dissolved gelatine.

Zabaglione

4 egg yolks	*Sherry 8 tablespoonfuls*
Caster sugar 3 oz.	*Sponge fingers*
1 egg white	

Whisk the egg yolks with the sugar till almost white, then add the sherry very gradually. Turn into a double saucepan and stir over a gentle heat till it thickens. On no account let it boil, or it will curdle. Remove from the heat and fold in the stiffly whipped egg white. Serve with sponge fingers.

Iced Desserts

If a Freezer is being used, the rules given with it should be followed.

Ices made in a Refrigerator. To obtain a smooth, evenly-textured ice cream in a refrigerator, the mixture must be frozen quickly and whisked well. Generally speaking, the best results are obtained by switching the freezing control to the coldest freezing point to start with, allowing the mixture about one hour before taking from the tray and beating it with cream, egg white, or evaporated milk until light and frothy. If the mixture is a rich one, return to the tray with the control left at freezing point. A thin, less rich mixture should have the control at half freeze. When the ice is frozen to the right consistency the switch should be turned back to normal.

Home-made cream pumped through a cream-making machine is an excellent foundation for ices.

Cream Ices are generally made with cream and custard, or, for a more economical mixture, condensed milk can be substituted for cream.

Water Ices require a sugar-and-water syrup as a foundation, to which fruit juices or purée are added.

Strawberry Cream Ice

Crushed strawberries 1 pint   *Cream ¼ pint*
Caster sugar 2–3 oz.   *Red colouring*
Custard ¼ pint

Add the sugar to the pulped strawberries, mix with the custard, and whisk lightly. Whip the cream till it will just hang on the whisk and add it to the strawberry mixture with a few drops of red colouring. Then freeze.

Other fruit ices are made in the same way. If tinned fruit is used, drain off most of the syrup.

For a more economical recipe, a rich custard can replace the cream.

Simple Sundaes

Put a small quantity of ice cream into a sundae glass or on a glass plate, and finish off in one of the following ways:

(1) Pour over 2 tablespoonfuls of well-flavoured fruit syrup, cover with whipped cream, and sprinkle with chopped nuts.

(2) Substitute crushed meringue for the chopped nuts.

(3) Coffee, chocolate, or butterscotch sauce can be used instead of fruit syrup.

(4) One tablespoonful clear honey sprinkled with chopped nuts.

Banana Sundae

Vanilla ice cream 1 pint   *Burnt almonds 2 oz.*
3 bananas   *Cream ¼ pint*
Honey ¼ teacupful

Divide the ice into six portions and place in glasses. Cover each portion with sliced banana and add a spoonful of honey. Cover with whipped cream and sprinkle with crushed burnt almonds (or almond rock).

Peach Melba

Put a slice of sponge cake into individual glasses and then a portion of vanilla ice cream. Place half a tinned peach on top and coat with Melba sauce (see page 294).

Ice Cream Sandwiches

Put a slice of ice cream brick between two thin slices of sponge cake. Put on individual plates, and put a spoonful of sieved strawberry, raspberry, or apricot jam on top.

Or omit jam and garnish with chilled tinned or stewed fruit, and top with marshmallow cream.

Baked Alaska

For this you will require a very stiffly frozen family-size ice-cream brick, a sponge cake about 7 by 10 inches and 2 inches thick, a meringue made with 4 egg whites and 6 oz. caster sugar.

The secret of success in making this hot ice cream dish is to make sure that the ice cream is completely covered with the meringue, so that the heat does not reach it, and that the oven is very hot, to set the meringue quickly.

First, heat the oven – 475–500°, Regulo No. 8–9.

Whip the egg whites to a stiff froth, gradually add the sugar, whipping all the time until the meringue stands in peaks.

Put the sponge cake on a baking dish and place the ice cream on top. Then pile the meringue on the top and sides of the ice cream, covering it completely and taking care that there is a thick layer where the ice cream and cake meet. Spread the meringue so that there are no cracks or spaces left. Sprinkle with caster sugar and place at once in the heated oven for 3–4 minutes, until the meringue is slightly coloured.

Serve immediately.

ICE CREAM SAUCES

Butterscotch Sauce

Brown sugar 6 oz.   *Golden syrup 1 tablespoonful*
Butter 2 oz.   *Milk 4 tablespoonfuls*

Cook all ingredients together in a double saucepan for ½ hour.
Serve warm over vanilla ice cream.

Chocolate Sauce

Caster sugar 4 oz.   *Arrowroot 1 teaspoonful*
Water ¼ pint   *Vanilla essence ¼ teaspoonful*
Chocolate 2 oz.

Boil the sugar and water together for 5 minutes, add the
grated chocolate and the arrowroot mixed smoothly with 1
tablespoonful of water, stir till the chocolate has melted, then
simmer gently for 5 minutes. Remove from the heat, add the
vanilla, whisk well, and use when cold.

Fudge Sauce

Put 1 tablespoonful of golden syrup and 2 tablespoonfuls of
evaporated milk in a small saucepan and simmer gently 3–4
minutes. Stand the pan in water till the sauce is cold.

Melba Sauce

Raspberry purée ¼ pint   *Arrowroot 1 teaspoonful*
Sugar 3 oz.   *Water 1 tablespoonful*

Use fresh or tinned raspberries and rub through a sieve. Put
the purée in a saucepan with the sugar and bring to the boil.
Blend the arrowroot with the water, add to the purée, stir till
boiling, and simmer for 5 minutes. Leave till cold and chill
before serving.

Or use raspberry syrup instead of raspberries. Simply bring
the syrup to the boil and thicken with arrowroot. Add sugar if
not sufficiently sweetened.

Note. If available, 1 or 2 tablespoonfuls redcurrant jelly can
be added to the sauce before boiling.

Strawberry Sauce

Sugar 3 oz.   *Strawberries ½ lb.*
Water ¼ teacupful

Boil sugar and water together for 5 minutes. Crush the strawberries with a fork, add to the syrup, leave till cold, and chill before using.

Savouries

A savoury is a tasty dish served either at the end of a meal, or as a luncheon or supper dish, or with cocktails (see pages 26–32). If served at a formal dinner it comes after the sweet, but at an informal meal it can easily *replace* the sweet – it makes a change and the menfolk often prefer it.

If served as a luncheon or supper course, it should be rather more substantial and served in larger portions than the dainty little after-dinner savoury.

The remains of all sorts of ingredients may be used up in savouries, provided they are sufficiently piquant.

They should be served on croûtons, toast, cheese pastry, or biscuits; or in little pastry cases or ramekin dishes. They can be served either hot or cold and should always be attractively garnished and daintily served.

Anchovy Puffs

Roll out some short or flaky pastry thinly and cut it into pieces the same length and double the width of anchovy fillets. Put one fillet on each piece of pastry, wet the edges, fold over, and press the edges well together. Brush over with beaten egg, sprinkle with grated cheese and a dust of cayenne. Bake in a quick oven (450°, Regulo No. 7) about 15 minutes and serve hot.

For Sardine Puffs. Use sardines sprinkled with lemon juice in place of the anchovies.

Anchovy Tartlets

Make some tartlets of flaky pastry and bake 'blind' (see pages 258–9).

When cold put a spoonful of whipped cream flavoured with anchovy essence in each. Put a curled anchovy on top and sprinkle with paprika or chopped capers.

Cheese Biscuits

Flour ¼ lb.   Fat 4–5 oz.
Pinch of salt   Cold water
Grated cheese 2 oz.

Use cooking fat, margarine, or a mixture.

Sieve the flour and salt, rub in the fat, add the grated cheese, and mix to a stiff paste with cold water. Knead lightly till free of cracks, then roll out very thinly, and cut into rounds with a fluted cutter. Bake in a hot oven (450°, Regulo No. 7) till lightly browned, 10–15 minutes. When cold garnish as follows:

(1) Piece of curled anchovy in the centre.
(2) A ring of overlapping slices of thinly-cut stuffed olives.
(3) Beat a little anchovy essence into some softened butter or margarine, and with icing forcers pipe a border round the biscuits. Sprinkle the centres lightly with paprika.

Cheese Fritters

Grated cheese 2 oz.   Whites of 2 eggs
Milk ¼ teacupful   Flour 2 oz.
Made mustard 1 teaspoonful   Salt and pepper

Mix flour and milk smoothly, add mustard and cheese, and season with salt and pepper. Then fold in the stiffly whipped egg whites. Fry (dessertspoonfuls at a time) a golden brown on both sides. Drain well and serve hot.

Cheese Straws

Flour 4 oz.   Butter or margarine 2 oz.
1 egg yolk   Salt, pepper, cayenne
Grated cheese 3 oz.

Rub fat into flour, then mix all ingredients together, binding with the egg yolk. Mix to a paste and roll out into a long thin strip about 3 inches wide. Cut across into straws about ¼ inch wide.

Knead the trimmings, roll out ¼ inch thick and cut into rings with two different sized biscuit cutters.

Bake on a floured tin in a quick oven (425°, Regulo No. 6) till lightly tinted – 10–15 minutes.

To serve put 3 or 4 straws through each ring.

Cheese Tartlets

Small pastry cases   *Margarine ½ oz.*
Grated cheese 3 oz.   *Flour ½ oz.*
Milk ¼ pint   *Salt and pepper*
1 egg

Roll out some short or biscuit crust thinly, cut into rounds, line 12 patty tins, prick the centres, and bake about 15 minutes in a hot oven (450°, Regulo No. 7).

Melt the margarine, stir in the flour and gradually add the milk, stir till boiling, and continue to stir while it simmers for 2 or 3 minutes. Remove from the heat, add the grated cheese and egg yolk, and season with salt and pepper. Whip the egg white till stiff, and fold it into the mixture. Fill the pastry cases and bake about 15 minutes in a moderate oven (400°, Regulo No. 5).

Herring Roes on Toast

8 fresh soft roes   *1 lemon*
Anchovy paste   *Margarine*
Salt, cayenne   *Toast*

Cut the toast into finger shapes, butter and spread with anchovy paste. Gently fry the roes till lightly browned, or grill them, put neatly on the toast, sprinkle with salt, cayenne, and lemon juice, and garnish with slices of cut lemon.

Savoury Éclairs

Make choux paste (see page 250), omitting vanilla essence. Put in a forcing bag with a ½-inch plain tube and force on to a greased baking tin, not too close together, and about 3½ inches long. Bake in a moderately hot oven (400°, Regulo No. 5) 30–40 minutes.

Remove from the tin, slit down the sides with a sharp

pointed knife and leave on a cake tray to cool; then fill with any savoury mixture.

Suggestions for Filling:

(1) Remove the skin and bone from some sardines, pound thoroughly with tomato ketchup, and season with salt and pepper.

(2) Pounded hard-boiled egg and tomato moistened with salad cream.

(3) Tiny roll of smoked salmon.

(4) Soft cream cheese, with chopped gherkin, olive, or chives.

(5) Mix 2 oz. grated cheese with 4 pounded anchovies, a little made mustard, and sufficient milk to form a soft paste.

Savoury Toasts

Cut slices of toast into rounds or fingers, spread with margarine, then with any of the following. Serve very hot.

(1) Finely flaked smoked haddock, moistened with white sauce. Garnish each with a slice of hard-boiled egg or a slice of pickled walnut. Or omit the garnish, sprinkle with grated cheese, and brown under the grill.

(2) Pound some sardines with vinegar and cayenne, make very hot and spread on fingers of toast. Garnish with capers.

(3) Skin 2 or 3 cooked sausages and cut into slices. Moisten 2 or 3 tablespoonfuls cooked rice with tomato ketchup or curry sauce. Heap up on the toast, arrange sausage overlapping on top, and heat in oven.

(4) Spread toast with chutney, then grated cheese, and brown under the grill.

(5) Grilled mushrooms. Sprinkle lemon juice and pepper.

(6) Grated cheese, sliced tomato on top and browned under the grill.

(7) Scrambled egg sprinkled with chopped olives or gherkins, or flaked cooked kipper warmed through in margarine.

(8) Spread toast with anchovy paste and sprinkle with chopped gherkins, or put an anchovy fillet on each finger of toast and garnish with paprika and chopped parsley.

Welsh Rarebit

Cheese 4 oz.	*Butter ½ oz.*
Milk 2 tablespoonfuls	*Made mustard 1 teaspoonful*
Cayenne	*Hot buttered toast*

Either grate the cheese or cut it in very thin slices. Melt the butter in a small saucepan, add the cheese, milk, mustard, and cayenne, and stir over a very gentle heat till the cheese has melted and the mixture is smooth. Pour on to rounds of buttered toast and brown under the grill.

Ground Rice Rarebit. Mix 1 oz. ground rice with a little cold milk. Boil the remainder of ½ pint milk, add the ground rice, and stir till thick. Add 2 oz. grated cheese, season with salt, cayenne, and made mustard, and continue to stir over a gentle heat till the cheese has melted. Pour on to hot buttered toast and brown under the grill.

Egg Dishes and Omelettes

Eggs are a highly concentrated form of food and, like meat, fish, and cheese, are first-class body-builders. In addition to protein and fat, they give us iron, calcium, sulphur, phosphates, and vitamins.

Boiled Eggs

To boil an egg, lower it slowly in a spoon into a saucepan of boiling water and boil gently for 3 or 4 minutes, according to taste and the freshness of the egg; a really new laid egg will take 4 minutes.

Never boil eggs straight from the refrigerator, or they will crack; if they have been forgotten, then place for a minute or two in a basin of warm water. It is a good plan to add a spoonful of salt to the water in which they are boiled, as this will prevent the white oozing out should they crack.

To boil hard for salads, etc., place in a saucepan of boiling water and cook gently for 10 minutes, then put immediately into cold water till the eggs are quite cold. This makes it easier to remove the shells and prevents the white becoming tough and a dark ring forming round the yolk.

To coddle an egg, which makes it lighter and more easily digested than boiling, see Invalid Cookery, page 317.

Poached Eggs

To every pint of water allow ½ teaspoonful salt and 1 table-spoonful vinegar.

Use a deep frying pan, break each egg in turn into a saucer, and when the water boils slip it in gently, tip the pan for a moment to envelop the yolk in the white, turn down the heat so that the water no longer boils, cover the pan, and leave for 5 minutes, or until the egg is lightly set, that is when the white becomes opaque. Remove carefully with a fish-slice or perforated spoon, and place on a round of buttered toast.

Steamed Eggs

Grease the small containers of an egg poacher with butter or cooking fat. Break an egg carefully into each, season with salt and pepper, place over the pan of boiling water, cover and cook till the whites are set – 3 or 4 minutes.

There are many dishes in which poached or steamed eggs can be used. They can be served on spaghetti, savoury rice or baked beans; or on spinach purée; or the hot buttered toast can first be spread with fish paste or creamed smoked haddock.

See also following recipes.

Fried Eggs

Melt a little butter or cooking fat in a frying pan, and when hot, break an egg into a cup, taking care not to break the yolk, and slip it carefully into the pan. Tip the pan to let the white run over the yolk. Cook over a gentle heat till just set, basting the fat over the top of the egg.

Baked Eggs

Individual china or glass fireproof dishes are the most convenient to use for baked eggs. Grease the dishes liberally, then carefully break an egg into each. Dust with salt and pepper and put a tiny knob of butter on top. Stand the dishes in a baking tin containing a little hot water and bake in a moderate oven till set – 10–15 minutes.

Variations:

(1) A little tomato purée in the bottom of the dish and a spoonful on top of each egg.

(2) Sprinkle greased dish with grated cheese, drop the egg carefully on top, and cover with grated cheese.

(3) Line bottom and sides of the dish with spinach purée, drop in the egg, and put a tiny knob of butter on top.

(4) Put a spoonful flaked, cooked smoked haddock or kipper moistened with white sauce in the bottom of the dish, drop in the egg, season with salt and pepper, and put a tiny knob of butter on top.

Eggs with Onion Sauce

3 hard-boiled eggs   Chopped parsley
Onion sauce ½ pint

Make the onion sauce (see page 197), season well with salt and pepper. Boil the eggs hard, shell, and cut in halves. Place in a hot dish and pour the sauce over. Sprinkle with chopped parsley.

Egg Cutlets

4 hard-boiled eggs   Lemon juice 1 teaspoonful
Thick binding sauce 4 table-   Fresh breadcrumbs 2 tablespoonfuls
    spoonfuls   Salt and pepper
Egg and breadcrumbs for   Fat for frying
    coating

Make thick binding sauce (page 204). Chop the eggs, add to the sauce together with the fresh breadcrumbs and lemon juice, and season with salt and pepper. Mix thoroughly, and spread on a plate to cool. When cold and firm divide into 4–6 equal portions, and shape into small cutlets. Dredge with flour, brush over with beaten egg, and coat with dry breadcrumbs. Fry in deep fat till golden brown. If possible, use a frying basket.

Egg Cutlets – Savoury

3 hard-boiled eggs
Fresh breadcrumbs 2 table-
    spoonfuls
Cooked rice 2 tablespoonfuls
Grated cheese 2 tablespoonfuls

Curry powder ¼ teaspoonful
1 raw egg
Salt and cayenne
Brown crumbs

Chop the eggs finely and mix with the rice, fresh breadcrumbs, cheese, and curry powder. Add the egg yolk and season with salt and cayenne. If at all dry, add a spoonful of milk. Form into cutlets, brush over with white of egg, coat with brown crumbs, and fry a golden brown.

Curried Eggs

4 hard-boiled eggs
Chopped onion 1 tablespoonful
Flour 1 tablespoonful
Butter 1 oz.
Chopped apple 1 tablespoonfuls

Curry powder 1 teaspoonful
Milk ½ pint
Lemon juice 1 teaspoonful
Boiled rice
Salt and pepper

Melt the butter, add the chopped onion and apple and fry till lightly browned, then stir in flour and curry powder, and gradually add the milk; stir till boiling, then simmer gently for 10 minutes, add lemon juice and seasoning to taste.

Cut the eggs in halves, pour over the sauce, and surround with a border of boiled rice.

If preferred, the eggs can be placed on rounds of fried bread before pouring over the sauce.

Note. Margarine or cooking fat can replace the butter, and vegetable or meat stock can be used in place of the milk when making the sauce.

Hard-Boiled Eggs on Risotto

4 hard-boiled eggs
Margarine 2 oz.
Concentrated tomato purée

Rice 4 oz.
Grated cheese
Salt and pepper

Boil the rice in salted water till tender, then strain. Add 1 oz. margarine, 2 tablespoonfuls of grated cheese and concentrated tomato purée to taste. Mix thoroughly, turn into a shallow fireproof dish and smooth neatly. Cut the hard-boiled eggs in half lengthways and place them cut side uppermost on the rice. Put a knob of margarine on top of each egg yolk, sprinkle with grated cheese and brown under the grill.

Scalloped Eggs

4 hard-boiled eggs *Capers 2 teaspoonfuls*
White sauce ¼ pint *Brown crumbs*
4 anchovy fillets

Boil the eggs while making the sauce. Chop the anchovy fillets and capers and add to the white sauce. Grease four individual dishes, place a sliced egg in each, pour over the sauce and sprinkle lightly with brown crumbs.

Reheat in a moderate oven for 10 minutes.

Nest Eggs

Separate the whites from the yolks, make some toast and cut into rounds. Beat the whites till very stiff and put some on each piece of buttered toast, leaving a hole in the centre. Put a small knob of butter in the hole, then drop in the yolk. Dust with salt and pepper and bake in a moderate oven (375°, Regulo No. 4) till set – about 15 minutes.

Poached Eggs with Savoury Sauce

Poach as many eggs as required and put each on a round of buttered toast. Make a sauce with ½ pint of milk, 1 oz. of margarine, and 1 oz. of flour. Simmer for a few minutes, then add 1 teaspoonful of anchovy sauce and 2 teaspoonfuls of Worcester sauce. Pour over the eggs and serve very hot.

Poached Eggs with Rice and Tomatoes

Rice 4 oz.   *Margarine 1 oz.*
Concentrated tomato purée *4 poached eggs*
 2 tablespoonfuls

Boil the rice in salted water till tender, then drain. Return to the saucepan, add the margarine and tomato purée mixed with

2 tablespoonfuls of rice water and reheat. Turn into a hot dish and place the poached eggs on top.

If preferred serve in individual dishes.

Poached Eggs in Broth
(See page 318)

Poached Eggs on Spinach
(See page 318)

Scrambled Eggs

Allow 1 tablespoonful milk or water and $\frac{1}{4}$ oz. butter or margarine to each egg. Beat up the eggs, add the milk or water, and season with salt and pepper. Melt the butter or margarine in a frying pan or small saucepan, pour in the eggs, and stir over a gentle heat until it thickens. Heap up on rounds of hot buttered toast, sprinkle with chopped parsley, and serve at once.

Variations:

(1) Any of the following can be added to the egg before it is cooked: chopped parsley, a pinch of mixed herbs, grated cheese, a little savoury sauce or vegetable extract, onion juice or finely minced shallots or chives, a few cooked green peas or cut-up beans.

(2) Croûtons. Cut some bread or potato into tiny dice and fry a golden brown. Add to the egg before cooking.

(3) The toast can be spread with savoury paste, or for a really substantial dish a layer of smoked flaked fish, moistened with white sauce, can be placed on the toast under the egg.

Scotch Eggs

3 eggs	*Egg and breadcrumbs*
Sausage meat $\frac{3}{4}$ lb.	*Fat for frying*

Boil the eggs hard, remove shells and coat with the sausage meat, keeping the shape of the egg. Brush over with beaten egg, coat with brown crumbs, and fry a golden brown. Cut through lengthways and serve on a bed of well-mashed potatoes.

Or leave till cold and serve with salad.

Surprise Eggs

4 hard-boiled eggs
Mashed potato 1 lb.
Grated onion 2 teaspoonfuls
Margarine 1 oz.

Chopped parsley 1 tablespoonful
Egg and breadcrumbs
Milk 2 tablespoonfuls

Boil the eggs hard and remove the shells. Mash the potato free of lumps, add the margarine melted in the milk, chopped parsley, and grated onion. Season with salt and pepper. Beat with a fork till smooth and creamy, mould round the eggs and proceed as for Scotch Eggs.

Eggs sur le Plat

Melt a small quantity of butter or margarine in a shallow fireproof dish, break the required number of eggs into it, season with salt and pepper, and cover with a greased paper. Bake in a moderate oven until the white is set, but not hard – 8–12 minutes at 425° (Regulo No. 6). Serve on the dish in which they are cooked.

This dish can be varied in the same way as Baked Eggs in individual dishes (see pages 301–2).

Swiss Eggs

Grease a shallow fireproof dish and line it with very thin slices of cheese. Dust with cayenne. Carefully break in as many eggs as will fit the dish. Pour over a little top milk, sprinkle with grated cheese, dot with small pieces of butter, and cook in a moderate oven 400° (Regulo No. 5) till the eggs are set – about 15 minutes.

Stuffed Eggs

Cut hard-boiled eggs in halves lengthways, remove the yolks, which can be pounded with various savouries. The yolks are then replaced and smoothed over with a knife dipped in water. Place each half on a slice of beetroot or tomato and garnish with watercress, small cress, or shredded lettuce. (See also pages 30–31.)

Suggestions for Fillings (the quantities given are for 4 eggs):

(1) One tablespoonful finely chopped olives, 2 teaspoonfuls butter or cream, salt and pepper.

(2) Three or four pounded sardines, a few drops vinegar or lemon juice, salt and pepper.

(3) Anchovy essence, 1 teaspoonful; curry powder, ½ teaspoonful; chopped parsley, 1 teaspoonful; salt and pepper.

(4) Minced tongue, 1 tablespoonful; moistened with horse-radish sauce, seasoned with salt and pepper.

(5) Chopped gherkins, 1 tablespoonful; mayonnaise sauce, 3 teaspoonfuls; salt and pepper.

(6) Smoked haddock or kipper (finely chopped), 1 tablespoonful; moistened with mayonnaise or French dressing.

(7) Grated cheese, 1 tablespoonful; butter, 2 teaspoonfuls; salt and pepper.

(8) Chopped chutney, 2 teaspoonfuls; curry powder, ½ teaspoonful; butter, 2 teaspoonfuls; salt and pepper.

Stuffed Anchovy Eggs in Tomato Cups

3 eggs	*Anchovy essence 1 teaspoonful*
6 tomatoes	*Butter 1 oz.*
Anchovy fillets	*Chopped parsley 1 teaspoonful*
Small cress	*Salt and pepper*

Use large tomatoes, cut a slice off the top of each, scoop out the centre, and season liberally with salt and pepper. Boil the eggs hard, shell them, and cut across in halves, remove the yolks and pound thoroughly with the butter, anchovy essence, and chopped parsley, season with salt and pepper. Fill the egg-whites with the mixture and place one half-egg in each tomato cup, cut side downwards. Either put the anchovy fillets cross-ways over the tops of the eggs, or in a circle round the bottom where they touch the tomatoes. Garnish with mustard and cress.

The scooped-out tomato can be used in soup, sauce, stews, etc.

Omelettes

It is not really a difficult matter to make an omelette, it only requires a little practice.

Omelettes are nourishing, very quickly made, and extremely useful for an emergency dish, so it is well worth the trouble of acquiring the knack of making them.

An omelette pan should be kept specially for the purpose of making omelettes. However, when this is not available, a smooth frying pan will do.

The less an omelette pan is washed, the better. It can be kept absolutely clean if, after use, it is rubbed over with crumpled kitchen paper and then with a dry cloth. If any pieces of egg should have stuck to the pan, rub them off with dry salt. Use cooking fat or fresh butter to grease the pan.

Everything should be ready before starting to mix the omelette; the dish on which it is to be served already warmed, and any garnishes or fillings required, prepared beforehand.

An omelette should be served as soon as it is made, or it will become tough and leathery.

Three eggs should make an omelette sufficiently large for two people, and it is best not to practise with more than this number until proficient.

Plain, sweet, and savoury omelettes are fundamentally the same, the difference being in what is added or used as a filling.

Plain Omelette

3 eggs　　　　　　　　　*Butter or cooking fat ½ oz.*
Water 2 tablespoonfuls　*Chopped parsley 1 teaspoonful*
Salt and pepper

Break the eggs into a basin and beat them only just sufficiently to blend the yolks and whites. Then add water and parsley and season with salt and pepper.

Place the omelette pan over a gentle heat, when quite hot put in the butter, and when melted tilt the pan in order to grease the sides, taking care that the butter does not brown. Then pour in the egg mixture and place over a moderate heat.

As soon as the omelette begins to set round the edge of the pan, loosen it with a palette knife to allow the uncooked part to run underneath. As soon as it is set at the bottom and no longer 'runny' on top, slip a palette knife round the side nearest the handle and double the omelette over, working it up gently with the knife. Leave in the pan for another moment, then slip the knife underneath to loosen it from the pan and turn it out on to a hot dish, so that the side that was next to the pan is on top.

The omelette should be soft and creamy inside with a smooth yellow surface.

Savoury Omelettes

Any of the following can be added to the egg before cooking: chopped chives, grated onion, pinch of mixed herbs.

Cheese Omelette. Add a tablespoonful of finely grated dry cheese to every two eggs, and sprinkle a little more over the top after it is dished.

Asparagus Omelette. Add a few asparagus tips before cooking, and garnish with a few more tips warmed in butter.

Separate Fillings. Odds and ends of cooked fish, meat, poultry, or vegetables, minced or finely diced, and warmed in thick sauce can be used as a separate filling. The mixture is placed in the centre of the cooked omelette just before folding over.

Mushroom Omelette

Allow 2 oz. mushrooms to 3 eggs.

Skin and wash the mushrooms and cut into thin slices; sauté in a little butter or margarine in a covered saucepan for 10 minutes. Season with salt and pepper.

Make the omelette and put mushrooms in centre before folding over.

Or a few mushrooms can be chopped finely and, after sautéing, added to the beaten eggs *before* making the omelette.

Puffy Omelette

3 eggs	*Seasoning*
Water 2 tablespoonfuls	*Butter 1 oz.*

Separate the yolks and whites of the eggs. Beat up the yolks until they are quite pale in colour; then add seasoning and the water (which should be warm), and beat together.

Whisk the whites of the eggs to a stiff froth; they should be so stiff that the bowl or plate can be inverted without their slipping out. Melt the butter in the omelette pan over a gentle heat. Fold the egg whites into the yolks and turn the mixture into the pan. Cook over a moderate heat until it is lightly browned underneath and the surface is full of breaking air bubbles. Then place under the grill until the omelette is dry on top. Loosen round the edge and underneath with a palette knife; mark it down the middle and double it over. Turn it carefully on to a hot dish and serve at once.

Sweet Omelette

Proceed as in previous recipe, adding a little sugar in place of the seasoning. Put a little warmed jam down the centre before folding over.

Casserole Cookery

The word 'casserole' includes all those fireproof dishes (with lids) in which food can be both cooked and served. They are so useful that they should find a place in every kitchen. They are made of earthenware, porcelain, or even glass, in all shapes and sizes. Some are just big enough for individual helpings, others sufficiently large to meet the needs of a big family.

Anything can be cooked in a casserole – meat, fish, vegetables, or fruit – in fact everything that requires slow, gentle cooking.

There are many real advantages in casserole cookery:

(1) Foods cooked in casseroles are better flavoured, because they are cooked slowly and all their goodness is retained.

(2) Saving of labour. As the food is served in the dish in which it is cooked, there is no extra saucepan to wash up.

(3) The food is always served really hot.

(4) Cheaper cuts of meat can be used, because the very slow method of cooking is just what is required to make them tender and taste equal to the more expensive cuts.

New casseroles should be 'seasoned' in the following manner: Fill with cold water, add a handful of salt, and place in the oven. Bring to the boil and leave in the oven for an hour;

then remove and let the water get cold in the casserole. This renders breakage much less likely.

Dried Peas, Butter Beans, and Haricot Beans

Soak in cold water for 24 hours. Then place in a casserole, add a pinch of salt and cover with boiling water. Put the lid on the casserole and cook in a moderate oven about 2 hours, or until quite soft.

Macaroni and Spaghetti

Allow about 1 pint boiling water to 4 oz. spaghetti or macaroni. Put the spaghetti in a casserole, pour over the water, add salt to taste, cover and cook in a moderate oven (400°, Regulo No. 5) till tender – 15–40 minutes, according to the type used. The 'quick-cooking' packet macaroni softens very quickly. Drain off any water that has not been absorbed, and reserve it for sauce or soup and use as required.

Rice can be cooked in exactly the same way.

Root Vegetables

Peel vegetables and cut into small pieces, put in a casserole, cover with boiling water, add salt to taste and cook in a moderate oven (so that the water is kept boiling) till tender – about 40 minutes. Drain, reserving the water for soup, add a small knob of margarine, and sprinkle with chopped parsley.

To Cook Conservatively. See Carrots en Casserole, page 90. Parsnips, swedes and turnips can be cooked in the same way.

Casserole of Vegetables (1)

Serve this as a course by itself, and vary vegetables according to what is available. Young carrots and turnips, peas, broad beans, new potatoes and spring onions make a delicious mixture. Prepare and cut up where necessary. Put a few spinach leaves at the bottom of the casserole. Shred a few outside lettuce leaves or a little cabbage, mix with vegetables that are being used and, when available, add a skinned and sliced tomato. Put into casserole, seasoning with salt and pepper, pour on sufficient boiling water to three parts fill the casserole, cover with a margarine paper, put lid on casserole, and bake in a slow oven for 1½ hours. Pour off liquid, thicken with flour and margarine and pour back over contents of casserole. Hand grated cheese separately.

Casserole of Vegetables (2)

Use a mixture of the following vegetables: cauliflower, sprouts, cabbage, carrots, parsnips, celery and tomatoes.

Prepare the vegetables in the usual way, wash thoroughly and cut into very small pieces. Allow 4 oz. margarine to every quart of vegetables.

Put the vegetables in a casserole, add a good seasoning of salt and pepper, pour over the melted margarine, and stir round, so that all the vegetables get coated. Add ½ teacupful hot water, cover closely and cook in a moderate oven for 1½ hours. The full flavour and valuable salts of the vegetables are retained by cooking in this manner.

Serve with steak or any kind of grill.

Dried Fruits

Figs, prunes, apricots, apple rings, etc., are excellent cooked *en casserole*. After soaking in cold water overnight, turn into the casserole, adding sugar and flavouring to taste. Use Demerara sugar; and sliced lemon is a great improvement to prunes and apricots. Cook in a slow oven, so that it just simmers, until the fruit is quite soft.

Chicken en Casserole

1 chicken	*Fat smoked beef (raw) 4 oz.*
1 onion	*Stock or water 1 pint*
Flour 1¼ oz.	*Mushrooms 4 oz.*
A bouquet garni	*Salt and pepper*

Cut the chicken into neat joints and dip in seasoned flour. Cut the smoked beef into dice. Melt some dripping in a frying pan and quickly brown the chicken and smoked beef; remove them, add the sliced onion, and fry this also till golden brown; then pour off most of the fat, stir in the flour, and when this is brown, add the stock and stir till boiling.

Wash and skin the mushrooms and put these with the chicken and beef into a casserole, season with salt and pepper and add the bouquet garni (a sprig of parsley and thyme, a bay leaf and a thin slice of lemon rind tied together) and pour the thickened gravy over. Cover and cook in a slow oven till tender – about 1½ hours. Remove the bouquet garni before serving.

Casserole of Duck

1 duck
Onion juice ¼ teaspoonful
Mushrooms 4 oz.
Stock

Shelled green peas ½ pint
Chopped mint 1 teaspoonful
Salt and pepper
Flour

Cut the duck into joints and dip in seasoned flour. Skin and chop the mushrooms. Put the prepared duck in the casserole, add the mushrooms, onion juice, and sufficient stock to just cover, put the lid on the casserole, and cook in a moderate oven for 40 minutes; then add the peas and mint and continue cooking till tender – about another 30 minutes.

Lamb en Casserole

Best end neck of lamb 2 lb.
Stock or water 1 pint
2 sticks celery
1 large onion
Tomatoes ¼ lb.
Vinegar 2 teaspoonfuls

Dripping 2 oz.
Chopped parsley 1 tablespoonful
Flour 1 oz.
Redcurrant jelly 2 teaspoonfuls
Salt and pepper

Divide the meat into neat chops and trim off some of the fat. Peel and slice the onion, skin and slice tomatoes and cut up the celery.

Melt the dripping in a frying pan, fry the onions a golden brown, lift them on to a plate, put in the chops and brown these lightly on both sides; then put them also on the plate. Stir the flour into the pan, stir till brown, add the stock or water and stir till it boils. Put the chops in a casserole, sprinkle over the vinegar, season with salt and pepper and put the onion, tomato and celery on top; season these also and sprinkle over the chopped parsley, then pour on the thickened gravy. Put the lid on the casserole and cook in a slow oven 2–2½ hours. Add the jelly and serve in the casserole.

Liver en Casserole

Sheep or ox liver 1 lb.	*Rice 1 teacupful*
Stock or water 1¼ pints	*1 large onion*
Worcester sauce 2 teaspoonfuls	*Small turnip*
Seasoned flour	*Medium-sized carrot*
Dripping	

Cut the liver into thin slices, dip in seasoned flour, then brown lightly on both sides in hot dripping. Prepare and slice the vegetables. Wash the rice. Put all ingredients together in a casserole, season with salt and pepper, cover, and cook in a very slow oven about 2 hours.

Stewed Steak with Pickled Walnuts

Stewing steak 1½ lb.	*2 carrots*
Stock 1 pint	*2 or 3 onions*
Dripping 2 oz.	*2 or 3 sticks of celery*
Flour 1 oz.	*Pickled walnuts*
Salt and pepper	

Cut up the steak in cubes. Cut the onions into thin slices, the carrots into dice and the celery into rings. Coat the steak with seasoned flour and fry it and the onions till lightly browned. Remove from the dripping, stir in the flour and when this is brown, gradually add the stock, and stir till boiling. Put the meat in alternate layers with the vegetables in a casserole, sprinkling the layers of meat with a little finely chopped pickled walnut. Season with salt and pepper, pour over the gravy, cover the casserole and cook in a slow oven about 2½ hours.

Pickled onions can be used in place of walnuts, in which case fresh onions can be omitted.

Veal Casserole with Mushrooms

Breast of veal 1 lb.	*6 olives*
Flour 1 tablespoonful	*Stock 1 pint*
Mushrooms 4 oz.	*1 or 2 onions*
Juice of ½ lemon	*Slice of smoked beef*
Dripping 1 oz.	*A glass of sherry*

Cut up the veal and put in a casserole.

Slice the onion and chop the beef and fry in the dripping till golden brown, then add the flour, brown this also, gradually add the stock, stir till boiling, season with salt and pepper, add the lemon juice and pour into the casserole. Cover and simmer gently in a slow oven for an hour, then add the sliced mushrooms, and cook for another hour. Add the wine and stoned olives before serving.

Further recipes for dishes cooked *en casserole* will be found in sections on meat, fish, poultry, luncheon and supper dishes.

Invalid Cookery

In cooking for the sick or convalescent the following rules should always be observed:

(1) Let each dish be as nourishing as possible and served in small quantities.

(2) Serve the food punctually at the time expected, neatly and daintily arranged on a tray with a spotless cloth, and where possible, use individual dishes in oven-glass or fireproof china.

(3) If the dish served is a hot one, see that it is really hot and not just lukewarm.

(4) Vary the menu as much as possible and do not let the patient know beforehand what is going to be served.

In addition to the recipes in this section, many other dishes suitable for the invalid will be found throughout the book.

Soups

Meat or good bone soups, such as chicken, veal or mutton broth, are all suitable for invalids. They must be absolutely free from grease and not too highly seasoned.

Thick vegetable soups are not easily digested and therefore are not suitable. Rice, barley, sago, semolina, or vermicelli can all be used for thickening.

Beef Tea

Gravy beef ½ lb.   *Water ¼ pint*
Salt

Shred the meat, put in a stone jar, sprinkle with salt, pour on the water and let it stand for 1 hour. Then stand the jar in a saucepan of water, cover and cook very gently 4 to 5 hours. Keep well stirred. Strain and when cold, remove the fat.

If preferred, make in a double saucepan, or in a casserole in a very slow oven.

Raw Beef Tea

This will not keep, so it must be made in very small quantities. Take 2 oz. lean, juicy beef, remove fat and skin, and shred finely. Put in a cup, add a pinch of salt and pour over ½ tea-cupful cold water. Let it stand for 1 hour, pressing the meat well from time to time with a fork. Strain and serve in a coloured glass to disguise the colour.

Soup for the Convalescent

A calf's foot   *Chopped parsley*
Gravy beef 4 oz.   *2 sticks of celery*
Water 3 pints   *A small piece of carrot,*
Seasoning   *   turnip and onion*

Cut up the calf's foot and shred the beef, put in a saucepan with the cold water, a little salt and 2 or 3 peppercorns, cover, and bring *very slowly* to boiling point. Skim, and add the prepared vegetables cut into small pieces; then continue simmering *very gently* until the calf's foot is quite tender and comes away from the bone quite easily. Strain and leave till cold. Remove fat and serve as required in a hot soup cup with a little of the calf's foot cut into tiny pieces and a little chopped parsley, together with fingers of toast.

Egg Flip

(1) Beat up a new-laid egg *very* lightly with ½ teaspoonful of sugar, add a tablespoonful of water and very slowly either a tablespoonful of brandy or a small glass of sherry or port. The wine or spirit must be added gradually and the mixture lightly beaten all the time, so that it does not curdle. Strain the mixture into a glass.

(2) Use the same ingredients as in (1), but separate the yolk and white of egg. Beat the yolk lightly, with sugar, water and wine or brandy. Whip the egg white to a stiff froth and fold in lightly.

(3) Beat the yolk of an egg very lightly with 1 teaspoonful of caster sugar, add 1 tablespoonful of brandy and, whisking lightly, gradually pour on ½ pint very hot milk. Strain and serve.

Calf's Foot Jelly

Cut up 2 calf's feet, wash and scrape thoroughly. Put the pieces in a saucepan, cover with cold water and bring slowly to the boil. Then strain, rinse the feet and return to the pan, cover again with cold water (4–5 pints), put the lid on the pan and simmer *very slowly* for 5 hours, when the liquid should be reduced to half the quantity, skimming if necessary from time to time. Then strain and leave till cold, when the stock should be a stiff jelly.

Remove every particle of fat. To 1 pint of stock allow the thinly peeled rind and juice of a lemon, 1 wineglass sherry, 2 tablespoonfuls sugar and 1 inch stick of cinnamon (optional).

Reheat the stock with the above ingredients, bring slowly to the boil and simmer for 5 minutes; then strain.

If the jelly is at all cloudy it can be cleared as follows:

Put the flavoured jelly in a saucepan (the pan should be only half full). Wash an egg and separate the yolk and white, put the white and crushed shell into the pan and whisk over a gentle heat until just beginning to boil; remove from the heat, cover and let stand for 10 minutes, then strain through a scalded cloth.

Note. The amount of sherry, lemon juice and sugar can be varied to suit individual taste.

Red wine can be used in place of sherry.

The juice of an orange can replace half the lemon juice.

Custards

Custards, sweet and savoury, are generally liked and are light and nourishing.

A steamed custard is quickly made. Beat an egg lightly with 1 teaspoonful of sugar, stir in ¼ pint of hot (but not boiling) milk, and add a drop or two of vanilla, strain into a basin or cup, cover, and put in a saucepan with hot water reaching just half-way up the basin. Put the lid on the saucepan and let the water boil *gently* until the custard is firmly set (about 12 minutes). If done in a steamer it will take a little longer.

Vary it by coating the basin with caramel (see page 269), or serve with chocolate sauce.

For Savoury Custard. Use ¼ pint of well-flavoured veal or chicken broth instead of the milk, and add salt to taste. Cut into dice and serve in chicken broth or other clear soup.

Coddled Egg

An egg 'coddled' is much lighter than a boiled one. Put sufficient water in a saucepan to completely cover the egg. Bring to the boil and when boiling fast, put in the egg, put the lid on the pan and place it where it will keep very hot, but the water must cease to boil. Let it stand for 6 minutes and then lift out. The white will be set without being tough and the yolk creamy.

Fluffed Eggs

Separate the white and yolk of an egg, keeping the yolk whole. Beat the white to a stiff froth. Grease a small fireproof dish or deep saucer with butter, put in the white of egg and carefully drop the yolk into the centre. Sprinkle with salt and pepper. Stand the dish in a tin containing a little water and bake in a moderate oven till set – 10–12 minutes.

Poached Egg in Broth

Take ¼ pint of well-flavoured chicken, veal or mutton broth, bring to the boil in a small saucepan and carefully drop in a fresh egg. Poach lightly. Lift the egg out and place it in the centre of a hot soup plate. Pour over the broth and serve with fingers of toast.

Poached Egg on Spinach

This makes a nourishing and well-balanced meal. One half to three quarters of a pound of spinach will be required. Remove the stalks and wash in several waters till free of grit. Put in a saucepan with just the water that clings to the leaves, add a little salt, press down well and bring to the boil. Cook till tender (about 20 minutes), then drain, pressing out all the moisture. Rub the spinach through a sieve; reheat with a little butter, while a fresh egg is poached or steamed. Shape the spinach purée into a neat, flat round. Place on a hot plate with the egg on top.

For a change, place the spinach in a small casserole, put the egg on top, then coat with white sauce and sprinkle with grated cheese. Brown quickly under the grill.

Note. The water strained from the spinach, flavoured with vegetable extract, makes a delicious bouillon.

Flaked Fish with Tomato Sauce

Use an individual glass casserole. Grease it thickly with butter and coat the inside with fine breadcrumbs. Flake some freshly-cooked white fish, season with salt, pepper and lemon juice, put in the casserole and cover with white sauce to which has been added a little tomato purée and finely chopped parsley. Sprinkle with breadcrumbs, dot with butter and bake in a moderate oven till lightly browned – about 20 minutes. Serve with potato purée.

Steamed Fish

Use fillets of sole, whiting, plaice, or fresh haddock, and remove the skin. Season with salt and lemon juice and either roll up the fillets or cut into neat pieces. Put these on a greased plate, dot with butter, cover with a greased paper and then with another plate or saucepan lid. Place over a saucepan of fast boiling water and cook till the fish looks white and creamy – about 15 minutes. Serve very hot with any juice that has run from the fish.

If allowed, coat with any kind of fish sauce, adding any liquor from the fish to it.

Chop en Casserole

Put a neatly trimmed chop in a casserole, sprinkle with salt, add 1 teaspoonful of washed rice, 2 skinned tomatoes and 1 tablespoonful of finely shredded celery. Pour over sufficient well-flavoured stock to cover, put the lid on the casserole and cook in a moderate oven for 1¼ hours.

Chicken Mould

Minced chicken 2 tablespoonfuls　*1 egg*
White breadcrumbs 2 tablespoonfuls　*Margarine ¼ oz.*
Chicken stock ¼ teacupful　*Seasoning*

Put the breadcrumbs in a small basin, add the margarine and pour over the hot stock. Cover and leave to soak for a few minutes. Then add the minced chicken, lightly beaten egg and seasoning, and mix thoroughly. Turn the mixture into a small greased basin, cover with a greased paper and steam slowly until firm to the touch – about 20 minutes.
Turn out on to a hot dish and serve with mashed potato and sieved spinach.

　Note. Minced veal can be used instead of chicken.

Sheep's Tongues and Mushrooms
(See pages 166–7)

Stewed Sweetbread

1 calf's sweetbread　*Yolk of an egg*
Stock ¼ pint　*Chopped parsley 1 teaspoonful*
Lemon juice 2 teaspoonfuls　*Seasoning*
Cornflour 1 small teaspoonful

Soak the sweetbread for 1 hour in cold water, then put in a small saucepan. Cover with cold water, bring to the boil and simmer for 3 minutes. Drain, put into cold water, and when cool remove skin and fat, and cut into 3 or 4 pieces. Put these in a small casserole and cover with stock (if this is not well-flavoured, add a small piece of carrot and onion). Cover and simmer very gently in a slow oven till tender (about ¾ hour). Strain off the liquid into a small saucepan, mix the lemon juice and cornflour and add them. Stir till boiling, and simmer for 5 minutes. Cool somewhat, then add the beaten egg yolk. Reheat *without boiling*, add the parsley and pour over the sweetbread. Garnish with snippets of toast.

For a change, omit the egg and lemon and add a few asparagus tips, or green peas, or skinned tomatoes.

Chocolate Rice Meringue

Milk ¼ pint	Plain chocolate 1 oz.
Rice 1 oz.	Sugar
White of an egg	Essence of vanilla

Put the rice and milk in a small casserole with 1 teaspoonful o sugar, cover and cook in a slow oven for 1 hour. Grate the chocolate into a cup and stand over hot water till it has dissolved; stir into the rice with a few drops of essence of vanilla, return to the oven and continue cooking uncovered until the rice is quite tender and the milk absorbed – about another hour. Whisk the white of an egg very stiffly, fold in 1 tablespoonful of caster sugar, heap over the pudding and return to a moderate oven till set and just tinted – about 20 minutes.

Snow Ball

Milk ¼ pint	1 egg
Sugar	Vanilla

Separate the yolk and white of the egg and beat the white to a stiff froth. Bring the milk to the boil in a shallow pan and drop in the white of egg in spoonfuls. When set on one side turn over and poach for a few seconds on the other. Lift out with a perforated spoon.

Beat up the yolk lightly, sweeten to taste and pour over the hot milk (not boiling) in which the white was cooked. Strain, add a few drops essence of vanilla and turn into a double saucepan; stir over a gentle heat till it thickens, but do not boil. Pour this custard over the white and serve cold.

For a change, add 1 teaspoonful coffee extract to the custard.

BEVERAGES

Albumen Water

Whites of 3 new-laid eggs　　*Pinch of salt*
Water 1 pint　　　　　　　*A few drops of lemon juice*

Beat up the egg whites lightly (*not* to a stiff froth) with the salt, and add the water – quite cold. Add a few drops of lemon juice and strain through muslin.

Clear Barley Water

Pearl barley 2 tablespoonfuls　　*¼ lemon*
Water 1 pint　　　　　　　　　*Sugar*

Wash the barley, put it in a saucepan, cover with cold water, bring quickly to the boil, then strain. Put the blanched barley in a jug with the rind and juice of the lemon and pour over 1 pint of boiling water. Add a little sugar if required. Cover, leave till cold, then strain, and it is ready for use.

Thick Barley Water

Pearl barley 2 tablespoonfuls　　*¼ lemon*
Cold water 2 pints　　　　　　*Sugar*

Blanch the barley as in previous recipe. Put the barley back into the saucepan, pour over the cold water and add the thinly-peeled lemon rind. Cover and simmer very gently for 2 hours. Strain, add the lemon juice and sugar, if required.

Note. Barley water can be made from the prepared patent barley. Full directions are given on the container.

Blackcurrant Tea

Put a heaped tablespoonful blackcurrant jam into a saucepan
with ½ pint water. Cover and simmer gently for 5 minutes,
then strain. Add a squeeze of lemon juice and sugar to taste.
Serve very hot for a cold or sore throat.

Sandwiches

The bread from which sandwiches are made should be 24 hours
old and of rather close texture.

Toasted bread is good for substantial sandwiches. Plain
biscuits, crispbread, bridge rolls, French bread and any kind
of brown bread can all be used as a basis for the various spreads.

The nature of the filling and the size of the sandwiches will
vary according to the purpose for which they are wanted.
There is the rather large, substantial sandwich for picnic
lunches and hikers, the somewhat daintier variety for the
refreshment buffet, and the afternoon tea sandwich, which is
little more than a mouthful.

Then there is the open sandwich – just one slice of French
bread, toast, biscuit, or split bridge roll, with the filling and
garnish arranged artistically on top, and here the housewife
has an opportunity to give full play to her imagination.

Use a very sharp knife to cut the bread and a pliable one to
spread the butter or vegetable margarine. If this is at all hard,
beat it up with a fork or wooden spoon till soft and creamy.
Do not always use plain butter or margarine on the bread;
peanut butter, thick salad cream or mayonnaise can be used
instead. Or the butter or margarine can be creamed and
flavoured with minced chives or grated onion, pimento, or
watercress.

For lunch or picnic sandwiches leave the crusts on the
bread.

For afternoon tea use very thin bread, remove the crusts
(dry these for crumbs), and cut up quite small with a sharp
knife or biscuit cutter.

To keep sandwiches fresh until required, cover with a
damp cloth. For picnics, etc., wrap in damp muslin, then in
plastic bags.

The Filling. For savoury fillings, meat, fish, poultry, fresh vegetables, nuts and cheese can all be used.

Salt, smoked, spiced, and fresh meat, tongue, and various kinds of sausages all make tasty sandwiches. Fresh meat needs the addition of something piquant (see detailed recipes later). The meat must be freed from skin and gristle and unless very tender, should be minced. When used in slices, cut very thin, small pieces and see that the fat is evenly distributed.

Open Sandwiches

Slices of French bread, rye bread, or split rolls are all excellent for open sandwiches. The bread should not be cut too thin. The garnishing of these sandwiches is very important and should help to make a very attractive supper table.

Smoked salmon or cod's roe need only a pinch of finely chopped or dried parsley in the centre. Other usual garnishes are thin slices of stuffed olive or gherkin; a tiny piece of pimento; sliced tomato; beetroot cut into fancy shapes or tiny dice; sliced radishes or very small radish roses; tiny tufts of watercress; a tiny sprinkle of hard-boiled egg yolk rubbed through a sieve.

Any of the Savoury Spreads mentioned in this section can be used, or any of the following:

(1) **Meat.** Cut very thin slices of veal, tongue, salt or smoked beef, or any kind of thinly sliced sausage. Garnish to taste, including some kind of pickle or grated horseradish.

(2) **Cheese.** Thin slices of cheese. Garnish with celery, chopped parsley and pimento or stuffed olive.

(3) **Fish.** (a) Flaked and moistened with mayonnaise. Garnish with cucumber and sliced radishes.

(b) Marinated or smoked herring. Cut into thin strips, arrange these diagonally and garnish with tiny radish roses, very small dice of beetroot and chopped parsley.

(c) Sardines or anchovies. Garnish with tomato and very small tufts of watercress.

(4) **Egg.** Add some chopped chives or anchovy essence to the butter before spreading it on the bread or rolls. Put a slice of tomato in the centre, cover this with a slice of hard-boiled

egg with a curled anchovy on top. Sprinkle with chopped parsley. A slice of stuffed olive can replace the anchovy.

(5) **Tomato and other Vegetables.** Spread slices of French or rye bread with a thin layer of any savoury mixture (see pages 324–6) and garnish with any of the following:

(a) A ring of sliced tomato round the edge and fill the centre with finely chopped celery moistened with mayonnaise. Sprinkle with chopped parsley.

(b) Mustard and cress, thinly sliced radish round the edge, and a small radish rose in the centre.

(c) Sliced tomato in the centre with a tiny tuft of watercress on top. Sprinkle edge with chopped chives.

(d) Tomato in the centre. Surround with sliced cucumber. Sprinkle with chopped parsley.

SANDWICH FILLINGS

Cream Cheese Spreads

Unless very soft add a spoonful top milk and mix thoroughly. Then add any of the following:

(1) Chopped walnuts and a few chopped capers. Salt and pepper to taste.

(2) Worcester sauce.

(3) Chopped olives or gherkins.

(4) Chopped chives or grated onion.

(5) Chopped watercress and paprika.

(6) Chopped pimento.

(7) Redcurrant jelly.

(8) Finely chopped pineapple.

(9) Two or three chopped stewed prunes and a few chopped nuts.

Grated Cheese Fillings

(1) Mix grated cheese to a paste with a little top milk or mayonnaise. Spread bread and butter first with made mustard.

(2) Mix grated cheese with an equal quantity of grated apple.

(3) To 4 tablespoonfuls grated cheese add 1 teaspoonful each anchovy essence and vinegar.

(4) To 3 tablespoonfuls grated cheese add 1 tablespoonful tomato ketchup, 1 teaspoonful grated onion (or chopped spring onion), or chopped chives and a dash of pepper.

Egg Fillings

(1) Two hard-boiled eggs, $\frac{1}{4}$ teaspoonful curry powder, a few drops anchovy essence, a squeeze of lemon juice, salt and pepper. Sieve the eggs, mix all ingredients, adding a little top milk to form a paste.

(2) Hard-boiled eggs, sieved, combined with grated cheese and flavoured with chopped tinned pimento and a very little grated onion.

(3) Hard-boiled eggs finely chopped, moistened with mayonnaise, seasoned with salt and pepper. Spread on bread and butter and cover with chopped watercress or lettuce or mustard and cress.

(4) Two hard-boiled eggs and a breakfastcupful cooked green peas. Rub through a sieve and add a teaspoonful chopped mint.

(5) Scrambled egg. Beat up the required number of eggs, adding 1 tablespoonful of water to 2 eggs, flavour with curry powder, savoury sauce, vegetable extract or grated onion. Add salt and pepper and scramble lightly. Remove from the heat as soon as it is set and leave till cold before spreading on bread and butter.

Fish Fillings

(1) **Flaked Salmon** moistened with mayonnaise and covered with thinly sliced cucumber.

(2) **Smoked Haddock,** flaked and moistened with skinned and chopped tomato.

(3) **Any Cooked White Fish,** flaked and moistened with salad cream and covered with thinly sliced radishes.

(4) **Salmon paste** mixed with chopped gherkin, covered with mustard and cress.

(5) **Kipper.** Pour boiling water over two kippers, leave for 5 minutes, then drain, remove all skin and bones, and pound to a paste, adding a little butter.

(6) **Bloater.** Pour boiling water over two bloaters, leave for a minute, then remove the skin and bones and put the fish in a small saucepan with 1 oz. margarine and a pinch of mace and cayenne. Simmer gently for 10 minutes, then pound to a paste.

(7) **Sardine.** Mash sardines to a paste, add vinegar and pepper to taste and cover with sliced cucumber.

Or spread some fingers of toast with parsley butter, put a boned sardine on each, sprinkle with pepper and lemon juice or vinegar and garnish with diced beetroot or sliced radish and small tufts of watercress.

Meat and Poultry Fillings

(1) **Beef.** Mince finely and add finely chopped pickle and leaves of watercress.

Or omit the pickle and cover meat with finely-grated apple.

(2) **Lamb.** Mince finely and moisten with mayonnaise and flavour with chopped mint.

(3) **Liver.** Mince some cooked liver, flavour with chutney and moisten with tomato ketchup.

(4) **Chicken,** minced and mixed with finely shredded celery. Moisten with salad dressing.

(5) **Chicken,** minced and mixed with half the quantity minced tongue or smoked beef. Add a little grated lemon rind and chopped parsley and moisten with salad dressing.

(6) **Liver Sausage.** Remove the skin from the sausage and mash to a paste. Spread between thin slices of rye bread.

Sweet Fillings

(1) **Strawberry Jam** beaten up with whipped cream.

(2) **French Plums, Figs, or Dates** minced with almonds and moistened with lemon juice.

(3) **Date Spread.** Chop some stoned dates and put in a small saucepan with sufficient water to barely cover, flavour with

cinnamon and simmer gently till of jam-like consistency – about 10 minutes.

(4) **Raisins** finely chopped and mixed with an equal quantity of grated apple. Flavour with cinnamon.

(5) **Banana.** Mash 4 bananas, add 2 finely-crumbled stale sponge cakes, and 1 tablespoonful redcurrant jelly.

(6) **Banana.** Thinly sliced, covered with grated chocolate. Grated apple can replace the bananas.

(7) **Lemon Curd** covered with chopped nuts.

(8) **Preserved Ginger.** Chop 2 oz. preserved ginger and an equal quantity of walnuts, mix together with enough whipped cream to make a paste.

(9) **Peanut Butter** mixed with an equal amount of jam, honey, syrup, or grated apple.

(10) **Honey** sprinkled with chopped nuts.

(11) **Chestnut.** Rub some boiled skinned chestnuts through a sieve and add sufficient sweetened condensed milk to make a stiff paste. Flavour with almond or vanilla essence. Spread between plain biscuits or bread and butter.

Salad Fillings

Shredded lettuce, watercress, mustard and cress, thinly sliced radishes, cucumber or tomatoes – all make excellent sandwiches, either singly or combined. Season with salt and pepper. If preferred, any savoury filling can be spread on the bread first.

Raw Brussels Sprouts cut into very thin slices and sprinkled with lemon juice, salt and pepper are also very good.

Root Vegetables. Chop cooked vegetables finely and moisten with mayonnaise.

Rolled Sandwiches

The bread for these must be new, sliced very thinly and the crusts cut off.

Rolled sandwiches may be made from one small slice of

buttered bread, or they may be made in long rolls, with any soft filling.

For those made with small slices of bread, after trimming off the crusts, spread with any soft savoury filling preferred, and roll up.

For Asparagus Rolls. Use canned or cooked asparagus tips 2–3 inches long. Roll a slice of buttered bread round each piece of asparagus, leaving about ½ inch exposed.

To make in Long Rolls. With a very sharp knife remove the crusts from the four sides of a sandwich loaf, then slice very thinly *lengthways*. Spread the slices with softened butter or margarine, then with a savoury filling, which preferably should be of a contrasting colour to the bread. Then roll up tightly like a Swiss roll. Press firmly and wrap in a cloth, greaseproof paper, or plastic bags, and leave in a cool place for a couple of hours. Then cut across into ¼- or ½-inch slices.

Harlequin Sandwiches

Cut some slices of brown and white bread ½ inch thick. Take two slices of white and two of brown; butter one of each on both sides and the remainder on one side only. Take one of the latter white ones and cover with any savoury filling, put a brown slice buttered both sides on top, and cover this with small cress, chopped watercress, or sliced cucumber. Repeat these two layers and press well together. Trim off the crusts and with a very sharp knife cut through into thin sandwiches.

Rainbow Sandwiches

Prepare four savoury fillings of contrasting colours, such as tomato, smoked cod's roe, chopped watercress and egg.

Slice *all* the crusts from a sandwich loaf with a very sharp knife. Then cut five ½-inch slices from the loaf lengthwise. Butter top and bottom slices on one side only and the remaining three on both sides. Spread the fillings evenly between the slices and press together. Then cover the loaf with greaseproof paper and wrap firmly in a damp cloth, press between two boards with a light weight on top for at least 2 hours.

Cut the loaf in thin slices and then cut each slice in half, either straight across or diagonally.

Buffet Suppers

Choose from the following for a buffet supper party: various kinds of sandwiches, patties, anchovy or sardine rolls, canapés, stuffed sticks of celery, savoury éclairs, savoury meringues, cheese straws, pastry cases filled with smoked fish moistened with mayonnaise, or a dish of salmon (or other fish) mayonnaise, egg or cheese savouries.

Recipes for these will be found in the sections on sandwiches, hors d'oeuvres and savouries.

Add also small dishes of olives, gherkins, salted almonds and potato crisps.

Sweets. Serve some of these in individual glasses. This makes for easy service. Trifles, fruit whip, ginger, coffee, or chocolate cream, can all be served in glasses. Chestnut meringues and brandy snaps filled with cream are great favourites with the younger folk.

Drinks. Cider cup and fruit cup are always popular; so are plain lemonade, orangeade and iced coffee. Later in the evening serve hot tea and coffee.

Sandwiches. These can be open or closed, or a selection of each. White and brown bread, bridge rolls, French or rye bread, or cheese pastry are all suitable as foundations for savoury mixtures. Pay special attention to the garnishing of open sandwiches; it makes all the difference to the look of the table. See pages 323–7 for hints on garnishing and choice of fillings.

Quantities to Allow. Allow 3 or 4 of the larger savouries (sandwiches, patties, etc.) per person, and 3 of the smaller ones (cheese straws, stuffed celery, savoury éclairs, etc.).

A 2-lb. loaf should give 24–30 slices.

Fruit salad: 1 pint for 4 people.

Ice cream: 1 quart for 12 people.

Cheese Dip

This appeals to the younger folk.

Mix together 1 lb. cream cheese and 1 dessertspoonful horseradish sauce, then add sufficient top milk — about 3 tablespoonfuls — to make a good dipping consistency; season with salt and pepper.

Turn into a bowl and stand it on a plate or covered tray. Serve with small wedges of brown bread, sliced French bread and crisp biscuits. The guests help themselves by dipping these into the bowl.

Variations:

(1) Add a little chopped preserved ginger.

(2) Omit the horseradish and add 2 tablespoonfuls of tomato ketchup and a few chopped olives or chives.

Picnic Fare

Choose things that will pack and carry well and are easy to eat.

Sandwiches, stuffed rolls, patties, hard-boiled eggs, buns, scones, plain cake and fresh fruit are all suitable. Cherries, apples, and bananas will carry better than the softer fruits, such as currants and raspberries.

Be generous with supplies; appetites are always keener in the fresh air. Use plastic cups and plates and paper serviettes. And take with you a large paper bag to wrap fruit skins, waste paper, etc., so that no litter is left to spoil the countryside.

Do not forget the salt and take this in a small container, not in a twist of paper from which it is likely to get spilt.

Use plastic bags for sandwiches, salads, etc. The food keeps in perfect condition for hours, and after use they can be washed and used over and over again. Use one of these also for a wet sponge for sticky fingers and take an old piece of towelling for drying.

Sandwich fillings can be prepared overnight and kept in the refrigerator or coolest part of the larder.

Hard-boiled eggs carry better in their shells.

If you are preparing a meal for a railway journey, make a separate package for each member of the party, for the passing backwards and forwards of bags can be somewhat annoying to other passengers in the carriage.

Sandwiches. For any savoury sandwiches some kind of salad placed on top of the mixture is a great advantage. It tastes good, is refreshing and will help to keep the bread moist. Shredded lettuce or watercress, mustard and cress, thinly sliced radishes, cucumber, or tomatoes can all be used.

A good selection of fillings will be found on pages 324–7.

Stuffed Rolls. Use either bridge rolls or ordinary rolls, and cover with lettuce leaves before adding the fillings.

'Cold Dogs' are also good. For these use large-size bridge rolls. Split through and remove a little of the crumb (dry this in the oven for bread rusks or brown crumbs). Spread with margarine and mustard, then place a *hot* grilled sausage in each, secure with elastic bands and wrap in greaseproof paper. The sausage will give its flavour to the whole roll.

Patties. Use any of the following fillings:

(1) Any cooked vegetables, mashed and moistened with curry or cheese sauce.

(2) Cooked fish flaked and mixed with one or more chopped hard-boiled eggs, moistened with anchovy or other savoury fish sauce.

(3) Tinned salmon; add a few chopped capers and moisten with mayonnaise.

(4) Any left-over meat or poultry, either diced or minced and moistened with thick gravy.

(5) Mix together 2 tablespoonfuls cooked rice, 2 oz. ground nuts, ½ teaspoonful curry powder, and 1 teaspoonful each tomato ketchup and liquid vegetable extract.

Beverages

HOT DRINKS

Cocoa

Cocoa 1½ *teaspoonfuls*	*Milk* ½ *pint*
Water 2 *tablespoonfuls*	*Sugar to taste*

Mix the cocoa and sugar to a smooth paste with the cold water, pour over the boiling milk, return to the saucepan and reboil.

Coffee

Coffee should always be freshly ground and stored in airtight tins.

Allow 1 heaped tablespoonful of coffee to ½ pint of water.

If a coffee machine is being used, make according to directions given. If no machine is available use an earthenware jug. Put in the coffee, pour over the boiling water and stir round with a spoon. Cover and let stand for 5 minutes, stir again, re-cover and let stand for another 10 minutes, by the end of which time the grounds should have sunk to the bottom of the jug. Strain, reheat and serve.

Tea

Water for making tea should be freshly boiled. Rinse out the teapot with boiling water and put in the tea, allowing 1 teaspoonful of tea per person and 1 teaspoonful extra if more than three. Half fill the teapot with boiling water, put on the lid, cover with a tea cosy and let stand for 3 minutes, then fill up the pot with boiling water and serve at once.

Russian Tea

Use China tea and infuse as above. Serve with slice of cut lemon instead of milk. The lemon should be wiped with a damp cloth and then slices cut through the rind and pulp, a slice being put in each cup.

COLD DRINKS
Blackberry Syrup

Blackberries 2 lb.   *Sugar 2 lb.*
Water ¼ teacupful

Pick and wash the fruit, put it in a large jar with the water, cover closely, and stand in a saucepan of boiling water. Cook over a gentle heat for 2 hours, then strain through a scalded cloth. Return to the saucepan, add the sugar and simmer gently for 20 minutes. When cold, bottle and cork securely.

A little of the syrup added to a tumbler of water or soda water makes a refreshing drink.

Loganberries, Mulberries, Blackcurrants or Raspberries can be used in the same way.

Cider Cup (1)

1 lemon　　　　　*Cider 1 quart*
Sugar 4 oz.　　　 *Soda water 1 quart*
Nutmeg (optional)

Add the sugar, thinly peeled lemon rind and juice and a grate of nutmeg to the cider, stir till sugar has dissolved, then chill. Strain and add the soda water just before serving.

Cider Cup (2)

China tea 1 pint　　*Cider 1 quart*
Sugar 2 oz.　　　　 *1 lemon*
2 oranges

Infuse the tea, pour on to the sugar and leave till cold, then add the strained orange juice and chill. Just before serving, add the chilled cider and the lemon cut into thin slices.

Claret Cup

1 bottle of claret　　*Sugar 2 oz.*
Water ¼ pint　　　　 *1 lemon*
Soda water 1 pint

Put the sugar, water and thinly peeled lemon rind in a small saucepan, bring to the boil, cover and simmer for 5 minutes; leave till cold, add the juice of the lemon and strain; add the claret and chill. Add soda water just before serving.

Iced Coffee

To 1 pint strong coffee add ¼ pint of milk and ¼ pint of cream slightly whipped. Stir in 1 tablespoonful of sugar, mix thoroughly and chill.

Note. Coffee extract added to the cold milk and sweetened to taste is also very good.

Lemonade

3 lemons   Brown sugar 3 tablespoonfuls
Water 3 pints

Peel the lemons *very* thinly. Put the rind into a saucepan with the sugar and ½ pint cold water, bring slowly to the boil and simmer for 10 minutes. Squeeze the juice from the lemons, pour on the remainder of the water and the contents of the saucepan. Leave till cold, then strain.

Lemonade Syrup (1)

4 lemons Sugar 1½ lb.
Water 1 pint Citric acid 1 oz.

Peel the lemons thinly. Put the rind into a saucepan with the juice, sugar and water. Bring to the boil, simmer for 5 minutes; then cover and leave till cold. Dissolve the citric acid in a little cold water; add to the syrup. Mix well, then strain and bottle. Dilute with water or soda water as required.

Lemonade Syrup (2)

Sugar 1½ lb. Citric acid 1 oz.
Water 1 pint Essence of lemon 2 teaspoonfuls

Put the sugar and water in a saucepan. Put over a gentle heat until the sugar has dissolved, then bring to the boil and cook steadily for 10 minutes. When cold, add the citric acid (dissolve in a little hot water) and the essence of lemon. Turn into a bottle and cork. When required, put 2 tablespoonfuls of the syrup in a tumbler and fill with water or soda water.

Mixed Fruit Cup

A mixed fruit cup can be made with almost any fresh or canned fruit juice.

Mix together a can each of pineapple juice and orange juice and add an equal quantity of soda water, the juice of 2 lemons and sugar to taste.

Chill, and before serving add slices of orange, tangerine segments and maraschino cherries.

Iced Tea Punch

China tea 1 pint   Juice of ½ lemon
Claret ¼ pint   3 or 4 slices cucumber
Sugar to taste

Mix all ingredients together and chill.

Tea and Fruit Drinks

Use China tea for choice. Make the tea in the usual way, allowing 2 teaspoonfuls to 1 pint of water. Infuse for 5 minutes, then pour off.

Sweeten with clarified sugar (see page 423), and flavour with fruit juice.

Use about 1 tablespoonful of sugar syrup and the same quantity of lemon juice to ½ pint of tea, add some small pieces of ice and any other fruit juice preferred.

Left-over juice from any kind of stewed or tinned fruit can be used.

Iced tea with the juice of fresh limes sweetened to taste makes a really satisfactory thirst quencher.

Ginger ale, ginger beer, or cider are all excellent mixed with an equal quantity of tea, poured over ice, flavoured with lemon juice and sweetened to taste.

Iced Fruit Cubes

These are attractive to serve in glasses of punch.

(1) Colour some water with green or red vegetable colouring. Put a small segment of orange or tangerine in the divisions in the ice trays, pour over the coloured water and freeze in the usual way.

(2) Dilute orange or lemon squash with water, add a few

drops of red colouring to the orange and green to the lemon, pour into ice trays and freeze.

Cakes

GENERAL RULES AND HINTS

First see to the oven. Light the gas or switch on the electricity 15 minutes before the cakes or biscuits are to be put in.

Where a heat-controlled cooker is in use, adjust according to directions given with the stove.

Large cakes need a moderate oven; small cakes a quick oven.

Have all ingredients and utensils collected before starting to mix the cakes.

Grease and prepare tins before mixing. Shallow tins used for layer cakes, etc., should be greased with melted cooking fat, butter, or margarine, using a pastry brush for this purpose. For rich fruit cakes grease the tin and line with one or more thicknesses of greased paper, which should come 2 inches above the sides of the tin.

Only fill the tins two-thirds full. Do not move a cake in the oven if it can possibly be avoided and then only when it is well risen, and always close the oven door gently. A sudden jar or draught of cold air will cause fruit to sink or the cake to fall in the centre.

Test a large cake to see if it is cooked through before removing from the oven. Do this with a *warmed* iron skewer or knitting needle. If it comes away clean the cake is done; if sticky, bake a little longer.

After removing from oven let a large cake stand in the tin for 10 minutes before turning out.

Cool all cakes and biscuits on a cake tray away from draughts, and never put away in tins till quite cold.

Always break eggs one at a time into a cup before using to see that they are quite fresh.

All dried fruit must be washed, picked over, and thoroughly dried before using. Damp fruit makes a heavy cake.

Weigh or measure all ingredients carefully.

There are three methods of preparing cake mixtures:
(1) By rubbing the fat into the flour.
(2) By creaming the fat and sugar.

(3) By beating or whisking the eggs and sugar.

To Rub Fat into the Flour. For this method have utensils, ingredients, and hands as cold as possible. Chop the fat coarsely in the flour with a knife. Using only the *tips* of the fingers and thumbs, rub lightly till the contents of the bowl looks like yellow breadcrumbs.

To Cream Fat and Sugar. Put the fat into a warm dry mixing bowl. Should the fat be very hard leave it in a warm place for a short time before using, but never allow it near a great heat so that it becomes 'oiled'. Beat the fat with a wooden spoon till it becomes whitish, soft, and creamy. Then add the sugar and continue beating till it is like whipped cream. Do not attempt to beat quickly, as if you were beating up an egg; experience will teach you that slow methodical beating is the quickest way of gaining your end.

To Beat Eggs and Sugar. See detailed recipes.

To Fold in White of Egg. Turn the stiffly whipped white of egg into the bowl of cake mixture. With a metal spoon cut down to the bottom of the bowl and turn the mixture on top of the egg white. Continue to do this 3 or 4 times, until the white is mixed in. On no account must the mixture be stirred round.

Consistency of Mixture. It is almost impossible to give the exact quantity of liquid required in any cake recipe because of the varying size of eggs and the varying dryness of flour. Unless otherwise stated the mixture should drop easily from the spoon. To test the correctness of the consistency, take a large spoonful of the mixture, hold it above the mixing bowl, and allow it to drop. If it pours it is too soft; if it has to be forcibly shaken out of the spoon it is too dry.

LARGE CAKES

Bola

Flour 1 lb.	Candied peel 6 oz.
Butter or margarine ½ lb.	Preserved ginger 4 oz.
Yeast ½ oz.	Soft brown sugar 1 oz.
Warm milk ½ pint	Ground cinnamon 2 teaspoonfuls
2 eggs	Ground almonds 4 oz.

Cream the yeast with a teaspoonful of caster sugar, then add the lukewarm milk. Sieve the flour into a warm bowl and rub in 2 oz. of butter; make a well in the centre. Pour in the dissolved yeast and leave to stand for 15 minutes. Add the eggs, mix to a dough. Cover with a cloth and leave in a warm place to rise for 1 hour.

Cut up the peel and ginger, and mix with the sugar, ground almonds, and cinnamon.

Roll out the dough, spread on half the remaining butter, fold over, and roll again. Spread on the rest of the butter and roll out again. Divide into two pieces, roll each piece quite thin, and cut each into two rounds. Warm two round shallow tins, line each with a round of dough, put half the peel mixture on each, and cover with dough.

Cover with a cloth and leave another $\frac{1}{2}$ hour in a warm place. Bake in a moderately hot oven (425°, Regulo No. 6) for $\frac{1}{2}$ hour; then brush over with syrup, reduce the heat and continue cooking another 20–30 minutes. When cooked, brush over again with syrup and sprinkle with hundreds and thousands.

For the Syrup. Boil together for 10 minutes 4 oz. sugar, 3 tablespoonfuls water, and 1 tablespoonful of syrup from the preserved ginger.

Cherry Cake

Flour 8 oz.	*Butter or margarine 5–6 oz.*
Caster sugar 5 oz.	*3 eggs*
Glacé cherries 3 oz.	*Milk 2 tablespoonfuls*
Candied peel 1 oz.	*Baking powder $\frac{1}{4}$ teaspoonful*
Essence of lemon	

Grease and line a cake tin 6–7 inches across. Sieve the flour and baking powder, cut up the cherries. Cream the fat and sugar, add the lightly beaten eggs one at a time, adding a teaspoonful of the flour with each, beat lightly, add a few drops essence of lemon, the cherries and peel, the remaining flour and milk. Mix lightly and turn into prepared tin. Bake on the middle shelf of a moderate oven (375°, Regulo No. 4) $1\frac{1}{4}$–$1\frac{1}{2}$ hours.

Seed Cake. Omit lemon essence, cherries, and peel, and add 3 teaspoonfuls caraway seeds.

Ginger Cake. Omit cherries, lemon essence, and peel, use only 1 tablespoonful milk, and add 4 oz. chopped preserved ginger and 1 tablespoonful ginger syrup.

Sultana Cake. Use 4 oz. sultanas in place of the cherries.

Walnut Cake. Add 2 oz. roughly chopped walnuts in place of the cherries and peel, and flavour with a few drops of almond essence.

For Small Cakes. Put 2 teaspoonfuls of the mixture into greased bun tins and bake on the second shelf of a moderately hot oven (400°, Regulo No. 5) 20–25 minutes. Makes 18 to 24 cakes.

Chocolate Cake

Self-raising flour 5 oz.   *2 eggs*
Caster sugar 4 oz.   *Milk 2 tablespoonfuls*
Margarine 4 oz.   *Essence of vanilla*
Chocolate 3 oz.

Grate or cut up the chocolate, put it in a small basin with the milk, and stand in a saucepan of hot water till dissolved; then cool. Sieve the flour. Cream the margarine and sugar, add the chocolate and a few drops essence of vanilla, and mix thoroughly. Then beat in one egg at a time, adding a spoonful of the flour with each, beat well, then add remaining flour. Turn into a well-greased shallow cake tin about 8 inches by 1½ inches, and bake in a moderate oven (400°, Regulo No. 5) about 35 minutes. Cool on a cake tray and before serving dredge the top with icing sugar.

If preferred, the cake can be cut through and sandwiched together with apricot jam or chocolate butter icing (see pages 369–70).

Iced Chocolate Cake

Self-raising flour 6 oz.   *Margarine 4 oz.*
Caster sugar 4 oz.   *2 eggs*
Cocoa 1 oz.   *Milk 3 tablespoonfuls*
Vanilla essence ½ teaspoonful   *Chocolate glacé icing*

Grease a 6-inch cake tin and line with greased paper.

Sieve flour and cocoa. Cream margarine and sugar till soft and white, then add the eggs one at a time, adding a spoonful of the flour with each, and beat well. Then add the vanilla essence and milk, and lastly the remaining flour and cocoa. Mix lightly and turn into prepared tin. Bake in a moderate oven (375°, Regulo No. 4) about 1¼ hours. Cool on a cake tray and when cold ice with chocolate glacé icing (see page 370).

Eggless Chocolate Sandwich

Self-raising flour 5 oz.	*Margarine 2 oz.*
Cocoa 1 oz.	*Golden syrup – a generous tablespoonful*
Sugar 1 oz.	*Milk and water 6 tablespoonfuls*
Bicarbonate of soda	
¼ teaspoonful	

Sieve flour, cocoa, sugar, and bicarbonate of soda into a basin. Put the margarine, syrup, and milk and water into a small saucepan, place over a very gentle heat till the margarine has melted, and when just tepid, pour on to dry ingredients and with a wooden spoon mix to a smooth batter. Turn into a greased deep sandwich tin (about 8 by 2 inches) and bake in a moderate oven (400°, Regulo No. 5) about 30 minutes. Cool on a cake tray, and when cold split through and spread with any chocolate icing preferred (see pages 369–70). The top can also be iced or simply sprinkled with icing sugar.

For a Steamed Chocolate Cake. This is useful if at any time an oven is not available. Turn the mixture into a greased cake tin 5 inches across, and cover with greased paper. Place in steamer, cover with a tightly fitting lid, and steam over a saucepan of gently boiling water for 1 hour. Remove paper from the tin and let it stand for a few minutes before turning out. Cool on a cake tray. Do not cut for at least 24 hours.

Coconut Cake

Self-raising flour 6 oz.	*3 eggs*
Desiccated coconut 2 oz.	*Caster sugar 4 oz.*
Butter or margarine 4 oz.	*¼ lemon*

Cream the butter and sugar, beat in each egg separately, then stir in flour and coconut lightly and lastly the grated rind and

strained juice of half a lemon. Turn into a greased 7-inch tin
and bake in a moderate oven (375°, Regulo No. 4) 1¼ hours.

Eggless Date Cake

Self-raising flour 5 oz.
Margarine 2 oz.
Mixed spice ¼ teaspoonful
Bicarbonate of soda 1 level teaspoonful

Sugar 2 oz.
Dates 4 oz.
Water ¼ teacup

Cut up the dates, put in a small saucepan with the water,
bring slowly to the boil, and simmer *very gently* for 5 minutes;
then cool.

Sieve the flour, spice, sugar, and bicarbonate of soda, rub in
the margarine, then pour over contents of saucepan and mix
thoroughly with a wooden spoon. Turn into a greased shallow
tin (about 8 inches by 2 inches), spread smoothly with a wet
knife, and bake in a moderate oven (375°, Regulo No. 4) for
40 minutes.

Dundee Cake

Flour 10 oz.
Sugar 6 oz.
Candied peel 2 oz.
Sultanas 6 oz.
Currants 6 oz.
Mixed spice ¼ teaspoonful

Glacé cherries 2 oz.
Butter or margarine 6 oz.
Baking powder ½ teaspoonful
3 eggs
Almond essence ¼ teaspoonful
Blanched almonds 1 oz.

Grease an 8-inch cake tin and line with greased paper. Sieve
flour, baking powder, and spice. Cut up peel and cherries.
Cream butter and sugar till very soft. Beat in the eggs one at
a time, adding a tablespoonful of the flour with each, beat
lightly, then stir in the remaining flour, fruit, peel, and
almond essence. Mix thoroughly, turn into prepared tin,
arrange blanched almonds over the top, and bake about 2
hours in a moderate oven (350°, Regulo 3–4).

Eggless Fruit Cake

Self-raising flour 8 oz.
Sugar 3 oz.
Mixed spice ½ teaspoonful
Candied peel 1 oz.

Dried fruit 8–10 oz.
Margarine 3 oz.
Water ¼ pint
Bicarbonate of soda ½ teaspoonful

If dates are being used, cut them up. Put the fruit, peel, margarine, sugar, and water into a saucepan, bring slowly to the boil and simmer for 3 minutes, then leave till nearly cold.

Sieve the flour and spice into a bowl; add the bicarbonate of soda to the contents of saucepan and pour on to flour. Mix thoroughly with a wooden spoon and turn into a 7-inch cake tin lined with greased paper. Smooth over with a wet knife and bake in a moderate oven about 1½ hours; the first hour 375°, Regulo No. 4, then reduce to 350°.

Do not cut for 2 days.

Fruit Cake

Flour 8 oz.	*Sugar 3 oz.*
Margarine 4 oz.	*Golden syrup 2 oz.*
Baking powder 2 level teaspoonfuls	*3 eggs*
Cinnamon 1 level teaspoonful	*Dried fruit 14 oz.*
Mixed spice 1 level teaspoonful	*Candied peel 2 oz.*
Lemon juice 1 teaspoonful	*Milk to mix*

Use any mixture of dried fruit preferred. Wash and dry thoroughly.

Cream the margarine, sugar, and syrup. Sieve flour, baking powder, and spices together, and add them alternately with the beaten eggs. Beat well, add the fruit and lemon juice and sufficient milk to make a fairly soft consistency. Turn into a 7-inch cake tin lined with greased paper, bake in a moderate oven for 2 hours – 375°, Regulo No. 4 for the first hour, then reduce slightly to finish.

Note. This is quite a good, not-too-rich cake, suitable for icing for festive occasions (see page 370).

Iced Fruit Cake

Flour 10 oz.	*Candied peel 4 oz.*
Margarine 8 oz.	*Glacé cherries 1 oz.*
Brown sugar 6 oz.	*Mixed spice ¼ teaspoonful*
Sultanas 8 oz.	*Dark treacle 1 tablespoonful*
Currants 8 oz.	*Almond paste (pages 368–9)*
Raisins 4 oz.	*Royal icing (page 370)*
4 eggs	

Line a 9-inch tin with greased paper, the top edge extending 1 inch above the side of the tin.

Stone raisins, wash and dry fruit thoroughly. Cream the margarine and sugar, then beat in eggs one at a time, then add flour, spice, fruit, and treacle. Mix very thoroughly; turn into prepared tin, spreading evenly with a wet knife.

Bake for 3 hours, the first hour 350°, Regulo No. 3, then reduce to 325°, Regulo No. 2.

Cool in the tin, then turn out on to a cake tray and leave till quite cold. This can be kept for a week or two before icing. First cover with almond paste and leave for a couple of days before covering with royal icing. See general directions for icing cakes, pages 367–8.

Genoa Cake

Self-raising flour 8 oz.   *Butter or margarine 6 oz.*
Caster sugar 6 oz.   *3 eggs*
Sultanas 4 oz.   *Currants 4 oz.*
Glacé cherries 2 oz.   *Candied peel 3 oz.*
Grated rind of ½ lemon   *Sliced almonds ½ oz.*
Milk 1 tablespoonful

Line a 7-inch tin with greased paper.

Cream the butter and sugar, add the eggs one at a time and beat well. Stir in the flour, then add the grated lemon rind, chopped peel, cherries cut in halves, the currants and sultanas, and the milk. Mix thoroughly. Turn into prepared tin, smooth over with a spoon dipped in milk, and place the sliced almonds on top. Bake in a slow oven (350°, Regulo No. 3) for about 2 hours.

Gingerbread (1)

Self-raising flour ¾ lb.   *Golden syrup ¾ lb.*
Ground ginger 1 teaspoonful   *Bicarbonate of soda 1 teaspoonful*
Candied peel 2 oz.   *Tepid water 1½ gills*

Grease well a loaf tin about 5 inches by 9 inches. Put flour and golden syrup into a basin. Mix the bicarbonate of soda and the ginger with the tepid water, pour on to the flour and syrup and mix to a smooth batter with a wooden spoon; add the peel

and turn into prepared tin. Bake in a slow oven (350°, Regulo
No. 3) for 1½ hours. When cold store in a tin for two days
before using. Serve cut into thin slices and buttered.

To weigh syrup, see page 22.

Gingerbread (2)

Flour 10 oz.	*Ground ginger 2 teaspoonfuls*
Golden syrup 6 oz.	*Mixed spice ¼ teaspoonful*
Brown sugar 2 oz.	*Milk 2 tablespoonfuls*
Margarine or cooking fat 3 oz.	*Bicarbonate of soda 1 teaspoonful*
1 egg	

Line a shallow greased tin about 10 inches by 8 inches with
greased paper.

Sieve the flour, ginger, and spice into a bowl and add the
sugar. Warm the margarine, syrup, and milk until the
margarine is melted, but do not make it hot. Pour on to the
flour and mix thoroughly. Dissolve the bicarbonate of soda in
a spoonful of milk, add this and the beaten egg, and beat
thoroughly. Turn into prepared tin and bake in a moderate
oven (375°, Regulo No. 4) for 45 minutes.

Honey Cake (I)

(Lekach)

Honey ½ lb.	*2 eggs*
Self-raising flour 12 oz.	*Ground ginger 1 teaspoonful*
Caster sugar 4 oz.	*Mixed spice ¼ teaspoonful*
Warm water ¼ pint	*Bicarbonate of soda ½ teaspoonful*
Oil 3 tablespoonfuls	*Shredded almonds*

Sieve the flour, ginger, spice, and bicarbonate of soda. Warm
the honey.

Beat the eggs and sugar till light and frothy, add the oil and
warmed honey, then the dry ingredients alternately with the
water. Mix to a smooth batter, then turn into a shallow greased
tin about 9 inches across, sprinkle with shredded almonds and
bake in a moderate oven (375°, Regulo No. 4) about 1 hour.

Honey Cake (2)

Flour 8 oz.	*Honey ½ lb.*
Butter or margarine 2 oz.	*1 egg*
Ground ginger 1 teaspoonful	*Mixed spice ¼ teaspoonful*
Bicarbonate of soda 1 level	*Milk ¼ teacupful*
teaspoonful	*Shredded almonds*

Sieve flour, ginger, and spice together. Put butter and honey in a mixing bowl and stand over hot water till the butter has dissolved; add the beaten egg, then stir in the sieved flour and lastly the bicarbonate of soda dissolved in the milk, which should be slightly warm. Mix thoroughly, turn into a greased shallow tin about 9 inches across, sprinkle with shredded almonds, and bake in a slow oven (350°, Regulo No. 3) about 1¼ hours.

Note. Three tablespoonfuls salad oil can replace the butter or margarine.

Kiddies' Cake

Self-raising flour 8 oz.	*Butter or margarine 4 oz.*
Caster sugar 4 oz.	*3 eggs*
Milk 2 tablespoonfuls	*A 2-oz. bar of chocolate*

Cream the butter and sugar. Add the beaten eggs one at a time, adding a tablespoonful of the flour with each, beat lightly, then add remaining flour and milk.

Cut up the chocolate into small pieces about ¼ inch square, and add to the mixture. Turn into a greased shallow tin about 8–9 inches across, and bake in a moderate oven (375°, Regulo No. 4) about 1 hour. Sprinkle the top with icing sugar before serving.

For a Birthday Cake. Ice with glacé icing sprinkled with grated chocolate or chocolate granules.

Madeira Cake

Flour 8 oz.	*Butter or margarine 5 oz.*
Baking powder 1 teaspoonful	*Caster sugar 5 oz.*
Essence of lemon	*3 eggs*
2 strips citron peel	*Milk 2 tablespoonfuls*

Line a greased cake tin 6–7 inches across. Sieve the flour and baking powder. Cream the butter and sugar, add the beaten eggs one at a time, adding a teaspoonful of flour with each, beat lightly, then add remaining flour, milk, and a few drops essence of lemon. Turn into prepared tin, lay the citron peel lightly across the top, and bake in a moderate oven (375°, Regulo No. 4) about 1¼ hours.

Mandelbrot

(*Komishbrot*)

Flour 10 oz.	*Baking powder 2 teaspoonfuls*
Sugar 4 oz.	*Cooking oil 6 tablespoonfuls*
Almonds 3 oz.	*Lemon juice 1 teaspoonful*
2 eggs	*Flavouring*

Blanch the almonds and chop coarsely.

Beat the eggs and sugar lightly, add the oil and lemon juice and a little grated lemon rind or almond essence.

Sieve flour and baking powder with a pinch of salt, add the egg mixture and the almonds and mix to a dough. With floured hands form into long thin rolls about 3 inches wide. Place on a well greased and floured baking tin and bake in a moderate oven (350°, Regulo No. 4) until very lightly browned – about 30–40 minutes. Leave till nearly cold, then cut across obliquely into slices about ¼ inch thick and return to the oven until lightly browned.

Orange Cake

Self-raising flour 12 oz.	*3 eggs*
Caster sugar 6 oz.	*Margarine 5 oz.*
1 orange	

Line an 8-inch cake tin with greased paper.

Separate the yolks and whites of the eggs. Melt the margarine, but do not make it hot.

Beat the sugar and egg yolks till light and frothy, add the melted margarine. Stir in the flour lightly and grated rind and strained juice of the orange. Then fold in the stiffly beaten egg whites. Turn into prepared tin and bake in a moderate oven (375°, Regulo No. 4) about 1¼ hours.

Iced Orange Cake

Self-raising flour 6 oz.	*2 eggs*
Caster sugar 4 oz.	*Butter or margarine 4 oz.*
Orange marmalade	*Glacé icing*
1 orange	

Cream the butter and sugar, add the lightly beaten eggs one at a time and a tablespoonful of the flour with each, beat well, add the grated orange rind and 2 tablespoonfuls strained juice, then the remaining flour. Spread evenly over 2 greased sandwich tins and bake in a moderate oven (400°, Regulo No. 5) 20–25 minutes. Cool on a cake tray, and when cold sandwich together with sieved orange marmalade, and ice with orange-flavoured glacé icing.

If preferred, omit icing and dredge top of cake with icing sugar.

Pound Cake

Flour 10 oz.	*Baking powder 1 teaspoonful*
Butter or margarine ½ lb.	*4 eggs*
Caster sugar ½ lb.	*Lemon rind*

Grease an 8-inch cake tin and line it with greased paper to come an inch above the sides.

Sieve the flour and baking powder. Cream the butter and sugar very thoroughly, then add the lightly beaten eggs one at a time, adding a tablespoonful of flour with each, then add the grated rind of a lemon and remaining flour.

Turn into prepared tin and bake in a moderate oven (375°, Regulo No. 4) about 1¼ hours.

Note. If fresh lemons are not available, flavour with essence of lemon.

Soda Cake

Flour 8 oz.	*Bicarbonate of soda ½ teaspoonful*
Margarine 6 oz.	*Cream of tartar ½ teaspoonful*
Sugar 5 oz.	*1 egg*
Currants 6 oz.	*Sour milk about ½ pint*

Sieve flour, cream of tartar, and bicarbonate of soda into mixing bowl. Rub in the margarine, add sugar and currants, and mix well. Add the beaten egg and sufficient sour milk to form a dropping consistency. Turn into a prepared 6-inch tin and bake in a moderate oven (375°, Regulo No. 4) about 1 hour.

Note. If no sour milk is available add 1 teaspoonful of lemon juice or a few drops of vinegar to $\frac{1}{4}$ pint fresh milk.

Walnut Layer Cake

Self-raising flour 8 oz.	*Butter or margarine 6 oz.*
Caster sugar 6 oz.	*3 eggs*
Walnuts 2 oz.	*Walnut filling*
Almond essence	*Glacé or American icing*
Milk 2 tablespoonfuls	

Line a 7-inch tin with greased paper.

Chop the nuts roughly; sieve the flour. Cream the butter (or margarine) and sugar till soft and white. Beat in the eggs one at a time, adding a spoonful of flour with each. Add the nuts, a few drops almond essence, and the milk, and lastly the flour. Mix lightly. Turn into prepared tin and bake in a moderate oven (375°, Regulo No. 4) $1\frac{1}{4}$ hours. Cool on a cake tray, and when cold cut through into three, spread with walnut filling and coat with vanilla glacé or American icing, and decorate with halved walnuts.

Walnut Filling. Cream together 2 oz. butter and 3 oz. sieved icing sugar, and add $\frac{1}{2}$ oz. finely chopped walnuts.

For Coffee Walnut Cake. After cutting through spread with coffee butter icing, coat the cake with it and decorate with walnuts.

Sponge Cakes, Sponge Sandwiches, and Swiss Rolls

GENERAL DIRECTIONS

Always prepare the tin before starting to mix the cake.

Sponge Cakes. Grease and warm the tin, then sprinkle with equal quantities of sieved flour and caster sugar. Then turn the tin upside down and tap sharply to remove any loose flour and sugar. Tie a band of greased paper round the outside of the tin to come 2 inches above the top. After baking allow the cake to get nearly cold, inverted on a cake tray, before turning out.

Sponge Sandwiches. Grease and warm two sandwich tins and sprinkle with sieved flour and caster sugar. Spread mixture evenly and bake according to directions. Fill and finish off as required.

Swiss Rolls. Grease a warmed Swiss roll tin and line it with greased paper. Spread mixture over evenly. While it is cooking, get the filling ready. If jam is being used, heat slightly. As soon as the roll is baked, turn it out top downwards on to a sheet of paper thickly dusted with caster sugar. Spread over the warm jam quickly, then trim off the edges all the way round, place the two hands under the sugared paper and roll up at once. Leave rolled in the paper for a minute to keep its shape, then cool on a cake tray.

American Sandwich

Flour 6 oz.	*Cream of tartar 1 teaspoonful*
Butter 2 oz.	*Bicarbonate of soda 1 level teaspoonful*
Caster sugar 4 oz.	*Milk ½ teacupful*
2 eggs	

Sieve the flour and cream of tartar. Separate the egg whites. Mix the bicarbonate of soda with the milk.

Cream the butter and sugar, add the beaten egg yolks and flour alternately, then the milk and soda. Mix lightly, beat the egg whites to a stiff froth and fold them in the mixture, then turn into two well-greased sandwich tins and spread evenly. Bake in a quick oven (450°, Regulo No. 7) 12–15 minutes. Cool on a cake tray, and when cold fill with any filling preferred.

The top can be dredged with icing sugar, or iced with butter or glacé icing.

Lemon curd for the centre with lemon-flavoured glacé icing is very good. Apricot jam, to which some shredded nuts have been added, or chocolate or coffee butter icing also make good centres.

The same mixture can be baked in a shallow round or square

9-inch cake tin, instead of in sandwich tins, in which case it will take about 30 minutes to cook in a less hot oven (400°, Regulo No. 5).

Another good topping is this. Spread the cake liberally with coffee butter icing. Mark across or round with a fork, sprinkle with shredded blanched almonds, then dredge lightly with icing sugar. If the cake has been baked in a square tin it can be cut into fingers before serving.

Sponge Cake (1)
(Plava)

Self-raising flour 5 oz.	*Vanilla essence*
3 eggs	*Hot water 2 tablespoonfuls*
Caster sugar 6 oz.	

Prepare a cake tin about 6½ inches across. See general directions.

Sieve the flour. Whisk the eggs, add the sugar, and beat until light and frothy and the mixture is nearly white. Add the flavouring and hot water and continue beating for another 5 minutes. Fold in the flour lightly with a metal spoon and turn into prepared tin. Bake in a slow oven (350°, Regulo No. 3) 50–60 minutes. Invert the tin on to a wire cake tray and leave till nearly cold before removing the cake from the tin.

Sponge Cake (2)
(Plava)

Flour 4 oz.	*Caster sugar 6 oz.*
4 eggs	*Lemon juice 1 tablespoonful*
Butter 1 oz.	*Lemon rind ¼ teaspoonful*

Prepare a 7-inch cake tin. Sieve the flour twice. Separate the yolks and whites of the eggs. Beat the yolks till thick and creamy; add the lemon juice and rind and beat again till very thick. Beat the egg whites till stiff, beat in the sugar a little at a time, then fold into the beaten yolks. Gradually fold in the sifted flour and melted butter, which must not be hot. Turn into prepared tin and bake in the centre of a slow oven (350°, Regulo No. 3) 1¼–1½ hours. Invert the tin on to a wire cake tray and leave for 1 hour before turning out.

Sponge Sandwich (1)

Self-raising flour 3 oz.   *Caster sugar 3 oz.*
3 eggs   *Water 1 tablespoonful*

Prepare the tins and sieve the flour. Whip the eggs for 2 or 3 minutes, then add the sugar and continue to whip them till the mixture is thick and nearly white – at least another 5 minutes. Then add the tablespoonful of hot water and fold in the sieved flour with a metal spoon. Spread evenly on the prepared sandwich tins and bake about 15 minutes in a moderate oven (400°, Regulo No. 5). Turn out and cool on a cake tray. When cold, sandwich together with any filling preferred.

For Small Sponge Cakes. Grease warm tins and sprinkle with sugar and flour, three-parts fill with the mixture and bake in a moderate oven (400°, Regulo No. 5) about 17 minutes. Leave for a minute after baking, then remove from the tins, and cool on a cake tray.

For a Large Cake, bake for 45 minutes (350°, Regulo No. 3).

Sponge Sandwich (2)

3 eggs   *Self-raising flour 3 oz.*
Caster sugar 3 oz.

Prepare tins. Sieve flour. Separate the yolks and whites of the eggs. Beat the whites to a stiff froth, then beat in the yolks one at a time, add the sugar, and whisk for 5 minutes. Fold in the sieved flour, turn into prepared tins, and bake in a moderate oven (400°, Regulo No. 5) 15–20 minutes.

If this mixture is used for a big cake, bake about 50 minutes at 350°, Regulo No. 3. Small sponge cakes will take about 17 minutes at 400°, Regulo No. 5.

Sponge Sandwich (3)

Flour 3 oz.   *Margarine 4 oz.*
Cornflour 2 oz.   *Caster sugar 4 oz.*
Baking powder 1½ teaspoonfuls   *2 eggs*
Warm water 1 tablespoonful   *Grated lemon rind*
Lemon curd   *Lemon glacé icing*

The addition of the cornflour gives a different texture from the previous recipes.

Prepare two 7-inch sandwich tins, sieve the flour, cornflour, and baking powder with a pinch of salt. Cream the margarine and sugar, add the lightly beaten eggs one at a time, then the sieved dry ingredients, warm water, and the grated rind of half a lemon. Mix lightly and turn into prepared tins. Bake 18–20 minutes in a moderately hot oven (400°, Regulo No. 5).

When cold, sandwich together with lemon curd and either ice the top with lemon glacé icing or simply sprinkle with icing sugar.

Swiss Roll

Use either mixture given for sponge sandwich and bake about 12 minutes in a quick oven (425°, Regulo No. 6). Directions for preparation of tin and rolling the cake will be found on page 349. Take care not to overbake the cake, or it will crack when being rolled.

Victoria Sandwich

Self-raising flour 6 oz.　*Butter or margarine 6 oz.*
Caster sugar 6 oz.　*Warm water 2 tablespoonfuls*
3 eggs

Sieve the flour. Grease two 8-inch sandwich tins and dredge with flour and caster sugar.

Beat the butter and sugar till soft and creamy, then beat in the eggs one at a time, adding a tablespoonful of the flour with each egg. Beat thoroughly, then add the water and remaining flour. Turn into prepared tins, spread evenly and bake in a moderate oven (400°, Regulo No. 5) about 20 minutes.

When cold, sandwich together with jam, lemon curd, or any filling preferred. Sprinkle the top with caster sugar or icing sugar, or spread with butter icing. (See sections on cake filling and icings.)

Biscuits and Small Cakes

For cutting biscuits have a set of plain round and fluted cutters. Single cutters can also be bought in fancy shapes.

When quite cold, store biscuits in tins with close-fitting lids. Never put cakes or scones in the same tin, for these always hold a certain amount of moisture which makes the biscuits soft.

If biscuits have lost their crispness, reheat them for a few minutes in a moderate oven.

Almond Macaroons

Ground almonds 4 oz. *Ground rice 1 oz.*
Caster sugar 8 oz. *Split almonds*
Whites of 2 large eggs *Rice paper*

Mix the almonds, ground rice, and sugar, then add the very slightly whipped egg whites and mix thoroughly.

Cover a greased baking sheet with rice paper and place teaspoonfuls of the mixture on it (or use a forcing bag and plain pipe), leaving room to spread. Put a split almond on each macaroon and bake in a slow oven (350°, Regulo No. 3) until a pale golden brown – about 35 minutes.

When cool, flake off surplus rice paper round the edges.

Biscuits
Basic Recipe

Self-raising flour 8 oz. *Butter or margarine 4–6 oz.*
Caster sugar 5 oz. *Flavouring*
1 egg yolk

Beat butter and sugar to a cream, add egg yolk and flavouring, then the flour. Mix thoroughly and knead to a pliable dough. Roll out $\frac{1}{4}$ inch thick on a lightly floured board, cut into rounds or crescents with a biscuit cutter. Place on a greased baking sheet and bake in a quick oven (400°–425°, Regulo No. 5–6) till lightly tinted – 10–15 minutes.

Lemon Biscuits. Add a few drops essence of lemon with the egg.

Cinnamon Biscuits. Add 1 level teaspoonful ground cinnamon to the flour.

Wine Biscuits. (1) Flavour basic mixture with lemon or vanilla essence and decorate the tops of the biscuits. First brush over with slightly beaten white of egg, sprinkle with chopped almonds, desiccated coconut or caraway seeds, or put a small piece of glacé cherry in the centre of each.

(2) Take small pieces of the dough, roll them on the board with the palm of the hand into pencil-shaped pieces about 4 inches long and shape into scrolls, twirls, or rings. Brush over with white of egg and dredge with caster sugar. Place on a greased baking tin, not too close together, and bake in a moderate oven (400°, Regulo No. 5) until very lightly tinted.

Spiced Biscuits. Add ¼ teaspoonful each of mixed spice, ground cinnamon, and ground ginger to the flour.

Jaffa Biscuits. Sandwich two biscuits together with seedless jam or lemon curd.

Coconut Biscuits. Add 1 tablespoonful desiccated coconut and ½ oz. finely chopped glacé cherries to basic mixture.

Brandy Snaps

Flour 4 oz.
Butter or margarine 4 oz.
Ginger 1 teaspoonful
Golden syrup 4 oz.
Demerara sugar 4 oz.
Lemon juice 1 teaspoonful

Sieve flour and ginger. Warm the syrup, butter, and sugar until the butter has melted, add the lemon juice, then stir in flour and ginger.

Grease a baking sheet and pour in teaspoonfuls of the mixture to form rounds, a good distance apart. Bake for 15 minutes in a moderate oven (375°, Regulo No. 4).

Remove from tin one at a time and shape round the greased handle of a wooden spoon. Work as quickly as possible, as they will not roll if allowed to get cold. They become pliable again if reheated for a moment in the oven.

Butter Cake

Self-raising flour 6 oz.
Caster sugar 4 oz.
A small egg
Butter 4 oz.
Ground cinnamon ½ teaspoonful

Grease two 8-inch sandwich tins.

Sieve flour and cinnamon. Cream butter and sugar, add the egg yolk and flour and knead to a pliable dough. Divide into two and press half in a thin layer in each tin. Brush over with beaten white of egg. Bake in a moderately hot oven (400°, Regulo No. 5) 25–30 minutes. Leave for 2 or 3 minutes to set, then cut across into 12 sections and leave in tin till cold.

If preferred, roll out the paste $\frac{1}{4}$ inch thick and cut into rounds. These will only take 12–15 minutes to bake.

Butterscotch Cookies

Self-raising flour 6 oz.   *Margarine 2 oz.*
Golden syrup 6 oz.   *Bicarbonate of soda $\frac{1}{4}$ teaspoonful*
Vanilla essence $\frac{1}{4}$ teaspoonful

Melt the margarine and syrup, stir in the vanilla and bicarbonate of soda, then pour on to flour and mix thoroughly. Leave till quite cold, then roll out *very thinly*, cut into rounds, and bake on greased tins in a moderate oven (400°, Regulo No. 5) 10–12 minutes.

Chocolate Pyramids

Caster sugar 1 tablespoonful   *Rice crispies 1$\frac{1}{2}$ oz.*
Cooking fat 1 oz.   *Cocoa 1 tablespoonful*
Golden syrup 1 level tablespoonful

Put fat, sugar and syrup into a small saucepan, stir over a gentle heat till melted and just beginning to bubble, but do not let it boil. Remove from the heat, stir in the cocoa and pour on to rice crispies and mix lightly with a fork until well coated. Spoon into 9 or 10 paper cases and leave till cold and set.

Note. Cornflakes mixed with 1 tablespoonful of desiccated coconut can be used instead of rice crispies.

Chocolate Wheels

Basic biscuit mixture   *Vanilla essence*
  (page 353)   *Cocoa 1 teaspoonful*

Divide the biscuit mixture in halves and knead the cocoa

thoroughly into one half, and add a few drops essence of vanilla.

Roll out the two pieces separately into even-sized oblong shapes. Brush over the plain one lightly with cold water and place the chocolate one on top. Roll up tightly like a Swiss roll, and leave in the refrigerator or other very cold place for at least ½ hour. Then with a very sharp knife cut across into thin slices. Place on a greased baking sheet and bake in a quick oven (425°, Regulo No. 6) till lightly coloured – 12–15 minutes.

Coconut Crisps

Desiccated coconut 2 oz.	Margarine 3 oz.
Rolled oats 2 oz.	Golden syrup 1 dessertspoonful
Flour 2 oz.	Bicarbonate of soda ½ teaspoonful
Caster sugar 3 oz.	Hot water 1 tablespoonful

Mix coconut, oats, flour, and sugar. Melt the margarine and syrup; dissolve the bicarbonate of soda in the hot water, add to the melted margarine, and pour on to dry ingredients and mix thoroughly. Put ½ teaspoonful of the mixture on to well-greased baking tins very far apart, as they spread considerably, and bake in a moderate oven (375°, Regulo No. 4) till a rich golden brown – about 15 minutes. Leave on the tin for ½ minute, then remove quickly with a pliable knife or palette knife. Cool on a cake tray.

Coconut Pyramids
(See pages 416–17)

Cornflake Crisps

Cornflakes 2 oz.	Demerara sugar 2 oz.
Rolled oats 1½ oz.	Golden syrup 1 dessertspoonful
Margarine 3 oz.	

Crush the cornflakes slightly and mix with the sugar and rolled oats. Melt the margarine and syrup, pour over dry ingredients, and mix thoroughly. Turn on to a well-greased shallow baking tin about 8 inches by 10 inches and press down evenly in a thin layer with a fork. Bake in a slow oven (350°, Regulo No. 3) for 30 minutes. Remove from the oven, leave for a minute to set, then cut into squares and remove carefully to a cake tray till cold.

Cherry Cookies

Self-raising flour 5 oz.   *Caster sugar 3 oz.*
Margarine 4 oz.   *1 egg*
Flavouring   *Glacé cherries*
Chopped nuts

Cream the margarine and sugar, add the egg yolk and a few drops of vanilla or lemon essence or 1 teaspoonful of lemon juice. Stir in the flour and knead to a pliable dough. Roll into tiny balls, dip in slightly beaten egg white, then roll in chopped nuts. Place on a greased baking tin, press a piece of glacé cherry on top of each, and bake in a moderate oven (400°, Regulo No. 5) 15–20 minutes.

Date and Honey Buns

Self-raising flour 6 oz.   *Honey 2 oz.*
Caster sugar 1 oz.   *Stoned dates 2 oz.*
1 egg   *Margarine 3 oz.*
Milk

Cream margarine, sugar and honey, add the lightly beaten egg, fold in the flour, adding sufficient milk to give a soft dropping consistency, and then add the finely chopped dates and mix lightly. Half fill well-greased patty tins or paper cases and bake in a moderately hot oven (400°, Regulo No. 5) about 20 minutes.

Dutch Butter Cake

Flour 8 oz.   *Butter or margarine 6 oz.*
Caster sugar 6 oz.   *1 egg*
Blanched almonds   *Cinnamon 1 level teaspoonful*

Sieve flour, cinnamon, and sugar into a bowl. Rub in the butter, add the egg yolk, and knead lightly. Put a thin layer into well-greased tins, brush over with white of egg, and sprinkle with chopped almonds. Bake in a moderate oven (400°, Regulo No. 5) about 30 minutes. After removing from the oven leave for a minute, then cut into squares, fingers, or any shape preferred, and remove from tin when cool.

Dutch Cookies

Self-raising flour 6 oz.   *Caster sugar 3 oz.*
Butter or margarine 3 oz.   *Chopped blanched nuts 1 oz.*

Rub butter into flour, add sugar and chopped nuts, and knead to a pliable dough. Roll out thinly on a floured board and cut into rounds. Bake in a moderate oven (400°, Regulo No. 5) till lightly browned – about 15 minutes.

Flapjacks

Rolled oats 8 oz.   *Butter or margarine 4 oz.*
Brown sugar 2 oz.   *Golden syrup 2 tablespoonfuls*

Mix the sugar and rolled oats together. Melt the butter and syrup, pour on to other ingredients and mix thoroughly. Turn into a shallow Swiss roll tin about 8 inches by 12 inches and press down smoothly. Bake in a moderately hot oven (425°, Regulo No. 6) for 25 minutes. Leave for a few minutes to set, then cut into fingers or squares and leave on the tin till quite cold.

Genoese Pastry

Self-raising flour 4 oz.   *Butter or margarine 3 oz.*
Caster sugar 4 oz.   *3 eggs*

Line a greased oblong tin (about 8 inches by 12 inches) with greased paper.

Melt the butter without letting it get too hot, and leave to cool, but not set.

Put the eggs and sugar in a basin, place over hot water and whisk about 8 minutes; remove the basin from the hot water and continue beating till the mixture is thick and white. Then add the melted butter and sieved flour, fold in carefully with a metal spoon, and pour the mixture into the prepared tin, which should be warm.

Bake in a moderate oven (375°, Regulo No. 4) till golden brown and firm to the touch – about 30 minutes.

Suggestions for Use:

(1) Leave plain, cut into fingers and serve with stewed fruit.

(2) Cut into two and sandwich together with lemon curd, butter icing, or any filling preferred.

(3) Spread with icing before cutting, and then cut into any shapes desired, or cut into shapes first and ice after.

(4) **Coffee and Nut Icing.** Brown 1 tablespoonful of shredded almonds in a moderate oven. Sieve 3 oz. icing sugar, add 2 oz. of butter and beat to a soft cream; add 1 tablespoonful of coffee essence and mix thoroughly. Spread this evenly over the slab, sprinkle over the nuts, and dust lightly with icing sugar. Trim edges with a sharp knife and cut into fingers.

(5) **Vienna Fingers.** Make butter icing as in previous recipe, but flavour with a little strong tea instead of coffee, and sprinkle top with finely chopped pistachio nuts.

(6) **Diamond Pastries.** Cut the slab into strips about $1\frac{1}{2}$ inches wide and then cut across into diamond shapes. Make some glacé icing (see page 370), leave half white, and colour the remainder green or pink; coat the diamonds with this. Garnish with glacé cherries, angelica, or crystallized violets or rose petals. Cut some of the cake into rounds with a biscuit cutter, ice with chocolate icing, and sprinkle with chocolate granules.

(7) **Almond Fancies.** Cut two strips of the cake about 2 inches wide. Put a narrow roll of marzipan down the centre, brushing over a little white of egg to keep it in position, and completely cover with glacé icing, coloured to fancy. Leave till set, then with a very sharp knife cut into pieces about 1 inch wide.

For the Marzipan. Mix together 4 oz. ground almonds, 2 oz. each caster and sieved icing sugar, 1 egg yolk, 1 teaspoonful of lemon juice, and few drops essence of vanilla. Knead thoroughly

till soft and pliable, and shape into a roll about ¾ inch across.
Use as directed.

Ginger Nuts

Self-raising flour 4 oz.   *Margarine 2 oz.*
Ground ginger 1 teaspoonful   *Ground cinnamon ¼ teaspoonful*
Golden syrup 4 oz. (2 level   *Bicarbonate of soda ½ teaspoonful*
tablespoonfuls)

Melt the margarine and syrup; sieve the dry ingredients into
mixing bowl, pour over melted margarine and syrup and mix
thoroughly. Put teaspoonfuls of the mixture on well-greased
baking tins (not too close together) and bake in a moderate
oven (375°, Regulo No. 4) about 12–15 minutes.

Kichals

Beat up 2 eggs lightly with 1 tablespoonful of caster sugar and
pinch of salt and 3 dessertspoonfuls of cooking oil, then add
sufficient self-raising flour to make a pliable dough. Knead
lightly, then roll out thinly on a floured board. Cut into
desired shapes and dredge lightly with caster sugar.
    Bake in a moderately hot oven (400°, Regulo No. 5) till a
light biscuit colour.

Macaroons

Rolled oats 4 oz.   *Self-raising flour 5 oz.*
Sugar 2 oz.   *Golden syrup 3 oz.*
Margarine 4 oz.   *Almond essence 2 teaspoonfuls*
1 egg   *Chopped nuts*

Cream the margarine, sugar, and syrup, add the almond
essence and well-beaten egg, then the flour and rolled oats,
and mix thoroughly. With hands dipped in cold water roll into
tiny balls, place on a greased baking tin, not too close together,
flatten slightly, and put a pinch of chopped nuts on each. Bake
in a moderate oven (400°, Regulo No. 5) 15–20 minutes.

Madeleines

Flour 4 oz.	*2 eggs*
Caster sugar 4 oz.	*Butter or margarine 3 oz.*
Milk	*Red jam*
Desiccated coconut	*Glacé cherries and angelica*

Sieve the flour. Cream the butter and sugar, beat in the eggs one at a time, adding a spoonful of the flour with each. Then add remaining flour and sufficient milk to make a rather soft consistency – about 2 or 3 tablespoonfuls. Half fill well-greased individual dariole moulds with the mixture and bake in a moderate oven (400°, Regulo No. 5) about 20 minutes. Cool on a cake tray and when quite cold brush over the tops and sides with warmed and sieved jam, holding the cakes on a skewer. Roll in desiccated coconut and put on each half a glacé cherry and leaves cut from strips of angelica.

Orange Cakes

Ground rice 3 oz.	*Flour 2 oz.*
1 orange	*Margarine 3 oz.*
Caster sugar 3 oz.	*Baking powder ¼ teaspoonful*
2 eggs	

Cream the margarine and sugar, then add the lightly beaten eggs. Sieve the flour, baking powder, and ground rice, then add the grated rind of the orange, and stir these lightly into the mixture. Add 1 tablespoonful or more of orange juice to make a fairly soft consistency. Mix lightly, put a dessertspoonful of the mixture into greased patty tins, and bake in a quick oven (425°, Regulo No. 6) about 15 minutes.

Petit Fours

Flour 6 oz.	*Baking powder 1 teaspoonful*
Caster sugar 4 oz.	*Butter or margarine 3 oz.*
3 eggs	*Milk 2 tablespoonfuls*

Cream the butter and sugar, beat the yolks of the eggs with the milk, and add them alternately with spoonfuls of the flour till both are mixed in; add the baking powder and beat lightly. Whisk the white of the eggs till stiff, fold them into the mixture, and turn into a well-greased shallow tin (about 8 inches by 12 inches), and bake in a moderate oven (400°, Regulo No. 5) 20–25 minutes.

Leave till the following day, then cut into any shape preferred – squares, triangles, or diamonds, or, with a biscuit cutter, into rounds and crescents. Ice with glacé icing and decorate with cherries and angelica.

Purim Cakes
('*Haman Taschen*')

Make Kuchen dough (see page 378). Roll out $\frac{1}{4}$ inch thick, cut into 4-inch rounds, and brush edges with melted margarine or oil; spread with desired filling and fold edges to form three-cornered cakes. Brush the top with warm honey, leave in a warm place to rise till bulk is doubled, then bake in a moderately hot oven (400°, Regulo No. 5) till golden brown.

Suggested Fillings:
(1) **Poppy-Seed Filling.** Put the following ingredients in a saucepan and cook over a gentle heat till thick: 1 teacupful ground poppy seeds, $\frac{1}{4}$ pint water, 2 oz. margarine, 2 oz. each chopped nuts and raisins, 1 tablespoonful golden syrup, 1 oz. sugar, and 1 oz. chopped peel.

(2) **Prune Filling.** Stone and chop $\frac{1}{2}$ lb. cooked prunes and add grated rind and juice of half a lemon.

(3) **Cream Cheese Filling.** Add a little sugar and a few currants to soft cream cheese.

Queen Cakes

Flour 6 oz.	*Caster sugar 3 oz.*
Butter or margarine 4 oz.	*Candied peel 1 oz.*
Glacé cherries 2 oz.	*Milk 2 tablespoonfuls*
Essence of lemon	*Baking powder 1 level teaspoonful*
2 eggs	

Cream the butter and sugar, add a few drops essence of lemon. Beat up the eggs lightly with the milk, and add these alternately with the sieved flour and baking powder. Add the chopped cherries and peel. Put dessertspoonfuls of the mixture into small greased tins or paper cases, and bake in a quick oven (425°, Regulo No. 6) about 15 minutes.

Sultanas can be used in place of cherries, and the tops can be sprinkled with chopped nuts.

Rock Cakes

Margarine 3–4 oz.	*Currants 3 oz.*
Self-raising flour 8 oz.	*1 egg*
Sugar 3–4 oz.	*A little milk*
Candied peel 1 oz.	

Rub the margarine into the flour, add the sugar, cleaned currants, and chopped peel; add the beaten egg and sufficient milk to form a dry stiff mixture. Put in rough heaps on a greased baking tin and bake in a moderately hot oven (425°, Regulo No. 6) about 20 minutes.

Scotch Shortbread

Flour 7 oz.	*Ground rice 1 oz.*
Butter or margarine 4 oz.	*Caster sugar 2 oz.*

Beat the butter and sugar till white and creamy, add the sifted flour and ground rice, and knead to a smooth pliable dough, free of cracks. Divide into two pieces and roll each into a round about ⅜ inch thick. Put on to a greased baking tin and pinch up the edges with finger and thumb. Prick all over with a fork and bake in a slow oven (350°, Regulo No. 3) till a light biscuit colour – about 40 minutes.

Remove to a cake tray, sprinkle with caster sugar, and leave till cold.

Shortbread Biscuits

Self-raising flour 6 oz.	*Ground rice 2 oz.*
Butter or margarine 5 oz.	*Caster sugar 3 oz.*

Sieve flour, sugar, and ground rice into a bowl, rub in the butter, then knead to a pliable dough. Roll out on a floured board ¼ inch thick and cut into pieces about 3½ by 1½ inches. Bake on a greased tin in a slow oven (350°, Regulo No. 3) till a light biscuit colour – about 20 minutes. When cool remove from the tin and dredge with caster sugar.

Shrewsbury Biscuits

Flour 8 oz.	*Butter or margarine 4 oz.*
Caster sugar 4 oz.	*Cinnamon $\frac{1}{4}$ teaspoonful*
1 egg	

Beat butter and sugar to a cream, add the flour, cinnamon, and beaten egg, and knead to a pliable dough. Roll out thinly on a floured board, cut into rounds, and bake on a greased tin in a moderate oven (375°, Regulo No. 4) until lightly browned – about 15 minutes.

Small Fancy Cakes

A variety of small fancy cakes can be made, using the same basic mixture with different fillings and toppings.

Basic Mixture

Self-raising flour 6 oz.	*Butter or margarine 4 oz.*
Caster sugar 4 oz.	*Flavouring*
2 eggs	

Cream the fat and sugar, add the lightly beaten eggs one at a time, then the flavouring (lemon, vanilla or almond essence), sieve the flour and fold it in lightly. The mixture should be a soft dropping consistency, so if necessary add a spoonful or two of milk.

Half fill well-greased patty tins or paper cases and bake in a moderately hot oven (400°, Regulo No. 5) about 20 minutes.

Variations:

(1) Cherry Cakes. Add a few chopped glacé cherries to basic mixture and when cold spread tops with glacé icing and garnish with cherries and angelica.

(2) Walnut Cakes. Add a few chopped walnuts to basic mixture and when cold ice with glacé icing with a piece of walnut in the centre of each; or spread tops with coffee-flavoured butter icing and sprinkle with chopped nuts and chocolate granules.

(3) **Chocolate Topped Coffee Cakes.** Add 2 teaspoonfuls of coffee essence to basic mixture and before baking sprinkle the top of each cake with a mixture of equal quantities of grated chocolate and chopped nuts.

(4) **Orange Cakes.** Flavour with grated orange rind and add 1 tablespoonful of orange juice to basic mixture. Ice with glacé icing mixed with strained orange juice instead of water.

(5) **Butterfly Cakes.** When cold cut a slice from the top of each cake and cut each slice in halves. Spread the cakes with whipped cream or jam and replace the two pieces of cake to represent wings. Sprinkle with icing sugar.

Stuffed Monkey

Flour 6 oz.	*1 egg*
Butter or margarine 4 oz.	*Cinnamon ½ teaspoonful*
Soft brown sugar 4 oz.	*Filling*

Sieve the flour and cinnamon, rub in the butter, add the yolk of the egg and sugar, and knead to a pliable dough. Roll out into two rounds to fit into a deep 8-inch sandwich tin. Grease the tin and put in one round, spread with the filling, and cover with the other half of the paste. Brush over with white of egg and bake in a moderate oven (375°, Regulo No. 4) about 30 minutes. Cool in the tin.

For the Filling

Chopped peel 2 oz.	*Ground almonds 2 oz.*
Margarine 1½ oz.	*Yolk of an egg*
Caster sugar 1 oz.	

Melt margarine and mix all ingredients.

Swedish Biscuits

Self-raising flour 6 oz.	*Caster sugar 1 tablespoonful*
Margarine 4 oz.	*Golden syrup 1 level tablespoonful*
Vanilla essence	

Put the margarine, sugar and syrup into a small saucepan and place over a gentle heat until the margarine is melted, then

add a few drops of vanilla and pour on to the flour. Mix
thoroughly, then leave till quite cold, in refrigerator if available. With wet hands roll into small balls, flatten and place on
greased baking tins. Mark the tops deeply with the prongs of a
fine fork and bake in a moderate oven (400°, Regulo No. 5)
15–20 minutes.

Teiglech

Flour ¼ lb.	*Ground ginger 1½ teaspoonfuls*
Syrup or honey 1 lb.	*2 large eggs*

Sieve flour with ½ teaspoonful of ginger and pinch of salt. Add
the lightly beaten eggs, mix thoroughly and knead to a smooth
dough. Roll out on a floured board about ½ inch thick and cut
into 1 inch squares.

Melt the golden syrup (or honey) in a saucepan, add remaining ginger and, when boiling, add the squares a few at a time,
then boil *slowly* until the teiglech are a pale biscuit colour –
about 20 minutes. Remove from the syrup with a perforated
spoon on to a wet board. With a wet wooden spoon pat into an
even thickness.

When cold cut into desired size.

If preferred, the dough can be rolled into tiny balls and,
after being removed from the syrup, rolled in chopped nuts or
desiccated coconut.

Vanilla Biscuits

Butter or margarine 2 oz.	*Self-raising flour 2 oz.*
1 egg	*Essence of vanilla*
Caster sugar 2 oz.	

Melt the butter without letting it boil. Beat the egg and sugar
together till frothy, add the melted butter and a few drops
essence of vanilla, then add the sieved flour. Put half-tea-
spoonfuls of the mixture on a greased baking sheet, not too
close together as they spread considerably, and bake in a quick
oven (450°, Regulo No. 7) until the edges are lightly browned
and the centres a pale biscuit colour; this will take about 10
minutes. As soon as they are baked, remove from tin immediately, as they set quickly and are rather brittle.

Cats' Tongues. This same mixture can be used for cats' tongues, in which case put the mixture into a forcing bag and squeeze out into fingers. Bake like the round biscuits.

Vanilla Cookies

Margarine 4 oz.   Self-raising flour 5 oz.
Caster sugar 3 oz.   1 egg yolk
Vanilla ¼ teaspoonful   Rolled oats

Cream the margarine and sugar, add the egg yolk and vanilla, then the flour, and mix thoroughly.

With hands dipped in cold water, roll the mixture into tiny balls. Coat with rolled oats, put on a greased baking tin, and bake in a moderate oven (400°, Regulo No. 5) about 20 minutes.

Viennese Fancies

Margarine 4 oz.   Icing sugar 1½ oz.
Flour 3 oz.   Flavouring
Cornflour 1 oz.   Red jam

Add the sieved icing sugar to the margarine and beat together till creamy. Add the flour and cornflour, flavour with vanilla or almond essence, and beat very thoroughly.

Put 8 paper cases on a baking sheet. Put the mixture into a forcing bag with a large rose pipe, and pipe the mixture into the paper cases, twice round, leaving a small space in the centre. Bake in a moderate oven (375°, Regulo No. 4) about 20 minutes.

When cold dredge with icing sugar and place a little jam in the centre of each.

Icings for Cakes

GENERAL DIRECTIONS

Icing sugar must always be rubbed through a fine sieve immediately before using.

Sugar icing needs really hard beating to get a smooth even texture.

When adding colouring never pour it from the bottle. Pour

a few drops first into a teaspoon. Red colouring for a pink icing is best dripped from the end of a skewer.

Put the cake to be iced on an upturned plate standing on a sheet of paper. Pour the icing over the middle of the cake and leave for a minute or two to let the icing run down the sides. Then dip a palette knife in hot water and smooth round the sides of the cake. Avoid touching the top if possible as this will give a smoother surface.

Let the icing set for ½ hour before adding any decorations. If writing or a design with forcers is being used, then let the top set completely before starting.

Cake Decorations

For decoration any of the following can be used:

Crystallized rose petals or violets *Glacé cherries*
Angelica *Almonds*
Silver balls *Desiccated coconut*
Chocolate granules *Pistachio nuts*

Nuts should be blanched and either sliced or chopped. When pistachio nuts are cut across into slices, they can be used to form little shamrocks. The finely chopped green nut makes an attractive border for white glacé or butter icing.

Blanched almonds can be browned in the oven before chopping.

Leaves can be made from angelica. It should be soaked in water to remove the sugar, then dried.

Coconut can be browned in the oven like almonds, or it can be coloured. Put a little colouring into a saucer, and work the coconut in it till it is a uniform colour.

Almond Paste

Ground almonds 1 lb. *Brandy 1 teaspoonful (optional)*
Lemon juice 2 tablespoonfuls *Caster sugar 4 oz.*
2 eggs *Vanilla essence 1 teaspoonful*
Icing sugar 12 oz.

Sieve the icing sugar and mix with the ground almonds, add flavourings and the well-beaten eggs; then with the hand knead to a soft, pliable dough.

Roll the paste out thinly, cut a strip wide enough and long enough to cover the sides of the cake and a round to fit the top. Brush cake lightly with white of egg or sieved and warmed apricot jam before applying the paste.

Leave for a couple of days to dry before covering with royal icing.

American Icing

Granulated sugar 1 lb.   *Whites of 2 eggs*
Water ¼ pint   *Vanilla essence*
Pinch of cream of tartar

Put the sugar and water in a thick saucepan. Let it stand for an hour or two, then place over a very gentle heat till the sugar has dissolved; add the cream of tartar, bring slowly to the boil and continue boiling till it reaches 240°. If no sugar thermometer is available, then boil steadily without stirring for 7 minutes after it has reached boiling point. Remove from the heat and add a few drops of vanilla.

Have the egg whites beaten to a stiff froth in a large bowl, pour the syrup over, beating continuously until the mixture is thick enough to coat the back of a spoon, then pour very quickly over the cake, which should have been previously coated with almond paste or brushed over with warm apricot jam.

This icing sets very quickly, so if any decorations are being used have them ready prepared.

Butter Icing

Butter or margarine 4 oz.   *Flavouring*
Icing sugar 6 oz.

Cream the butter, add the sieved icing sugar and beat till smooth and creamy. Add flavouring to taste.

Chocolate Butter Icing

Icing sugar 6 oz.   *Butter or margarine 3 oz.*
Grated chocolate 1 oz.   *Vanilla essence*
Milk 1 tablespoonful

Dissolve the chocolate in the milk by slightly warming it. Cream the butter, add the sieved sugar and dissolved chocolate, and a few drops essence of vanilla. Beat hard till thoroughly blended.

Glacé Icing

This icing is suitable for small cakes, petit fours, sandwich and layer cakes.

Put $\frac{1}{2}$ lb. sieved icing sugar in a small saucepan, add 2 tablespoonfuls warm water, and the flavouring (vanilla, coffee essence, almond essence, or 1 teaspoonful lemon juice). Stir over a gentle heat till just warm; be sure it does not get too hot.

It should be thick enough to coat the back of a spoon. If too thin add more sugar, or more water if too thick. Use at once.

If colouring is being used, this should be added just before pouring over the cake.

For Chocolate Glacé Icing. Melt 2 oz. grated chocolate in 2 tablespoonfuls water, bring to the boil, then cool. Add $\frac{1}{2}$ lb. sieved icing sugar and $\frac{1}{2}$ teaspoonful essence of vanilla. Stir over a very gentle heat till just warm.

Royal Icing

Icing sugar 1 lb.   Lemon juice 2 teaspoonfuls
2 egg whites

Sieve the sugar twice through a very fine sieve. Make a well in the centre and add slightly beaten egg whites and lemon juice. Beat vigorously with a wooden spoon till the icing is very smooth.

Spread icing smoothly over the cake and when quite set decorate using an icing bag and tubes.

To keep the icing for decoration scrape down from the sides of the basin, cover the bowl with a folded cloth wrung out in cold water, and place a plate on top. Redamp the cloth if necessary, and do not leave the icing exposed to the air.

Cake Fillings

Butter Cream

Butter or margarine 4 oz.   *Flavouring*
Icing sugar 6 oz.

Cream the fat until soft and beat in the sieved icing sugar by degrees, adding a few drops essence of vanilla.

Chocolate Filling. Melt a 2-oz. bar of chocolate in a basin over hot water, add to creamed fat and sugar, and mix thoroughly.

Coffee Filling. Add 1 tablespoonful of coffee essence.

Coconut Filling. Add 2 tablespoonfuls desiccated coconut.

Ginger Filling. Add 1 oz. chopped preserved ginger and 1 teaspoonful of ginger syrup.

Orange or Lemon Filling. Add 2 teaspoonfuls orange or lemon juice and a little grated rind in place of vanilla essence.

Nut Filling. Add 2 tablespoonfuls finely chopped toasted almonds.

Walnut Filling. Add 2 tablespoonfuls chopped walnuts to coffee filling.

Confectioner's Custard

Butter or margarine 1 oz.   *2 egg yolks*
Flour 1 oz.   *Milk ¼ pint*
Caster sugar 1 oz.   *Essence of vanilla*

Melt the butter in a small saucepan, add the flour, cook for a minute, then gradually add the milk, stir over a gentle heat till boiling and simmer gently for 2 or 3 minutes; stir in the sugar and remove from the heat. When cool add the lightly beaten egg yolks and ½ teaspoonful vanilla essence, beat well and stir over a gentle heat till it thickens, but do not reboil.

Cream Fillings

Thick cream ¼ pint   *1 white of egg*
Icing sugar 2 tablespoonfuls   *Flavouring*

Whip the cream till thick and light. Whisk the white of egg to a stiff froth, fold it into the cream, together with the sugar and flavouring. This can be plain vanilla, or for coffee flavour add a little coffee extract as well. Chopped nuts, crushed burnt almonds, or peanut brittle can also be added.

Nut and Apricot Filling

Ground almonds 3 table-   Chopped walnuts 1 tablespoonful
spoonfuls   Apricot jam 3 tablespoonfuls
Flavouring

Chop the nuts finely; warm and sieve the jam; mix all ingredients, flavouring with a teaspoonful lemon or orange juice or $\frac{1}{4}$ teaspoonful vanilla.

This filling is good for biscuits, sandwich cakes, or petit fours (see Genoese pastry, page 359).

Bread, Buns, and Scones

When using yeast, the flour, water, mixing bowl, etc., must be warm.

Yeast should be fresh and moist in appearance; when fresh it liquefies quickly when mixed with sugar.

When the dough is put to rise, cover with a cloth to exclude draughts, and leave in a warm, but not hot, place.

A larger proportion of yeast is required for a small quantity of flour than for a large amount.

Allow $\frac{1}{2}$ oz. yeast up to $1\frac{1}{2}$ lb. flour.
Allow 1 oz. yeast to $1\frac{1}{2}$–$3\frac{1}{2}$ lb. flour.
Allow $1\frac{1}{2}$ oz. yeast to $3\frac{1}{2}$–7 lb. flour.
Allow 2 oz. yeast to 7–14 lb. flour.

Bread

Yeast 1 oz.   Flour 3$\frac{1}{4}$ lb.
Warm water about 1$\frac{3}{4}$ pints   Salt 3 teaspoonfuls
Caster sugar 1 teaspoonful

Cream the yeast and sugar and stir in about $\frac{3}{4}$ pint warm water·
Warm the flour and sieve into a warmed bowl with the salt·

Make a well in the centre and pour in the yeast mixture. Sprinkle over a little flour from the sides, cover with a cloth, and leave in a warm place for 20 minutes; then work in all the flour with the hands, using sufficient tepid water to form an elastic dough. Knead thoroughly, then again cover the bowl and leave in a warm place to rise – about 1½ hours. Turn on to a floured board, knead lightly and shape into loaves. Put into greased loaf tins, which should only be half filled. Leave another ½ hour in a warm place, or until the dough rises to the top of the tin. Bake about 45 minutes; the first 15 minutes in a hot oven (450°, Regulo No. 7) then reduce to moderate (375°, Regulo No. 4). When the loaf is cooked sufficiently it draws away from the sides of the pan.

Rolls. Make dough as for bread, shape into small rolls or twists and bake in a quick oven (450°, Regulo No. 7) 15–20 minutes.

Cholla

Flour 3¼ lb.	Salt 2 teaspoonfuls
Yeast 1oz.	Warm water about 1¾ pints
Caster sugar 1 teaspoonful	Poppy seeds

Sift the salt and flour into a large bowl and make a well in the centre. Cream the yeast and sugar together and stir in about ½ pint of warm water. Pour this into the centre of the flour; sprinkle over a little flour from the sides of the bowl. Cover with a cloth and stand in a warm place for 20 minutes. Work in all the flour with the hand, adding as much more warm water as necessary to make into a firm dough and knead for 5–10 minutes. Cover the bowl and stand in a warm place until the dough has doubled its bulk – about 1½ hours. Turn on a board and knead lightly.

Divide the dough in halves and each piece into three. With the palm of the hand roll each piece into a long thin roll and form the rolls into two plaits. Place on a floured tin in a warm place and leave for 15 minutes. Then brush over with beaten egg, sprinkle with poppy seeds and bake about 50 minutes. Start at 450°, Regulo No. 7, and after 15 minutes, reduce to 375°, Regulo No. 4. Bake in the upper part of the oven, which should be lit at least 15 minutes before putting in the bread.

Bagels

Flour 1 lb.	Milk or water bare ½ pint
Margarine 2 oz.	Caster sugar 1 oz.
Salt 1 teaspoonful	Yeast ½ oz.
1 egg yolk	

Cream the yeast with a teaspoonful of the sugar.

Put the margarine, milk, remaining sugar and salt into a saucepan and place over a very gentle heat until the margarine is melted. Leave till just lukewarm, then mix with dissolved yeast. Add this with the beaten egg yolk to the flour and knead to a firm dough. Cover with a cloth and leave in a warm place till just beginning to rise – about 1 hour. Then knead again and roll into small pieces the width of a finger and about 5 inches long. Shape into rings, pinching the ends well together. Leave on a floured board in a warm place till just beginning to rise – about 10 minutes. Then drop one at a time into a saucepan half full of water that is just simmering. Cook very gently until they rise to the top. Remove with a fish slice on to greased baking tins and bake in a moderately hot oven (400°, Regulo No. 5) until golden brown and crisp – 20–30 minutes.

Note. The bagels can be sprinkled with caraway seeds or salt before baking.

Three tablespoonfuls cooking oil can be used in place of the margarine.

Baking-powder Rolls

Flour 1 lb.	Baking powder 2 teaspoonfuls
Salt 1 level teaspoonful	Milk and water to mix

Sieve flour, salt and baking powder, and add sufficient milk and water – about 1½ teacupfuls – to form a soft dough. Knead lightly. Divide into 8 or 9 equal portions and roll into balls. Place on a floured baking tray, brush over the tops with milk and bake in a hot oven (475°, Regulo No. 8) about 15 minutes.

Soda Bread

Flour 1 lb.
Salt 1 teaspoonful
Milk ½ pint
Butter or cooking fat 1 oz.

Bicarbonate of soda 1 level
teaspoonful
Cream of tartar 1 heaped
teaspoonful

Sieve flour, salt, cream of tartar, and bicarbonate of soda in a bowl, rub in the butter and mix to a soft dough with the milk. Knead lightly and shape into a rather flat round. Place on a greased and floured baking tin and prick with a fork. Bake in a quick oven (425°, Regulo No. 6) about 30 minutes.

Sultana Loaf

Flour 1 lb.
Caster sugar 1 oz.
Milk bare ½ pint
Candied peel 1 oz.

Butter or margarine 1 oz.
Yeast ½ oz.
Sultanas 4 oz.
Mixed spice ½ teaspoonful

Dissolve butter in the milk until it is just warm. Cream the yeast with a teaspoonful of the sugar and add it to the milk.

Mix sugar, sultanas, peel, and spice with the warmed flour, pour in the yeast mixture and mix to a soft dough. Cover and leave in a warm place to rise for 1½ hours. Then with floured hands knead lightly. Half fill two greased loaf tins with the mixture and leave in a warm place for another ½ hour. Bake in a hot oven (450°, Regulo No. 7) for 15 minutes, then reduce to 375°, Regulo No. 4, until nicely browned and cooked through – another 30–40 minutes. Mix 1 teaspoonful of sugar with 1 teaspoonful of milk, brush the loaves over with this and return to the oven for 5 minutes.

For Milk Rolls. Make dough as above, omitting the sultanas and peel. After the final kneading shape into small rolls or twists, place on greased warm trays, and leave in a warm place for 15 minutes. Brush over with milk and bake in a moderately hot oven (425°, Regulo No. 6) for 25 minutes.

Bath Buns

Flour 1 lb.	*Yeast 1 oz.*
Butter or margarine 3 oz.	*Caster sugar 3 oz.*
Milk ¼ teacupful	*Candied peel 1 oz.*
2 eggs	*Grated rind of ¼ lemon*
Sultanas 2 oz.	

Rub butter into flour. Cream the yeast in a cup with a tea-spoonful of the sugar. Warm the milk slightly and add it to the yeast. Pour this on to the flour, also the well-beaten eggs, and mix together. Cover and leave in a warm place to rise for 1½ hours. Then add the finely chopped peel, sultanas, sugar, and grated lemon rind. Turn on to a floured board and divide into 12 buns. Place on a greased baking tin, leave in a warm place for another 10 minutes, then brush over with milk, and sprinkle with coarsely crushed loaf sugar. Bake in a quick oven (450°, Regulo No. 7) about 20 minutes.

Currant Buns

Flour 1 lb.	*Butter 2 oz.*
Sugar 1¼ oz.	*Yeast ¾ oz.*
Currants 2 oz.	*Candied peel 1 oz.*
Mixed spice ¼ teaspoonful	*Milk about ½ pint*
Salt ¼ teaspoonful	

Warm the flour, then sieve it with the salt and spice into a warm bowl, rub in the butter and add the cleaned currants and chopped peel.

Cream the yeast and sugar, add the tepid milk and leave for 10 minutes; then add to other ingredients, and mix to a light dough. Cover and leave in a warm place till it has doubled its bulk. Then turn on to a floured board, knead thoroughly and divide into 12 portions. Roll into buns, place on a floured baking tray, flatten slightly, cover with a cloth and leave in a warm place about ½ hour. Bake in a moderately hot oven (425°, Regulo No. 6) for 20 minutes.

To Glaze. Dissolve 1 tablespoonful of sugar in a little water and brush this over the buns as soon as they are removed from the oven.

Doughnuts

Flour 1 lb.	*Margarine 2 oz.*
Pinch of salt	*Milk ½ pint*
Yeast 1 oz.	*1 egg*
Caster sugar	*Deep fat for frying*
Jam	

Sieve flour and salt into a warm basin. Add 2 teaspoonfuls of caster sugar to the yeast and stir till liquid. Melt the margarine in a small saucepan, add the milk and when just lukewarm stir on to the yeast, add the beaten egg and pour into the centre of the flour. Mix thoroughly into a stiff dough. Then cover and leave in a warm place to rise for 2 hours. Then turn on to a floured board and knead lightly for 5 minutes. Divide into 18 pieces, roll each into a smooth ball, flatten and put a small quantity of jam in the centre of each. Then again form into a ball, completely covering the jam. Leave on a floured tin in a warm place for another 20 minutes; then fry 3 or 4 at a time in deep hot fat till golden brown, turning them over so that they brown evenly. This will take about 5 minutes. Drain thoroughly on absorbent paper and roll in caster sugar.

If liked, a little ground cinnamon can be mixed with the sugar.

Doughnut Rings

Flour 8 oz.	*Baking powder 2 teaspoonfuls*
Cinnamon ¼ teaspoonful	*Margarine 1¼ oz.*
Caster sugar 3 oz.	*1 egg*
Milk to mix	*Deep fat for frying*

Sieve all dry ingredients into a bowl, add the melted margarine, beaten egg, and sufficient milk to form a soft dough.

Roll out on a floured board ¼ inch thick, cut into rounds, then with a smaller cutter cut a piece from the centre of each, leaving a ring a good ½ inch in width.

Fry the rings a few at a time in deep hot fat till golden brown, turning over when brown on one side. Drain on absorbent paper and roll in caster sugar and cinnamon, allowing 1 level teaspoonful cinnamon to 1 tablespoonful caster sugar.

Fruit Milk Loaf

Self-raising flour 8 oz.
Bicarbonate of soda 1 teaspoonful
Golden syrup 2 tablespoonfuls
  (4 oz.)

Sultanas or currants 2 oz.
Milk ¼ pint
Butter or margarine 1 oz.

Grease a small loaf tin (about 7 by 4 inches) and line with greased paper.

Put syrup, butter and milk in a small saucepan over a gentle heat till the butter has melted. Sieve flour and bicarbonate of soda into mixing bowl, pour over this the tepid milk mixture and mix to a smooth batter, add the dried fruit and turn into prepared tin. Bake in a moderate oven about 45 minutes. Start at 375°, Regulo No. 4 and reduce slightly after ½ hour. Serve sliced and buttered.

This quickly prepared loaf will keep fresh for several days in a covered tin.

Kuchen Dough

Flour 1 lb.
Caster sugar 2 oz.
Milk ¼ pint
Pinch of salt

Yeast ½ oz.
Margarine 2 oz.
1 egg

Cream yeast with a teaspoonful of the sugar. Melt the margarine in the milk and when just *lukewarm* pour it on to the creamed yeast. Sieve flour and salt into a *warm* basin, make a well in the centre and pour in the yeast mixture. Gradually work in the flour from the sides and knead to a smooth dough; cover and leave in a warm place to rise 1½–2 hours. Then add sugar and beaten egg and knead thoroughly. Roll out and use as required.

For Plain Coffee Kuchen. Roll out risen dough ½ inch thick, place in a shallow buttered tin. Cover and leave in a warm place for another ½ hour. Pour a little melted butter over the top and sprinkle with sugar, cinnamon and chopped nuts, or with streusel. Bake in a moderate oven (375°, Regulo No. 4) about 30 minutes.

Coffee Kuchen

Flour 1¼ lb.	*Butter or margarine 3 oz.*
Yeast ¾ oz.	*Sultanas 4 oz.*
Sugar 3 oz.	*Currants 2 oz.*
Milk and water ½ pint	*Candied peel 2 oz.*
1 egg	*Salt ¼ teaspoonful*

Place the flour in a warm basin, rub in the fat, and add sugar and salt.

Cream the yeast with a teaspoonful of the sugar. Beat up the egg, pour on the milk and water, which must be just tepid, and add it, together with the creamed yeast, to the flour, mix thoroughly and knead to a smooth, elastic dough; then cover the bowl with a cloth and leave in a warm place until the volume has been doubled – about 1½ hours – then add the fruit and peel and knead lightly.

Warm 2 loaf or cake tins and grease well, half fill with the mixture and leave in a warm place for another ½ hour.

Pour a little melted margarine over the top and sprinkle with caster sugar or streusel, bake in a moderately hot oven (400°, Regulo No. 5) for 15 minutes, then reduce the heat to 375°, Regulo No. 4 until well risen and brown – about another 30 minutes.

Bun Ring

Divide risen kuchen dough into 3 equal pieces. Roll each piece with the hands into a long strand, then form the three into a plait. Place in a circle on a well-greased baking tin and leave in a warm place for ½ hour. Brush the top with melted margarine, sprinkle with caster sugar and chopped nuts and bake in a moderately hot oven (425°, Regulo No. 6) for about 20 minutes.

Streusel

Flour 2 oz.	*Cinnamon ¼ teaspoonful*
Sugar 3 oz.	*A few chopped almonds*
Butter 2 oz.	

Sieve the flour and cinnamon, mix in the sugar, then rub in the butter until like breadcrumbs. Add a few chopped almonds, and sprinkle over coffee kuchen that has been brushed with melted butter.

Plain Scones

Flour ½ lb.	*Bicarbonate of soda ½ level*
Butter or margarine 2 oz.	*teaspoonful*
Milk ¼ pint	*Cream of tartar 1 level*
Salt ¼ teaspoonful	*teaspoonful*

Sieve flour, bicarbonate of soda, salt, and cream of tartar into a basin, rub in the butter and mix to a soft dough with the milk. Roll out on a floured board ½ inch thick and cut into rounds. Place on a floured baking tray, brush over with milk and bake in a quick oven (450°, Regulo No. 7) about 15 minutes.

If preferred, 2 level teaspoonfuls baking powder can be used instead of the bicarbonate of soda and cream of tartar.

For Sultana Scones. Add 1 or 2 oz. sultanas and 1 table-spoonful of caster sugar before adding the milk.

Cheese Scones

Self-raising flour 8 oz.	*Grated cheese 4 oz.*
Milk ¼ pint	*Pinch of salt*

Mix flour, cheese and salt to a fairly soft dough with milk. Roll out ¾ inch thick and cut into small rounds. Bake in a hot oven (450°, Regulo No. 7) till brown. Split through, butter and serve hot.

Drop Scones
(Scotch Pancakes)

Flour ½ lb.	*Pinch of salt*
1 egg	*Bicarbonate of soda ½ level teaspoonful*
Milk to mix	*Cream of tartar 1 level teaspoonful*
Sugar 1 tablespoonful	

Sieve the flour, sugar, salt, cream of tartar and bicarbonate of soda into a bowl, add the egg and sufficient milk to make a thick batter — about ½ pint.

Drop tablespoonfuls on to a hot greased girdle, a little distance apart, and cook for 3 or 4 minutes; then turn and cook on the other side.

Serve hot or cold, buttered.

A very thick frying pan can be used instead of a girdle.

Jams, Jellies, and Preserves

The making of jams, jellies, and preserves does not require much skill, but in order to get the best results, it is essential to pay attention to a few important details.

GENERAL HINTS

(1) Use a cast aluminium or heavily enamelled iron preserving pan. Do not have the pan more than two-thirds full, or the jam will boil over.

(2) Stir with a *wooden* spoon.

(3) Grease the bottom of the pan with a little oil. This will help to prevent the jam from sticking.

(4) Jars should be washed, dried and heated thoroughly. Jam put into damp jars will not keep.

PECTIN

The success of the jam or jelly will to a great extent depend on the amount of pectin present in the fruit.

Pectin is the gelatinous substance found in fruit, which, combined with sugar and acid, causes the jam or jelly to set. This is present in greatest quantity when the fruit is just *under-ripe*, and is hardly present at all when the fruit is over-ripe. Therefore, it is essential to use the fruit when it is slightly under-ripe.

Fruits containing insufficient acid require the addition of lemon juice, tartaric or citric acid, *or* should be combined with the acid fruits. See detailed recipes.

Pectin can be bought in bottles, and if this is used, follow the directions.

Apple Pectin

To 2 lb. apples or apple skins and cores add 2 pints water and 1 level teaspoonful tartaric acid. Boil for 30 minutes, then strain. Reboil for 10 minutes.

If not to be used immediately, turn into a preserving jar and sterilize as for bottled fruit (see pages 396–8).

METHOD OF MAKING JAM

Pick over all fruit carefully, rejecting any that is unsound. Wash quickly through a colander.

Place prepared fruit in a greased preserving pan (with water if necessary) and place over a very gentle heat till the juice begins to flow; then increase heat slightly and bring to the boil. *Cook slowly till fruit is quite soft.*

During this time put the sugar in a basin in a cool oven to get warm – but not very hot – leaving the oven door open. Add the warmed sugar to the softened fruit, stir till dissolved, then *boil quickly till the jam sets when tested.* Start testing after 10 minutes.

Testing for Setting Point. Place a little jam on a cold plate and cool quickly; if setting point has been reached, the jam will wrinkle when pushed with the finger.

When the jam is ready, remove scum with a metal spoon which has been dipped in boiling water.

Pour into heated jars, fill to within ¼ inch of the top. A special jam funnel is useful for this purpose and will prevent the edges and outside of the pots becoming sticky.

Cover at once with disks of waxed paper, wax side down, and press them down over the surface, then tie down immediately or when quite cold with damped parchment or cellophane covers, and wipe jars with a cloth wrung out in hot water. Label and store in a cool, dry, dark cupboard.

Apple Ginger

Apples 6 lb.	*Preserved ginger 8 oz.*
Root ginger 2 oz.	*Sugar 4 lb.*
Water 1¼ pints	*3 lemons*

Peel, core and slice the apples. Bruise the root ginger and tie it in a piece of muslin with the peel and cores. Put all together in a saucepan, add the water, cover the pan and simmer gently till the apples are soft. Then remove the muslin bag and mash the apples to a pulp. Turn into a preserving pan, add the grated rind and juice of the lemons, the finely cut up ginger and the sugar. Stir till boiling and cook steadily till it sets when tested. Start testing after 10 minutes. Pot into warm, dry jars.

Apple Jam

Sound windfalls can be used, preferably sour ones. Allow 1 pint of water to 3 lb. fruit.

Cut up the apples, leaving the peel and core, removing any blemishes and the stalks. Put in a saucepan with the water, put the lid on the saucepan, bring very slowly to the boil, then simmer very gently till reduced to a pulp, keeping it covered all the time. Then rub through a sieve.

Weigh the pulp and allow 12 oz. sugar to each pound, also the grated rind and juice of half a lemon and ½ teaspoonful ginger. Stir till sugar has dissolved, then boil *hard* till it sets when tested – about 10 minutes.

Dried Apricot Jam

Dried apricots 1 lb.　　*Juice of a lemon*
Cold water 3 pints　　*Blanched almonds 1 oz.*
Sugar 3 lb.

Wash apricots thoroughly. Cut them into pieces, put in a bowl, pour over the water and leave for 24 hours. Next day turn into a preserving pan, bring to the boil and *simmer gently* for 45 minutes. Add the warmed sugar and lemon juice, and boil hard till it sets when tested. Start testing after 15 minutes. Add the blanched almonds and pot and tie down as directed.

Fresh Apricot Jam

Apricots 4 lb.　　*Sugar 4 lb.*
Water ¾ pint　　*Juice of a lemon*

Wash the fruit, cut in halves and remove the stones. Crack a few of the stones and blanch the kernels.

Put the fruit, water, lemon juice and kernels into the preserving pan, bring to the boil and cook gently till the fruit is tender; add the warmed sugar, stir till boiling, then boil hard till it sets when tested. Start testing after 15 minutes.

Blackberry and Apple Jam

Blackberries 4 lb. *Sour apples 3 lb.*
Water ¾ pint *Sugar*

Put the blackberries in a pan with ¼ pint of the water, simmer gently till tender, then rub through a sieve.

Peel, core and slice apples, add remaining ½ pint water, and cook gently till tender; then mash to a pulp, add the sieved blackberries and weigh. Put into preserving pan with ¾ lb. warmed sugar to every pound of fruit, stir till boiling, then boil quickly till it sets when tested. Start testing after 20 minutes.

Note. It is important to use blackberries that are just ripe. Those that are over-ripe and soft do not set well.

Blackcurrant Jam

As the skins of blackcurrants are always tough, it is necessary to add quite a lot of water to the fruit and to simmer until it is quite tender. This must be taken into account when reckoning the amount of sugar required. The following quantities should yield about 10 lb. of jam:

Blackcurrants 4 lb. *Sugar 6 lb.*
Water 3 pints

Stalk and wash fruit and put into preserving pan with the water and simmer gently till the fruit is quite tender; stir frequently and crush the fruit with a wooden spoon.

Add warmed sugar, stir till dissolved and boil hard till it sets when tested. Start testing after 10 minutes.

Cherry Jam (1)

Redcurrants 2 lb.   *Morello cherries 2 lb.*
Water ¼ pint   *Sugar 3 lb.*

Wash the currants, put them in a saucepan with the water, simmer very gently for 30 minutes, then strain through a cloth.

Stone the cherries and put in preserving pan with the redcurrant juice, and cook slowly till the cherries are quite soft – 10–15 minutes. Then add the warmed sugar, stir till dissolved and boil hard till it sets when tested. Start testing after 10 minutes.

Cherry Jam (2)

Morello cherries 4 lb.   *Citric or tartaric acid*
Sugar 3¼ lb.   *2 level teaspoonfuls*

Stone the cherries and remove the kernels from 2 or 3 dozen. Put the kernels with the stoned cherries and the acid mixed with 1 tablespoonful of water in a preserving pan, cook over a very gentle heat till the juice begins to flow, then bring slowly to boiling point, and simmer gently for 30 minutes. Add the warmed sugar, stir till it is dissolved, then boil quickly till it sets when tested. Start testing after 10 minutes.

Damson Cheese

Damsons 6 lb.   *Sugar 1 lb. to 1 lb. fruit pulp*
Water 2 pints

Wash the damsons and cook gently with the water till tender, then rub through a sieve. Weigh the pulp and put in a preserving pan with an equal weight of sugar. Stir till boiling, then simmer about 15 minutes, keeping it well stirred. Test for setting and pot as usual.

Damson Jam

Damsons 4 lb.   *Sugar 4 lb.*
Water 1½ pints

JC–25

Put damsons with the water in a preserving pan and bring to the boil. Simmer gently till damsons are quite soft – about 20 minutes – then add warmed sugar and stir till it is dissolved. Boil quickly till it sets when tested – about 10 minutes – removing as many stones as possible as they come to the surface.

Gooseberry Jam

Gooseberries 6 lb.   *Sugar 6 lb.*
Water 2 pints

Top and tail gooseberries and put with the water into preserving pan. Cook very gently till the fruit is quite soft, then add warmed sugar, stir till dissolved and boil rapidly till it sets when tested.

Greengage Jam

Greengages 6 lb.   *Sugar 6 lb.*
Water 1¼ pints

Wash fruit, cut in halves and remove the stones. Break a few of these and remove kernels. Put the greengages, water, and kernels into preserving pan and simmer gently till the fruit is quite soft. Then add warmed sugar, stir till dissolved and boil quickly till it sets when tested. Start testing after 15 minutes.

Lemon Curd

Butter or margarine 3 oz.   *Caster sugar 8 oz.*
3 lemons   *3 eggs*

Put the butter, sugar, grated rind and strained juice of the lemons into a double saucepan, stir occasionally and when sugar has dissolved, add the well-beaten egg. Stir till it thickens, but do not boil.

Turn into warm dry jars and tie down.

This is best made in small quantities and should be kept only a short time.

Loganberry Jam

Sugar 1 lb. to 1 lb. fruit

Put washed and hulled berries in preserving pan, and place over a very gentle heat till the juice begins to flow, then simmer gently for 20 minutes, stirring occasionally. Add warmed sugar, stir till dissolved, then boil quickly till it sets when tested. Test after 10 minutes.

Marrow Jam

Prepared marrow 4 lb.   *Sugar 4 lb.*
Bruised ginger 1 oz.   *3 lemons*

Weigh marrow after removing peel and seeds. Cut into $\frac{1}{2}$-inch cubes, put into a bowl with the sugar and leave overnight.

The following day turn into a preserving pan, add the grated rind and juice of the lemons and the bruised ginger tied in muslin. Bring to the boil and boil steadily till it sets when tested – $1\frac{1}{2}$ to 2 hours.

Note. Marrows used for preserves should be quite hard. They are usually ready in October.

To Bruise Ginger. Wrap ginger in paper, place on a hard surface and beat with a weight or hammer.

Plum Jam

Plums 4 lb.   *Sugar 4 lb.*
Water 1 pint

Stone the plums and cook gently with the water till the plums are quite soft. Add warmed sugar, stir till dissolved, then boil rapidly till it sets when tested. Yield about 7 lb.

Raspberry Jam

Raspberries 4 lb.   *Sugar 4 lb.*

Put fruit in preserving pan, place over a very gentle heat till the juice begins to flow, bring slowly to the boil and simmer for 10 minutes. Add the warmed sugar, stir till dissolved, then bring to the boil and boil till it sets when tested. Test after 10 minutes. Yield about 7 lb.

Raspberry and Redcurrant Jam

To 1 lb. raspberries and 1 lb. redcurrants allow 1¾ lb. sugar. Prepare fruit, put into preserving pan over very gentle heat till the juice begins to flow. Bring to the boil, simmer for 5 minutes, add the warmed sugar, stir till dissolved, then boil quickly till it sets when tested.

Rhubarb Jam

Rhubarb 6 lb.   *Sugar 6 lb.*
2 lemons   *Bruised ginger 2 oz.*

Cut rhubarb into 1-inch lengths, put in a bowl in layers with the sugar and leave overnight. The following day put in preserving pan with the lemon juice and the bruised ginger and lemon rind tied in a piece of muslin, bring slowly to the boil, then boil quickly till it sets when tested.

Strawberry Jam

Strawberries are lacking in pectin and acid. In order to get a good set it is essential to add acid in some form, such as lemon juice, tartaric acid, or a prepared pectin. Or the strawberries can be mixed with some fruit rich in pectin and acid, such as gooseberries, apples or redcurrants.

If using a commercial pectin, follow the directions given on the bottle.

Recipe using Lemon Juice. Allow 14 oz. sugar and the juice of 1 lemon to each pound of strawberries. Remove stalks and hulls of the strawberries, put in preserving pan with the lemon juice and simmer gently for 30 minutes. Add the warmed sugar, stir till dissolved, then boil till it sets when tested. Start testing after 15 minutes.

When sufficiently cooked, allow to cool, stirring occasionally. When half cold, turn into jars, cover with waxed paper circles and tie down when cold.

Using Tartaric Acid. In place of lemon juice use 1 level teaspoonful tartaric acid to every 2 lb. strawberries and proceed as above.

Using Gooseberry or Redcurrant Juice. To 4 lb. strawberries and 4 lb. sugar use 2 lb. gooseberries or redcurrants. Wash gooseberries or currants, put in a pan with sufficient water to cover, bring to the boil, mash them and simmer for 20 minutes; then strain through a jelly bag or cloth.

Cook prepared strawberries in this extract for 30 minutes then add warmed sugar and finish as in first recipe.

Strawberry Jam
(*Quick Method*)

Strawberries 2 lb.   *Caster sugar 3 lb.*
Juice of a lemon

Choose small fruit, and it must *not* be over-ripe.

Slightly crush the fruit, put in a pan in layers with the sugar. Add strained lemon juice. Stand pan on an asbestos mat and stir till boiling all over, then continue stirring while it boils *hard* for 3 minutes.

Turn into hot jars and tie down at once.

This should yield about 4¾ lb. jam.

JELLY MAKING

Choose firm, sound fruit and wash quickly through a colander.

It is *not* necessary to stalk currants or top and tail gooseberries, but remove all leaves.

Jelly making requires two processes: first, the cooking of the fruit with or without water; then, the cooking of the *strained* liquid with the sugar.

If a jelly bag is not available to strain the juice, a cloth attached to a kitchen chair will serve the purpose. This is how it is done:

Turn a kitchen chair seat downwards on a table and put a basin on it. Then tie a linen cloth to the ends of the four upturned legs. The cloth should first be scalded and then wrung as dry as possible and tied securely with strong tape, so that it will not slip with the weight of the fruit pulp.

In order to get a clear bright jelly, the straining process

must not be hurried. Leave it to drip overnight and do not squeeze it, or the jelly will be cloudy.

Apple Jelly

Sour apples 6 lb.   *Sugar 1 lb. to every pint of juice*
2 lemons   *Water*

Wash the apples and cut into thick slices, but do not peel or core them. Put into preserving pan with the lemon juice and sufficient water to cover well. Add the thinly peeled rind of the lemons and simmer slowly till the apples are soft and pulpy.

Drain through a cloth or jelly bag and leave to drip overnight.

Measure the juice and bring to the boil, add the warmed sugar and boil quickly till it sets when tested.

Note. Windfalls can be used quite successfully, as long as they are not sweet dessert apples, which do not contain enough pectin to set well. Remove any bruised or damaged portions.

Bramble Jelly (1)

Blackberries 4 lb.   *Water ½ pint*
Tartaric acid ½ oz.   *Sugar*

The fruit should be just ripe. Cook with the water and acid very slowly till the fruit is quite tender, mashing it occasionally.

Drain overnight through a cloth or jelly bag, and finish like Apple Jelly.

Bramble Jelly (2)

Make like Apple Jelly, adding 1 lb. blackberries for every 3 lb. apples.

Crab Apple Jelly

Crab apples 6 lb.   *Water 4 pints*

To each pint of juice allow 1 lb. sugar and juice of half a lemon.

Choose apples that are not too ripe, cut them into quarters, and put in a preserving pan with the water. Boil till reduced to a pulp. Strain through a jelly bag overnight. Measure the juice, then put in the preserving pan and bring to the boil, add the warmed sugar and lemon juice, stir till the sugar has dissolved, boil for a few minutes, test, and when ready, pot in small jars.

Redcurrant Jelly

Redcurrants 3 lb.   *Sugar*
Water 1 pint

Wash the fruit; do not remove stalks. Put into preserving pan with the water and cook gently until the fruit is quite pulped. Strain through a jelly bag and leave to drip overnight. Measure the juice, put it into preserving pan and bring to the boil. Add 1 lb. sugar to each pint of juice, stir till the sugar is dissolved, then bring to the boil. Boil briskly till it sets when tested. Start testing after 7 minutes. When ready, pot into small jars.

Mint Jelly

Sour green apples 4 lb.   *Water 2 quarts*
Sugar   *2 lemons or 2 level teaspoonfuls*
A bunch of mint   *citric acid*

Wash and cut up the apples, but do not peel or core. Put into preserving pan with the water, the thinly peeled rind and juice of the lemons (or the citric acid), and half a dozen sprigs of mint. Cook to a soft pulp, then drain through a jelly bag or cloth overnight.

Measure the extract and put into preserving pan with 1 lb. sugar for every pint. Stir till sugar has dissolved, then boil quickly till it sets when tested. Skim if necessary and add 2 tablespoonfuls finely chopped mint before potting into small jars.

Serve with roast lamb or mutton.

MARMALADE

Choose fruit that is just fully ripe, for that is the time when the greatest amount of soluble pectin is present.

Small, dried-up oranges will not make good marmalade, nor will *over-ripe* fruit.

If cutting peel by hand, use a *very sharp knife*, if possible a stainless one, and resharpen frequently.

Seville Orange Marmalade (1)

6 Seville oranges Sugar and water
2 lemons

Wash and dry fruit, cut in quarters and remove pips. Put these in a small basin and pour over ½ pint cold water.

Remove pulp, cut in small pieces and shred rind finely.

Weigh empty preserving pan.

Weigh pulp and rind, put it into a large bowl and pour over 2 pints cold water to every pound and leave till the following day. Then turn into a greased preserving pan, add the strained water from the pips and the pips tied in a muslin bag and boil gently till the peel is quite tender – about 1½ hours.

Remove pips, squeezing the bag well. Weigh pan and contents and deduct weight of empty pan to obtain weight of pulp. Add 1½ lb. preserving sugar to every pound.

Stir till the sugar has melted, then bring to the boil and boil quickly till it sets when tested.

Turn into warm, dry jars, place waxed paper circles in position, and tie down.

Seville Orange Marmalade (2)

10 Seville oranges *Preserving sugar 8 lb.*
2 sweet oranges *Cold water 9 pints*
2 lemons

Wash and dry fruit, cut in halves, remove pips, and squeeze the juice. Shred peel finely, put in a bowl with the juice and water, and leave till the following day. Put pips in a small basin and pour ½ pint cold water over.

Put the contents of the bowl into the preserving pan, add the strained water from the pips and the pips tied in a muslin bag.

Bring to the boil and boil slowly till the peel is quite soft and the contents of the pan reduced by about half. Then remove bag of pips, squeezing well, add warmed sugar, stir till melted, then boil rapidly till it sets when tested. Start testing after 15 minutes.

Pot as in previous recipe.

Seville Orange Marmalade (3)

Seville oranges 2 lb.   *1 lemon*
Cold water 5 pints   *Sugar*

Put the washed fruit into pan with the water, cover and cook gently till tender — about 2 hours. When cool, remove from the water, cut in halves, remove and discard pips, and shred the peel and pulp. Measure the fruit and water in which it was cooked and allow 1½ lb. sugar to every pint. Put together in preserving pan, stir till sugar has dissolved, then boil quickly till it sets when tested.

Mixed Fruit Marmalade

6 Seville oranges   *6 tangerines*
2 Jaffa oranges   *2 lemons*

Prepare and cut up fruit as in Seville Orange Marmalade (1). Put into a bowl with 2 pints water to every pound of fruit and put the pips in a small basin with ½ pint cold water. Leave till the following day, then finish like first recipe, but only allow 1¼ lb. sugar for every pound.

The mixed fruit gives a delicious flavour. The above quantities should yield about 22 lb. marmalade, but one cannot estimate exactly, as the size of fruit varies considerably.

Grapefruit Marmalade

2 large grapefruit   *4 lemons*
Sugar   *Water*

Prepare and cut up fruit as in first recipe, but discard the centre pith and pips of the grapefruit. Put the pips from the lemons in a small basin with ¼ pint cold water.

Put the cut-up fruit in a bowl and pour on 2 pints cold water to every pound. Leave till the following day.

Turn into preserving pan, strain in water from the pips,

and add the pips tied in a muslin bag. Boil gently till the peel is very soft — at least 1½ hours. Remove bag of pips, squeezing thoroughly, and weigh contents of pan; add 1½ lb. preserving sugar to every pound, stir till sugar has melted, then boil quickly till it sets when tested.

Lemon Marmalade

Prepare lemons as in first recipe; put pips in a small basin with ½ pint cold water. Weigh the lemons and put in a bowl with 3 pints cold water to each pound and leave till the following day. Then continue exactly as for Seville Orange Marmalade (1).

Mincemeat

Raisins ½ lb.	Apples 1 lb.
Currants ¼ lb.	2 lemons
Sultanas ¼ lb.	1 orange
Beef suet ¼ lb.	Cinnamon ¼ teaspoonful
Candied peel 4 oz.	Mixed spice ¼ teaspoonful
Almonds 2 oz.	Demerara sugar ¾ lb.
Salt ¼ teaspoonful	

Chop the suet finely; blanch the almonds; stone the raisins; peel and core the apples; wash and dry the currants and sultanas.

Put the raisins, currants, sultanas, peel and almonds through a mincing machine. Mix all ingredients together, using the grated rind and juice of the lemons and orange. Turn into jars and tie down. If to be kept for any length of time, omit the orange juice and add a little brandy or sherry.

Fruit Bottling

It is not essential to have a special sterilizing outfit for fruit bottling, but it is a great help when a large amount of bottling is done.

In any case it is important to sterilize carefully and follow directions exactly in order to destroy any bacteria that would otherwise cause the fruit to deteriorate.

Fruit can be preserved in water or in syrup by sterilizing it in bottles either on top of the stove or in the oven.

Bottles should be examined to see that the top rim and lids are free from chips.

New **rubber rings** should be used each time, and both these and the bottles should be scalded before use.

PREPARATION OF FRUIT

The fruit chosen for bottling should be dry, sound and not over-ripe. Prepare fruit according to kind.

Apples, Pears, Quinces. Wash, peel and core, and cut into convenient-sized pieces. The pieces should be dropped into weak brine (1 tablespoonful salt to 1 quart of water) to prevent discoloration.

Peaches and Apricots. Remove the skins. To do this place fruit in a colander, stand it in a large bowl, cover with boiling water, and leave for 1 minute. Then plunge it quickly into cold water, after which peel off the skins, using a stainless or silver knife. Cut in halves and remove stones.

Plums, Damsons, Greengages, Cherries. Remove stalks. If plums are very large they can be cut in half and the stones removed.

Raspberries and Loganberries. Pick over, hull, and wash very carefully, for raspberries and loganberries sometimes contain little maggots.

Gooseberries. Top and tail.

Currants. Remove stalks.

Whenever possible grade fruit according to size and ripeness. Pack the fruit tightly into the bottles without crushing. Use the handle of a spoon, if necessary, to push the fruit gently into place. When the bottle is half full, tap it firmly on a folded cloth, which will make the contents settle better.

Syrup for Fruit Bottling

Allow ¾ lb. sugar to each quart of water.

Put sugar and water in a saucepan and stir over a gentle heat till the sugar is dissolved. Bring to the boil and simmer for 5 minutes.

If sugar is in short supply, the quantity can be reduced and, if necessary, more sweetening can be added when the fruit is used.

To Sterilize on Top of the Stove

Scald bottles, lids, and rings and pack with prepared fruit up to the neck of the bottle; then completely cover with cold syrup (or cold water), adjust rubber rings and lids, and screw bands or clips in position.

If screw bands are used, screw down tightly, **then unscrew one half-turn.**

If a special sterilizer is used, carefully follow directions supplied with the outfit. If no special sterilizer is available, use a fish kettle, very large saucepan, or clothes boiler. Whatever is used must be deep enough for the water to cover the jars. The jars must not touch the bottom of the pan, so put in several thicknesses of newspaper or a piece of old blanket or felt.

Put in the jars, which must not touch each other or the side of the pan, cover with cold water and put on the lid.

Heat very slowly until the temperature reaches 165° in $1\frac{1}{2}$ hours. If no thermometer is available, heat till the water is slowly simmering. Maintain this heat for 15 minutes.

Plums, cherries and pears require to be brought to a slightly greater heat – (180°–190°) – and this heat should be maintained for 20 minutes.

When sterilizing is complete, remove bottles from the water and stand on a wooden board or table till cold. Do not stand them on a metal surface, such as an enamel-top table, for there is a risk of the bottles cracking owing to sudden change of temperature.

If screw-top bottles have been used, the bands must be tightened immediately and again after a short interval. Leave till the following day, then remove screw bands and lift the bottles by the lids. If the seal is perfect, the lids will remain in position. Lightly grease the inside of the band before rescrewing on the bottle.

If clips have been used, remove these and test lids in the same manner.

Any bottles that have not closed must be resterilized. Examine rubber rings and bottle carefully, and if these are in any way faulty, use others.

Jars with Synthetic Skin Covers. Fill the jars to within ½ inch of the top, and tie a piece of synthetic skin over with strong fine string. Put into pan, completely cover with cold water, put on the lid and bring the water gradually to *boiling point* and keep at this temperature for 3 minutes for soft fruit and 6 minutes for hard fruit. By this time the skin should have risen ½ to 1 inch above the top of the jar. It is not advisable to allow the skin to rise too high.

Remove from pan and leave till quite cold, when, if properly sealed, the skin will be tight as a drum and be drawn down into the neck of the bottle.

Sterilizing in the Oven
First Method

A very cool oven is required – about 250° or Regulo No. ½. Pears need a slightly higher temperature – Regulo No. 1 or 300°.

Scald the jars, rings and glass tops in boiling water and pack with prepared fruit (see page 395).

Stand the jars on a board and pour *boiling* syrup or water over the fruit to within ½ inch of the top. Adjust rings and lids and screw on bands tightly, then unscrew one half-turn.

Put the jars in the oven, standing in a baking tin containing 1 inch of water, allowing a little space between each jar. Leave in the oven as long as required, according to the fruit used.

Gooseberries, greengages, damsons and plums will take 45 minutes, all other fruit 1 hour.

Pears should be prepared in the following manner. Choose firm fruit, very slightly under-ripe. Peel them, cut in halves and remove cores with a teaspoon. Put in a saucepan with cold syrup and bring very slowly to boiling point. Then pack the fruit in hot jars and pour over boiling syrup to within ½ inch of the top. Adjust rings and tops as for other fruit and heat in the oven for 1 hour, at a temperature of 300°, Regulo No. 1.

Screw tightly as for other fruit and the following day test for sealing.

Second Method

Sterilize jars, etc., and fill with fruit as in the first method. Cook in the oven at the same temperature and for the same length of time as in the first method, but without any liquid, covering the jars with a baking tin.

Remove from oven one at a time, stand on a board and immediately pour in boiling water or syrup, filling the jar to overflowing. Adjust rubber ring, lid and screw band as quickly as possible, screwing quite tight. Leave till following day and test for sealing.

Bottled Fruit Pulp

This is a simple way to bottle stewed fruit.

Stew the fruit with very little water and sugar to taste. When thoroughly pulped turn into hot jars and seal immediately. See 'To Sterilize on Top of the Stove' (pages 396–7).

Put the jars in a pan of boiling water sufficient to completely cover them and boil for 5 minutes. Remove from the pan, tighten screws and the following day test for sealing.

Bottled Tomatoes (1)

Allow 1 teaspoonful each salt and sugar to each pound of tomatoes.

Skin the tomatoes – the best way to do this is to tie them in muslin, dip them in boiling water, then plunge into cold. After removing skin, cut in halves or, if very large, in quarters and pack closely in sterilized jars to within 1 inch of the top, sprinkling with sugar and salt in the proportion suggested. Do *not* add any water.

Adjust rings, lids and screw bands or clips and either sterilize in the oven for 1½ hours at 250°, Regulo No. ½, *or* on top of the stove, following directions given for fruit. Bring water in sterilizer to 190° in first hour and maintain at that temperature for another 30 minutes.

Bottled Tomatoes (2)

Choose small, rather under-ripe tomatoes. Remove stalks and pack tightly into jars, taking care not to break the skins. Add 1 teaspoonful salt to each pound and cover with water to within 1 inch of the top. Finish off as in previous method, using boiling water if sterilized in the oven, and cold water if done on top of the stove.

Bottled Tomato Pulp

Cut up tomatoes and put in a saucepan with 1 teaspoonful each of sugar and salt to each pound. Bring to the boil, stirring frequently, then cook very gently to a thick pulp. Sieve and pour into warmed jars and sterilize as in the first method for bottled tomatoes.

Bottled Vegetables

Vegetables should *not* be bottled unless a pressure cooker is available. Follow instructions issued by the maker of the cooker that is being used.

To Preserve Fruit Without Cooking

Fruit can be preserved without cooking by using Campden Fruit Preserving Tablets dissolved in water.

Dilute the tablets in tepid water according to directions on the bottle. Prepare the fruit, pack into jars, pour over the solution to cover the fruit completely and seal at once.

To Use the Fruit. Turn fruit and liquid into a saucepan, bring to the boil and simmer gently with the lid off the saucepan about 20 minutes, or until all smell and taste of sulphur has disappeared. Add sugar to taste and cook for a few minutes longer.

Blackberries, Currants, Pears and Tomatoes should *not* be preserved in this way.

Pickles, Chutneys, Ketchups, etc.

Use only the best ingredients, first-quality vinegar, sugar, and spices, and vegetables that are fresh, sound, and not over-ripe.

Use either an aluminium or an unchipped enamel-lined saucepan. Copper, iron or tin saucepans must never be used, as the vinegar acting on the metal produces a harmful poison.

Store in glass jars, and make sure the vinegar completely covers the vegetables.

Some pickles are improved by soaking in brine overnight. The brine draws some of the water out of vegetables, makes them crisper, and helps to preserve them.

Brine for Pickles

Add 4 oz. salt to 1 quart of water. Bring to the boil and use when cold.

Spiced Vinegar

Most pickles are made with spiced vinegar. A supply can be made in advance of the pickling season. It improves with keeping.

Vary spices to suit your own taste. These proportions are suggested as suitable for most palates.

For each quart of vinegar use $\frac{1}{4}$ oz. each cloves, whole allspice and mace, a few peppercorns, a 3-inch stick of cinnamon, and 1 oz. sugar, *or* 1 oz. mixed pickling spices.

Bring the spices, sugar, and vinegar to boiling point in a covered saucepan and stand for 2 hours without any further heating. Strain and use as required.

Apple Chutney

Sour apples 3 lb.
Seedless raisins 1 lb.
A few chillies
Brown sugar 1 lb.
Ground ginger 1 teaspoonful
Onions $\frac{1}{2}$ lb.
Vinegar $\frac{3}{4}$ pint
Salt 2 oz.
Mixed spice 1 teaspoonful

Peel and core apples and peel onions. Put them and the raisins and chillies through the mincing machine. Put all ingredients in a preserving pan, bring slowly to the boil, and simmer gently, stirring well until reduced to a soft pulp – about 1 hour.

Pot and tie down when cold.

Pickled Cucumbers (1)

Choose young, green, medium-sized cucumbers. Wash them and leave to soak in cold water for 24 hours, then dry thoroughly. Put into wide-necked jars or an earthenware bowl, filling containers three-quarters full. Sprinkle over a little pickling spice, and fill up with cold brine. Put a plate or saucer on the surface of the brine (to keep the cucumbers under the brine), cover with muslin, and leave in a cool, airy place for about 3 weeks. Once a week remove scum, wash saucer, and replace. If the brine evaporates, fill up container with weak salt water.

For the Brine. Allow 3 oz. salt to each quart of water; boil together for 3 minutes. Use when cold, adding $\frac{1}{4}$ pint of boiled vinegar to every quart of brine.

Pickled Cucumbers (2)

Cut cucumbers into pieces, soak 12 to 24 hours in a brine of 2 tablespoonfuls salt to each pint of water, allowing 1 pint brine to 1 lb. cucumbers. Drain off the brine, rinse in cold water, and drain thoroughly.

Put cucumbers into jars, cover with *cold* spiced vinegar (see page 400), which should be at least $\frac{1}{2}$ inch over the cucumbers. Seal and store in a cool place.

Pickled Cucumbers (3)

Wash and dry cucumbers, cut in pieces, put in a bowl or jar, add 1 teaspoonful mixed pickling spice and 3 or 4 bay leaves. Pour over the cold vinegar mixture, place a small plate or saucer on top to keep the cucumbers under the vinegar, and cover with a large plate. The cucumbers can be used after 10 days.

For the Vinegar Mixture. To 1 quart water allow 2 tea-spoonfuls acetic acid, 1 tablespoonful salt, 2 tablespoonfuls sugar. Boil water, pour on to sugar and salt, add acetic acid, and leave till cold. Taste before using, and if too strong, add a little more cold boiled water. The amount of sugar and strength of the vinegar can be varied to suit individual tastes.

Mixed Vinegar Pickles

Choose any vegetables available — cauliflower, cucumber, gherkins, small green tomatoes, small onions, marrow, beans, cabbage, etc.

Prepare the vegetables: slice tomatoes; peel onions; remove the ends of the cucumbers, then cut into small pieces; shred cabbage; separate cauliflower into small flowerets.

Put all the vegetables in a large bowl and cover with brine (see page 400), and leave for 24 hours; then drain and dry. Pack into jars and cover with boiling spiced vinegar (see page 400). Cover and leave at least a month before using.

Note. When marrow is included, dice this after removing peel and seeds, and sprinkle with dry salt instead of brine.

Piccalilli

Vegetable marrow	*To every 2 quarts vinegar :*
Cucumber	Sugar ¼ lb.
Gherkins	Curry powder ¼ oz.
French beans	Mustard 1½ oz.
Cauliflower	Flour 1 oz.
Button onions	Root ginger ¼ oz.
Vinegar	Turmeric ¼ oz.
Salt	Few peppercorns

Any of the above vegetables can be used. Prepare them in the usual way. Cut the marrow in cubes, divide the cauliflower into small branches. Choose small young beans, string them, and leave whole. Peel onions and leave them whole.

Spread the vegetables on dishes, sprinkle with salt, and leave till the following day, then drain thoroughly. Estimate the amount of vinegar to cover them.

Mix the flour, mustard, turmeric, and curry powder with some of the cold vinegar. Bruise the ginger and tie in muslin with the peppercorns.

Put the vegetables with the remaining vinegar and bag of

spices in a saucepan, and simmer gently for 20 minutes; then add the sugar, mustard, etc., and stir while it boils for 2 or 3 minutes. Pot into warm jars and tie down when cold.

Pickled Onions

Choose very small silver onions. Put them in a bowl, cover with boiling water, leave for a minute, then drain. This makes them easier to peel.

With a stainless steel knife remove the skins. Soak in brine (see page 400) for 24 hours. Then drain off the brine, rinse in cold water, and drain thoroughly.

Put into jars, leaving sufficient room for the vinegar to come $\frac{1}{2}$ inch above them; then pour over the cold spiced vinegar (see page 400) and seal.

Leave a month before using.

Pickled Red Cabbage

1 red cabbage	Vinegar 1 quart
Salt	Mixed pickling spice 1 tablespoonful

Choose a hard cabbage, trim off the coarse outside leaves, cut in four, and remove the thickest stalks. Then shred the cabbage very finely, using a long sharp knife. Put the shreds in layers on a dish, sprinkling each layer with salt, and leave till the following day. Boil the spices in the vinegar for 5 minutes, then leave till cold.

Drain off all moisture from the cabbage and put into jars. Pour over the cold spiced vinegar, which should come 1 inch above the cabbage, and tie down.

It will be ready to use after a fortnight. After 2 months it tends to soften.

Bottled Mint Sauce (1)

Take enough mint leaves to fill a breakfastcupful when well pressed down, $\frac{1}{2}$ pint vinegar, 4 oz. granulated sugar.

Remove leaves from the stalks and discard any that are coarse or brown at the edge, then wash and dry them thoroughly.

Put the vinegar and 3 oz. of sugar in a saucepan, bring to the boil, simmer gently for 2 or 3 minutes, then leave till cold.

Put mint leaves on a chopping board, sprinkle over the remaining sugar and chop finely. Pack into small glass jars and pour over the cold vinegar, which must be sufficient to saturate the mint and ½ inch above, then seal.

When using dilute with a little water and vinegar.

Bottled Mint Sauce (2)

Put a few spoonfuls of golden syrup in a basin and stir in as much chopped mint as it will absorb. Turn into a jar and seal. When using, add a little hot water and vinegar to taste.

To Dry Parsley for Winter Use

Wash and dry thoroughly.

Cut off the stalks and place parsley in a single layer on baking tin. Bake in a moderate oven till dry and crisp, but be sure not to let it get brown.

Rub through a sieve or gravy strainer, and store in small screw-top jars.

To Preserve Eggs

Eggs for preserving should be at least 24 hours old. Eggs put down in the spring keep better than those laid later in the year.

Never wash eggs before preserving. If slightly soiled, wipe with a cloth, but if they are very dirty, have a rough shell, or are cracked, they should not be preserved.

Ducks' eggs are not suitable for preserving.

Dry Method of Pickling

There are various preparations on the market for coating eggs; either a liquid preparation in which the eggs are dipped with the dipper supplied for the purpose; or a greasy preparation which is rubbed on with the palms of the hands. Full directions for their use are supplied by the manufacturer, and they should be used accordingly.

Preserving in Waterglass

Mix and use the waterglass according to the directions given on the packet. With the different brands the quantities vary somewhat.

The solution should be quite cold before using, and sufficient will be required to three-parts fill the container, which can be a bucket, a stoneware crock, or a galvanized iron bath.

If possible, place the eggs pointed end downwards. Put some kind of lid over the container to keep out the dust and prevent evaporation. The eggs must always be kept covered with the solution, more of which can be added if necessary. More eggs can be added as they become available until the container is full.

Confectionery

The recipes in this section are all quite simple, and can be made without the use of a sugar thermometer.

A good variety of sweets can be made that require no cooking, but these should be made just before they are to be used, as they do not keep well. They are best eaten when they are two days old. They do not keep fresh much longer than a week.

French Cream
(Foundation Mixture for Uncooked Fondants)

Icing sugar 1 lb.   *Cream of tartar ¼ teaspoonful*
White of an egg   *Cream or top milk 1 tablespoonful*

Sieve the sugar and add the cream of tartar. Whip the white of egg slightly, add half the sugar and cream (or top milk), mix together, then add remaining sugar. Dust the hands with icing sugar and knead to a firm paste. Use as required.

Chocolate Cream Fondants

French cream ¼ lb.   *Plain chocolate ¼ oz.*
Cream 1 dessertspoonful   *Vanilla essence*

Grate the chocolate very finely, add a few drops essence of vanilla and the cream, and knead it with half of the French cream. When thoroughly mixed, roll into tiny balls. Roll out the remainder of the French cream thinly, take a small piece and coat each chocolate ball with it. Dip the fingers in icing sugar to prevent sticking. Roll in sugar and leave for 24 hours to dry.

Coconut Cubes

French cream ¼ lb.   *Green colouring*
Desiccated coconut 2 oz.   *White of egg 1 dessertspoonful*

Knead the coconut and white of egg into the French fondant and mix thoroughly. Divide into two portions and colour one half green. Roll out each portion on a sugared board quite thin. Cut into even strips and place one on top of another in alternate colours, four together. Cut into cubes and leave on a sugared tin for 24 hours to dry.

Fudge

Granulated sugar 1 lb.   *Margarine 2 oz.*
A small tin condensed milk   *Golden syrup 3 oz.*
Milk 2 tablespoonfuls   *Vanilla essence 1 teaspoonful*

Put the margarine, syrup, sugar, and milk into a strong saucepan that has been rinsed with cold water. Place over a gentle heat till the sugar is quite melted, then add the condensed milk, and boil steadily till a little dropped in cold water forms a soft ball – about 15–20 minutes. Remove from the heat, add the vanilla essence, and beat until it becomes thick and creamy; then turn into greased tins, and when cool cut into squares. Remove from tins when quite cold.

Marzipan

Ground almonds ¼ lb.   Lemon juice 1 dessertspoonful
Icing sugar 4 oz.   Orange flower water
Caster sugar 4 oz.   Vanilla
1 egg

Rub the sugars through a very fine sieve, then put them in a
basin with the almonds, beaten egg, lemon juice, a few drops of
vanilla, and orange flower water. Knead thoroughly till a
smooth workable paste is formed.

This paste can be used in various ways:

(1) Remove the stones from some dates or French plums and
put a little ball of the mixture inside, with just a little showing
on the outside.

(2) Shape the mixture like little potatoes. Make 'eyes' with a
knitting needle, and roll the potatoes in cocoa.

(3) Take some large walnuts. Make little balls of the mixture,
and press one in between two halves of walnut.

(4) Divide the mixture in halves. Colour one half green.
Roll out about ¼ inch thick. Brush over the top of one piece
with water, press on the other, and cut into fancy shapes.

Grapefruit Sticks

(Pomerangon)

Cut the skins of 2 grapefruit into quarters, cut away most
of the pith and any blemishes. Put in a saucepan, cover with
cold water, and bring to the boil, then strain. Repeat this
twice. The last time simmer for at least 1 hour till the peel is
soft, then strain.

Cut the peel into strips ¼ inch wide, weigh them, and to
every 4 oz. allow 5 oz. sugar and 2 tablespoonfuls of the water
in which the skins were cooked.

Put sugar and water in a saucepan, and when the sugar has
dissolved, bring to the boil, put in the peel, and simmer until
it is transparent – about 20 minutes. Drain off the syrup, roll
the sticks in granulated sugar, and leave on a cake tray for a
few hours to dry.

Peppermint Creams

Icing sugar 1 lb.   *Water 1 tablespoonful*
White of egg   *Oil of peppermint*

Sieve the icing sugar and put it in a basin; add the water and sufficient white of egg to form a pliable, but not sticky, paste. Flavour with a few drops of oil of peppermint. Roll out on a sugared board about ¼ inch thick and cut out with a tiny round cutter. Leave on a sieve overnight to get quite dry.

Toffee

Brown sugar 8 oz.   *Butter or margarine 2 oz.*
Golden syrup 4 oz.

Put all ingredients into a strong saucepan over a very gentle heat till the sugar has dissolved, then bring to the boil and boil rapidly until a drop hardens immediately when dropped in cold water. Turn into a well-buttered tin and leave till set.

Honeycomb Toffee

Loaf sugar 1 lb.   *Golden syrup 4 oz.*
Pinch of cream of tartar   *Bicarbonate of soda 1 level teaspoonful*
Water ¼ pint

Put the water, syrup, sugar, and cream of tartar into a strong saucepan over a very gentle heat till the sugar has dissolved, stirring occasionally, then boil without any further stirring until it sets when tested in cold water. Mix the bicarbonate of soda with 1 dessertspoonful warm water, and stir into the boiling toffee after removing from the heat. Stir gently, turn into a greased tin, and mark into squares when half set.

Russian Toffee

Demerara sugar 1 lb.   *Golden syrup 2 tablespoonfuls*
Butter or margarine 4 oz.   *A small tin condensed milk*

Put butter, sugar, and syrup into a saucepan over a gentle heat and stir till the sugar has dissolved; bring to the boil, then add the milk. Boil for 20 minutes. Pour into greased tins and when cool mark into squares.

The Seder Table

The following are required for the traditional *Seder* table:

Three Matzot. For the *Seder* Service it is customary to have specially prepared *Matzot*, known as *Shemura Matzot* (and sometimes referred to as *Mitzvot*). If not available, ordinary *Matzot* may be used. In the absence of a special *Matzot* cover, fold a large napkin in four and place one *Matzo* in each of the three folds, making sure that the *Matzot* do not touch each other. Then put on a plate.

Roast Shank-bone of a Lamb, representing the Paschal Lamb.

One Roasted Egg, representing the Festival offering.

Bitter Herbs. Some small pieces of horseradish are normally used.

The shank-bone, the egg, and the horseradish are put together on a dish or plate which is then placed next to the three *Matzot*.

Charoseth, a recipe for which is given on page 410.

Parsley or Lettuce, accompanied by a small bowl of salt water.

All the items listed above are placed in front of the man conducting the service.

Wine. Sufficient wine should be provided for four full glasses for each person present.

Elijah's Cup. This is a spare goblet of wine which, though placed on the table, is not used during the ceremony. It is a guest cup set aside for any visitor who may enter the family circle unexpectedly.

Passover Cookery

Fine matzo meal or potato flour or arrowroot should be used for thickening soups and sauces.

When frying fish, first coat with fine matzo meal, then dip in beaten egg. Or if to be served hot, dip the fish first in egg, then coat with fine or medium meal and fry in a pan with sufficient oil to cover the fish. In veal stuffing substitute mashed potato for breadcrumbs. Cutlets should be brushed over with beaten egg and then coated with matzo meal.

Charoseth

Apples ¼ lb.   Almonds 2 oz.
Raisins 2 oz.   Cinnamon

Peel and core the apples and chop finely, together with the almonds and raisins. Mix together, adding cinnamon to taste. Then form into a neat block and place in a glass dish, or roll into tiny balls and coat with chopped nuts.

Raisin Wine (1)

Cut 1 lb. raisins in halves, put in a saucepan with 3 pints cold water and simmer *very gently* until the water is reduced by one third. This should take several hours. When cold, strain through muslin. If additional sweetness and flavouring are required, add a little sugar and cinnamon before boiling.

Raisin Wine (2)

Seed and chop 1 lb. raisins, put into a stone jar with ½ lb. loaf sugar and half a sliced lemon. Pour over 2 quarts boiling water and stir till sugar has dissolved. Cover with muslin and stir every day for a week. Then strain and bottle. Ready for use in 10 or 12 days.

Almond Balls for Soup

Ground almonds 2 oz.   1 egg
Grated lemon rind   Salt

Separate the yolk and white of the egg. Beat up the yolk, add the almonds, grated rind of half a lemon and a little salt. Whip the white of the egg to a stiff froth, add to the other ingredients and mix lightly. Drop a little from the end of a small spoon into very hot fat and when puffed up and brown, drain well. Put into soup just before serving.

Matzo Meal Noodles

Beat up 2 eggs with ½ teaspoonful of salt, add 2 tablespoonfuls of matzo meal and mix thoroughly.

Melt a little dripping in a small frying pan and pour in sufficient of the mixture to cover the bottom; when cooked on one side, turn and cook on the other. Roll up each pancake and cut across into 'noodles' ¼ inch wide.

Drop into boiling soup and cook for 2 or 3 minutes.

Matzo Kleis (1)

2 matzot	Chicken fat or vegetable fat 2 tablespoonfuls
1 onion	Salt and pepper
Matzo meal	Ginger
2 eggs	

Soak matzot in cold water till soft, then drain and squeeze dry. Put in a basin and beat up with a fork. Chop onion finely and fry a golden brown; then add, with the fat, to the soaked matzot. Season with salt, pepper and ginger, stir in beaten eggs and sufficient fine meal to bind the mixture.

With hands dipped in fine meal roll into tiny balls and roll in fine meal. Drop into fast-boiling soup or stew 20 minutes before serving. These are best made in advance and left for a few hours in a cool place or refrigerator before cooking.

Matzo Kleis (2)

(Kneidlech)

Matzo meal (medium) 1 breakfastcupful	Chopped parsley 1 teaspoonful
Boiling water 1 breakfast-cupful	Chicken fat 2 tablespoonfuls
	Salt and pepper
1 egg	Nutmeg and ginger

Pour boiling water over the meal and stir well till blended; then add the egg, fat, parsley, and seasoning. Mix thoroughly and put in refrigerator or very cold place for at least 1 hour. With hands dipped in cold water roll into tiny balls. Drop into boiling soup and simmer gently for 15 minutes with the saucepan uncovered.

Filled Matzo Kleis

Make Matzo Kleis (1) mixture and form into small flat cakes.
Put a cooked stoned prune on half, cover each filled cake with
another. Press firmly together, roll into balls and coat with fine
meal. Drop into fast-boiling water and cook for 20 minutes.

Serve coated with fried onions. These should be sliced and
fried till golden brown in chicken or vegetable fat. Pour any fat
remaining in the pan over the kleis with the onions.

Scrambled Eggs with Matzot

Break 2 matzot into small pieces, put in a colander, pour
boiling water over and drain quickly. They should be moist,
but not soggy. Add 3 lightly beaten eggs and season with salt
and pepper. Melt 2 oz. butter or vegetable fat in a frying pan,
put in the mixture and cook over a gentle heat like ordinary
scrambled eggs, keeping it well stirred.

Halibut Stewed with Egg and Lemon Sauce

Head and shoulders of halibut	*Chopped parsley*
2 onions	*2 eggs*
Oil 2 tablespoonfuls	*2 lemons*
Potato flour 1 dessertspoonful	*Water 1½ pints*
Matzo meal	*Cod's liver*
Salt, pepper, ginger	

Cut the fish up into convenient-sized pieces for serving. Slice
the onions and fry them in the oil in a stewpan till lightly
browned. Then lay in the fish, season with salt, pepper and a
pinch of ginger. Pour over 1½ pints of hot water, cover and
cook gently till the fish is done – about 30 minutes. Put in the
liver balls when the fish is half cooked.

Arrange the fish in the centre of a dish, with the liver balls
around. Pour over the egg and lemon sauce. Serve cold; add
finely chopped parsley.

For the Liver Balls. Boil some cod's liver in salted water for
10 minutes, then strain and chop finely. Add the whites of 2
eggs, a little chopped parsley and sufficient matzo meal to

bind; season with salt and pepper. Dust the hands with meal and roll into small balls.

Egg and Lemon Sauce. Pour the strained juice of 2 lemons on to the potato flour. Mix smoothly and add ¾ pint of the fish stock. Stir till boiling and simmer for 5 minutes, then cool. Beat up the egg yolks lightly; gradually pour the sauce on to them. Return to the saucepan and stir till it thickens. Do not reboil, or it will curdle.

Stewed Steak with Matzo Balls

Stewing steak 1½ lb.	*3 or 4 onions*
Potato flour 1 tablespoonful	*Carrots ½ lb.*
Stock or water 1½ pints	*Matzo balls*
Seasoning	

Cut the steak into cubes and season with salt and pepper Prepare and cut up the vegetables. Melt a little dripping in a frying pan, add the meat and brown quickly. Remove from the pan, add the onion and brown this also; then pour in stock and when boiling, add the potato flour mixed smoothly with a spoonful of cold water. Stir till boiling; season to taste.

Put the meat and carrots in a stewpan or casserole, pour over the gravy and onion, cover and simmer gently on top of the stove or in the oven 2–2½ hours.

Matzo Balls. Make Matzo Kleis (1) mixture (see page 411). Roll into balls, coat with fine meal and drop into boiling salted water. Boil gently for 10 minutes, then add to the stew 15 minutes before serving.

Blintzes

Potato flour 8 oz.	*2 eggs*
Meat filling	*Water*

Put the potato flour into a basin, make a well in the centre and break in the eggs. Mix to a thin batter with cold water – ¾–1 pint will be needed.

Heat a small frying pan, grease lightly and pour in sufficient batter to make a thin pancake, tilting the pan so that the entire surface is covered. Cook on one side only till the pancake is set; continue till they are all made. Fill each pancake with a spoonful of the meat filling, fold into three-cornered pieces and fry in chicken fat.

Meat Filling. Chop 2 small onions and fry a golden brown in a little chicken fat. Add 1 large cupful of minced cooked meat, season with salt and pepper and bind with a beaten egg.

Potato Pancakes

Peel and grate potatoes, then drain very thoroughly. To each pint add 2 well-beaten eggs and sufficient fine matzo meal to form a batter. Season with salt and pepper.

Melt a very little fat in a thick frying pan and fry the mixture in spoonfuls, turning when brown on one side.

These can be served with the meat course or as a sweet. If the latter, omit the pepper and serve with jam or stewed fruit.

Fried Matzot

Break some matzot into neat equal pieces. Soak in milk until slightly soft, but not soggy. Drain, dip in beaten egg and fry a light brown on both sides.

Serve sprinkled with cinnamon, sugar and grated lemon or orange rind.

Pie Crust (1)

Margarine or vegetable fat 2 oz.   1 egg
Fine matzo meal 4 oz.   Pinch of salt
Mashed potato 4 oz.

Rub fat into the meal, add the salt, well-mashed potatoes and the egg, and mix to a paste, adding a very little cold water if necessary. Roll out on a board dusted with meal.

It can be used for tartlets or a flan case, with sweet or savoury filling. It should be baked 'blind' and the filling added after it is cooked. For tartlets, cut into rounds with a cutter; for a flan case, shape well into a deep, greased sandwich tin and bake in a quick oven (450°, Regulo No. 7) about 20 minutes.

For Savoury Fillings. Mixed cooked vegetables in well-flavoured sauce can be used, or flaked fish in sauce, or finely diced cooked meat moistened with thick gravy.

For Sweet Fillings. Use fresh or dried stewed fruit or tinned fruit. Strain the fruit and arrange in the pastry. Thicken the fruit juice with potato flour, using 1 rounded teaspoonful to $\frac{1}{4}$ pint of juice and spoon over the fruit when cold.

Pie Crust (2)

2 matzot	*Margarine or other fat 1 oz.*
2 eggs	*Sugar 2 tablespoonfuls*
Pinch of salt	*Fine matzo meal $\frac{1}{2}$ teacupful*

Soak the matzot in cold water till soft, then drain and squeeze very dry.

Put into a basin, beat up with a fork, then add melted margarine, beaten eggs, sugar, salt and meal and mix very thoroughly. Press into a greased pie plate, having the mixture about $\frac{1}{4}$ inch thick. Bake in a slow oven (350°, Regulo No. 3) about 30 minutes.

This can be baked 'blind' and the filling added afterwards, or the fruit filling can be cooked with the flan, in which case it will take a little longer to cook.

Apple Filling. Peel, core and chop finely 1 lb. cooking apples, add the grated rind and juice of a lemon, 2 tablespoonfuls currants or chopped raisins and sugar to taste. Spread over the flan and bake as directed.

For other fruit fillings, see previous recipe.

CAKES AND BISCUITS
Almond Cakes

2 eggs	*Caster sugar 2 oz.*
Fine meal 1$\frac{1}{2}$ oz.	*Grated lemon rind*
Ground almonds 2 oz.	

Separate the yolks and whites of the eggs. Beat up the egg yolks with the sugar till light and frothy, add meal and almonds and beat for another 5 minutes. Add the grated lemon rind, then fold in the stiffly whipped egg whites. Turn into

small greased patty tins or paper cases and bake in a quick
oven (450°, Regulo No. 7) 12–15 minutes.

Almond Macaroons

Make according to the recipe on page 353, but substitute 3
teaspoonfuls fine matzo meal for the rice flour and bake on a
well-greased tin instead of rice paper.

Chocolate Buns

Potato flour 4 oz.   *Butter or margarine 4 oz.*
Cocoa 1 tablespoonful   *Bicarbonate of soda ½ teaspoonful*
3 eggs   *Milk 1 tablespoonful*
Fine meal 2 oz.   *Sugar 4 oz.*

Sieve the potato flour, meal and cocoa. Beat the butter and
sugar to a cream, beat in the eggs one at a time, adding a
tablespoonful of the dry ingredients with each egg, mix the
bicarbonate of soda with a tablespoonful of warm milk, add this
and remaining dry ingredients. Half fill small greased patty
tins with the mixture and bake in a quick oven (450°, Regulo
No. 7) about 15 minutes.

Cinnamon Balls

White of 1 large egg   *Caster sugar 2 oz.*
Ground almonds 4 oz.   *Icing sugar*
Cinnamon 2 teaspoonfuls

Beat the egg white to a stiff froth, add caster sugar, cinnamon
and ground almonds and mix thoroughly. Roll into small balls
and bake on a greased tin in a slow oven (350°, Regulo No. 3)
for 18 minutes. Remove from the tin and when cold roll in
icing sugar.

Coconut Pyramids (1)

Desiccated coconut 6 oz.   *Potato flour 1 oz.*
Caster sugar 4 oz.   *Whites of 2 eggs*

Mix the coconut, sugar and potato flour together. Whip the
egg whites to a stiff froth, then fold in the dry ingredients

lightly. Put in little rough heaps on a well-greased baking tin and bake very slowly (325°, Regulo No. 2) till crisp and a light biscuit colour – about 40 minutes.

Coconut Pyramids (2)

Desiccated coconut ½ lb.   *2 eggs*
Caster sugar 5 oz.

Mix all ingredients thoroughly and with hands dipped in cold water form into pyramids. Bake on a greased tin in a moderate oven (375°, Regulo No. 4) till lightly browned.

Lemon Biscuits

Potato flour 4 oz.   *Butter or margarine 2 oz.*
Fine matzo meal 1 oz.   *Caster sugar 2 oz.*
Grated rind of ½ lemon   *1 egg*

Sieve the potato flour and meal into a bowl, rub in the butter with the tips of the fingers, then add lemon rind and sugar. Mix to a dough with the beaten egg. Unless it is a very small one, only about three quarters of the egg will be required. Knead lightly and roll out on a board dusted with potato flour. Cut into fingers about 1 inch by 3 inches and place on a greased baking sheet. Bake in a slow oven (350°, Regulo No. 3) until lightly tinted – about 15–20 minutes. Handle carefully, as these biscuits are very light and break easily.

Butter Cake

Fine matzo meal 6 oz.   *1 egg*
  (or cake meal)   *Flavouring*
Caster sugar 4 oz.   *Chopped nuts*
Butter 4 oz.

Cream the butter and sugar, add the yolk of the egg, then the meal and a little cinnamon or vanilla sugar, and knead to a pliable dough. Press into a greased baking tin (the mixture should be about ¼ inch thick), brush over with white of egg and sprinkle with chopped nuts. Bake in a moderate oven (400°, Regulo No. 5) till lightly browned – about 25 minutes.

After removing from the oven, leave for 2 or 3 minutes, then cut into squares or fingers. Leave in the tin for a few minutes longer, then remove and cool on a cake tray.

Wafer Biscuits

Fine matzo meal 1 oz.	*Caster sugar 2 oz.*
Potato flour 1 oz.	*Butter 2 oz.*
1 egg	*Flavouring*

Melt the butter, but do not let it boil.

Whip the egg and sugar till light and frothy; add the melted butter and either a little grated lemon rind or 1 teaspoonful of vanilla sugar; whisk again; then stir in the matzo meal and potato flour. Grease a baking tin thoroughly with cooking fat and put the mixture on it a teaspoonful at a time and very far apart, since it spreads considerably. Bake in a hot oven (450°, Regulo No. 7) until the mixture has set and the edges are lightly browned.

Remove biscuits from the tin immediately and cool on a cake tray.

Rout Cakes

Ground almonds ¼ lb.	*Yolks of 3 eggs*
Caster sugar ¼ lb.	*Royal icing*

Mix sugar and almonds together, then add the egg yolks, using just sufficient to form a pliable mixture. Dredge a pastry board with icing sugar, roll out the paste ⅓ inch thick and leave in a cool place for 1 hour. Then form into any shapes preferred. It can be rolled out thinly and cut into diamonds or fingers; or rolled into pencil-shaped pieces and formed into rings, scrolls or twirls. Place on a well-greased tin and bake in a cool oven (325°, Regulo No. 2) till firm. Decorate to taste with royal icing.

Sand Cake

Butter 6 oz.	*3 eggs*
Caster sugar 6 oz.	*Fine matzo meal 2 oz.*
Potato flour 4 oz.	*Grated lemon rind*

Separate the yolks and whites of the eggs. Melt the butter, but do not make it hot. Sieve meal and potato flour together.

Beat the egg yolks and sugar till very light, add the melted butter, then the potato flour, meal and grated lemon rind. Beat the egg whites to a stiff froth and fold them in lightly. Turn into a greased 8-inch cake tin and bake in a moderate oven (400°, Regulo No. 5) 1–1¼ hours.

Note. The grated rind of an orange can be used instead of lemon and the cake can be iced with orange glacé icing.

Sponge Cake (1)

Fine matzo meal 2 oz.   *Potato flour 4 oz.*
Butter (or margarine) 6 oz.   *Caster sugar 6 oz.*
3 eggs

Grease and line an 8-inch cake tin.

Melt the butter, but do not make it very hot. Separate the yolks and whites of the eggs; sieve the meal and potato flour together.

Beat the egg yolks and sugar till very light, add the melted butter, then the potato flour and meal. Then fold in the stiffly whipped egg whites. Turn into prepared tin and bake in a moderate oven (375°, Regulo No. 4) about 1¼ hours. When cooked invert on to a cake tray and leave till nearly cold before turning out.

Note. This can be flavoured with vanilla sugar or grated lemon or orange rind.

For Small Sponge Cakes. Turn into greased patty tins and bake 15–20 minutes in a somewhat hotter oven (400°, Regulo No. 5).

Sponge Cake (2)

Caster sugar 6 oz.   *Fine matzo meal 3 oz.*
4 eggs

Grease a 7-inch cake tin and dust with sugar and potato flour.

Put the eggs and sugar in a large bowl and stand over a saucepan of hot water and whisk briskly until the mixture is very light and fluffy. Fold in the meal lightly, using a metal spoon. Turn into prepared tin and bake 1–1¼ hours in a slow oven (350°, Regulo No. 3). When cooked invert on to a cake tray and leave till nearly cold before turning out.

Note. The mixture can be flavoured with vanilla sugar or grated lemon rind.

For a Sponge Sandwich. Grease 2 sandwich tins and dust with sugar and potato flour. Put half the mixture in each and bake in a moderate oven (400°, Regulo No. 5) 25–30 minutes. When cold sandwich together with jam or butter icing.

PUDDINGS AND SWEETS

Almond Pudding

Caster sugar 5 oz.   *Ground almonds 4 oz.*
4 eggs

Separate the yolks and whites of the eggs. Whisk the yolks and sugar till very light, add the ground almonds and beat for a few minutes longer, then fold in the stiffly whipped egg whites. Turn into a greased baking dish and bake in a slow oven (350°, Regulo No. 3) about 50 minutes. Serve cold sprinkled with caster sugar.

Apple Charlotte

Apples 1 lb.   *Sugar*
Margarine 2 oz.   *Medium matzo meal 1 breakfastcupful*
A few sultanas   *Grated rind and juice of ¼ lemon*

Peel and core the apples and cut them into small pieces. Rub 1½ oz. margarine into the meal and add 2 tablespoonfuls of sugar.

Grease a baking dish and put in one third of the meal, cover with half the apples and sprinkle with sugar, sultanas, lemon juice and grated rind. Repeat the layers and pour over 4 tablespoonfuls of water. Put the remaining meal on top, sprinkle with sugar, dot with margarine and bake in a moderate oven (375°, Regulo No. 4) 1–1¼ hours.

For Rhubarb Charlotte substitute cut-up rhubarb for the apple.

Apple Fritters

Cooking apples 1 lb.
Fine meal 2 tablespoonfuls

Sugar, cinnamon
2 eggs

Peel and core the apples and cut into thick slices. Separate the yolks and whites of the eggs. Beat up the yolks lightly with the meal, then stir in the stiffly whipped whites. Dip each apple slice in this batter and fry slowly in shallow fat a golden brown on both sides. Drain well and serve hot sprinkled with cinnamon and sugar.

Apple Pudding (1)

2 large cooking apples
2 eggs
Shredded suet 2 oz.
Brown sugar 2 oz.

2 matzot
Currants 2 oz.
Raisins 2 oz.
Cinnamon, lemon rind

Soak matzot in cold water, then squeeze very dry and beat up with a fork. Peel, core and chop the apples, stone the raisins and clean the currants. Mix all ingredients thoroughly, adding grated lemon rind and cinnamon to taste. Turn into a greased oven dish and bake in a moderate oven (375°, Regulo No. 4) about 1¼ hours.

Apple Pudding (2)

Cooking apples 1 lb.
Fine meal 3 tablespoonfuls
Ground almonds 1 tablespoonful
Cinnamon ½ teaspoonful

Sugar 4 oz.
3 eggs
1 lemon

Peel, core and grate the apples. Beat up the egg yolks lightly with the sugar. Add the grated apple, meal, almonds, the grated rind and juice of the lemon and cinnamon. Mix thoroughly, then fold in the stiffly whipped egg whites. Turn into a greased oven dish and bake in a moderate oven (375°, Regulo No. 4) about 1 hour.

Coffee Chocolate Cream

Strong coffee 1 pint   *Potato flour 1 oz.*
2 eggs   *Sugar 2 oz.*
Chopped almonds   *Cocoa 1 oz.*

Mix cocoa, sugar and potato flour with a little cold coffee, boil remainder and pour it over. Beat up the eggs and add to the mixture. Turn into a double boiler and stir till it thickens. Whisk lightly and serve cold sprinkled with chopped almonds.

Grimslich

2 matzot   *2 eggs*
Fine meal 2 oz.   *Dried fruit 4 oz.*
Ground almonds 2 oz.   *Sugar 2 oz.*
Cinnamon ¼ teaspoonful   *Melted fat 2 tablespoonfuls*

Soak the matzot in cold water till soft, then squeeze very dry and beat up with a fork. Separate the yolks and whites of the eggs, add the beaten yolks and remaining ingredients. Mix thoroughly, then fold in the stiffly whipped egg whites. Drop in spoonfuls in hot shallow fat and fry a golden brown on both sides. Sprinkle with sugar and serve hot.

Lemon Cream

2 lemons   *2 eggs*
Water 1 pint   *Potato flour 1 oz.*
Sugar 3 oz.   *Shredded almonds*

Peel the lemons thinly. Put the rind into a saucepan, add the water, juice of the lemons, and the sugar, bring to the boil slowly, simmer for 2 or 3 minutes, then cover and leave till cold; then strain. Mix the potato flour with a little of the lemon syrup, add to the beaten eggs; heat the remaining liquid and pour on to the egg and lemon mixture. Turn into a double saucepan and stir till it thickens. Serve cold sprinkled with shredded almonds.

Lemon Sponge

Potato flour 2 oz.   Whites of 2 eggs
Sugar 4 oz.   Water 1 pint
2 lemons

Peel the lemon rind as thinly as possible, put in a saucepan
with the sugar and water, bring to the boil slowly, simmer for
5 minutes, cover and leave till cold; then strain and reheat.
Mix the potato flour smoothly with a little cold water, add the
strained lemon juice and the hot syrup and stir over a gentle
heat while it simmers for 5 minutes.

Whip the egg whites to a stiff froth, gradually pour on the
potato flour mixture, beating lightly all the time; then beat
another 2 or 3 minutes. Turn into a wetted mould and leave
till set. Serve with stewed fruit.

Matzo Fritters (1)
(Beolas)

3 eggs   Clarified sugar
Fine matzo meal   Ground cinnamon
  3 tablespoonfuls   Oil for frying

Beat the eggs till light and frothy, then add the meal and beat
again for 5 minutes. Drop in spoonfuls into hot deep fat or oil.
When lightly browned on one side, turn and brown the other.
Drain well and put into a glass dish, sprinkle lightly with
ground cinnamon and pour over clarified sugar. Serve cold.

Clarified Sugar

Sugar 4 oz.   Water ¼ pint
Lemon rind

Put sugar and water in a small saucepan, add a few strips of
thinly peeled lemon rind. Boil for 5 minutes, leave till cold,
then strain.

Matzo Fritters (2)

Fine meal 3 oz.   2 eggs
Sugar 1 tablespoonful   Milk or water ¼ pint

Mix the meal and sugar, beat up the egg yolks lightly and add the milk or water, pour on to the meal and mix thoroughly; then fold in the stiffly whipped egg whites.

Thoroughly grease a thick frying pan and when hot, pour the mixture on to it in spoonfuls, not too close together. When full of bubbles, turn with a broad knife and brown the other side.

Serve hot with jam or sprinkled with sugar and lemon juice.

Matzo Pudding

2 matzot	Matzo meal 2 tablespoonfuls
Mixed spice	Shredded suet 2 oz.
Mixed dried fruit 6 oz.	2 eggs
Brown sugar 3 oz.	

Break up the matzot and soak in cold water till soft, then drain and squeeze very dry. Put in a basin and beat up with a fork; add mixed spice to taste, and remaining ingredients, reserving 1 oz. of the sugar. Mix thoroughly and turn into a greased baking dish. Sprinkle over remaining sugar and bake 50 minutes in a moderate oven (400°, Regulo No. 5). Serve with Rum Sauce.

Rum Sauce

Yolks of 2 eggs	Sugar 1 tablespoonful
Water ¼ pint	Rum 1 wineglassful
1 lemon	

Beat up the egg yolks with the sugar. Add the water, strained juice of the lemon and the rum. Turn into a double boiler and stir over a gentle heat till the sauce thickens, but do not let it boil.

Meringue Pudding

Fine meal 4 oz.	Cooking apples ¾ lb.
Caster sugar 5 oz.	2 bananas
2 eggs	1 lemon

Peel, core and grate the apples, add the very lightly beaten egg yolks, 3 oz. sugar, the grated rind and juice of the lemon and the matzo meal. Beat lightly, turn into a greased oven dish and bake in a moderate oven for 40 minutes. Then cover the top with the thinly sliced bananas. Whisk the egg whites to a stiff froth, fold in remaining 2 oz. caster sugar, and heap up over the pudding. Return to a cool oven till the meringue is set and lightly browned – 15–20 minutes.

Carrot Candy
(Ingber)

Carrots 1 lb.	Caster sugar 1 lb.
Chopped nuts 4 oz.	Ground ginger ¼ teaspoonful

Scrape and wash the carrots, then grate on a fine grater. Put into a saucepan with the sugar, place over an asbestos mat and stir over a very gentle heat till the sugar has dissolved; then continue cooking *very slowly* till all moisture is absorbed and the mixture is very thick, keeping it very well stirred. Test a little on a plate and when it sets hard add the nuts and ginger, and remove from the heat.

Spread on a damp board, and when cool mark with a knife. When cold break into pieces along the marks.

Traditional Jewish Dishes

Within the framework of their dietary laws, Jews in every land have adapted and adopted local dishes and from each country added new ones to their now formidable list of 'traditional dishes'. Many of these can be traced very easily to the land of origin. For example, recipes for savoury fish, such as Brown Stewed Fish and Fish with Sweet and Sour Sauce, as well as Gefillte Fish, are all common to the non-Jewish in- habitants of places situated inland at a great distance from the sea and are designed to give flavour to fresh-water fish. They are eaten very generally in Poland, whereas among Sefardic Jews, who lived in maritime countries where saltwater fish was available, Gefillte Fish was scarcely known.

Similarly, in modern times a new list of traditional Jewish dishes has necessarily been evolved among the pioneers and settlers in Israel. One of the first tasks the Wizo had to set itself through its institutions in the early days of the Jewish

National Home in Israel was to re-educate Jewish women from cold Northern European countries to form a diet suitable for Israel and possibly, in time, meals consisting of salads and uncooked vegetables, in which carrots predominate, will come to be looked upon as traditionally Jewish.

Jews in India, the Levant, and North Africa all have special local dishes which they claim as 'traditional', while such combinations as brussels sprouts cooked with chestnuts, which are very popular throughout Holland and Belgium, have come to be included among Jewish 'traditional' dishes.

As regards the dishes looked on as being traditionally associated with the *Yomtovim*, it follows that there is also a considerable divergence of choice and opinion, varying often from family to family. Broadly speaking and taking into consideration the local variations referred to above, these are the most generally accepted among the majority of Jewish families:

Passover. Any of the dishes found in the section on Passover Cookery, pages 409–25.

Purim. 'Haman Taschen', page 362. 'Haman's Ears', page 283. Purim Fritters, page 242.

Shevuoth – Pentecost. Cheese Cake, pages 255–6. Cheese Blintzes, page 114.

Rosh Hashana – New Year. Honey Cake, pages 344–5.

Succoth – Tabernacles. Stuffed Cabbage Leaves, page 181.

Chanucah. Potato Latkes, pages 105–6.

Miscellaneous

Cottage Cheese

Take a pint or more of milk that has gone sour, put it in a jug and let it stand in a warm place for 24 hours, or until it is quite thick. Then turn it into a muslin bag, tie it at the top and hang it up over a basin until all the whey has dripped out; put into a small basin and beat up with a little salt. Then put it back on the muslin, roll it up and tie the two ends like a roly-poly pudding (this is just to shape it), and it will be ready in about one hour. It can be rolled into small balls and served on lettuce leaves.

Eggless Batter

When eggs are in short supply, a flour and water batter can be used instead for coating fish, cutlets, etc.

Mix 2 oz. flour with a pinch of salt, then gradually add sufficient cold water to mix to a thin cream – about ¼ pint.

First dip the fish or cutlets in seasoned flour, then in the batter and coat with breadcrumbs. Leave on a board for a while to dry before frying.

Uses for Stale Bread

There is no need to waste a single crust of stale bread, for there are endless ways in which it can be used:

(1) **An uncut stale loaf** can be freshened by just heating through in a moderate oven.

(2) **Left-over Sandwiches.** Use in any of the following ways:

(a) Toast on both sides and spread with butter or margarine.

(b) Dip in frying batter and fry a golden brown in hot fat.

(c) If the sandwiches have a meat filling, put the entire sandwich through the mincer and use in rissoles or a meat loaf.

(d) Fish sandwiches can be fried and served with cheese sauce.

(3) **Raspings.** Place any crusts and odd scraps of bread on a tin in a moderate oven and dry slowly till crisp. Then either crush till quite fine with a rolling pin, or put through the mincing machine, using a fine cutter. Store in an airtight container and use for crumbing cutlets, rissoles, fish, etc., or to sprinkle on top of vegetable or fish pies.

(4) **Croûtons and Bread Rusks.** See pages 47–8.

(5) **Soaked Bread.** The stalest bread, including crust, can be used for puddings, etc., if properly prepared. Break up bread into small pieces, put into bowl, cover completely with cold water and soak till soft. If the bread is to be used for a savoury, then soak in vegetable water. When soft, drain off water and squeeze the bread *very dry*. Put back in bowl and beat with a

fork till it is quite free from lumps and pieces of crust and the mixture is smooth and creamy. Beat thoroughly and the result will be a smooth, spongy texture instead of a dull, heavy pudding.

Recipes for puddings, savoury stuffings, meat dishes, etc., containing stale bread will be found in the various sections throughout the book.

Index

More about Penguins and Pelicans

Penguinews, which appears every month, contains details of all the new books issued by Penguins as they are published. From time to time it is supplemented by *Penguins in Print*, which is a complete list of all available books published by Penguins. (There are well over four thousand of these.)

A specimen copy of *Penguinews* will be sent to you free on request. For a year's issues (including the complete lists) please send 30p if you live in the United Kingdom, or 60p if you live elsewhere. Just write to Dept EP, Penguin Books Ltd, Harmondsworth, Middlesex, enclosing a cheque or postal order, and your name will be added to the mailing list.

Note: *Penguinews* and *Penguins in Print* are not available in the U.S.A. or Canada

The Philosopher in the Kitchen

Jean-Anthelme Brillat-Savarin

'Whoever says "truffles" utters a great word which
arouses erotic and gastronomic memories among the
skirted sex, and memories gastronomic and erotic among
the bearded sex.

'This dual distinction is due to the fact that the noble
tuber is not only considered delicious to the taste, but
is also believed to foster powers the exercise of which
is extremely pleasurable.'

' "Rejoice, my dear," I said one day to Madame
de V—; "a loom has just been shown to the Society for
Encouragement on which it will be possible to
manufacture superb lace for practically nothing."

' "Why," the lady replied, with an air of supreme
indifference, "if lace were cheap, do you think anybody
would want to wear such rubbish?" '

Jean-Anthelme Brillat-Savarin (1755–1826), Mayor
of Belley, cousin of Madame Récamier, Chevalier de
l'Empire, author of a history of duelling and of a
number of racy stories (unfortunately lost), whose
sister died in her hundredth year having just finished a
good meal and shouting loudly for her dessert, is now
best known for his *Physiologie du Goût*, here brilliantly
translated as *The Philosopher in the Kitchen*, which
was first published in December 1825. The work has a
timeless appeal – being wise, witty and anecdotal,
containing some of the best recipes for food and some
of the most satisfactory observations on life.

Elizabeth David

Elizabeth David is well known for the infectious
enthusiasm with which she presents her recipes.

'She has the happy knack of giving just as much detail
as the average cook finds desirable; she presumes
neither on our knowledge nor on our ignorance' –
Elizabeth Nicholas in the *Sunday Times*

Mediterranean Food

A practical collection of recipes made by the author
when she lived in France, Italy, the Greek Islands and
Egypt, evoking all the colour of the Mediterranean
but making use of ingredients obtainable in England.

French Country Cooking

Some of the splendid regional variations in French
cookery are described in this book.

French Provincial Cooking

'It is difficult to think of any home that can do without
Elizabeth David's *French Provincial Cooking* . . . One
could cook for a lifetime on the book alone' – *Observer*

Italian Food

Exploding once and for all the myth that Italians live
entirely on minestrone, spaghetti and veal escalopes,
this exciting book demonstrates the enormous and
colourful variety of Italy's regional cooking.

Summer Cooking

A selection of summer dishes that are light (not
necessarily cold), easy to prepare and based on the food
in season.

English Cooking Ancient and Modern 1
Spices, Salt and Aromatics in the English Kitchen

Elizabeth David presents English recipes which are
notable for their employment of spices, salt and
aromatics. As usual, she seasons instruction with
information, explaining the origins and uses of her
ingredients.